Under Confucian Eyes:
Writings on Gender in Chinese History

Under Confucian Eyes

Writings on Gender in Chinese History

Edited by Susan Mann
and Yu-Yin Cheng

UNIVERSITY OF CALIFORNIA PRESS
Berkeley · Los Angeles · London

University of California Press
Berkeley and Los Angeles, California

University of California Press, Ltd.
London, England

Library of Congress Cataloging-in-Publication Data

Under Confucian eyes : writings on gender in Chinese history / edited by Susan Mann and Yu-Yin Cheng.

p. cm.
Includes bibliographical references.
ISBN 0-520-22274-1 (cloth : alk. paper)—
ISBN 0-520-22276-8 (pbk. : alk paper)
1. Women—China—History. 2. Women in literature. I. Mann, Susan, 1943– II. Cheng, Yu-Yin.

HQ1767 .U53 2001
305.4'0951—dc21 2001027090

Printed and bound in Canada

10 09 08 07 06 05 04 03 02 01
10 9 8 7 6 5 4 3 2 1

The paper used in this publication is both acid-free and totally chlorine-free (TCF). It meets the minimum requirements of ANSI/NISO Z39.48-1992 (R 1997) (*Permanence of Paper*). ∞

Contents

Illustrations

Acknowledgments

This book is a companion volume to *Women and Confucian Culture in Premodern China, Korea, and Japan,* also to be published by the University of California Press, and edited by Dorothy Ko, JaHyun Kim Haboush, and Joan Piggott. Both books are the result of a long-term project seeking to rethink Confucianism in East Asia by using gender as a category of analysis. Planning for these volumes began in September 1994, when Susan Mann convened a workshop in Davis, California, funded by the Joint Committee on Chinese Studies of the Social Science Research Council and the American Council of Learned Societies, as well as the SSRC's East Asia Regional Research Working Group. The colleagues who attended the workshop laid the groundwork for the documents collection and proposed an international conference, which was held in the summer of 1996 at the La Jolla campus of the University of California, San Diego, under the leadership of Dorothy Ko.

The editors of this volume are indebted to all of the scholars who have contributed translations—among them many participants in the original workshop and conference—for their enthusiastic and even delighted responses to our call for "texts on gender." We have accumulated many additional debts in the course of preparing the manuscript for publication. We thank the Office of Research and the Dean of Social Sciences at the University of California, Davis, for funds supporting word processing and disk preparation. Alison Book and Denise Forestek transcribed the first two drafts with efficiency and skill. John Ziemer made invaluable suggestions after reading an early version of the manuscript. We are grateful to anonymous reviewers for their astute criticism, to Carolyn Bond and Jan Spauschus Johnson for sensitive editing, and especially to Sheila Levine for her steadfast interest and support.

S.M.
Y.Y.C.

Editors' Introduction

We chose the title of this book to underscore the sometimes ironic relationship between Confucian viewpoints and women's visibility in Chinese historical documents. Although women have been marginalized in Western accounts of Chinese history, China's documentary record on gender relations is rich.[1] Chinese texts invite historians to sharpen their focus by cutting through what the writers of those texts considered the "outer" spheres of government and community to look more closely at the "inner" world of family and household. In the eyes of Chinese writers, family and household were the crucial sites of production and reproduction on which the larger polity depended to flourish and endure. Precisely because of that conviction, Chinese historical texts are a barely tapped resource for all scholars interested in women and gender relations.[2]

Confucian beliefs about the importance of family relations continually brought female relatives—and the female relatives of friends—into the writings of the literati elite. In a cultural context where Buddhist and Daoist beliefs were readily syncretized with Confucian ideas, female deities cap-

1. Recent studies in law, medicine, and technology point to the rewards of mining hitherto neglected texts on women and gender. See Matthew Sommer, *Sex, Law, and Society in Late Imperial China* (Stanford: Stanford University Press, 1999); Charlotte Furth, *A Flourishing Yin* (Berkeley: University of California Press, 1998); Francesca Bray, *Technology and Gender: Fabrics of Power in Late Imperial China* (Berkeley: University of California Press, 1997).

2. The title is indebted to scholarship on the relationship between power and the writer's vantage point, or gaze, especially work by Mary Louise Pratt, *Imperial Eyes: Travel Writing and Transculturation* (London: Routledge, 1992); and Chandra Talpade Mohanty, "Under Western Eyes: Feminist Scholarship and Colonial Discourses," in *Third World Women and the Politics of Feminism,* edited by Chandra Talpade Mohanty, Ann Russo, and Lourdes Torres (Bloomington: Indiana University Press, 1991), 51–80.

tured the imagination of narrators and the devotion of worshippers. Women symbolized the "other" in literati accounts of cultures or status groups different from their own. Women figure too in fiction and fantasy by literati writers exploring sexuality and passion, when a Confucian idiom did not suffice. Finally, the emergence of female writers in the Ming and Qing periods brought women's own voice into the canon of poetry and prose that dominates Confucian culture. Thus, despite the Confucian principles of separation that marginalized women in official historical and philosophical records, a vast body of Chinese historical texts lend themselves readily to gender analysis.

In China, as in most Western cultures, the bulk of documentary evidence used by historians comes from the so-called public sphere of politics, economy, and society. Domestic life, for the most part, was concealed from view, and properly so, since respectable women were not supposed to move about freely outside their homes. (At least this was the case from the tenth century, when Confucian norms stressing separation between the sexes gained increasing currency among the elite.) Early Confucian classics tell us that "women's words should not be heard beyond the inner quarters" *(nei yan buchu men wai),* making the publication or even the circulation of women's writings a source of concern and debate in late imperial times.[3] Yet, as Dorothy Ko has shown,[4] the Chinese conceptions of "inner" and "outer" used to delineate the proper spheres of women and men do not correspond directly to Western notions of "private" and "public." Rather, "inner" and "outer," in Chinese parlance, were shifting and mutually dependent boundaries linking men's and women's worlds into a coherent and balanced whole. Women's influence extended into the "outer" sphere, mainly through moral instruction. As Patricia Ebrey's study of women in the Song dynasty (960–1279) emphasizes,[5] women's influence reached from the inner quarters into the outer realm by other means as well: through emotional and sexual ties affecting men's behavior, through personal networks centered on a married woman's natal family, and in the form of investments made with her savings or her dowry. A woman "inside" could be influential "outside" through her personal reputation for learning or virtue; through the reputations of her daughters as wives and daughters-in-law; and through the successes of her sons. Many scholars believe that Chinese women resorted to dramatic ways of publicly displaying their virtue—committing suicide to defend their

3. Susan Mann, "Classical Revival and the Woman Question: China's First Querelle des Femmes," in *Family Process and Political Process in Modern Chinese History,* edited by Institute of Modern History, Academia Sinica (Taipei: Institute of Modern History, Academia Sinica, 1992), 1:377–411.

4. Dorothy Ko, *Teachers of the Inner Chambers: Women and Culture in Seventeenth-Century China* (Stanford: Stanford University Press, 1994).

5. Patricia Buckley Ebrey, *The Inner Quarters: Marriage and the Lives of Chinese Women in the Sung Period* (Berkeley: University of California Press, 1993).

chastity, winning imperial awards as faithful widows, or lodging a petition in a court of law—in order to bring honor to their husbands' families as well as to their own persons. In this way, a woman's action could erase what Western historiography might mistake for a boundary between "private" and "public."[6] In other words, although Chinese sources drew a sharp line to separate inner (women's) and outer (men's) spheres, the line was drawn precisely in order to emphasize the interdependency between the two parts. The boundary was not spatial. It was constantly shifting. And its intent was never to marginalize or privilege one over the other.

Where marginalization undeniably took place was in the larger discourse that dominated the production of texts. That discourse focused on the outer realm, where men were visible. Textual production included everything from statecraft and government documents (the dominant industry) to literary collections, and in all these arenas women were marginalized. Women were automatically shut out of the government spheres of writing by virtue of their exclusion from the entire civil service system. Moreover, the separation of spheres so defined kept "inner" matters, as much as possible, from intruding into the documented workings of "outer" government.

By the same token, but for rather different reasons, women's presence in literary collections was constrained by the expectations and pressures of their roles "inside." First, women wrote far less than men because they had less time to write, being required in upper-class families to devote most of their energy to other matters considered proper to their "inner" duties. Second, very few women wrote prose. Prose writing by women was considered unusual enough that when a woman produced a *wenji* (prose collection), it was cause for extended comment among her peers and admirers.[7] Most of what women wrote was poetry, a short form requiring less mastery of history and philosophy than prose. By the same token, few women wrote in the parallel prose style favored by men, which required years of practice to master. Since women never prepared for the civil service examinations, they were rarely pushed to master any sort of essay form. And since women generally were not pulled into the daily rounds of correspondence on matters political, philosophical, and aca-

6. See Mark Elvin's interesting observations about the public honoring of private virtue in his pathbreaking study of female virtue and the state in China ("Female Virtue and the State in China," *Past and Present* 104 [1984]: 111–52). Here Elvin unconsciously uses Western dichotomies to draw a distinction that would not be recognizable in emic terms (see p. 151).

7. See, for example, the effusive preface to the modest two-chapter collection of prose by Zhang Wanying, composed when Zhang's works were printed in 1849–1850. Wu Jin's preface invokes the memory of Ban Zhao when he remarks on how few women after Zhang have mastered ancient prose, because "mastery of *guwen* requires both talent and study, and the combination is not easy to achieve for those confined to the inner quarters." See Zhang Wanying, *Canfengguan wenji,* second preface, 1a–b, manuscript copy, Shanghai Municipal Library.

demic that absorbed their male relatives, they were rarely called upon to communicate in prose in any systematic or sustained fashion. As a result, the prose writing by women that does survive generally takes the form of short prefaces, letters, and diaries.

In only two domains of Chinese historical writing are women prominent and ubiquitous. One of these domains is fiction and drama; the other is the genre referred to as "random jottings" or "notes" *(biji* or *suibi)*. Not surprisingly, though most of these works were written by men, women are central to any plots or notes that are based on observations of ordinary life. Both fiction and drama, along with the random jottings of literati, were relegated to an inferior position in the Confucian literary canon of the imperial period; like their female subjects, these genres occupy marginal literary spaces, and perhaps for that reason their impact on studies of Chinese history has been relatively limited.

This combination of circumstances—scant literary production by women and exclusion of women from the domain of state-structured and canonical Confucian writing—means that Chinese women often appear far less visible than men to Western historians relying on written records. But we must never mistake historiographic artifacts for historical facts. Women's marginality in written documents does not mean that they played a marginal role in elite culture. On the contrary, women's low profile in historical documents may deceive us, masking their central place in the emotional and material lives of the men who dominate the written record. To compensate, we must pay the closest possible attention to sources where women do appear. Women are far more visible in personal, intimate, homely, or local texts than they are in texts produced by the imperial scholarly apparatus, or in formal "official" prose.

Herein, of course, lies another potential source of error or distortion. Isn't it accurate, we might ask, to marginalize texts that are themselves marginal? Isn't it the case that women were screened out of the public sphere and in that sense play only a marginal role in the stories history has to tell us? Aren't we understanding quite accurately the marginal role women played by seeing the marginal place they occupy in the written historical record? The answer is no, and the reason is that our own biases about the importance of a "public" sphere are getting in the way. In our view, if the public record dominates, then the private record must be commensurately insignificant. In fact, though, in Chinese history the "inner" realm is never reduced in importance relative to the "outer" realm: it merely occupies less visible textual space at certain times. Inner and outer are always interconnected: the texts themselves tell us so. So the historian's job is not to consign the inner sphere to marginality because it is less visible in the record, but rather to piece together—as painstakingly as possible—the fragmentary evidence from the inner sphere in order to be certain that the total picture described in the "outer" sphere is complete, accurately capturing the understanding and lived experience of our subjects.

In the texts that follow we call attention to questions about reading that engage any scholar who is looking at documents from the past: discerning the many voices in which a text can speak, distinguishing ideal from practice, heeding the relationship between gender and text, being alert to notions of the body embedded in textual expression, and finally, appreciating the sheer narrative power of Chinese classical prose. At every level, the texts in this anthology supply a counterpoint, critique, or confirmation of the dominant Confucian discourse on normative gender relations.

VOICE AND TEXT

Historians reading primary sources are more aware now than ever before that every text speaks with many voices. We hear the author, of course, but we also hear representations of persons, events, and ideas that the author sets before us, and further, we imagine the author's audience and its own reception of the text. Other voices intrude as well, for we as readers are hardly the audience the author had in mind; on the contrary, separated as we are by time, space, and culture from the original production of these texts, we have no alternative but to translate them into another language, which is freighted with the voices of its own cultural assumptions.

Ultimately, how much we can learn from a text depends on how carefully we manage to discern all of these voices. Readers are invited to approach the documents that follow with conscious attention to the writing strategies of the translator as well as the original author, and to the reading strategies of the intended audience as well as the present readers. With this in mind, each translator has prepared for the reader not only an introduction but also a short note explaining her or his relationship to the text.

IDEAL AND PRACTICE

The texts that follow assume that readers know what is ideal or expected in the world where the text was produced. Virtually every text relies for its power on an understanding of Confucian values. Some criticize, some celebrate, some parody, and others express alienation, but all derive their authority from the pervasive awareness of Confucian discourses. Readers attuned to the dialogue between Confucian values and norms and the texts that follow will immediately notice that Confucianism frames and encloses discourses that are actually contending with Confucianism for authority. For example, men and women received different messages, even from normative Confucian didactic works. This is shown most dramatically in Patricia Ebrey's juxtaposed translations of excerpts from separate renditions of the *Book of Filial Piety* for women and for men (chapter 3).

Moreover, in a Confucian context, where separation of the sexes is a premise governing all normative human action, texts by and about women show that women's voices and women's experiences are to some degree autonomous domains, requiring particularized forms of address and demanding special attention from writers. This is most apparent in letters, where conventional and highly stylized forms governed the exchanges between men and women (chapters 10, 11, 12), but it is also plain in the topoi of biography, which demanded that writers take account of particular qualities in women's character, such as purity, devotion to service, diligence, frugality, and resourcefulness (chapters 4, 6, 7, 9, 14).

Although much of the writing on gender relations and Confucianism locates women in the domestic life of the family (the "inner quarters"), the texts translated in this book show that domesticity is a Confucian construction: a representation of the principle of separation that imposes boundaries on women's political, religious, and social practices. These texts, read closely for what they reveal about author and audience, also make clear that even the most homebound womanly practices reached far beyond the domestic sphere and well outside the conventional forms of the family. Chen Liang's writings about his female relatives (chapter 4), Luo Rufang's memoirs (chapter 6), Gu Ruopu's admonitions to her sons (chapter 9), Wang Duanshu's reflections on Ming loyalists (chapter 12), and Zhang Xuecheng's biographies of women (chapter 14) all point to the ways in which women stood at the center of political, social, scholarly, and philosophical networks spanning the divide between the "inner quarters" and the world that surrounded it. Religious belief and practice, by contrast, provide spaces where women can secede or withdraw from Confucian family relationships, as shown in chapters 1, 2, and 8.

GENDER AND TEXT

In part because of the artifice of the conventions that dominate Confucian writing, women's relationship to written texts was not the same as men's. Didactic texts about women, written by men, were intended to be read by men and then "translated," so to speak, onto women. Viewed in this light, the text becomes a mode of discipline in which men explain how women should behave, especially how they should comport themselves. The poems on women picking tea (chapter 15) derive their subversive quality from this feature of Confucian writing, as do the short stories by Pu Songling (chapter 13).

Women as writers employed Confucian vocabularies consciously to display their own mastery of *wen,* high culture,[8] especially in poetry and letters (see chapters 11 and 12). But while men's writing about women reads as a mode of discipline or a form of hagiography, women's writing about themselves conveys spiritual and emotional power, steadfast resolve, hardheaded practical reasoning, and dazzling creativity. This anthology includes several bold examples of self-defining prose by women, including an autobiographical religious statement by Ji Xian (chapter 8), a dramatic self-exploratory tableau by Wu Zao (chapter 16), and several short reflective pieces by Wang Duanshu (chapter 12). In addition, the short women's letters translated by Yu-Yin Cheng show women deploying the conventions of letter-writing to suit their own imaginative purposes (chapter 11).

BODY AND TEXT

Because in Confucian thought knowledge and action are one, bodily images in every text convey important messages about moral meanings. The overwhelming bodily image of women in Confucian texts is of women devoted to the management of household and family affairs. Appreciating this normative Confucian setting for the female body in texts helps us to appreciate the inherently disruptive nuance of a story about a Daoist saint (the biography of Wang Fengxian in chapter 1) or a female bodhisattva (the legend of Miaoshan in chapter 2), or a poem about a bare-armed girl singing on a hillside (chapter 15). A Confucian sensibility spices up the flavor of ethnographic or fictional accounts of minority women or non-Han ladies who violate the principles of cloistering, described with detailed fascination by Li Jing (chapter 5) and Ding Shaoyi (chapter 17). And it sharpens readers' attention to the Manchu flavor of the "youth books" popular in Beijing during the nineteenth century (chapter 18).

The body is the obsessive subject of the ghost stories translated here by Judith Zeitlin (chapter 13). Female ghosts, unencumbered by the constraints of Confucian convention, enable both male and female characters to indulge in explorations of their sexuality and to experiment with performances that embodied persons can only dream about or, as in the case of Wu Zao (chapter 16), invent as fantasy or play. The body is also the site of female religious experience: it is subject to discipline through fasting and mutilation, bound to reproductive and productive service by Confucian norms that can be escaped only through widowhood. Ji Xian's struggle with her parents over her fate as a married woman (chapter 8) echoes the timeless tension between

8. See Maureen Robertson, "Changing the Subject: Gender and Self-Inscription in Authors' Prefaces and *Shi* Poetry," in *Writing Women in Late Imperial China,* ed. Ellen Widmer and Kang-i Sun Chang (Stanford: Stanford University Press, 1997), 171–217.

Confucian parental desires for continuing the descent line and individual desires to pursue a Buddhist spiritual quest. This great contest, recapitulated in the life of the princess Miaoshan and embodied in the iconic figure of the Bodhisattva Guanyin (chapter 2), lies like a template over the life struggles of millions of young Chinese women in the historical record.

Most men's writing about women focuses on what women do with their bodies, rarely exploring how they think with their minds. Even biographies such as those by Zhang Xuecheng (chapter 14), which were intended to exalt the mental and moral capabilities of their female subjects, stress bodily tasks and bodily labor. This reflects men's own understanding of the Confucian principle of hierarchy articulated first by Mencius: the distinction between "those above" who labor with their minds and "those below" who labor with their hands. Normative texts stressing women's work and women's bodily comportment are telling us that women by definition fall into the latter category. Some of the poems on tea-picking (chapter 15), on the other hand, express a different Confucian perspective: female labor becomes an emblem of the exploitation of the poor or the oppression of peasant families by the rich and powerful.

NARRATIVE AND POWER

The power of Confucian writing about women derives at least as much from narrative style as it does from the images and ideas conveyed by the writer. Stories about women are engaging because they feature dramatic plots: violent temper tantrums, cruel vendettas, heartless wrongdoers, selfless sacrifice, public suicide, or (as in chapter 13) seductive ghosts. A Daoist female saint ascends to heaven in broad daylight (chapter 1), and a filial daughter contrives to avoid marriage altogether by enduring cruel tests of her spiritual resolve (chapter 2). The lives of these unusual women are melodramas, but their predicaments are revisited in mundane Confucian injunctions about jealous wives (chapter 3), faithful widows (chapter 7), omnicompetent matriarchs (chapter 14), inspiring mothers (chapter 6), and admiring or nostalgic poems about women at work (chapter 15).

Just as examples from fiction often enlivened the pages of didactic texts and inspired the pens of letter-writers, so the embellishments of narrative style—drawn from short story, novel, and drama—weave through the stories about women in the documents that follow, inviting readers past and present to turn the page.

Guide for Students and Teachers

This book is for teachers, students, scholars, and interested readers looking for primary sources on the history of Chinese women. The translators were invited to select texts that would open up issues in gender relations. With a few exceptions, we have included only complete texts and avoided excerpts in order to let the documents and their authors speak for themselves in their entirety. Even so, because translating classical Chinese is a creative project that defies literal or mechanical equivalencies, and because—as the reader will see—a text may have distinctly personal meanings for a translator, we asked each translator to introduce herself or himself to the reader as the agent who has re-created the text as well as brought it to our collective attention. This translator's preface is followed by a more formal introduction that supplies details about historical context, textual history, authorship, and so forth for the selected text. We have kept sinological annotations to a minimum, but have provided glossaries for interested readers.

The texts are arranged chronologically to supplement the readings in any history course that deals with China, East Asia, or the world between the dynasties of Tang (618–906) and Qing (1644–1911). Materials from the late Ming (1368–1644) and Qing (1644–1911) periods predominate, reflecting the importance of Ming print culture for the publication of letters, stories, and other works by and about women.[1] Few writings by Chinese women dated before the seventeenth century survive, and most of those that do have the didactic or hagiographic quality characteristic of the texts from the Tang and Song (960–1279). For an intimate insight into the private

1. See Dorothy Ko, *Teachers of the Inner Chambers: Women and Culture in Seventeenth-Century China* (Stanford: Stanford University Press, 1994), 29–67.

emotional world of women and their relationships, we must rely mainly on late Ming and Qing writings. On the other hand, the translations of Song and Yuan (1279–1368) work presented here contain rich materials for readers interested in women or gender relations—topics that these writings were not intended to reveal much about. No Chinese text describing a non-Han people fails to mention the sexual practices and gender norms of that society. And few Chinese men writing a tribute to a friend or family member will fail to allude to the nurturing support and diligent labors of a mother. In that sense, as the following readings demonstrate, texts by both men and women from most periods in Chinese history may be read with a view to understanding gender relations.

Considering these texts chronologically, chapter 1 treats Daoism in Tang times and its religious significance for women. Chapter 2 lends itself to the study of Buddhism and its syncretization in Chinese local cults and Confucian family relationships in China's middle period. It also shows Buddhism's special significance for women in Chinese society. Chapters 3 and 4 supply evidence on Confucian views on women in Song times and on the importance of Confucian values in Chinese family relationships. Since the Song dynasty was the period when the Chinese family system and family rituals were first widely embraced among the emerging "gentry" class, these texts are particularly significant in calling attention to the importance of women's roles in the family.

Chapters 5 and 17 dramatize the expansion of Han civilization under Yuan rule and Manchu rule. Rulers of both of these dynasties were non-Han people who took a special interest in the pacification and Confucianization of border regions and minority peoples. Chapters 6 through 16 and chapter 18 all illustrate the broad impact of Ming print culture and the world of letters on women and gender relations from the seventeenth century through the nineteenth century. Historians interested in distinguishing the Ming from the Qing period should make use of chapter 12, which stresses the Ming-Qing transition through a series of memoirs for Ming loyalists, or chapter 6, which shows the influence of Wang Yangming Confucianism on views of women in the thought of a leading proponent of Wang Yangming's school of thought. Poems translated in chapter 15 can be used effectively in discussions of women's work, the feminization of poverty, and the use of female images of oppression, as well as in analyzing the representation of the female body in poetry and aesthetics.

We assume that readers will find additional methods for using the readings in this volume beyond the strictly chronological approach suggested by the order of the texts. The topical guide that follows may be useful for courses on women's history, comparative literature, religious studies, or East Asian studies.

TOPICAL APPROACHES

The Unmarked Male Subject

Chapter 3 dramatizes the fact that virtually all Confucian classics were written about an unmarked male subject—a feature of classical Chinese writing that is masked by the absence of gendered pronouns. Works intended specifically for women, such as the *Book of Filial Piety for Women* excerpted here, specify "female" or "women" *(nü)* in the title. For further reading, consult the study of Ban Zhao's *Admonitions for Women* by Yu-shih Ch'en ("The Historical Template of Pan Chao's *Nü Chieh,*" *T'oung Pao* 72, no. 4–5 [1996], 229–57).

Kin Relations

All but a very few of these texts can be studied for an understanding of the complexity of kin relationships in the Chinese family system. Chapter 4 illustrates how relatives were carefully identified through kinship terminology that distinguished mother's from father's descent lines, or relatives related by blood from those related by marriage. Readers will also appreciate the heavy social burden associated with writing eulogies and other kinds of biographical memoirs for one's own kin and for those of friends or others to whom one was obligated. For talented writers like Chen Liang or Zhang Xuecheng, composing eulogies was a major professional activity. Perhaps because of the expressive opportunities that women's lives offered a biographer, women as subjects of epitaph, eulogy, and biography often spark an empathic or even intimate tone in male writers.

Gender as Performance: The Behavior of Ethnic Minority Groups

Chapters 5, 17, and 18 give readers a chance to see how prejudice and stereotype about members of other ethnic groups were expressed in descriptions of their customs. Chapter 5, which concerns the western borderlands at a relatively early stage in their development, conveys a Han Chinese reaction to the dress and social practices—especially sexual behavior and kin relations—of non-Han minority peoples. The text displays the determination to classify minority peoples in a manner that remains characteristic of Han Chinese governments today. Chapter 17, concerning Taiwan, reveals how recently that island remained a frontier site in the eyes of Confucian literati. Chapter 18, harking back to the time of the Manchu conquest, recalls ethnic differences that were defined in the traumatic period immediately following the fall of the Han Chinese Ming dynasty in 1644, after which Manchu policy forbade Manchu women to bind their feet. Because the Manchus failed to enforce footbinding bans among the Han Chinese population, unbound feet remained a powerful cultural and ethnic marker throughout the Qing dynasty, which ended in 1911.

Fiction and Nonfiction

The fiction works translated here, Chapters 13 and 18, give readers a chance to see the frank and explicit attention to sexuality and humor in narrative fiction. Moreover, as chapter 10 shows, the line between fiction and nonfiction, especially in letter writing, was often blurred beyond recognition. Readers will be interested to notice how much nonfiction biography adheres to the lines of a fictional narrative, with bursts of dialogue and excerpts from letters and other writings interwoven with the factual details of a life. Many biographies seem intended to be read like contemporary soap operas, lavishing attention on dramatic conflict and human passion. This is generally more true of biographies of women than biographies of men, which can be filled with details of career moves and educational achievements.

GENRES

Biography/Hagiography

The texts in the first two chapters of this volume are hagiographic, providing examples of what might be called accounts of saints' lives. But these are only one form of biography, the broad genre that makes up one of the richest sources for Chinese women's history. Many other texts in the volume also supply biographies. There are epitaphs and eulogies (chapters 4, 6, 14), which tend to be more intimate and less stylized than the formal, didactic biographies of "exemplary women" that fill Chinese history books. Grace Fong's translation (chapter 8) provides one of the few extant examples of a woman's autobiography. Students would find it an interesting exercise to read an essay about biographies of men and then use the texts in this volume to develop a different set of criteria for biographies of women. Two fine essays on Chinese biography, both written with reference to male subjects, are by Denis Twitchett: "Chinese Biographical Writing," in *Historians of China and Japan,* ed. W. G. Beasley and E. G. Pulleyblank (London: Oxford University Press, 1961); and "Problems of Chinese Biography," in *Confucian Personalities,* ed. Arthur F. Wright and Denis Twitchett (Stanford: Stanford University Press, 1962). On autobiography, see Wu Pei-yi, *The Confucian's Progress: Autobiographical Writings in Traditional China* (Princeton: Princeton University Press, 1990).

Letters

Making effective use of the letters in this volume (chapters 7, 9, 10, 11, 12) poses a particular challenge to students unfamiliar with Chinese culture, who may be unaware that writing letters was hardly a "private" pursuit. In fact, most well-educated people wrote letters with the idea that their letters would likely be saved, if only for progeny to read. In the Qing period, especially in the Jiangnan region, it was common for letters to be published together with other writings in volumes of "collected works" *(wenji)* compiled and edited by devoted sons, brothers, grandsons, and occasionally spouses. Most *wenji* comprised the writings of men, but thousands of women in Qing times, and hundreds in the Ming period as well, were also honored by the posthumous publication of their collected writings. The many letters included in this volume show the range of occasions on which a woman was required to send an elegant letter. In addition, Kathryn Lowry's extensive discussion of letter-writing manuals (chapter 10) reveals the rules and the imagination that together inspired most letter-writing women. Readers will be struck, especially on encountering Lowry's translations from letter-writing handbooks, by the close overlap of fiction and letter-writing. Her long introduction stresses the ways in which the print culture of the seventeenth century influenced the style and content of letters and also expanded the audience for fiction, especially among women. Yu-Yin Cheng's translations of the writings of Luo Rufang (chapter 6) suggest that his own sensibilities were influenced by the print culture of his day, which might have piqued his interest in women as philosophers and as sources of emotional support. See also the "letter" quoted in Zhang Xuecheng's biography of Jiang Lan (chapter 14). Since women rarely, if ever, wrote formal prose, letter-writing was one of the few ways in which a woman could display her prose style, especially her command of classical allusions and her virtuosity in classical learning.

Fiction, Poetry, and Other Genres

Because so much Chinese fiction is already available in translation, this volume contains only a few selections: two short stories by a master of the genre, Pu Songling (chapter 13); a singular example of a dramatic tableau composed as a soliloquy by a female writer (chapter 16); and a rare example of the Manchu oral performance texts known as "youth books" (chapter 18). Students will recognize Pu Songling's name if they are familiar with Jonathan Spence's well-known book *The Death of Woman Wang* (Harmondsworth: Penguin Books, 1978), in which Pu's fiction plays a major role. The fascination with sexuality and the uninhibited exploration of sexual identity and sexual attraction in these stories remind us that Confucian injunctions about purity may have had little success in discouraging curious readers, male and female, who were drawn to fiction out of their own inchoate desires.

Desire figures as well in the sensual conversation between Wu Zao and her image in a portrait (chapter 16), giving readers a chance to view this work as a miniature theatrical performance that underscores the importance of the theater in the internal erotic and emotional lives of young women during the late imperial period. Readers interested in theater and in the visual representation of dramatic performance in illustrated books of the period should consult two important articles: Ann Waltner, "On Not Becoming a Heroine: Lin Dai-yu and Cui Ying-ying," *Signs* 15, no. 1 (Autumn 1989), 61–78; and Katherine Carlitz, "The Social Uses of Female Virtue in Late Ming Editions of *Lienü Zhuan*," *Late Imperial China* 12, no. 1 (1991), 117–48. Finally, Mark Elliott's translation of a hybrid Manchu-Chinese performance text (chapter 18) gives us the flavor of neighborhood Beijing at the end of the Qing dynasty, when Manchu and Han populations shared a common urban culture in which jokes relied partly on everyone's appreciation of ethnic diversity and gender roles were a primary avenue for the display and invention of that diversity.

Only a few poems are included in the present volume, since a major anthology of Chinese women's poetry in translation is at last available. Readers will want to consult Kang-i Sun Chang and Haun Saussy, eds., *Chinese Women Poets: An Anthology of Poetry and Criticism from Ancient Times to 1911* (Stanford: Stanford University Press, 1999).

RELIGIOUS STUDIES

Many of the texts included here contain insightful detail and nuance concerning female spirituality and religious life. Chapters 1 and 2 present formal hagiographies, with obvious significance for religious studies. But they also supply tropes that can be identified in the interstices of many other texts in the volume. The most obvious is Grace Fong's translation of Ji Xian's struggle with her parents over her religious and spiritual autonomy (chapter 8). Luo Rufang's account of the spiritual journeys of women he admired reveals a different kind of spirituality—that of older women past their child-bearing years (chapter 6). Zhang Xuecheng's biography of Lady Xun makes no attempt to conceal Lady Xun's own disparagement of the Buddhist beliefs of her husband's concubine (chapter 14). Interested students will want to consult Ann Waltner's study of the Ming dynasty Daoist adept Tanyangzi: "T'an-yang-tzu and Wang Shih-chen: Visionary and Bureaucrat in the Late Ming," *Late Imperial China* 8, no. 1 (1987), 667–87; and P. Steven Sangren,

"Female Gender in Chinese Religious Symbols: Kuan Yin, Ma Tsu, and the 'Eternal Mother,'" *Signs* 9, no. 1 (1983), 4–25. For additional translations, see Donald S. Lopez, Jr., ed., *Religions of China in Practice* (Princeton: Princeton University Press, 1996).

FURTHER READING

At the back of the book are lists of references for each text; translators have placed asterisks beside the works that are especially recommended for further reading.

Fig. 1. Portrait of a woman in white. Yuan dynasty, fourteenth century. Hanging scroll, ink and color on silk; 93.7 cm. x 43.7 cm. This painting is traditionally said to depict Lu Meiniang, another ninth-century southern woman who became a Daoist nun. Her biography appears in Du Guangting's *Records of the Assembled Transcendents of the Fortified Walled City*. Courtesy of the Freer Gallery of Art, Smithsonian Institution, Washington, D.C. F1917.114.

ONE

Biography of the Daoist Saint Wang Fengxian by Du Guangting (850–933)

Translated by Suzanne Cahill

TRANSLATOR'S PREFACE

I first became interested in hagiographical accounts of medieval Daoist holy women because they were among the few records I could find of actual women of the Tang dynasty (618–907). Tang dynastic histories and poetry written by Tang men mostly repeat standard images of women as evil empresses, bewitching concubines, or faceless victims of the Confucian patriarchy. The references are brief, and the women do not grow or develop. After reading a few biographies of female saints in the Daoist canon,[1] I realized that they tell compelling and entertaining stories. These accounts counteract simple stereotypes of medieval Chinese women, revealing a rich and complicated reality. The biographies introduce distinctly individual women of diverse geographic and class backgrounds. These people change over time, negotiate solutions to conflicts between personal goals and traditional roles, and act creatively within the limitations imposed upon them by the medieval Chinese social context. Wang Fengxian is one of these resourceful characters; her life is both exemplary and unique. When viewed from the perspective of traditional Chinese women's roles, the unmarried Daoist nun Wang emerges strongly out from under the Confucian gaze as an oppositional figure. Yet Wang remains under Confucian eyes as she faces the expectations of her parents that she marry, of her local officials that she assist them, and of her emperor that she glorify his reign by joining his harem. She circumvents the power structures of family and state to pursue her own religious objectives, but she never ignores those structures. In fact, her biographer claims that her life demonstrates a higher filial piety and loyalty than the norm because her Daoist practices help her whole family, her community, and her state.

INTRODUCTION

By the time the Tang dynasty ruled China, Daoism already had a long history as China's native major religion. Since the second century of the Common Era, Daoists had revered a host of deities, engaged in numerous rituals, and practiced self-cultivation to attain perfection, which included eternal life and residence in the Daoist heavens. During the fourth and fifth centuries, two great schools arose that continued into the Tang. These are the Shangqing or "Supreme Clarity" (after the Daoist highest heavens), and Lingbao or "Numinous Treasure," schools. The Shangqing tradition emphasized perfection through individual practices such as meditation and asceticism; it found adherents among the imperial family and the elite of the Tang. The Lingbao school favored collective ritual and community worship and provided many rites for the state and the people of the Tang. Our author, late-Tang Daoist master and courtier Du Guangting (850–933), was a Shangqing master. In his writings Du tried to unite the two main traditions of his time under the leadership of his own Shangqing school. All his works, including the present one, are meant to glorify both Daoism and his school.

Du Guangting's hagiographical account of Daoist holy women, entitled *Records of the Assembled Transcendents of the Fortified Walled City (Yongcheng jixian lu),* contains twenty-seven biographies of varying lengths.[2] The author narrates the lives of the nine saints, including Wang Fengxian, who lived closest to his own time, in the richest detail. These accounts all follow a similar structure, which derives from the official biographies in dynastic histories. The organization and style have also been influenced by the "exemplary women" *(lienü)* biographies and by earlier biographies of Buddhist nuns.[3]

Du Guangting's style is dense and allusive. His biographies begin with information about the saint's family and place of origin, followed by an account of her childhood, including any special religious tendencies or practices. Her childhood ends with the crisis of the marriage quandary: she must marry or remain celibate. If she marries, she will not be able to give full attention to her Daoist religious practice; if she remains single, she will not be doing her filial duty to her family. After resolution of the marriage dilemma, the saint carries on with her mature religious practice and may obtain special gifts, such as perpetual youthfulness, as a result. Finally, she departs from this world, leaving evidence of her sanctity, and ascends to heaven, where she takes up an office in the celestial bureaucracy. Wang Fengxian's biography adheres closely to this pattern. Each saint models a Daoist path to salvation; the individual details of each one's life make her unique.

Du Guangting's book of holy women has several expressed purposes. In the course of the text, he states his desire to save Daoist records from the chaos attendant upon the end of the Tang dynasty, to record the lives of women saints whom other sources have neglected, to show the variety of valid paths to the Dao (the Way), and to praise the Tang dynasty for producing such auspicious signs of Heaven's approval as living saints. A careful reading of the text suggests that he also wishes to encourage imperial patronage of the Daoist church, promote the Daoist religion as a means of salvation in times of trouble, argue for the superiority of Daoism over Buddhism, support the belief that human beings can become perfected through their own efforts, and exalt the teachings of his school of Daoism over those of other schools.

For our purposes, Du Guangting's text provides an opportunity to explore several issues affecting women within the social context of medieval China. His work is the only one in the Daoist canon that presents female figures exclusively. We are able to examine their loyalty, filial piety, marriage, and social roles. We can also observe, through examination of the traces of Wang Fengxian and others like her in the historical, religious, and literary records of the time, that Daoist spiritual paths allowed some women during the Tang dynasty considerable scope for literacy, cultural contribution, and leadership.[4]

The fascinating tale of the life of Wang Fengxian (ca. 835–885), an important Daoist saint of the late Tang dynasty, is recorded in Du Guangting's work. Born in the south to a family of poor weavers, Wang Fengxian lived in a time and place of great turmoil. During her lifetime of forty-eight or fifty years, the south was the starting point for rebellions that plunged the country into chaos and signaled the beginning of the end of the three-hundred-year reign of the Tang.[5] Although unrest surrounded her, Wang's early life in the countryside is described as idyllic. After a childhood of eccentric behavior that revealed her religious inclinations, she became a renowned Daoist nun and revered teacher. She was known for her ascetic practices, skill in meditation, magical travels, services to the community of religious, and popular following.

Throughout his narration of the life of Wang Fengxian, Du Guangting repeatedly shows how her Daoist faith helps her overcome obstacles. First she avoids marriage by becoming a nun. She evades her powerful pursuers and escapes a life in the imperial harem by hiding in a temple. She moves serenely amid the bloody chaos attendant upon the collapse of the Tang dynasty and helps save others with her Daoist practices and teachings. Through Wang's exemplary biography, Du Guangting recommends Daoism as a means of saving grace in terrible times. He also commends to his readers the cult of Wang Fengxian as efficacious and worthy of reverence. The asceticism and meditation stressed by Du Guangting as part of Wang Fengxian's saintliness are precisely the practices most valued by his school, the Shangqing tradition. Wang Fengxian's victory is indirectly presented by Du as a triumph for the teachings of Shangqing Daoism.

Wang Fengxian's biography makes a great story. It also brings up important issues in the history of Chinese religions. Du Guangting's writing shows the rivalry of Daoism and Buddhism in medieval times. In their competition for the hearts and minds and patronage of the people and the imperial court, representatives of Buddhism and Daoism constantly tried to make clear distinctions between the two religions, while at the same time continuously borrowing from each other and reinterpreting their own traditions. We see this in the account of Wang Fengxian. She is called Guanyin after a major Buddhist deity and takes refuge in a Buddhist temple, where she is revered by common people. Du Guangting calls the Daoist emperor of the highest heavens—the deity who gives Wang the elixir of immortality and predicts her celestial return—the Heavenly Honored One, which is probably a title borrowed from Buddhism. A few sentences later, Master Du instructs the reader on the superiority of Daoism to Buddhism, and he aligns Daoism with Confucian teachings.

In fact, the biography of Wang Fengxian forces us to examine what is sometimes termed the polar opposition between Confucianism and Daoism. Such an opposition seriously misrepresents the true situation, at least in medieval times. Daoist leaders like Du Guangting are quick to claim that their religion upholds the supposedly Confucian values of filial piety within the family and loyalty to the state. They see these virtues as cultural norms shared by all people of the Tang, rather than as exclusively Confucian values. Du Guangting characterizes Wang as careful to support the family and the state even as she resists their demands on her own life. She has found strategies—such as the claim that by pursuing a religious life the Daoist ascetic submits to a higher form of filial piety and loyalty than the householder—that enable her to move outside the confines of the traditional roles of wife and mother without challenging their importance.

In addition to shedding light on the relations between Daoism, Buddhism, and Confucianism, Wang Fengxian's biography illuminates aspects of women's culture in the Tang dynasty. Clearly, some medieval Chinese women were able to create space for themselves within the limitations posed by the prevailing culture. A small number of women religious were able to make friends, travel, become literate, speak in public, wield power, and live independent lives. Wang Fengxian and others like her engaged in the same religious practices, such as fasting, ingesting elixirs, and meditating, as the male Daoists of their time. They hoped for the same results: immortality and celestial office. They were revered by both men and women and numbered both men and women among their disciples. After the Tang, Daoist practices for men and women were separated, and women's ability to leave the home was curtailed. But for a short period of time a few Daoist holy women managed to lead lives that should cause us all to question the image of the timeless, traditional Chinese woman hobbled by bound feet. Wang Fengxian was such a person.

ORIGINAL TEXT[6]

Wang Fengxian ["Offering to the Transcendents"] was the daughter of a peasant family from Dangtu county in Xuan prefecture [in modern Anhui]. Her household was poor. Her father and mother wove and spun to provide for themselves.

Once when Fengxian was about thirteen or fourteen, as she ate her provision of rice [lit., "laborer's ration"] in the fields, she suddenly saw ten or more young girls.[7] After she played with them for a long time, they scattered and departed. Another day, she saw them again, just as before. From that time on, whenever she was in the fields eating her provision of rice, the flocks [of young girls] coming to play became a regular thing. For more than a month, various girls met at night in her house, talking and laughing the whole evening until dawn, when they would disperse. Some brought along strange fruits; others set out rare delicacies. None of it was anything we have in this world. Although her room was narrow and confined and the flock that came was numerous, it did not seem too constrained.

Her father and mother, hearing their talk and laughter, became suspicious. So they spied upon the visitors in order to scrutinize them, whereupon they just disappeared again. In addition, Wang's parents suspected she was being misled by bewitching goblins, so they examined her in great detail. Of course, she used other [evasive] words to answer them. From this time on, the various girls did not descend at night again.

The girls often came and went during the daylight hours. Sometimes they took her along on prolonged and distant journeys. Skimming the void, drifting far and returning, there was no place they did not reach. By evening she would return home. In addition, she never drank or ate. Day by day, she grew increasingly odd. One day, towards evening, her mother saw her throwing herself to the ground from the tips of bamboo plants growing in the corner of the courtyard [she was learning to fly]. Growing more and more worried and anxious, her mother begged Wang to tell her why she did this. So she told her mother and father about the things she had encountered. Finally, before she had even finished discussing the whole matter, the various girls [suddenly appeared and] cut Fengxian's hair, exposing her eyebrows in front and leaving just enough hair hanging down in back to reach the tops of her shoulders.[8] From this time on, for several years, her hair simply did not grow longer.

She did not eat for a year or more.[9] Her flesh and muscles were rich and lustrous, as clean as ice or snow. With a cicada-shaped head and a rounded [lit., "maggot"] neck, she seemed made of luminous matter, with bright pupils. Her appearance was like that of a heavenly person. She was brilliant and perceptive in knowledge and argument. People south of the Yangtze River called her Guanyin.[10]

At the end of the Total Comprehension reign period (860–874), the Official Who Assists the Nation [Prime Minister], Common-Lord Du Shenquan, pacified the Jinling region, while Common-Lord Linghu Tao settled and held together the Yangzhou region.[11] Their reputation for writing poetry and making donations [to Wang Fengxian] was widespread south of the Yangtze River. Later Qin Yan requested that she remain in Jiangdu.[12]

The extended multitudes revered her. She received with ceremony lofty officials and community leaders. Energetic and diligent men who indeed took uprightness and rectitude to heart, they suspected something might be heterodox, so they visited and questioned her. Welcoming them, Wang treated them with reverence. She spoke of the Dao for several days. The community leaders asked about the basic principles of what she discussed and whether or not these principles were more or less in harmony with the essentials [of the Dao]. They also asked why she had the title of [the Buddhist deity] Guanyin. Fengxian said: "What I have encountered is the Dao. What I have gained is transcendence. Babbling common folk just flatter me with the name of Guanyin."

Some years passed and then Common-Lord Du sought her [at her hermitage] beneath Penglai and Mount Mao, intending to offer her as tribute for the consorts' apartments inside the imperial palace. She avoided this by abruptly cutting off her hair.[13] When he still would not allow her to return home to serve her parents, she remained inside a [Buddhist] temple. In the lanes and alleys people did not really understand her victory, but their gossip and praise of her reached the point where they burned incense in reverence to her, offered candles, gave her treasures, and dropped coins [in donation]. Thus some years passed. Up to the present, nobody really understands her hiding [in the Buddhist temple].[14]

Subsequently her ascetic practices and nurturing [the breaths] were not restrained or restricted to those of the rear courtyard [women's quarters]. She also did such brilliant services as performing stygian prayers [prayers for the dead] of the realized transcendents, cutting hair [to ordain nuns], and arranging and directing [convents]. Still she was not satisfied with what she had obtained. But if we were to say she made a pair with the Dao, there would be no obstacle [error]. As Master Zhuang said: "If people consider me an ox, then I'll act like an ox. If they consider me a horse, then I'll act like a horse. Forgetting form and body, realized ones do not take the names of things as binding. Therefore they do not despise people."[15]

Moreover, whenever anyone saw her, she looked like a girl of eighteen or nineteen. Her face and appearance were different from those of ordinary people. She wore a garment with huge sleeves, made of damask and embroidery with patterns of clouds and auroral mists. What she held were transcendent flowers and numinous grasses. What she chanted and intoned were transcendent classics and chapters from the *dong* [lit., grottoes, referring to the three main divisions of the Daoist canon]. What she spoke about were matters pertaining to techniques of the divine transcendents for prolonging life and escaping from this world. Consequently, whenever she went about she could ramble at leisure or rush in a hurry, but she never experienced fatigue. She went to heavenly palaces and transcendent watch towers, golden-storied buildings and jade audience halls, narrow corridors and broad courtyards, mushroom fields and cloud orchards full of divine birds, heavenly wild animals, gemstone trees, and numinous fragrant plants—places not seen in this world.[16]

Passing over the Xinghan [Starry Han River: the Milky Way], going who knows how many thousands of myriads of *li,* she attended court to pay a formal visit to the Heavenly Honored One.[17] Inside the broad basilica in the palace of the Heavenly Honored One, feathered guards were densely arrayed. The Heavenly Honored One declared to Fengxian: "After you have lodged your life in the human world for fifty years, then you will certainly return here."[18] He ordered his attendants to the left and right to take a single cup of jade broth and give it to her to drink. When she finished, he warned her: "As for the produce of the hundred grains or fruits of the grasses and trees, eating them kills people in their youth. If you want longevity, then you should cut them off." From this time on, she did not eat for twenty years.

Now, the Heavenly Honored One performs his transformations in heaven, teaching people by means of the Dao, extending people by means of life, ruling and guiding all the myriad created things, protecting and nurturing universally on all sides: he is like a father among people of this world. [In contrast], Shakyamuni [Buddha] performed transformations on earth, urging people to stop evil and inducing people to seek blessings: he was like a mother among the people in this world. And Zhongni [Confucius] taught the classics to the people, showing them by means of the instructions of the five constants [the five human relationships] how to take up a hundred courses [of good behavior]: he was like an older brother among people of this world. A baby in this world only recognizes its mother; it does not know its father and older brother should be revered. Thus among ordinary people, those who know the Dao are few and those who respect scholars are scarce. This is nothing to wonder at.[19]

In addition, among the people from above the heavens who have been seen, the males wear cloud caps and feathered clothes or tufted chignons and blue aprons, while the females have golden hairpins with kingfisher ornaments and either three hair coils or a pair of horn-shaped chignons. In their hands they hold jade tablets; on their necks they wear round and radiant [jewels]. They fly along, riding the void. No one can fathom their transformations. There are also riders on dragons, *qilin,* simurghs, and cranes [all auspicious creatures], as well as stalwarts with feathered standards and rainbow tallies. They are like thearchs or rulers among humans. Can't you see? As for images of bodhisattvas and Buddhas and Buddhist monks, those that emerge from paintings offered [by Buddhists] are extremely numerous. They all look like the forms of heavenly people, thearchic kings, lords of the Dao, and flying transcendents; they do not represent the actual appearance of monks and Buddhas.[20]

During the Total Comprehension (860–874) and Radiant Disclosure (874–888) reign periods, altogether about forty years, she wandered around the Wanling region of the Huai and Zhe Rivers.[21] Whenever she arrived, spectators gathered like clouds. In her preaching to the masses, she often took up the Dao of loyalty, filial piety, uprightness, and rectitude. She used words that were clear, clean, temperate, and simple; she taught the essentials of the secret (Daoist) practices for refining the body [self-cultivation].[22] Therefore everyone from far and near respected her, setting money and precious substances before her. Rejecting all the million myriads of things she was given, she departed, never looking back. She followed the rolling waves and billows of the Sanhuai region, stopped to perch in the four wildernesses, always seeming naturally unconcerned and unworried.[23] There were imposing tyrants, such as Sun Ru, Zhao Hongbi, and Shi Tao, who oppressed the masses; they wanted to annoy her with improper behavior and coerce her with white [metal] swords, so as to look secretly at the appearance of her spirits.[24] But without even knowing what they were doing, they bowed, knelt, and extended to her the rites of disciples. Afterwards she lived at Mount Dongting in the company of two women disciples who had entered the Dao.[25]

At the beginning of the Radiant Disclosure reign period (885), she moved up to Mount Qianqing in the region of Yuhang.[26] The people beneath the mountain built her a floriate cottage to dwell in. After over a year, she was transformed without ever getting sick. She was forty-eight years old. Auspicious tokens of cloud cranes and strange fragrances were present. This tallied precisely with the period of fifty years mentioned [by the Heavenly Honored One]. In addition, she had not eaten for thirty years. She had a youth's complexion and snowy flesh as if she had remained a virgin. If not through the work of gold and cinnabar elixirs and jade fluid, how could she have reached this point? Also her spirits frequently wandered to the borders of heaven, and she could sit upright for a whole month. Sometimes she descended to inspect the affairs of earthly bureaus or stygian passes, or she sat and looked to the eight extremities; many times she spoke about this with people who possessed the Dao. People in this world do not recognize that [all her accomplishments] are on account of sitting in forgetfulness [meditation]. She is now a companion of the Primal Ruler of the Southern Pole and of the Divine Mother of the Eastern Tumulus.[27]

NOTES

I would like to thank Sue Fernsebner, Liu Lu, Cecily McCaffrey, Elena Songster, Ye Wa, and an unidentified reader for comments on this translation.

1. I use the term "saint" to mean a person in any major religious tradition who is believed to have overcome human limitations, achieved perfection, and become a focal point of veneration. Saints typically become conduits for communication with the divine as well as creators of community. I have argued elsewhere that Chinese Daoist saints are made through a process that draws upon traditional Chinese ideas to verify and then legitimize sanctity. A life of religious practice and a body that does not rot after death verify sanctity. The Daoist saint is then legitimized using the two major modes of ordering the world in traditional China: lineage and bureaucracy. The saint is accepted in a religious lineage and granted a post in the celestial bureaucracy. See Cahill, "Smell Good and Get a Job: Verification and Legitimization of Saints in Medieval Chinese Daoism."

2. The biography of Wang Fengxian discussed and translated here is found in *Records of the Assembled Transcendents of the Fortified Walled City (Yongcheng jixian lu),* completed around 910 by Du Guangting, and reprinted in the Song dynasty Daoist encyclopedia, *Yunji qiqian,* HY 1026, *juan* 114. That text is found in the *Daozang,* or Daoist canon, Zhengtong edition, reprinted in 1976, where Du Guangting's *Yongcheng jixian lu* appears in volume 38, 30344–46 (hereafter DG). Daoist

texts are referred to here by the letters HY, followed by the number assigned to the text in Weng Tu-chien, *Tao tsang tsu mu yin te.*

Du Guangting is the subject of a study by Franciscus Verellen *(Du Guangting [850–933]: Taoiste de cour à la fin de la Chine medievale).* Portions of the *Yongcheng jixian lu* have been studied and translated in Schafer, "Three Divine Women of South China"; Kohn, "The Mother of the Tao"; Cahill, "Practice Makes Perfect: Paths to Transcendence for Women in Medieval China"; Cahill, *Transcendence and Divine Passion: The Queen Mother of the West in Medieval China;* and Cahill, "Pien Tung-hsuan: A Taoist Holy Woman of the T'ang Dynasty (618–907 AD)." A brief biography of Wang Fengxian appears in a text compiled in 1154 by Chen Baoguang (*Sandong qunxian lu,* HY 1238, volume 53, 43316). For the history of the Daoist religion in China, see Bokenkamp, *Early Daoist Scriptures;* and Robinet, *Taoism: Growth of a Religion.*

3. The *lienü* biographical literature, dating back to the Han dynasty work of Liu Xiang, entitled *Biographies of Women (Lienü zhuan),* is studied in Sung, "The Chinese *Lieh nü* Tradition"; and in Raphals, *Sharing the Light: Representations of Women and Virtue in Early China.* The first great collection of biographies of Chinese Buddhist nuns, the *Biqiuni zhuan* by Shi Baochang, is studied and translated in Tsai, *Lives of the Nuns: Biographies of Chinese Buddhist Nuns from the Fourth to the Sixth Centuries.* For an example of a *lienü* biography, see chapter 14.

4. For a study of a young Chinese woman who became a great saint within the confines of Ming society, see Waltner, *The World of a Late Ming Visionary: T'an-yang-tzu and Her Followers.*

5. The garrison revolt of Pang Xun, the most serious uprising of the sixties, paved the way for the disastrous Huang Chao rebellion of 878–884. Both began in the south, originating in popular unrest and lack of faith in the imperial government. On the Pang Xun rebellion, see Twitchett, *Sui and T'ang China,* vol. 3, part 1 of *The Cambridge History of China,* 695–700. On the Huang Chao rebellion, see the same work, 723–47.

6. Source: Du Guangting, *Yongcheng jixian lu.*

7. These are minor Daoist goddesses, a sign of her vocation and selection.

8. Her hair is left too short in front for the coiffure of a married woman. Her parents never have a chance to refuse her permission to enter religious life. Divine intervention in the form of an ordination ritual circumvents the question of marriage, which precipitates crises in the lives of other Daoist holy women, before it arises. Wang Fengxian is now a Daoist nun, ready to undergo further austerities. Cutting the hair is a traditional part of Daoist and Buddhist ordination practices. By Tang times, Daoist nuns no longer shaved the head but left the hair long enough to gather in coils that replicated the fashions of female immortals. On ordination of Daoist nuns in the Tang, see Despeux, "L'ordination des femmes Taoistes sous les T'ang"; and Benn, *The Cavern-Mystery Transmission.*

9. On fasting, an important Daoist ascetic practice, see Levy, "L'abstinance des céréales chez les taoistes"; and Maspero, *Taoism and Chinese Religion.* On the significance of fasting and eating for women's religious practice in medieval Europe, see Bynum, *Holy Feast and Holy Fast: The Religious Significance of Food to Medieval Women.*

10. Guanyin, the Bodhisattva of Compassion who saves people from catastrophes and grants their wishes, was the most popular Buddhist deity in Tang China (see chapter 2). Guanyin is the Chinese name of the bodhisattva called Avalokiteśvara in Sanskrit and Kannon in Japanese. As a female deity, she won devotees throughout

East Asia. Guanyin figures prominently in chapter 25 of the Lotus Sutra, a scripture well known even to illiterate people of the Tang. See the translation by Leon Hurvitz (*Scripture of the Lotus Blossom of the Fine Dharma,* 311–19). Calling a Daoist saint by the name of a Buddhist deity suggests intermingling of the two religions on the popular level. The change from male to female in this deity's image may already be under way here; Chün-fang Yü's forthcoming study of the cult and transformations of Guanyin addresses this transformation.

11. Du Shenquan, an official who passed the imperial examinations and served as a minister under Xuanzong (846–859), was appointed military governor in the south under Yizong (859–873). During the Pang Xun rebellion of 868–869, he was instrumental in restoring peace. Du Shenquan has official biographies in Liu Xu, *Jiu Tang shu* (hereafter JT), volume 14, *juan* 177, 4610–11, and Ouyang Xiu, *Xin Tang shu* (hereafter XT), volume 12, *juan* 96, 3863. Jinling is a city in the south, near present-day Nanjing, in Jiangning county. Linghu Tao (802–879), another official who passed the imperial examination and served as a minister under Xuanzong, held a military post under Yizong and played a part in the Pang Xun rebellion. He has official biographies in JT, volume 14, *juan* 172, 4465, and XT, volume 16, *juan* 166, 5101. Yangzhou is a city in the south of China, to the southeast of Xun, near present-day Jiangning county. These two top military governors were not embarrassed to write poems to this young woman and to support her with donations.

12. Qin Yan (d. 888), was a former thief who became a leader in the Huang Chao rebellion. He has official biographies in JT, volume 14, *juan* 182, 4715, and XT, volume 20, *juan* 224, 6401. Jiangdu is a city in the south, in present-day Jiangsu province, near Jinling.

13. Presumably, she cut her hair to make herself unattractive.

14. This episode, suggesting that she lived and received homage for a time in a Buddhist temple, perhaps passing as a Buddhist nun, perplexes her Daoist biographer. He protests that he cannot understand why she would spend such a long time in a rival institution. Wang's residence in a Buddhist temple suggests that her cult was widespread among common folk of the Tang and that she was claimed as a holy figure by Daoists and Buddhists alike. If, as I suspect, Buddhists also once claimed her as their saint, Du Guangting's perplexity on this episode is disingenuous.

15. This quotation, attributed to the Warring States Daoist thinker Zhuang zi, does not exist in any current recension of the *Zhuang zi* text. The words suggest that Wang is unconcerned with her reputation and only cares for the good of the people. The statement may also be an attempt to justify Wang's indifference to whether people consider her a Buddhist or a Daoist nun. For Du Guangting, she is one of the *zhen ren* (realized ones, or Daoist perfected). Du suggests that her brilliance, compassion, and skill in teaching rival those of Guanyin, after whom she is mistakenly called. Du Guangting implies that Wang Fengxian possesses *upaya* or "skill-in-means," the foremost teaching tool of compassionate Mahāyana bodhisattvas, such as Guanyin, to whom she has just been compared. Using skill-in-means, the bodhisattva teaches all listeners according to their ability. This miraculous skill in communication is demonstrated in the famous parable of the burning house in chapter 3 of the Lotus Sutra. See Hurvitz, *Scripture of the Lotus Blossom of the Fine Dharma,* 49–83.

16. Du Guangting describes Wang as dressing like a goddess and obtaining miraculous herbal medicines. She chants Daoist texts revealed by the high gods and gains access to scriptures only known to initiates. Possessed of the secrets of longevity, transcendence, and celestial travel, she journeys to the Daoist heavens.

17. "Heavenly Honored One" (Tian Zun) is an honorific title bestowed on the highest gods of Daoism. Here Du Guangting refers either to the deified Lao zi or to a ruler of one of the three Daoist heavens. Buddhists use the same title for the Buddha.

18. The god's prediction of immortality for Wang Fengxian helps her biographer establish her legitimacy as a holy figure. The importance of prediction in Daoist lore closely parallels that in Buddhist tales, in which Buddhas of the past give predictions of future Buddhahood to bodhisattvas. Co-opting this device of prediction, Du Guangting asserts the priority of Daoism over Buddhism.

19. Du Guangting pauses in the course of his story to deliver a sermon in which he denigrates Buddhism (and mothers), while he elevates Daoism and aligns it with Confucianism. Here we see Du Guangting the court official as well as the Daoist master. He also explains why people do not revere the Dao or respect scholars and might mistakenly favor Buddhism. Notice that in comparing the Heavenly Honored One to the father, the Buddha to the mother, and Confucius to the elder brother, he places them in order of relative importance.

20. Du Guangting makes the interesting claim that the many and ubiquitous Buddhist images are not true representations of the appearances of Buddhist deities but are really copies of Daoist deities. This sheds light on a question that has been puzzling me for over a decade: if Daoism is so important in the Tang dynasty, where are all the Tang Daoist images? Maybe they have been hiding in plain sight under the guise of Buddhist images. This is an important subject that needs more work.

21. Wanling is in modern-day Anhui province and includes Xuan city, Wang Fengxian's hometown.

22. Despite her life of celibacy, which seems to contradict the demands of tradition that a woman marry and supply male descendants to her husband's ancestral line, Du Guangting stresses Wang's support of the Confucian values of filial piety and loyalty. He asserts elsewhere that her saintly life embodies a higher form of filial piety and loyalty: by attaining transcendence she gains blessings for her whole family and for the state. See DG, 30346.

23. Sanhuai (the "three Huai") is a region named for the three tributaries of the Huai River in the south. The "four wildernesses" refers to lands beyond Chinese civilization in each of the four directions.

24. Sun Ru, a great military leader at the time of the Huang Chao rebellion, has an official biography in XT, volume 17, *juan* 188, 5466–68. I have not identified Zhao Hongbi or Shi Tao.

25. The Mount Dongting intended here is a mountain in Jiangsu, rather than the more famous mountain of that name (also called Mount Zhun) near Lake Dongting in modern Hunan.

26. Mount Qianqing is located near Yuhang in present-day Zhejiang province.

27. The titles designate two great goddesses of *Shangqing* Daoism.

Fig. 2. The execution of Miaoshan. Ca. sixteenth century. Fresco at Dahui si, Beijing. Source: Wang Guanghao, ed., *Mingdai Guanyin dian caisu*, 111.

TWO

Biography of the Great Compassionate One of Xiangshan by Jiang Zhiqi (1031–1104)

Translated by Chün-fang Yü

TRANSLATOR'S PREFACE

I first heard the story of Princess Miaoshan from my maternal grandmother when I was five. She was a devotee of Guanyin. She kept enshrined in her room a white porcelain statue of Guanyin, to which she would offer incense and prayer every morning. Many years later, in 1986–1987, when I was in China doing research on my book on Guanyin, many of the women pilgrims I interviewed in different parts of China, from Zhejiang to Yunnan, were familiar with this story. Many Chinese people, men as well as women, see Guanyin as Miaoshan. The story has served as a powerful medium for the transmission of the cult of Guanyin in China. It also has special appeal to Chinese women.

INTRODUCTION

The great Buddhist bodhisattva Guanyin (Avalokiteśvara) has been linked with the story of Princess Miaoshan since the twelfth century. The Chinese believe that the princess was the incarnation of the deity. The story tells how Miaoshan, a king's daughter, refused to marry because she wanted to practice Buddhism, how she was persecuted and executed by her angry father, how she was restored to life by the gods and achieved enlightenment, how she saved her father from death by offering him her eyes and hands as medicine, and finally, how she converted her father to Buddhism. It ends with her appearance as the deity titled Great Compassionate One (Dabei), the Tantric form of the bodhisattva with a thousand hands and eyes, popular since the Tang (618–907). By refusing to obey her father's order to marry, she committed the greatest Confucian offense: she was unfilial. At the same time, however, by sacrificing parts of her body to save her dying father, she became the true embodiment of compassion. Her story describes the great conflict between an individual's quest for spiritual autonomy and the pressures from the individual's family to fulfill social expectations—a conflict experienced by countless women in imperial China. Miaoshan's triumph in this story offered such women inspiration and hope. The following translation is from a stele inscription that provides us with the earliest version of this legend.

The Miaoshan story serves another important function. By identifying the pan-Buddhist bodhisattva Guanyin as Princess Miaoshan, a real woman who lived and died in Henan, the Miaoshan legend humanized and "sinified" (made Chinese) a mythical deity who was originally not bound by any place or culture. The legend also transformed Xiangshan, a county in central China, into a holy land. After the story appeared it became widely known through its use in plots of dramas and novels. Most importantly, beginning in the Ming (1368–1644) the legend was transcribed as a sacred text, the *Xiangshan baojuan* (Precious volume of Xiangshan baojuan; the earliest extant version is dated 1773). It is mainly through this story that Chinese of all social strata and both sexes have come to know Guanyin first and foremost as a strong-willed yet filial girl who refused to get married.

Glen Dudbridge was the first scholar to pay serious attention to the origin and evolution of this legend. According to him,[1] the earliest documentary evidence of the legend was a text about Miaoshan's life written by Jiang Zhiqi (1031–1104) while he served as prefect of Ruzhou (in modern Henan) briefly in 1100. This text was copied by the prime minister and calligrapher Cai Jing (d. 1126) and engraved on stone later that same year. Jiang had heard the story from the monk Huaizhou, the abbot of Xiangshan Monastery, which housed a stupa dedicated to the Great Compassionate One. The abbot, in turn, attributed the story to the famous Vinaya master Daoxuan (596–667), who had learned it from a divine spirit. Although the legend claimed to bear such a miraculous and hoary origin, Dudbridge convincingly argues that its dissemination in the early twelfth century was closely tied to the rising fame of Xiangshan Monastery as an important regional pilgrimage center.

Three years after Jiang served at Ruzhou, he was the prefect of Hangzhou for a year—from November 1102 to either September or October 1103. Most likely he brought this story to Hangzhou with him, for the original text was later re-engraved and re-erected by a monk of the Upper Tianzhu Monastery, a major cultic center for Guanyin worship in Hangzhou. Inspired by Dudbridge's research,[2] Lai Swee-fo (Lai Ruihe) tracked down the three extant rubbings of the Upper Tianzhu stele in existing collections and pointed out that they contained only the second half of the story. He also proved that a work titled "An Abridged Biography of Bodhisattva Guanshi yin" ("Guanshi yin pusa zhuan lüe"), written in 1306 by Guan Daosheng (1262–1319; wife of the famous painter and calligrapher Zhao Mengfu [1254–1322]), which has survived in stele collections, was based on the stele text.[3] But because the local gazetteer did not record the Xiangshan stele and the extant three rubbings of the Upper Tianzhu stele only recorded its latter half, the fate of the original stele at Xiangshan and its entire content have long been a mystery. Dudbridge theorized that the Upper Tianzhu rubbing was from the second of two original stelae and that the first slab was either destroyed or lost.[4]

The mystery has now been resolved. In 1993 Lai Swee-fo reported that on a trip to Xiangshan Monastery, in Baofeng, Henan, he had seen the stele, which had been re-erected in 1308, with the inscription originally composed by Jiang Zhiqi.[5] The stele is very tall and wide (2.22 meters in height and 1.46 in width) because the text is very long, containing over three thousand characters. The top portion was damaged during the Cultural Revolution and later repaired, resulting in the loss of about ten characters in each line. The second half of the stele corresponds exactly to what has been preserved from the Upper Tianzhu stele. Lai explains why the first half of the text, running twenty-four lines, was not handed down: because the slab is so wide, in fact twice the width of a normal stele, it would have required two separate pieces of paper to make the rubbing. Most likely, the rubbing from the first half of the stele got misplaced or lost early on and thus has remained unknown to scholars until now.

Dudbridge had translated the second half of the stele in 1978.[6] He also compared the story as it is found in two later sources. The first of these is the *Comprehensive Record of Buddhism Compiled in the Longxing Era (Longxing fojiao biannian tonglun)*, a chronicle of Buddhist history in China from 64 to 957 C.E. written in 1164 by Zuxiu, a monk of Longxing fu (the present Nanchang); the second is the *Jin'gang keyi,* a vernacular annotation of commentaries on the Diamond Sutra compiled by Juelian with a preface dated 1551. With the discovery of the entire stele of Xiangshan, we can now say with some confidence that both Zuxiu and Juelian knew of Jiang's inscription, for they at times used phrases identical to those in the stele in their own works, which were much shorter and less detailed. The biography of 1100 can safely be regarded as the source of all later compositions.

The following is the translation of the entire stele, setting forth the life of the Great Compassionate One. Dr. Lai provided the transcription of the first half of the text and kindly gave me permission to translate it. The second half, starting with "When the envoy arrived," follows Dudbridge's translation.[7] Missing words are indicated by ellipsis dots within parentheses, while possible reconstructions based on related sources are enclosed within parentheses.

ORIGINAL TEXT[8]

(Lü Master Daoxuan's) pure conduct moved the divine spirit who came to attend him. One day the Master asked the divine spirit, "I have heard that the Mahasattva [Great Being] Guanyin has special affinity with this land. Of all the places where the bodhisattva's efficacious traces are manifested, which is the most excellent?" The divine spirit answered, "Guanyin's appearances follow no fixed rule, but Xiangshan is most excellent because the bodhisattva left the trace of her flesh-body there." The Master asked, ("Where is this Xiangshan?" The spirit replied:

Two hundred *li* south of Mount Song there stand three hills. The middle one is Xiangshan, where) the bodhisattva achieved enlightenment. To the northeast of the hill there was in the past a king whose name was Zhuang. His lady was named Baode. The king followed heterodox ways and did not respect the Three Treasures. He had no crown prince, only three daughters: the eldest Miaoyan, the second Miaoyin, the youngest Miaoshan. Of these three daughters, two were already married. Only the third (was not married).

(At the time of her birth, fragrance filled the air and light) shone both inside and outside the palace. People of that country were astounded, saying that a fire had broken out in the palace. She was born that very evening. At birth she was clean without being washed. Her holy marks were noble and majestic, her body was covered by five-colored auspicious clouds. The people all wondered, saying, "Could it be that a holy person has appeared in the world?" The king marveled at this and named her "Miaoshan" [Wondrous Goodness].

When Miaoshan grew up, her conduct and appearance far transcended the ordinary. (She always wore dirty clothes and did not adorn herself. She would eat only once a day.) When it was not the proper time (i.e., past noontime), she would not eat. In her conversations she always gave people good advice. She would talk about cause and effect and about everything being impermanent and illusory. In the palace she was called Buddha's Heart. All those who listened to her turned to good. They fasted and practiced the Way without faltering in their resolve.

When the king heard this, he said to his wife, "Our young daughter Miaoshan is teaching my ladies-in-waiting to practice the Way in the palace. They have given up adornment and cosmetics . . ." (The king) said to his daughter, "You have now grown up and should obey my instruction. Do not delude and confuse the ladies in the inner palace. Your father has a country to rule and does not like what are doing. Your mother and I will find a husband for you. From now on you should follow the correct path and refrain practicing the heterodox way, thus corrupting the customs of our country."

When Miaoshan heard what the king said, she smiled and replied, "Royal Father, (. . .) So that you may not be deceived (I must tell you that) I would never, for the sake of one lifetime of glory, plunge into aeons of misery. I have pondered long on this matter and deeply detest it [marriage]. I want to leave home to practice the Way in order to realize Buddhahood and attain enlightenment. I can then repay the kindness of my parents and save sentient beings from suffering. If you order me to marry, I dare not obey. Father, please understand and pity me."

The king told his wife, "Our daughter does not (want to marry. Please talk to her and make her change her mind." The mother then tried to persuade Miaoshan, who answered,) "I will obey Mother's command only if it will prevent three misfortunes." The mother asked, "What are the three misfortunes?" She answered, "The first is this: when people are young, their faces are as fair as the jade-like moon, but when they grow old, their hair turns white, their faces are wrinkled; in walking, resting, sitting, or lying down they are in every way worse off than when they were young. The second is this: one's limbs may be strong and vigorous, one may walk as briskly as if flying through the air, but when one suddenly becomes sick, one lies in bed (without a single pleasure in life. The third is this: a person may have a large group of relatives and) be surrounded by his flesh and blood, but when death comes, even such close kin as father and son cannot take the person's place. If a husband can prevent these three misfortunes, I will marry him. But if he cannot do so, I vow never to marry. People of the world are all mired in these kinds of suffering. If one desires to be free from these sufferings, one must leave the secular world and pass through the gate of Buddhism. Only when one practices religion and obtains its fruit can one deliver all people from suffering. This is why I have undertaken my quest (for enlightenment . . ."

The king became) ever more angry and exiled her to the garden in the back of the palace. Cutting off her food and drink, he ordered everyone in the palace not to go near her. Her mother was sad and missed her. She secretly asked a palace maid to take food and drink to Miaoshan. The king said to the queen, "I exiled her to the back garden, but she does not seem to fear death. Nor does she eat. Why don't you go to her with Miaoyan and

Miaoyin and persuade her to change her mind? If she does, father and child will meet again. Otherwise (. . .)"

When they came to the back garden, they saw Miaoshan seated in deep meditation. She paid no attention to her mother. The lady embraced her and cried aloud, "Ever since you left the palace, my two eyes are almost dried up and my liver and innards are breaking into pieces. How can you be at peace seeing your mother thus? Your father is so troubled by you that he cannot hold audience in the palace nor take care of state affairs, so he told me to come with Miaoyan and Miaoyin to talk to you. Please think of your father (. . .)"

Miaoshan said, "I am not suffering here. Why are Father and Mother so unhappy? In all the emotional entanglements of this world there is no period of spiritual release. If close kin are united, they must inevitably be sundered and scattered. Even if one stays with one's parents for a hundred years, when death arrives, we still must be parted. Rest at ease, Mother. Luckily you have my two sisters to care for you and there is no need for me. Please go back and say that I have no desire to go back on my resolve."

Then Miaoyan and Miaoyin said to Miaoshan, "(. . .) Look at those who have left the home and become nuns. Who among them is able to shine light, shake the earth, attain Buddhahood, or become a patriarch so that she can repay kindness above and save all beings below? Isn't it better to get married in accordance with the rites? Why do you worry our parents so?"

Miaoshan replied to her two sisters, "You are attached to glory, luxury, and conjugal love. You are bound by the pleasure of the moment. But you do not know that pleasure is the cause of pain (. . .) As daughters, we cannot be excused from attending parents. But can your husbands do this for you? Sisters, each of us has to live her life. Please think it over and take care of yourselves, but do not keep advising me what to do. The reality of my decision is right in front of you. There is no use in empty regret. Please persuade Mother to go back to the palace, and tell Father that empty space may have a limit, but my vow is limitless. Whether I live or die is up to Father to decide." Miaoyan and Miaoyin returned to tell (. . .) The queen further reported to the king, who then became even more enraged.

There was a nun by the name of Huizhen. The king sent for her and told her, "My youngest daughter Miaoshan does not follow righteousness and propriety but insists on leaving home. There is no way to dissuade her. You people must try to devise a way to persuade her. I will allow my youngest daughter to stay in your place for seven days to be instructed by you. If she listens to me, I will decorate your (nunnery . . .)" A messenger was dispatched to go with the nun to the back garden. She invited Miaoshan to accompany her to the nunnery. Five hundred nuns came out to welcome her and escort her to the main hall to burn incense. The next day the nuns said to Miaoshan, "You were born in the palace and grew up there. Why do you seek loneliness? You had better go back to the palace, which is so much superior to a temple."

Miaoshan heard what they said and replied with a smile, "(. . . I want to) save all sentient beings. What you show me about your knowledge is truly pitiable and despicable. If even Buddhist disciples such as yourselves say things like this, no wonder worldly people blame me for what I do. My father, the king, is angry and hateful toward you people and does not allow me to leave the householder's life. Doesn't he have a reason? Don't you know the reason for having a shaved head and wearing a square robe? One who has left the householder's life detests vainglory, luxury (. . .) and sexual love (. . . Your behavior, on the other hand,) accords very little with what is demanded of a monastic. The Buddha has left clear instructions: a monastic should give up makeup and adornment, wear rag robes, carry a begging bowl, and sustain herself by begging. Why are all of you interested in luxury, wearing beautiful clothes, and behaving in such a bewitching and seductive manner? You entered the gate of Buddhism wantonly, corrupted the pure rules, and accepted the offerings from the faithful undeservedly. You are monastics in name only, and your hearts are not in accordance with the Way!" The nuns had nothing to say when Miaoshan rebuked them thus.

At that point, Huizhen became worried and told Miaoshan, "The reason why the nuns tried to persuade you just now (to give up the idea of renouncing the world) is because they were following the king's order." She then told Miaoshan about the king's decree, as mentioned before, and asked her to change her mind so that the nuns could be spared and the nunnery would be safe from disaster.

Miaoshan said, "Don't you know (the stories) about Prince Mahasattva's realization of no-birth as a result of throwing himself off the cliff in order to feed the hungry tigers, or about King Sivi's attaining the other shore as a result of cutting his flesh to save a dove? Since you have already left the life of a householder, you should regard this illusory body as impermanent and detestable, and the four great elements as temporarily coming into being but originally nonexistent. You should want to be delivered from transmigration in your every thought and seek for release in every moment of consciousness. Why do you fear death and love life? Don't you know that attachment to this dirty and smelly leather bag [the body] is an obstacle? (. . .) You want to escape death by obeying the king's wish. But be at ease. When I achieve enlightenment I will save you from transmigration. Do not worry."

When the nuns heard this, they conferred among themselves and decided that because Miaoshan grew up in the palace, she did not know the difficulties of ordinary life outside the palace and so believed that leaving the world would be a happy experience as well. So now she must be made to feel the pain and humiliation of hard manual labor so that she would know fear and thus repent. They told Miaoshan, "If you want to be a monastic, you [should] (. . .) labor earlier than everyone else and work in the kitchen. You must work at chores no one else is capable of doing. There are no vegetables in the vegetable garden, but you must serve food in a timely fashion without fail."

Miaoshan went to the vegetable garden and seeing how few vegetables there were, she became worried about the next day, not knowing how to get food to serve the nuns. But just when she was thinking thus, the dragon spirit of the temple came to her help, and with divine assistance (. . .) she served the nuns without difficulty (. . .) Obtaining water was also very difficult, and Miaoshan was troubled. But a spring appeared miraculously on the left side of the kitchen. The water from the spring was very sweet. Huizhen then knew that Miaoshan was not an ordinary person, for she could move the dragon spirit to help her. So she reported this to the king, who became greatly angered and said to his attendants, "My youngest daughter has practiced the heterodox way for a long time. I put her in a nunnery, but she used magic to delude the people and insult me (. . .)"

(When the king's envoy arrived at the nunnery,) Miaoshan obeyed the royal command and said to the community of nuns, "Retire at once, all of you. I am to suffer execution." Miaoshan then came out (to meet) her death. At the moment when she was about to endure the blade, the mountain god of Longshan—who knew that Miaoshan, the bodhisattva of great power, was on the point of fulfilling her spiritual destiny and delivering the multitude of living beings and that her evil royal father was wrongly about to behead her—used his divine powers to produce (. . .) dark, violent wind, thunder, and lightning. He snatched Miaoshan and set her down at the foot of the mountain. The envoy, no longer knowing where Miaoshan was, rushed in haste to report to the king.

The king, again shocked and enraged, sent off five hundred soldiers to behead the entire community of nuns and burn all their buildings. His lady and the royal family all wept bitterly, saying that Miaoshan was already dead and beyond hope of rescue. The king said to his lady, "(. . .) Do not grieve. This young girl was no kin of mine. She must have been some demon who was born into my family. I have managed to get rid of the demon; that is cause for great delight!"

Now that she had been snatched away by divine power to the foot of Longshan, Miaoshan looked around and found no one there. With slow steps she climbed the mountain. Suddenly she noticed a foul, reeking smell and thought to herself: "The mountain forests are secluded and quiet; why is there this smell?"

The mountain god took the form of an old man and met Miaoshan with the words: "Kind one, where do you want to go?" Miaoshan said, "I wish to go up onto this mountain to practice religion." The old man said, "This mountain is the abode of creatures with scales and shells, feathers and fur. It is no place for you to practice your cultivation, kind one." Miaoshan asked, "What is the name of this mountain?" He said, "It is Longshan. Dragons live on this mountain; hence it is named after them." "What about the range to the west of here?" He answered, "That too is an abode of dragons, and for that reason it is called Lesser Longshan. However, between the two mountains there is a small ridge named Xiangshan. The place is pure and clean, a fit place for you to pursue your cultivation, kind one."

Miaoshan said, "Who are you, that you are showing me the place to live?" The old man answered, "Your disciple is not a man but the god of this mountain. You, kind one, are going to fulfill your spiritual destiny, and I, your disciple, have sworn to protect and keep you." With these words he vanished.

Miaoshan went to Xiangshan, climbed to the summit, and looked around. It was peaceful, without any trace of human beings, and she said to herself, "This is the place where I shall transform my karma." So there on the summit she built a shelter for practicing religious cultivation. She dressed in grasses, ate from trees, and no one knew [of her] (. . .) for three whole years.

Meanwhile her father, the king, sickened with jaundice on account of his sinful karma. It spread all over his skin, and he found no rest in sleep. The best doctors throughout the land were unable to heal him. His lady and the royal family were anxious about him morning and night.

One day a strange monk stood in front of the inner palace, saying, "I have a divine remedy that can heal the king's sickness." The king's attendants hastily reported these words to the king, and on hearing them he summoned the monk into the inner palace. The monk addressed him: "I, a poor man of religion, have medicine to cure the king's sickness." The king said, "What medicine do you have that can cure my disease?" The monk replied, "I have a prescription that requires two major ingredients." The king asked what, and the monk replied, "This medicine is made using the arms and eyes of one who is without anger."

The king said, "(. . .) Do not speak so frivolously. If I take someone's arms and eyes, will they not be angry?" The monk said, "Such a one does exist in your land." The king asked where that person might be, and the monk replied, "In the southwest of your dominion is a mountain named Xiangshan. On its summit is a hermit practicing religious cultivation with signal merit, though no one knows of it. This person has no anger." The king said, "How can I get this person's arms and eyes?" The monk said, "No one else can seek them; they are available only to you, the king. In the past this hermit had a close affinity with you. If you obtain this hermit's arms and eyes, your sickness can be cured instantly, without any doubt."

When the king heard this, he burned incense and offered this prayer: "If my terrible sickness can really be cured, may I receive this hermit's own arms and eyes, bestowed without stint or grudge." His prayer completed, he commanded an envoy to go to the mountain bearing incense.

When the envoy arrived, he saw a hermit whose body was stately and impressive sitting cross-legged inside a thatched hermitage. He burned fine incense and announced the royal command: "The king of the land has suffered jaundice now for three years. The great physicians and the wonder drugs of all the land are unable to cure him. A monk has presented a (remedy): by using the arms and eyes of one without anger a medicine can be made up. And now, with deep respect, we have heard that you, holy hermit, practice religion with signal merit, and we believe that you must be without anger. We venture to beg you for your arms and eyes to cure the king's sickness."

The envoy bowed twice, and Mianshan reflected: "My father, the king, showed disrespect to the Three Treasures, he persecuted and suppressed Buddhism, he burned monastic buildings, he executed a community (of nuns). He invited the retribution of this sickness. With my arms and eyes I shall save the king from his distress." With this resolve she said to the envoy, "It must be your king's refusal to believe in the Three Treasures that has caused him to suffer this evil malady. I shall give my arms and eyes to provide medicine for him. My one desire is that the remedy may match the ailment and drive out the king's disease. The king must direct his mind towards enlightenment and commit himself to the Three Treasures; then he will achieve recovery."

With these words she gouged out both her eyes with a knife, then told the envoy to sever her two arms. At that moment the whole mountain shook, and from the sky came a voice commending her: "Rare, how rare! She is able to save all living beings, to do things impossible in this world!" The envoy was terrified, but the hermit said, "Have no fear. Take my arms and eyes back to the king, and remember what I have said." The envoy accepted them and returned to report to the king.

When the king received the arms and eyes, he felt a deep shame. He told the monk to blend the medicine; then he (took) it. Before ten days had passed, he had recovered completely. The king and his lady, his kin, his officials, and all down to the subjects of his realm began to rejoice. The king sent for the monk to give him thank-offerings, saying: "No one but you, (Master), could save us from that terrible sickness." The monk said, "It was not my power. How could you have recovered without the hermit's arms and eyes? You should go up the mountain to offer thanks to the hermit." With these words he vanished.

The king was astounded. He brought his palms together and said, "So slight a cause as mine has moved a holy monk to come and save me!" And then he commanded his attendants: "Tomorrow I shall go to visit Xiangshan and make thank-offerings to the hermit."

The next day the king had carriages prepared and with his lady, his two daughters, and the palace retinue, set out from the walled city and came up Xiangshan. (Reaching) the hermitage, they lavishly laid out the finest offerings. The king burned incense and offered thanks with the words: "I could not have recovered from that foul disease without your arms and eyes, hermit. Today, therefore, I have personally come with my closest kin to visit the mountain and offer thanks to you."

When the king with his lady and palace maidens moved forward to gaze upon the hermit who was without arms or eyes, they were moved to sorrowful thoughts because the hermit's physical impairment had been brought about by (the king). His lady made a minute examination, gazed at the hermit's physical characteristics, and said to the king, "When I look at the hermit's appearance, she is very like our daughter." And with these words she found herself choking with tears and lamentation.

The hermit suddenly spoke, "My lady mother! Do not cast your mind back to Miaoshan: I am she. When the king, my father, suffered that foul disease, your child offered up her arms and eyes to repay the king's love."

Hearing these words, the king and his lady embraced Miaoshan with loud weeping, stirring heaven and earth with their grief. He said, "My evil ways have caused my daughter to lose her arms and eyes and (endure) this suffering. I am going to lick my child's two eyes with my tongue and rejoin her two arms. I desire the gods and spirits of heaven and earth to make my child's withered eyes to grow again, and her severed arms once more to be whole!"

As soon as the king had expressed this resolve but before his mouth had touched her eyes, Miaoshan suddenly vanished. At that moment heaven and earth shook, radiance blazed, auspicious clouds gathered, divine musicians began to play. (And then) the All-Compassionate Guanyin of the Thousand Arms and Thousand Eyes appeared, solemn and majestic in form, radiant with dazzling light, lofty and magnificent, like the moon amid the stars.

When the king with his lady and palace maidens beheld the form of the bodhisattva, they rose and struck themselves, beat their breasts with loud lament, and raised their voices in repentance: "We, your disciples, with our mortal sight failed to recognize the Holy One. Evil karma has obstructed our minds. We pray you to extend your saving protection to absolve our earlier misdeeds. From this time on we shall turn towards the Three Treasures, we shall rebuild Buddhist monasteries. We pray you, Bodhisattva, in your great compassion, to return to your original body and permit us to make offerings."

In a moment the hermit returned to her original person, with her arms and eyes quite intact. She sat cross-legged, brought her palms together, and with great solemnity passed away, as though entering into meditation.

The king and his lady burned incense and made a vow: "We, your disciples, will (provide) an offering of fragrant wood, will commit your holy body to the funeral pyre, and when we return to the palace, will raise a stupa and make offerings to it in perpetuity." Having made his vow, the king surrounded the transcendent body with all kinds of pure incense, cast flames upon it, and burned it. When the fragrant fuel was consumed, the transcendent body loomed there still and could not be moved. The king made another vow: "It must be that the bodhisattva will not depart [from] this place and wishes to cause all living beings to see and hear and make offerings." Having said these words, the king and his lady together lifted the body, and immediately (at their touch) it rose lightly.

The king then reverently established a precious shrine with the bodhisattva's true body inside, and outside he built a precious stupa. With great solemnity he buried her on the summit of the mountain, beneath the site of her hermitage. And there on the mountain, with court and kin, he watched and protected her day and night without sleeping.

At length he returned to his capital. He rebuilt Buddhist monasteries, increased the ordination of monks and nuns, and paid reverence to the Three Treasures. He drew resources from his private treasury and built at Xiangshan a pagoda with thirteen stories to cover the true body of the bodhisattva.

(The divine spirit said:) "Master, you have asked me, your disciple, about the holy traces of the bodhisattva, and I have given a brief account of the broad essentials. As for the bodhisattva's secret incarnations, these are not known to me."

The Vinaya Master [of that school of monastic discipline] again asked, "What is the present state of the precious stupa on Xiangshan?"

The divine spirit said, "The stupa has long been abandoned. Now (there remains only) the pagoda, and few know of it. The traces left on earth by a holy one prosper and decay in their due time. Only after three hundred years will a revival occur."

Now that his questions were finished, the Vinaya Master brought his palms together and uttered these words of praise: "How great is the spiritual power of the Mahasattva Guanyin! Were it not for the amplitude of the bodhisattva's vow, these signs could not have been revealed. If the living beings of that land had not brought their karmic conditions to maturity, they could not have attracted this response. How mighty, this merit without measure! It cannot be conceived!"

He told his disciple Yichang to set the story down in writing, on the fifteenth day of the second summer month in the second year of Shengli [April 20, 699].

Written in the third month of the third year of Yuanfu [May 1100].

Erected in the seventh month of the first year of Zhida [August 1308] by monks of the Public Chan Monastery of the Great Universal Gateway on Xiangshan.

NOTES

1. Dudbridge, "Miao-shan on Stone: Two Early Inscriptions."
2. Dudbridge, *The Legend of Miao-shan.*
3. Lai Swee-fo, "Miaoshan zhuanshuo de liangchong xin ziliao."
4. Dudbridge, "Miao-shan on Stone."
5. Lai Swee-fo, "Wanli xunbei ji."

6. Dudbridge, *The Legend of Miao-shan;* Dudbridge, "Miao-shan on Stone."
7. Dudbridge, "Miao-shan on Stone."
8. Source: Stone stele inscription originally dated 1100, calligraphed by Cai Jing (d. 1126), Xiangshan Monastery, Baofeng, Hunan; and Dudbridge, *The Legend of Miao-shan.*

Fig. 3. *Illustrations of the Book of Filial Piety for Women* (detail), handscroll attributed to twelfth-century artist Ma Hezhi. The section here illustrates "Serving One's Parents-in-Law." Courtesy of the National Palace Museum, Taipei, Taiwan, Republic of China.

THREE

The *Book of Filial Piety for Women* Attributed to a Woman Née Zheng (ca. 730)

Translated by Patricia Buckley Ebrey

TRANSLATOR'S PREFACE

Confucian didactic tracts written for the education of girls are, on the whole, predictable. Few would be amazed to find that girls were told to cultivate Confucian virtues like filial piety, faithfulness, loyalty, diligence, trustworthiness, and sincerity, and warned against such evils as scheming, selfishness, and sensual indulgence. Nevertheless, I thought it would be worthwhile to translate the *Book of Filial Piety for Women* because it parallels so neatly the original *Book of Filial Piety*. Miss Zheng, the author of the *Book of Filial Piety for Women,* has given us her understanding of how the moral man and the moral woman differed by adapting one of the most widely circulated moral primers to make it more appropriate to girls. Although the language of the *Book of Filial Piety,* like that of many other Confucian texts, is gender-neutral as though it was addressed to both males and females, Miss Zheng was well aware that it was implicitly addressed to males and needed considerable adaptation to make it suit females. Here excerpts from the two texts are lined up to encourage readers to read them against each other. The historical interest of the *Book of Filial Piety for Women* lies in the ways it differs from the original, unmarked *Book of Filial Piety.*

INTRODUCTION

By Song times, several didactic texts considered useful for the education of girls were in circulation. The two most famous had been written approximately a thousand years earlier and required a relatively high degree of literacy—these were the two classics of the Han period, Liu Xiang's *Biog-*

raphies of Women (Lienü zhuan) and Ban Zhao's *Admonitions for Women (Nü jie)*.[1] Many women's biographies state that their subjects had studied these texts, and leading neo-Confucian scholars urged that parents instruct their daughters in them.[2] In addition, however, there were at least two short works written in later centuries and composed in a style simple enough to be used as primers: the *Book of Filial Piety for Women (Nü xiaojing)* and the *Analects for Women (Nü lunyu)*. These texts are not mentioned very often in the writings of leading Song scholars, perhaps because they were considered too elementary. That the *Book of Filial Piety for Women* circulated in Song times, however, can be seen in the paintings made to illustrate it, some of which have survived.[3] Moreover, along with the *Analects for Women,* it was copied into the fourteenth-century compendium, the *Shuofu,* and in subsequent centuries into other collectanea, the last in the late nineteenth century.[4]

Evidence for the dating of the *Book of Filial Piety for Women* is scanty. The preface is signed by a Miss Zheng, the wife of an official named Chen Miao. She says that she wrote the text for her niece, who was about to marry Prince Yong. The Tang histories mention a Prince Yong who was the sixteenth son of Emperor Xuanzong, which would date this text to around 730.[5]

In terms of its moral message, the *Book of Filial Piety for Women* could have been written at almost any period after the Han.[6] Its primary goal is to expand the message of the *Book of Filial Piety* to apply to girls and women. Like its prototype, the *Book of Filial Piety for Women* presents filial piety as the supreme virtue required of everyone in society. The moral vision presented is one in which seemingly small acts can have major consequences as one person's virtue transforms those he or she comes into contact with, and they can in turn transform others, in ever-widening circles. Thus, even women who do not leave their homes can exert a moral influence that extends outward to people they never meet. For instance, a daughter-in-law, through her influence within the household, can by degrees transform others, beginning with her relatives and working outward; and the wife of the Son of Heaven (the Emperor), through her influence on her husband, can have an impact that reaches everywhere in the realm. Such a theory of moral influence is well attested in early Confucian texts, such as the *Analects* and the *Great Learning*. Moreover, *Biographies of Women* supplies many concrete examples of women who transformed the men around them and thus indirectly had an impact on larger political realms. Still, Miss Zheng may be the first author to be so direct in implying that women's moral power is comparable to men's.

Differentiation by station is also central to this text, as it is to the original *Book of Filial Piety*. Miss Zheng aims not merely to convince girls that filial piety applies to them, but also to convey to them the ways in which the station of a woman determines how she expresses her filial piety. Positive evaluation is placed on wives who admonish their husbands, mothers who educate their children, and widows who refuse to remarry. Condemned as immoral and unfilial are wives who become jealous of their husbands' concubines and concubines who use their sexual allure to lead men astray. Miss Zheng's debt to Liu Xiang's *Biographies of Women* is particularly noticeable in her selection of examples. By contrast, even though Miss Zheng casts Ban Zhao as the female equivalent of Confucius in this text, she borrows relatively little from the *Admonitions for Women* other than to use the language of yin and yang. Ban Zhao's work focuses on the relationship between a woman and her husband, and Ban quotes the saying that "To obtain the love of one man is the crown of a woman's life; to lose the love of one man is to miss the aim of a woman."[7] By contrast, the *Book of Filial Piety for Women* gives no more attention to a woman's relationship with her husband than to her relationship with her parents-in-law or children.

The translations that follow are not full translations of either text (about a quarter of each has been omitted to save space), but include enough to give the flavor of each.[8]

ORIGINAL TEXTS

The *Book of Filial Piety*[9]

Opening the Discussion and Explaining the Principles

Confucius was at home and Zengzi was attending him. Confucius said, "The former kings had the highest virtue and the essential Way. By recourse to them they kept the world ordered and the people in harmony, and neither superiors nor inferiors resented each other. Is this something you know about?"

Zengzi rose from his mat and replied, "Since I am not clever, how can I know about this?"

Confucius said: "Filial piety

The *Book of Filial Piety for Women*[10]

Opening the Discussion and Explaining the Principles

Lady Ban was at home at leisure and the women were sitting in attendance. Lady Ban said, "In antiquity, the two daughters of the Sage Emperor [Yao] had the filial way and went to the bend of the Gui River [to marry Shun]. They were humble, yielding, respectful, and frugal; they concentrated their thoughts on the way to be a wife. Wise and well-informed, they avoided problems with others. Have you heard about this?"

is the root of virtue and the source of civilization. Sit down again and I will explain it to you. Since we receive our body, hair, and skin from our parents, we do not dare let them be injured in any way. This is the beginning of filial piety. We establish ourselves and practice the Way, thereby perpetuating our name for future generations and bringing glory to our parents. This is the fulfillment of filial piety. Thus filial piety begins with serving our parents, continues with serving the ruler, and is completed by establishing one's character."

In the Daya [section of the *Book of Poetry*], it says, "Think of your ancestors and maintain the practice of their virtues."[11]

The Feudal Lords

"Although in superior positions, they are not arrogant and thus can hold lofty positions without

The women rose from their seats and apologized, "We women are ignorant and have not yet received all of your teachings. Could you tell us about it?"

Lady Ban said, "Study involves gathering information, questioning and evaluating it, and discarding the doubtful. In this way one can become a model for others. If you are willing to listen to my words and put them into practice, I will explain the principles to you.

"Filial piety expands heaven and earth, deepens human relationships, stimulates the ghosts and spirits, and moves the birds and beasts. It involves being respectful and conforming to ritual, acting only after repeated thought, making no effort to broadcast one's accomplishments or good deeds, being agreeable, gentle, pure, obedient, kind, intelligent, filial, and compassionate. When such virtuous conduct is perfected, no one will reproach you."

This is what is meant by the passage in the *Book of Documents,* "Filial piety is simply being filial and friendly to one's brothers."[12]

The Noble Ladies

"Although occupying honored positions, they are able to show restraint and thus they can peril. By exercising restraint and caution they can have plenty without going to excess. Holding a lofty position without peril is the way to preserve high rank for a long time. Having plenty without going overboard is the way to preserve wealth for a long time. If they retain their wealth and rank they will later be able to protect their heritage and keep their people in peace. This is the filial piety of the feudal lords."

In the *Book of Poetry,* it says: "Be as cautious as if you were standing on the edge of a chasm or treading on thin ice."[13]

hold their positions without relying on partiality. They observe the diligent toil [of others] and understand their viewpoints. They can recite the *Poetry* and *Documents;* they can perform the *Rituals* and *Music.* As a consequence, they consider it a misfortune to be well-known but unworthy, and a calamity to be great in status but little in virtue, and in fact take a warning from such cases. By first ensuring that their persons conform to propriety whether at rest or in motion, they are able to get along well with their children and grandchildren and preserve the ancestral temple. This is the filial piety of the noble ladies."

The *Book of Changes* says: "He wards off depravity and preserves his integrity," and "His virtue spreads far and transforms others."[14]

The Ministers and High Officers

"They dare not wear garments not prescribed by the former kings; they dare not use words not approved by the former kings; they dare not behave in ways outside the virtuous ways of the former kings. Thus, they will not speak improper words and will not follow anything against the Way. Their words are not

The Wives of Officials

"They dare not wear garments not prescribed by the ritual codes; they dare not use words not modeled on the *Poetry* and *Documents;* they dare not behave in any way outside the virtuous ways based on honesty and moral principle. There is nothing better than not saying what one wishes others would not hear, arbitrary, nor their actions capricious; their words reach all in the world, yet offend no one; their actions fill the world, yet give no one cause for complaint. Those who fulfill these three conditions are able to preserve their ancestral altars. This is the filial piety of the ministers and high officers."

The *Book of Poetry* says: "Never negligent morning or night in the service of the One Man."[15]

THE COMMON PEOPLE

"They follow the laws of nature to utilize the earth to the best advantage. They take care of themselves and are cautious in expenditures in order to support their parents. This is the filial piety of the common people. Thus, from the Son of Heaven to the common people, unless filial piety is pursued from beginning to end, calamities will surely result."

not doing what one wishes others would not know, and not performing what one wishes others would not pass on. Those who fulfill these three conditions are able to preserve their ancestral altars. This is the filial piety of the wives of officials."

The *Book of Poetry* says: "She picks the artemisia by the pond and on the islands for use in service to the lords."[16]

THE COMMON PEOPLE

"They follow the way of the wife and utilize moral principle to the best advantage. They put others first and themselves last in order to serve their parents-in-law. They spin and weave and sew clothes; they prepare the sacrificial foods. This is the filial piety of the wife of a common person."

The *Book of Poetry* says: "Women do not have public affairs [for if they did] they would stop their weaving."[17]

SERVING PARENTS-IN-LAW

"With regard to a woman's service to her parents-in-law, she is as reverent as to her own father, as loving as to her own mother. Maintaining this attitude is

THE THREE POWERS

Zengzi said, "How exceedingly great is filial piety!"

Confucius responded, "Filial piety is the pattern of heaven, the standard of the earth, the norm of conduct for the people. When people follow the pattern of heaven and earth, they model themselves on the brilliance of heaven and make use of the resources of the earth and through these means comply with all under heaven. Thus, [a ruler's] instruction succeeds without being stringent, and his

a matter of duty, and adhering to it is a matter of ritual. When the cock first crows, she washes her hands, rinses her mouth, and gets dressed to make her morning call. In the winter she checks that [her parents-in-law] are warm enough, in the summer cool enough. In the evening she checks that they are settled, in the morning that they are getting up. She is reverent in correcting inside matters, principled in her dealings with the outside. She establishes herself as a person of principle and decorum and then acts on them."

The *Book of Poetry* says: "When a woman departs, she distances herself from her parents and brothers."[18]

THE THREE POWERS

The women said, "How exceedingly great is the husband!"

Lady Ban responded, "The husband is heaven. Can one not be devoted to him? In antiquity, when a woman went to be married, she was said to be going home. She transfers her heaven to serve her husband. The principle in this is vast. It is the pattern of heaven, the standard of the earth, the norm of conduct for the people. When women follow the nature of heaven and earth, model themselves on the policies are effective without being severe. The former kings, realizing that their instruction could transform the people, showed them an example of universal love. As a consequence, men did not neglect their parents. These kings set an example of rectitude and virtue, and as a consequence the people enthusiastically copied them. The kings showed an example of respectful yielding, and the people did not contend with each other. They taught through ritual and music, and the people lived in concord. They made clear to them the difference between good and evil, and as a consequence the people knew restraint."

The *Book of Poetry* says: "How dignified is Master Yin! The common people all look on him with reverence."[19]

Bringing Order through Filial Piety

Confucius said, "Formerly the illustrious kings brought order to the world through filial piety. They did not dare neglect the ministers of small states—not to mention their own dukes, marquises, earls, counts, and barons. Therefore they gained the support of all the states, making them better able to serve the

brilliance of heaven, make use of the resources of the earth, guard against idleness, and adhere to ritual, then they can bring success to their families. On this basis, a wife acts first to extend her love broadly, then her husband will not forget to be filial to his parents. She sets an example of rectitude and virtue, and her husband enthusiastically copies it. She takes the initiative in being reverent and yielding, and her husband is not competitive. If she follows the path of ritual and music, her husband will join in harmoniously. If she indicates the difference between good and evil, her husband will know restraint."

The *Book of Poetry* says: "Intelligent and wise in order to protect her person."[20]

Bringing Order through Filial Piety

Lady Ban said, "In ancient times, virtuous women brought order to their nine relations through filial piety. They did not dare neglect the lowest ranking concubine, not to mention their sisters-in-law. Therefore they gained the support of their six relations, making them better able to serve their parents-in-law. Those placed in former kings. The rulers did not dare insult the widows and widowers—not to mention the upper class or the common people. Therefore they gained the support of all the people, making them better able to serve their former rulers. The heads of families did not dare mistreat their servants and concubines—not to mention their wives and children. Therefore they gained their support, making them better able to serve their parents. Accordingly, while living, parents were well taken care of; after their deaths, their ghosts received sacrifices. In this way the world was kept in peace and harmony. Calamities did not occur, nor was disorder created. Such was the way the former illustrious kings brought order to the world through filial piety."

The *Book of Poetry* says: "The states in the four directions will follow the one whose conduct is truly virtuous."[21]

The Rule of the Sages

Zengzi said, "May I ask if there isn't anything in the virtue of the sages that surpasses filial piety?"

Confucius replied, "Of all the creatures in heaven and earth, man is the most important. Of all man's acts, none is greater

charge of family business did not dare insult the chickens and dogs—not to mention the lower-ranking family members. Therefore they gained the support of their superiors and inferiors, making them better able to serve their husbands. Those in charge of the women's quarters did not dare mistreat the servants—not to mention the master. Therefore they gained the support of the people, making them better able to serve their parents. Accordingly, while living, parents were well taken care of; after their deaths, their ghosts received sacrifices. In this way the nine relations were kept in peace and harmony. Pettiness did not occur, nor disorder arise. Such was the way virtuous women brought order to superiors and inferiors through filial piety."

The *Book of Poetry* says: "Not erring, not forgetting, conforming in all matters to the old rules."[22]

Wisdom

The women said, "May we ask if there isn't anything in the virtue of a wife that surpasses wisdom?"

Lady Ban replied, "Human-kind is patterned on heaven and earth; yin and yang are interdependent. Making use of than filial piety. In the practice of filial piety, nothing is greater than respecting one's father. For respecting one's father, nothing is greater than placing him on the level with heaven.

"The person who did all this was the Duke of Zhou. In former times the Duke of Zhou sacrificed to the Spirit of Agriculture, placing him on a level with heaven. He sacrificed to his father, King Wen, in the Bright Hall, placing him on a level with the Supreme Lord. Therefore, within the four seas all of the lords, according to their stations, came to sacrifice. Thus, how can there be anything in the virtue of the sages that surpasses filial piety? From infancy a child's desire to care for his parents grows daily more respectful. The sages used this natural reverence for parents to teach respect and used this natural affection to teach love. Thus, the teachings of the sages were effective though not severe, and their rule was orderly though not harsh. This was because they relied on what was basic to human nature.

"The proper relation between father and son is a part of nature and forms the principles that regulate the conduct of rulers and ministers. Parents give life—no tie is stronger than this. Rulers one's intelligence is always beneficial, especially when done in a purposeful manner.

"In former times, King Zhuang of Chu was holding court in the evening. Lady Fan entered and said, 'Why don't you end this court session? It is so late. Aren't you tired?' The king said, 'Today I have been talking with a wise person and have been so happy, I have not noticed the time.' When Lady Fan asked the identity of the wise person, the king said Yu Qiuzi. Lady Fan covered her mouth and laughed. The king, perplexed, asked her what made her laugh. She answered, 'Yu Qiuzi may be wise but he is not loyal. For eleven years I have had the favor of occupying a place in your rear chambers, where I still attend to you with wash basin, towel, and comb and clean up. During this time I have introduced nine other women. Today two of them are wiser than I am, and the other seven are my peers. Even though I know how to safeguard your love for me and snatch your favor, I would not dare keep you in the dark [about other women] for selfish reasons. Rather, I wish that you be broadly informed. Now, Yu Qiuzi has been prime minister for ten years, but the only people he has recommended are his descendants personally watch over the people—no care is greater than this. Therefore to love others without first loving one's parents is to reject virtue. To reverence other men without first reverencing one's parents is to reject the rules of ritual. If one copies such perversity, the people will have no model to follow. Although a person who does not do good but only evil may gain a high position, a man of honor will not esteem him. The practice of a man of honor is different: his speech is praiseworthy, his behavior is pleasing, his standards are respected, his management of affairs can be taken as a model, his deportment is pleasant to observe, his movements are deliberate. When a man of honor deals with his people, they look on him with awe and affection; they imitate and seek to resemble him. Thus he can carry out his moral instruction and put into effect his political directives."

The *Book of Poetry* says: "The good man, the true gentleman, his deportment is impeccable."[23]

or his collateral relatives. I have never heard of him recommending someone wise or demoting someone unworthy. Can he be called wise?'

"When the king repeated this to him, Yu Qiuzi, in his confusion, abandoned his home and slept outside. The king sent someone to invite Sun Shuao, and on his arrival made him prime minister. Thus because of the wisdom of a single person's advice, the feudal lords did not dare attack, and in the end King Zhuang became the paramount leader of the states. All this was due to the efforts of Lady Fan."[24]

A poem says: "Those who obtain the right men prosper; those who lose them are defeated." The *Book of Poetry* says, "When language is harmonious, the people will be united."[25]

Filial Conduct

Confucius said, "Let me comment on the way a filial son serves his parents. While at home he renders the utmost reverence to them. In

Virtuous Conduct

Lady Ban said, "Let me comment on the way a woman serves her husband. From the time her hair is arranged and she meets him supporting them he maximizes their pleasure. When they are sick he takes every care. At their death he expresses all his grief. Then he sacrifices to them with full solemnity.

"Only a son who has fulfilled these five requirements is truly able to serve his parents. He who really loves his parents will not be proud in a high position. He will not be insubordinate in an inferior position. And among equals he will not be quarrelsome. If he were proud in a high station, he might be ruined. If he were insubordinate in an inferior position, he might incur punishment. If he were quarrelsome among his equals he might end up fighting. Thus, unless these three evils are eliminated, a son cannot be called filial—even if every day he supplies his parents with the three choice meats."

[during the wedding ceremony], she maintains the formality appropriate between an official and the ruler. When helping him wash or serving him food, she maintains the reverence appropriate between father and child. When reporting her comings and goings, she preserves the manner appropriate between siblings. She always keeps agreements, thus maintaining the trust appropriate among friends. Her words and actions are unblemished, giving her the capacity to manage the family.

"Only a woman who has fulfilled these five requirements is truly able to serve her husband. Such a woman will not be proud in a high position. She will not be insubordinate in an inferior position. And among equals she will not be quarrelsome. If she were proud in a high station, she might be ruined. If she were insubordinate in an inferior position, she might incur punishment. If she were quarrelsome among her equals, she might end up fighting. Thus, unless these three evils are eliminated, a woman cannot be called wifely—even if she harmonizes with her husband as well as the lute with the zither."

The Five Punishments

Confucius said, "There are three thousand offenses subject to the five punishments, but of these the most heinous is lack of filial piety. To use force against the ruler is to defy authority. To deny the sages is to be unprincipled. And to decry filial piety is to renounce kinship ties. These are the roads to chaos."

The Five Punishments

Lady Ban said, "There are three thousand offenses subject to the five punishments, but of these the most heinous is jealousy. It is the first among the seven grounds for divorce. The teachings of the sages are encompassed in purity, obedience, rectitude, straightforwardness, gentleness, absence of jealousy, orderliness in the inner quarters, absence of contact with the outside, and the ability to not be so stimulated by sights and sounds that desires are pursued recklessly. You women should put this into practice."

The *Book of Poetry* says: "Fine his deportment and appearance! He models himself on the ancient rules and applies himself to attaining dignity."[26]

Elaborating on the Idea of Highest Virtue

Confucius said, "A man of honor in teaching the duties of filial piety need not go daily to the people's homes to observe them. He merely teaches the principles of filial piety and all the fathers in the world receive the filial respect due to them. He teaches the principles of fraternal love and all the elder brothers receive the respect due to them.

Elaborating on the Idea of Preserving Trust

"The way of establishing heaven is called yin and yang; the way of establishing earth is called gentle and firm. Yin and yang, gentle and firm, these are the beginnings of heaven and earth. Men and women, husbands and wives, these are the beginnings of human relationships. *Qian* and *kun*[27] are interconnected and pervasive, with no space between them. The

He teaches the duties of subjects and all the rulers of the world receive the reverence due to them."

The *Book of Poetry* says: "Affectionate the man of honor, a father and mother to the people."[28] Unless he possessed the highest virtue, who could educate the people to such an extent?

wife is earth, the husband is heaven; neither can be dispensed with. But the husband has a hundred actions, the wife has a single purpose. For men there is the principle of successive marriages, but there is no text authorizing women to marry more than once.

"Formerly, King Zhao of Chu took a trip and left [his wife] Miss Jiang at Qian pavilion. The river flooded and the king sent someone to get the lady, but because the messenger should have carried a tally, she would not go with him. Miss Jiang said, 'I have heard that a chaste woman, as a matter of principle, does not break an agreement, just as a brave soldier does not fear dying. Now I know that I will surely die if I do not leave. But without a tally I dare not break the agreement. Although if I leave I will surely live, to live without faith is not as good as dying to preserve principle.' It happened that when the messenger returned to get the tally, the water rose above the pavilion and she drowned. Such was the way she preserved trust.[29] You should strive to emulate her example."

The *Book of Changes* says: "The crying crane resides in yin; its child joins it in harmony."[30]

ELABORATING ON THE IDEA OF PERPETUATING ONE'S NAME

Confucius said, "The man of honor's service to his parents is filial; the fidelity involved in it can be transferred to his ruler. His service to his elder brothers is deferential; the obedience involved in it can be transferred to his superiors. Self-disciplined at home, he can transfer his good management to official life. When his conduct is perfected at home through these means, his name will be perpetuated to later generations."

ELABORATING ON THE IDEA OF PERPETUATING ONE'S NAME

Lady Ban said, "A daughter's service to her parents is filial; the fidelity involved in it can be transferred to her parents-in-law. Her service to her sisters is deferential; the obedience involved in it can be transferred to sisters-in-law. Self-disciplined at home, her reputation for discipline will reach the six relations. When her conduct is perfected at home through these means, her name will be perpetuated to later generations."

ADMONISHING

Zengzi remarked, "I understand your teachings concerning kind affection, loving respect, comforting one's parents, and bringing glory to one's name. May I ask if a son who obeys all of his father's commands can be called filial?"

Confucius replied, "What kind of talk is this? What kind of talk is this? In ancient times if the Son of Heaven had seven ministers to point out his errors, he would not lose his empire, even if he were imperfect. If a feudal lord had five good ministers to point out his errors, he would not lose his state, even if he were imperfect. If a high officer had three officials to point out his

ADMONISHING

The women said, "We now understand your teachings concerning modest purity, filial principles, serving one's mother-in-law, respecting one's husband, and bringing glory to one's name. May we ask if a wife who obeys her husband's orders can be called worthy?"

Lady Ban replied, "What kind of talk is this? What kind of talk is this? In ancient times when King Xuan of Zhou [stayed in bed so long he] was late for court, Queen Jiang [accused herself of leading him astray and] took off her hairpin and earrings to wait for her punishment at the end of the alley. This brought errors, he would not lose his patrimony, even if he were imperfect. If a gentleman had a friend to point out his errors, he would not lose his good name. And if a father had a son to point out his errors, he would not fall into doing wrong. Thus, when he might do something wrong, a son must not fail to warn his father against it, nor a minister fail to warn his ruler. In short, when it is a question of doing wrong, one must admonish. How can following a father's orders be considered fulfilling filial piety?"

King Xuan to his senses.[31] When Emperor Cheng of the Han dynasty ordered Consort Ban to board the carriage he was in, she declined, saying, 'I have heard that in the three dynasties enlightened kings all had wise officials at their side. I have never heard of one who rode with a favored woman,' which caused Emperor Cheng to change color.[32] Because King Zhuang of Chu was fond of hunting, Lady Fan would eat nothing from the wilds, which moved the king and led to his giving up hunting.[33]

"Viewed in this way, if the Son of Heaven had ministers to point out his errors to him, he would not lose his empire, even if he were imperfect. If a feudal lord had ministers to point out his errors to him, he would not lose his state, even if he were imperfect. If a high officer had officials to point out his errors to him, he would not lose his patrimony, even if he were imperfect. If a gentleman had a friend to point out his errors to him, he would not lose his good name. If a father had a son to point out his errors to him, he would not fall into doing wrong. And if a husband had a wife to point out his errors to him, then he would not slip into incorrect ways. For instance, Lady Wei reformed Duke Huan of Qi so that he no longer listened to lewd music,[34] and it was because Qi Jiang sent Duke Wen of Jin that he became hegemon.[35] Thus, when a husband might do something wrong, a wife warns against it. How can following a husband's orders be considered wise?"

The *Book of Poetry* says: "When his plans are not farsighted, it is time to admonish strongly."[36]

Mutual Interaction

Confucius said, "In ancient times, because the illustrious kings were filial to their fathers, they were able to serve heaven intelligently. Because they were filial to their mothers, they were able to serve earth with circumspection. Superiors could govern inferiors because the young obeyed their elders. Thus, because heaven and earth were served with intelligence and care, the spirits manifested themselves brilliantly. Even the Son of Heaven had someone he paid reverence to, that is to say, his father. He had someone he deferred to, that is to say, his elder brothers. At the ancestral temple he was reverential, not forgetting his parents. He cultivated his character and acted prudently, for fear of disgracing his ancestors. When he paid

Prenatal Education

Lady Ban said, "With regard to the way people receive the five constant virtues, at birth they have an intrinsic nature, but much is also learned. If they are exposed to good, then they will be good; if exposed to evil, they will be evil. Even while they are in the womb, how can they not be given education! In ancient times, when women were with child, they did not lie on their side while sleeping, nor sit to one side, nor stand on one foot, nor eat anything with a strange taste, nor walk on the left side of the road, nor eat anything not cut straight, nor sit on a mat that was not laid straight, nor look at or listen to any evil sights or sounds, nor utter any wild words, nor touch any deviant objects. At night they would recite the classical texts; in the reverence at the ancestral temple, the ghosts and spirits sent blessings. When his filial piety and fraternity were perfected, his influence reached the spirits. He illuminated the four seas; there was no place his virtue did not penetrate."

The *Book of Poetry* says: "West, east, south, north, no one fails to submit to him."[37]

Serving the Ruler

Confucius said, "In serving his superior the man of honor makes every effort to be faithful when he is in office. In retirement he tries to make up for his shortcomings. He encourages his superior in his good inclinations and tries to keep him from doing wrong. In this way, the relations between superiors and inferiors can be cordial."

The *Book of Poetry* says: "In his heart is love. Why not admit it? He stores it in his heart. When could he forget it?"[38]

morning they would discuss ritual and music. When these women gave birth, their children's form was correct and their talent and virtue surpassed that of others. Such was their prenatal education."

Maternal Proprieties

Lady Ban said, "Anyone who is a mother needs to understand the ritual proprieties. Get along with your child through kindness and love. Offer a model to your child by being stern and correct. Your movements should conform to ritual forms; your words must have principles behind them.

"When your sons reach six, teach them the names of numbers and directions; at seven see that they do not sit on the same mat or eat together with girls; at eight have them study elementary learning; at ten have them study with a teacher. They must report when they are going out and come to see you in person on their return. Their amusements must have some regularity to them; their studies must have some substance to them. When at home, they should not occupy the innermost place; they should not sit in the middle of a mat, nor walk in the middle of the road, nor stand in the middle of the doorway. They should not climb high places or stand on the edge of deep chasms. They should not make unwise oaths or laugh foolishly. They should keep no private property. When standing they should be straight and square. Their ears should not be swayed by what they hear. They should maintain the separation between males and females to avoid cause for suspicion and should share neither towel nor comb.

"As for your daughters, at seven you should teach them the four virtues.

"Such is the way of maternal proprieties. The aunt of Huangfu Shi'an once said, 'The mother of Mencius moved three times to help form his character and bought meat to teach him to preserve trust. By not properly selecting the neighborhood we live in, I am responsible for making you so obtuse.' "[39]

The *Book of Poetry* says: "Instruct and advise your children so that they come to resemble you."[40]

Removing Evils

The women said, "We have reverently heard your instructions

Mourning for Parents

Confucius said, "When mourning a parent, a filial son weeps

without wailing loudly; he performs the rites without attention to his appearance; he speaks without attention to the beauty of his words; he feels uncomfortable in elegant clothes; he gets no joy from hearing music; he does not relish good food—all of this is the emotion of grief. After three days he eats again to show men that the dead should not hurt the living and that the suffering should not lead to the destruction of life. This was the regulation of the sages. The period of mourning is not allowed to exceed three years, thus showing the people that everything ends. [The filial son] prepares a double coffin and grave clothes. When he sets out the sacrificial vessels, he grieves. Beating his breast, jumping up and down, and crying, he bids a last sad farewell. He divines to choose the burial place where the body can be placed to rest. He prepares an ancestral altar, so that the ghost can receive sacrifices. Spring and autumn he offers sacrifices thus thinking of the dead one every season. When his parents were alive he served them with love and reverence; in death he grieves.

"With the man's fundamental duty fulfilled, relations between the living and the dead are on the way of the wife. Even though we, your pupils, are not clever, we wish to devote our lives to putting your teachings into practice.

"May we ask, were there also any bad women in antiquity?"

Lady Ban responded, "The rise of the Xia dynasty was because of [the wife of the founder], Tushan.[41] Its fall was due to [the concubine of the last king], Moxi.[42] The rise of the Yin dynasty was because of [the wife of the founder], Youxin;[43] its fall was due to [the concubine of its last king], Danji.[44] The rise of the [Western] Zhou dynasty was because of [the mother of the founder], Tairen;[45] its demise was due to [the concubine of the last king], Baosi.[46] It was because of women that the kings of these three dynasties lost the realm, their lives, and their states. This is even more true at the level of feudal lords, greater officers, and common people. Thus the calamity that befell Shensheng [the crown prince of Jin] resulted from [the slander of his father's concubine], Linu.[47] The demise of [the last heir of the Liang dynasty], Minhuai began with [the Jin empress] Nanfeng.[48]

"When viewed in this way, there are women who deserve credit for founding their families complete, and the filial son's service to his parents is finished."

and others who destroyed their families. Then there is the case of Miss Xia, the wife of Chen Yushu, who brought about the deaths of three husbands, a son, and a ruler, chased away two ministers, and brought on the destruction of a state—this must be the most extreme case of evil.[49] It is appalling to think that a single woman could destroy the patrimony of six families.

"If, however, you practice the way of goodness, you will never reach such extremity."

NOTES

1. On these two texts, see O'Hara, *The Position of Woman in Early China according to the* Lieh nü chuan, *"The Biographies of Eminent Chinese Women"*; Raphals, *Sharing the Light: Representations of Women and Virtue in Early China;* Swann, *Pan Chao: Foremost Woman Scholar of China;* Ch'en, "The Historical Template of Pan Chao's *Nü Chieh.*"

2. See Ebrey, *Inner Quarters: Marriage and the Lives of Chinese Women in the Sung Period,* 120–24.

3. See Murray, "Didactic Art for Women: The *Ladies' Classic of Filial Piety*"; and Murray, "The *Ladies' Classic of Filial Piety* and Sung Textual Illustration: Problems of Reconstruction and Artistic Context."

4. See Martin-Liao, "Traditional Handbooks of Women's Education."

5. Ji Yun et al., *Siku quanshu zongmu tiyao* (95:1949), give the husband's surname as Houmochen—an unusual three-character surname—perhaps because this is given as the surname of the consort of the prince in Liu Xu, *Jiu Tang shu* 10:243.

6. Some scholars have tried to assign a date to the *Book of Filial Piety for Women* on the basis of its message, but they have not agreed on its message. Some say it celebrates women's moral influence and thus deserves a mid-Tang date; others argue that it reinforces constraints on women and thus deserves a late Tang or early Song date. For my part, I find most such arguments flawed: in neither period was only one set of ideas expressed, and the ideas expressed in texts never correspond to behavior in a simple way. Just because Empress Wu did not define herself in terms of the Triple Obedience does not mean that people in the seventh century no longer admired the mother of Mencius or read the *Biographies of Women.* So also, the fact that Emperor Taizong did not define himself in terms of submission to his father and elder brother does not mean that no one read the *Book of Filial Piety* or admired the

Twenty-Four Filial Sons anymore. However, I do consider it worth noting that due largely to the spread of printing, the *Book of Filial Piety for Women* seems to have circulated more widely in Ming and Qing times than in Tang or Song.

7. Swann, *Pan Chao,* 87.

8. In the translation, the honorific title "Dagu" is translated "Lady Ban," and the title "Zi," meaning "the Master," is translated "Confucius." An alternative would have been to use "the Instructress" and "the Master."

9. Source: Chen Menglei, *Qinding gujin tushu jicheng,* "Jiafan dian," 11:12a–13a.

10. Source: Chen Menglei, *Qinding gujin tushu jicheng,* "Guiyuan dian," 3:1a–5a.

11. *Shi jing,* Mao 235; cf. Legge, *The Chinese Classics,* 4:431. The quotations from the classics are translated here in the sense in which I think they were intended by the authors of these texts, even if this differs from modern scholars' interpretations of the original meanings of the passages.

12. *Shu jing* 49 (Zhoushu, Junchen); cf. Legge, *The Chinese Classics,* 3:535.

13. *Shi jing,* Mao 195; cf. Legge, *The Chinese Classics,* 4:333.

14. *Yijing* hexagram 1; cf. Lynn, *Classic of Changes,* 133.

15. *Shi jing,* Mao 260; cf. Legge, *The Chinese Classics,* 4:543.

16. *Shi jing,* Mao 13; cf. Legge, *The Chinese Classics,* 4:22.

17. *Shi jing,* Mao 264; cf. Legge, *The Chinese Classics,* 4:562.

18. *Shi jing,* Mao 39; cf. Legge, *The Chinese Classics,* 4:63.

19. *Shi jing,* Mao 191; cf. Legge, *The Chinese Classics,* 4:309.

20. *Shi jing,* Mao 260; cf. Legge, *The Chinese Classics,* 4:543.

21. *Shi jing,* Mao 256; cf. Legge, *The Chinese Classics,* 4:511.

22. *Shi jing,* Mao 249; cf. Legge, *The Chinese Classics,* 4:482.

23. *Shi jing,* Mao 152; cf. Legge, *The Chinese Classics,* 4:222.

24. Based on *Lienü zhuan* 2, no. 5; cf. O'Hara, *Position of Woman,* 56–58.

25. *Shi jing,* Mao 254; cf. Legge, *The Chinese Classics,* 4:500. The first quotation is not found in the *Book of Poetry.*

26. *Shi jing,* Mao 260; cf. Legge, *The Chinese Classics,* 4:542.

27. *Qian* and *kun* are the first two hexagrams of the *Yijing.*

28. *Shi jing,* Mao 251; cf. Legge, *The Chinese Classics,* 4:489.

29. Based on *Lienü zhuan* 4, no. 10; cf. O'Hara, *Position of Woman,* 117–18.

30. *Yijing* hexagram 61; cf. Lynn, *Classic of Changes,* 524.

31. Based on *Lienü zhuan* 2, no. 1; cf. O'Hara, *Position of Woman,* 49–50.

32. Based on *Lienü zhuan* 8, no. 14; cf. O'Hara, *Position of Woman,* 230–35.

33. Based on *Lienü zhuan* 2, no. 5; cf. O'Hara, *Position of Woman,* 56–58.

34. Based on *Lienü zhuan* 2, no. 2; cf. O'Hara, *Position of Woman,* 50–52.

35. Based on *Lienü zhuan* 2, no. 3; cf. O'Hara, *Position of Woman,* 52–54.

36. *Shi jing,* Mao 254; cf. Legge, *The Chinese Classics,* 4:499.

37. *Shi jing,* Mao 244; cf. Legge, *The Chinese Classics,* 4:463.

38. *Shi jing,* Mao 228; cf. Legge, *The Chinese Classics,* 4:415.

39. A fuller and somewhat different version of this conversation between Huangfu Mi (215–282) and his adoptive mother, Miss Ren, is found in Fang Xuanling, *Jin shu,* 51:1409.

40. *Shi jing,* Mao 196; cf. Legge, *The Chinese Classics,* 4:334.

41. Cf. *Lienü zhuan* 1, no. 4; cf. O'Hara, *Position of Woman,* 20–21.

42. Cf. *Lienü zhuan* 7, no. 1; cf. O'Hara, *Position of Woman,* 186–87.

43. Cf. *Lienü zhuan* 1, no. 5; cf. O'Hara, *Position of Woman,* 21–22.

44. Cf. *Lienü zhuan* 7, no. 2; cf. O'Hara, *Position of Woman,* 187–89.
45. Cf. *Lienü zhuan* 1, no. 6; cf. O'Hara, *Position of Woman,* 22–25.
46. Cf. *Lienü zhuan* 7, no. 3; cf. O'Hara, *Position of Woman,* 189–92.
47. Cf. *Lienü zhuan* 1, no. 3; cf. O'Hara, *Position of Woman,* 19–20.
48. The logic here seems to be that the cruel and perverse streak apparent in one of the royal women in the Jin led inexorably to cruel and perverse progeny among subsequent rulers, though in this case there had been three intervening changes of dynasty. This case is from relatively recent history and therefore not from the *Lienü zhuan.*
49. Based on *Lienü zhuan* 7, no. 9; cf. O'Hara, *Position of Woman,* 201–4.

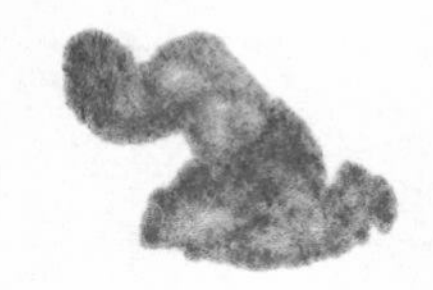

Fig. 4. A man offering prayers before the ancestral altar. From a Qing morality book. It was in a setting such as this that Chen Liang would have burned his sacrificial prayers to his maternal aunt, younger sister, and sister's husband. Source: *"Guandi bao xun" xiang zhu* (1731; reprinted 1882), 4:26. Courtesy of the East Asian Library, University of California, Berkeley.

FOUR

Funerary Writings by Chen Liang (1143–1194)

Translated by Beverly Bossler

TRANSLATOR'S PREFACE

I began looking at Chinese funerary writings many years ago, as part of an effort to understand social change between the Tang and the Song. Although I was not primarily interested in gender issues at that point, it soon became apparent that even the most stylized of these sources contained a great deal of information useful for analysis of gender roles. Moreover, although all inscriptions present us with highly idealized images, when men wrote about women to whom they were especially close—their mothers, but also their sisters and occasionally their wives—their emotion sometimes conjures up traces of the actual woman underlying the stereotype. As an aspiring official in the Southern Song, Chen Liang was known for his candor and even rashness. Fortunately for us, some of that candor comes through in the funerary inscriptions he composed for those close to him.

INTRODUCTION

The following selection consists of three *jiwen* (sacrificial prayers), and one *muzhiming* (commemorative funerary biography, or eulogy) composed by the Song dynasty scholar Chen Liang (1143–1194). The prayers were addressed respectively to the spirits of his younger sister's husband, his younger sister, and his maternal aunt; the eulogy was written in commemoration of his wife's paternal aunt.

In China of the Song period, as in more recent eras, it was understood that the comfort and repose of the deceased's spirit—and the consequent prosperity of his or her descendants—were dependent on ritual sacrifices offered by those descendants. Sacrificial prayers such as those translated here were composed to accompany offerings of meat and wine that were made to the deceased at regular intervals. As ritual writings, sacrificial prayers were subject to certain stylistic conventions. The writer addressing the spirit generally adopted a grief-stricken persona (which could, of course, be quite genuine), and in many cases, part or all of the prayer was in verse, perhaps because it was meant to be chanted out loud during the ritual.[1] The prayers often end by inviting the deceased to partake of the sacrifice.

In addition to regular sacrifices, proper burial was also considered important for the lasting peace of the deceased's spirit. Among the upper classes a proper burial was not complete without the composition of a commemorative biography that would ensure that some record of the deceased was preserved for posterity. These commemorative biographies could take various forms, but probably the most common was the *muzhiming*, in which the biography was carved on stone, covered, and buried with the deceased. Like sacrificial prayers, commemorative biographies were subject to constraints of form and content. The biographies were expected to provide certain basic information about the deceased's family background and to detail the deceased's life history in suitably flattering terms.

Within these conventions, however, both the style and the content of funerary biographies for women changed considerably between the Tang and the Song periods.[2] Under the influence of the "ancient-style prose" (*guwen*) movement, the elaborate and highly allusive language of Tang inscriptions shifted in Song times to more simple and straightforward expository prose. Similarly, reflecting shifts in Chinese social structure that took place between the Tang and the Song, Tang descriptions of beautiful, nobly born, and ritually correct women gave way in the Song to equally idealized but different images: dutiful daughters-in-law personally administering to ailing in-laws, and impoverished widows carefully schooling their orphaned sons. Thus in spite of their stylized nature, inscriptions are important sources for discerning historical change in gender ideals.

The texts of sacrificial prayers and commemorative biographies from the Song survive today because such writings were often included in the *wenji* (collected works) of Song scholars.[3] These comprised the writings a man (and occasionally a woman) composed over the course of his or her lifetime. Such writings were passed down to descendants and, if the author was sufficiently eminent, were eventually published. The majority of writings included in collected works tend to be concerned with political or intellectual careers and issues of state; but sacrificial prayers and commemorative biographies—like poetry and some letters—could be very personal in nature. As such, they sometimes touch on matters not revealed in more public genres. In particular, they are one of the few places where one can catch a glimpse of men's family lives and their emotional relationships with women.

Chen Liang, the author of the texts translated here, is somewhat unusual among the men whose writings survive from the Song. Although the Chen kin group as a whole was undoubtedly affluent by Song standards, Chen Liang tells us that his branch of the kin group had suffered a decline, as unexpected illness and deaths forced them to turn repeatedly to kinsmen for aid.[4] As the eldest son of an only son, Chen Liang was seen as the family's main hope of a comeback. Liang's grandmother had dreamt about a young boy taking first place in the examinations and upon awakening decided that the child in her dream must have been Liang. Defying the ridicule of neighbors, she named Chen Liang after the boy in the dream and insisted that he be educated.[5] Chen Liang lived at a time when the Song dynasty was beleaguered by constant threats from the Jurchen Jin dynasty, which had taken over northern China in 1127. As a young man he was infatuated with military history and strategy, and as he reached adulthood his impassioned essays on military affairs earned him the attention and support of powerful men. Still, success in the examinations eluded him—and without an examination degree and an official post, outlets for Chen Liang's talents were limited. Chen Liang's grandmother died a disappointed woman: it was more than a year after her death that—ironically, after he had changed his name—Chen Liang took first place in the first level of the examinations, in 1168.[6]

Even after he passed the preliminary examinations things did not go smoothly for Chen Liang. He spent most of his time studying and writing at home, but he proved to be anything but a model scholar. Arrogant and given to drunken outbursts, he more than once got himself thrown in jail. It was not until the age of fifty that Chen Liang finally passed the higher-level examinations and was awarded a top-ranking *jinshi* degree. But fate was to have the last laugh: within a year, Chen Liang was struck down by illness while en route to the official post he had longed for all his life.[7] He died without ever having taken up office.

The sacrificial prayers Chen Liang wrote for his relatives are historically valuable in several respects. First, they are a potent reminder of the precariousness of prosperity and of life itself in Song times. In this regard the sacrificial prayer for Liang's sister is particularly interesting, for it shows us a Song family in crisis. The crisis began with the early death of Chen Liang's mother in 1165, just a few months after Chen Liang's marriage. This tragedy was followed shortly by his father's incarceration in prison on charges that are now obscure.[8] Worry over this affair, Chen Liang says, subsequently caused the deaths of both of his grandparents in 1167. In the face of these disasters, the relatives of Liang's wife fetched her home, and Liang's brother opted to abandon the family and strike out on his own. The text suggests that Chen Liang, too, was eventually implicated in his father's crime, and he blames the events of this period—and his own inability to manage them—for the illness that eventually led to his sister's death.

In the end, the Chens were able to surmount this crisis,[9] but their affines, the Huangs, were less lucky. In the sacrificial prayer for his maternal aunt, Chen Liang reveals that his mother, née Huang, and her younger sister were orphaned at a young age by the sudden deaths of their parents and all six of their brothers. The two girls were subsequently taken in by their father's sister, who turns out to have been Chen Liang's paternal grandmother. By prior arrangement, the elder Huang girl was ultimately married—at an extremely tender age[10]—to her cousin (Chen Liang's father); the younger girl married a man surnamed Zhou. In other sources we discover that the Huangs had had a prior affinal connection with the Zhous as well,[11] such that Chen Liang's aunt was also marrying her cousin (her mother's brother's son). Although marriage between people of the same surname was forbidden by law and custom in Song China, marriage between cousins of differing surnames (e.g., between the children of a man and his sister, or between children of two sisters) was very common in the Song as well as in later eras. The Chen, Huang, and Zhou families evidently made quite a habit of cousin marriage, for in the sacrificial prayer for Chen Liang's sister's husband we learn that the families' interconnections were perpetuated in the succeeding generation, when the two Huang sisters arranged for *their* children to marry each other. Thus Chen Liang's brother and sister both married Zhou cousins. Some sense of the extremes to which the families were willing to go to maintain such marriage connections is conveyed in Chen Liang's prayer to his sister, in which he hints that her marriage to her mother's sister's son was extremely awkward, even humiliating. The prayer for her husband reveals why: the cousin their mother had arranged for her to marry was nine years younger than she.

In these prayers, then, we also see that relationships made through women were a critical resource when families were in trouble. It was a married aunt, rather than any male kinsman, who took in the orphaned Huang girls. Chen Liang's mother, distraught at the thought that her natal family's line had died out, impressed upon *her* son—rather than any Huang kinsmen—his responsibility for seeing that the sacrifices to her ancestors continue. Similarly, when Chen Liang's mother died, it was their mother's sister to whom Chen Liang and his siblings turned. We also see that women were not passive instruments in these relationships, but rather were frequently responsible for critical family decisions. The marriages of Chen Liang's siblings and cousins were arranged by his mother and her sister, and their plans were upheld by the males in the family (including Chen Liang) even when the latter did not fully approve of them. It was Chen Liang's grandmother, rather than any male in the family, who chose her grandson's name and determined that he should be educated.

The commemorative biography of Chen Liang's wife's aunt (her father's sister) gives us a somewhat different perspective both on Chen Liang's family life and on Song social life in general. Chen Liang tells us here that his wife was the daughter of a wealthy and prominent family, the niece of the up-and-coming scholar and *jinshi* degree holder He Ke (Maogong). It is not entirely clear why her family was interested in a connection with Chen Liang, who observes that most of the Hes' other affines disapproved of the match and that he himself felt unworthy of it.[12] But in any event the marriage was carried out, and Chen Liang was thereby brought into a family circle considerably more prosperous and well ordered than his own seems to have been.

Two final points seem particularly noteworthy here. One is the closeness of Chen Liang's relationships with his wife's natal kin. The biography suggests that Chen Liang was accustomed to visiting his affines with some regularity, and he was sufficiently intimate with his wife's aunt that the two were able to joke together. Whereas in the sacrificial prayers we see evidence for the importance of relationships through women in times of crisis, here we see that those relationships were also a significant part of everyday life. The second interesting aspect of this biography is what it has to say—perhaps implicitly more than explicitly—about values regarding female behavior. Chen Liang depicts his wife's aunt as open and forthright, fond of parties, guests, and conversation. Chen Liang implies that her directness is both admirable and a quality seldom found in women. But in the very act of admiring qualities in this woman that he says few women are able to achieve, Chen Liang shows us, paradoxically, that women did not always conform to the stereotyped images men had of them.

ORIGINAL TEXTS

"Sacrificial Prayer for My Younger Sister's Husband, Zhou Yingbo"[13]

Alas! My father had few siblings, and my mother had only one younger sister. Alone and in dire straits, they relied on one another to get by. Eventually, [the sister] married into the Zhou family: she was Yingbo's mother. Accordingly, Yingbo's older sister also married my younger brother. But my younger sister was older than Yingbo by nine years: the reason my mother also agreed to marry her to Yingbo was that she wanted to see the devotion between affinal relatives perpetuated without end, to the utmost of intimate affection. Some seven or eight years after my mother passed away [lit., abandoned her orphans],[14] Yingbo gradually matured and my sister ultimately married him; we did not dare to repudiate [lit., eat] my mother's stated wishes.

That Yingbo when young studied with me and wanted to dedicate himself to military affairs was a measure of what was appropriate to his disposition. That, ambitions unfulfilled, he devoted himself to family affairs in order to provide a decent living, leaving my sister without a moment's worry, was what exhausted his heart and strength. That we exchanged seasonal greetings, that we helped each other out in difficulties, that he answered my needs even for the most trivial things was because out of consideration for my sister's lot in life, he was dutiful to me. That I have made use of the available wood and stones, that the beams and tiles used were sufficient, that I have renovated this residence[15] to sparkling newness is because I have assumed the cares of the venerable worthy [i.e., the deceased] and taken the responsibility on myself.

The elders had already passed away, and then you followed along;
A widowed wife, a tiny babe, suddenly lost what they relied upon.
In trouble with those in power, trapped in a net was I.
I forbore dying to clear my name; the light shines from on high.
Alone and solitary in the prison, no relatives by my side,
Now you have also abandoned me; such despondency who could abide!
My younger sister's thoughts were anxious, and before long her
consciousness lapsed.
What good is my surviving?! This, too, can be asked.
I keep the mourning in greatest grief, to the spirits I am obliged;
I ought to go with your honored son and subsist in the high and wide.[16]
In death they share a grave and cherish these ten feet of space.
I scatter the wine and express my sincerity; O soul, come and partake!

"*Funerary Ode for My Younger Sister*"[17]

Formerly, our mother at the age of fourteen *sui* gave birth to me; two years later she gave birth to your second elder brother, and two years after that to a boy who did not survive. The following year she then gave birth to you, and from that point on had no further children. When I was twenty-three, our mother, in the prime of life, abandoned her several orphans and passed away. Before the mourning was complete, our father encountered obstacles and was bound up in prison. Our grandfather and grandmother grew ill from worry, so that one after the other they both perished: three funerals in progress, and me rushing around frantically to save the living. My wife was born and reared in a wealthy home; when we encountered such bizarre ill fortune, her family in the end fetched her back. My younger brother also took his wife and lived with no regard for honor in a small hovel by the road. Only you and a maidservant[18] kept the mourning for these three, noble in the midst of shame.[19] What no person can bear you had to your right and to your left. Bitter tears filled your heart, paining all who saw you. I cried out to Heaven, but got no response. At the time I had no plan; in attending to one matter, neglecting the next, in such great grief I wanted to die, coming and going heedlessly. Thinking of you [living] in such extremes, I hoped to protect you even unto death, so I am all the more ashamed that I wasn't able to save you. Another time we will escape [these calamities] and share equally in poverty or wealth.[20]

Marriage between cousins had been our mother's intention for a long time; if in the middle of things I had wanted to alter [the arrangement], who would have taken responsibility for explaining it? My meager powers were not adequate to make [your marriage] perfect, and so it was completed in this humble manner: you donned [lit., completed] the bridal veil, but in the end it was I whose face was ashamed. My wife looked on you more fondly than a daughter; would we be willing to be remiss at the seasonal inquiries? Heaven and earth know whether or not my heart is exhausted; when you see our mother under the earth, you can report these things to her one by one. In those three years' time, disasters and worries converged like the spokes of a wheel. People in power wanted to kill me, their punishments not easy to bear. Helpless, I awaited my fate: all will become clear in the light of day! Relatives and friends turned away: who was not my enemy? You and my wife were weeping and wasted; coming back to see me off, ill, you collapsed. I was even more panicked, hoping only for Heaven's help. Wailing, we parted; the whole affair an absurd mistake! I was victim of a frame-up, and my fate was in men's hands. You had already lost your husband, your son was still young; thinking of this, you were at wits' end, and your illness also became chronic. You could not ascend to Heaven; earth would not answer your pleas, so you closed your eyes and departed, like a dog seeking refuge in its den. I was caught in a net, like a deer in a pen; obstructed on all sides, dazed by this dreadful time. Life and death are eternally separated: how can one say there will be a chance to meet? Your obligations have not ended; my disasters continue to accumulate. I ought to see to it that your son can somewhat distinguish the fragrant from the foul.[21] One can bear not to die,[22] and the coffin [lit., the wood] is difficult to enter.

Crawling on my knees, I consign myself to the universe. What else is there for me to say? I have nothing with which to struggle with the stone.[23] If you have consciousness, partake of this sacrifice.

"Sacrificial Prayer for My Maternal Aunt, Madame Zhou, Née Huang"[24]

Alas! Previously, my maternal grandfather had six boys and two girls, and my late paternal grandmother was in fact my maternal grandfather's younger sister. Therefore he agreed to marry his daughter to my late father. But my maternal grandparents passed away one after the other, and in the same space of time their six sons all perished. Thus my aunt was reared from a young age by my paternal grandmother, and when she reached marriageable age [lit., when her hair was pinned] she was married to the Zhou family. Thereafter, these two females were the only survivors of the Huang family. Every time my mother thought about this, she did not want to live. Consequently, the seasonal sacrifices were entrusted to the Chen family. From the time I was very small, I recognized my mother's sadness and distress, and always feared that my strength would be insufficient to fulfill my obligations as her descendant. Before long my mother, though still in the prime of life, abandoned her orphans. My younger brother and younger sister were entrusted to the Zhou family, and again there was only my aunt to raise them: it was not only the responsibilities of the Huang family that fell on the shoulders of my aunt alone. All under Heaven have the distress of losing their parents, and my aunt also got an illness in her limbs; still, she took medicine in order to keep herself going. Whenever she became very sick, she would say to me: "You will be able to establish yourself: my sister was counting on you so that she could die in peace. But the Huang family is now ending—can it be that your mother does not have lingering worries?!" Wiping at my tears, I told her: "I will uphold [my mother's] wish for a hundred years: don't say such inauspicious things!" But in my heart I was still apprehensive and never expected that it had come to this! O Heaven, the cruelty! O Heaven, the pain! Due to my unfilial [lack of success], I fear the demise of the Chen family; how will I be able to preserve the graves of the Huang family and sacrifice to their spirits so as to bring lasting peace to the souls of my mother and my aunt?! When I think of my aunt, it is as if my mother is alive. If by dying I could take her place, would I dare to begrudge this body? Now she is gone; who will take on the obligations? In great grief I wail and inform my descendants.

"Commemorative Biography of Madame Liu, Née He"[25]

At the end of the Shaoxing period [1131–1162] I had been residing in Lin'an [the Southern Song capital of Hangzhou] for three years; my parents desired a daughter-in-law and ordered me to return home. He Maogong of Yiwu wanted to marry his elder brother's daughter to me. At that time, "wealthy" in Yiwu meant the He family. Both Maogong and his brother were literati, and Maogong's reputation was especially eminent. I was extremely poor and feared that I was not up to the match. All of Maogong's affinal relatives were opposed: only Mr. Liu Shuxiang of Wuyi vigorously endorsed Maogong's words and, moreover, advised my father to hasten with the betrothal gifts. The following year, in the first year of the Qiandao reign period [1165–1173], I went to their house for the wedding ceremony. All the affinal relatives were there, and Shuxiang's wife was Maogong's younger sister. At the time, Maogong's mother was over seventy, and she, her two sons, and her daughter relied on one another to get by. Their household had begun to flourish, and harmony filled the air: those who entered their gates were naturally moved to esteem. She loved her granddaughters like daughters, but especially considered my wife to be like herself. Because of this, her Aunt Liu regarded her with special favor, and Shuxiang was even more kind to me.

Maogong retired from office in Yongxin county in Ji prefecture; the various gentlemen competed to recognize his talent, and onlookers also felt that it would not be difficult for him to rise to the top at lightning speed. But one day in the spring of 1177, with no sign of illness, he died. Another three or four years later, his mother also departed this world. Shuxiang and his wife attended the funeral, and thereupon Shuxiang died. Not long after that, Maogong's wife died as well. My wife's father passed away in 1183, his death like that of Maogong. Only Aunt Liu and my wife's mother were still without infirmity.

In the spring of 1186, we all gathered at my in-laws' home. Aunt Liu said to me, "I was born on the twenty-eighth day of the seventh month; if on my birthday you take the trouble to send gifts but don't come even once to see me, it will be as if you haven't sent anything!" I laughed and replied, "That was always my intent; now I certainly will have to fulfill it!" When the date arrived, I went over, and she came out to greet me with a smile. It was a great gathering of the relatives; the wine flowed until dawn and still her interest did not flag. The following night, the celebrations continued; the wine glasses had not yet circulated when she lifted her hand to her head and declared herself ill. When I went to see her, she was already dead. O woe! The vicissitudes of fortune follow one upon the other, there is no point in trying to calculate them; as for the moment of life and death, who can possibly do so! But to have her brothers die as one person—even I did not realize how bitterly she cried! In these twenty and more years—how many months? how many days?—the transformations among the Hes and the Lius have been so rapid, yet I am as poor as I was in the beginning. Only when it reaches me does the Way of constant change come to rest! This, too, is something to sigh about!

Madame's surname was He. Her great-grandfather was [named] Jing, her grandfather Xian, her father Ju. At the age of seventeen she married into the Liu family; at her death she was fifty-three. She had three sons: Sanfu, who was a Supervisor in Northern Quzhou,[26] Sanyu, and Sanjin. She had three daughters, [two of whom] married Huang Hua and Huang Shugu. Both of them were superior young men, and Shugu was once sent up to the upper-level examinations from the National University.[27] The youngest daughter is not yet married. There are three grandsons and three granddaughters, all still young.

Madame's aspirations were broad and open, her speech clear and forthright. When dealing with kinsmen senior and junior, she treated all in a kind and orderly fashion, without regard to wealth or position. In general she resembled her father and was not like women and girls usually are. She liked it when others drank but she did not drink herself; she talked and laughed all day without saying anything one could take exception to. Her virtuous behavior in the inner quarters even a young maiden could not surpass. Is it not that she achieved the pure virtue of yin [the female principle] without its gloomy and selfish aspects?! This too [made her] extraordinary among women.

Initially, Shuxiang was buried in the eastern field of Jintang, five *li* from their home. In 1187 her orphans were going to bury her with him and said to me, "Will you see to it that our mother, though dead, will not perish?" My strength is surely insufficient; I will rely on friends to help myself. The inscription reads:

> Ambitions and thoughts open and clear,
> Cherish them in death.
> Buried together with your husband,
> Bless your descendants.

NOTES

1. Observers of contemporary funerary rituals describe various types of *jiwen* used today, all of which seem to be read aloud or chanted as part of the funeral ritual. See Watson and Rawksi, *Death Ritual in Late Imperial and Modern China,* 122, 222.

2. For a fuller discussion of the changes in funerary inscriptions between Tang and Song, see Bossler, *Powerful Relations: Kinship, Status, and the State in Sung China (960–1279),* 12–24. Research in progress suggests that there were similar shifts in later periods: for example, widow chastity seems to become a much more prominent theme in funerary inscriptions in the Yuan and after.

3. A relatively small number of Song *muzhiming* have been published in inscription collections after having been recovered from Song tombs in later dynasties. Archeological excavations in China today also occasionally turn up *muzhiming* of Song date.

4. Chen Liang, *Chen Liang ji,* 27:395–96; 28:411–12.

5. Chen Liang, *Chen Liang ji,* 22:343–44. The name she gave him was "Runeng," which loosely translated means "you can do it!"

6. The Song examination system in this period consisted essentially of two major steps: passing the preliminary examinations at the prefectural level qualified a man to sit for the *jinshi* examinations, which were held roughly every three years in the capital. In theory, only by passing the *jinshi* examinations could a man hope to be awarded an official post.

7. For Chen Liang's biography, see Tuo Tuo et al., *Song shi,* 436:12929–43; Tillman, *Utilitarian Confucianism: Ch'en Liang's Challenge to Chu Hsi,* 69–114.

8. Chen Liang's biography in the *Song History (Song shi)* gives one version of the story (Tuo Tuo et al., 436:12941), but there are several inconsistencies. See also Tillman, *Utilitarian Confucianism,* 74–75.

9. It is not clear exactly how Chen Liang managed to get his father freed, but evidently he was able to prevail on powerful officials from his native prefecture for help (Tillman, *Utilitarian Confucianism,* 74–75; and Chen Liang, *Chen Liang ji,* 21: 317).

10. In fact, both Chen Liang's mother and his aunt were married off at ages quite young by Song standards: as the sacrificial prayers reveal, Chen Liang's mother was only fourteen *sui* (so quite possibly only thirteen by Western reckoning) when she gave birth to him. Similarly, we know from a funerary inscription for his aunt that she was married off at fourteen *sui* (Chen Liang, *Chen Liang ji,* 30:434). Other funerary biographies of Sung women indicate that it was far more common for females to be married in their late teens (note that in a Song data set considered by Patricia Ebrey, the mean age at marriage was 19 *sui*; Ebrey, *The Inner Quarters: Marriage and the Lives of Chinese Women in the Sung Period,* 74–75). This early marriage is probably attributable to their orphan status: Yuan Cai, the author of a famous advice book on Song family life, pointed out the awkwardness of having sexually mature but unmarried non-kin females around (see Ebrey, *Family and Property in Sung China: Yüan Ts'ai's Precepts for Social Life,* 218–19).

11. Chen Liang, *Chen Liang ji,* 27:407–8.

12. It is tempting to dismiss these remarks as merely rhetorical humility, but the evidence suggests that in fact Chen Liang's family did *not* share the social position of his in-laws. I have argued elsewhere that Chen Liang in fact represented something

of a marital gamble for the Hes, a gamble based on Chen Liang's local reputation as a scholar. See Bossler, *Powerful Relations,* 197–99.

13. Source: Chen Liang, "Ji meifu Zhou Yingbo wen," in *Chen Liang ji,* 23:362. Much of this prayer is constructed around a particular grammatical pattern, which I have maintained as much as possible in the English, in spite of the rather awkward diction it creates. In a few instances I have altered the grammatical pattern in favor of keeping the meaning of the original clear. For an alternative translation of the first few lines of this ode, see Ebrey, *The Inner Quarters,* 77.

14. "Abandoned the orphans" was a conventional way of referring to a parent's death.

15. It is not entirely clear what edifice Chen Liang renovated. The term he uses implies a residence of some type, though from the context it also seems plausible that he rebuilt the ancestral hall of the Zhou family, on which his sister's tablet would have been placed along with that of her husband.

16. The phrase *xing ying gao chang* used here comes from Sima Qian's *Records of the Historian,* where a man too poor to bury his mother was said to have gone to a high and open place to make a living.

17. Source: Chen Liang, "Ji mei wen," in *Chen Liang ji,* 25:385–86.

18. This "maidservant" seems to have borne a child by Chen Liang's father. Cf. Bossler, *Powerful Relations,* 193 and 322–23, n. 99.

19. The remainder of this prayer is written in four-character rhyme, which leads to a certain awkwardness in the diction. I have not attempted to preserve the rhyme scheme in this translation, though I fear the awkwardness persists!

20. "Escape" here has Buddhist overtones, in the sense of escape from karmic cycles of death and rebirth, or at least from one karmic cycle into a better one.

21. In other words, Chen Liang feels he ought to take some responsibility for educating his sister's son.

22. The expression used here has the sense that one continues to live in a situation where death would be preferable.

23. It is unclear to me what is meant by "struggle with a stone" here, unless perhaps the idea is struggling with the ink stone (i.e., with the creative process).

24. Source: Chen Liang, "Ji yimu Zhou furen Huang shi wen," in *Chen Liang ji,* 25:375–76.

25. Source: Chen Liang, "Liu furen He shi muzhiming," in *Chen Liang ji,* 30:437–38.

26. I have been unable to discover the precise nature of what he was supervising: the title that Chen Liang attributes to him does not appear in any of the standard reference works on Song official titles.

27. For a discussion of the National University and its role in the examination system, see Chaffee, *The Thorny Gates of Learning in Sung China: A Social History of the Examinations,* 103–5.

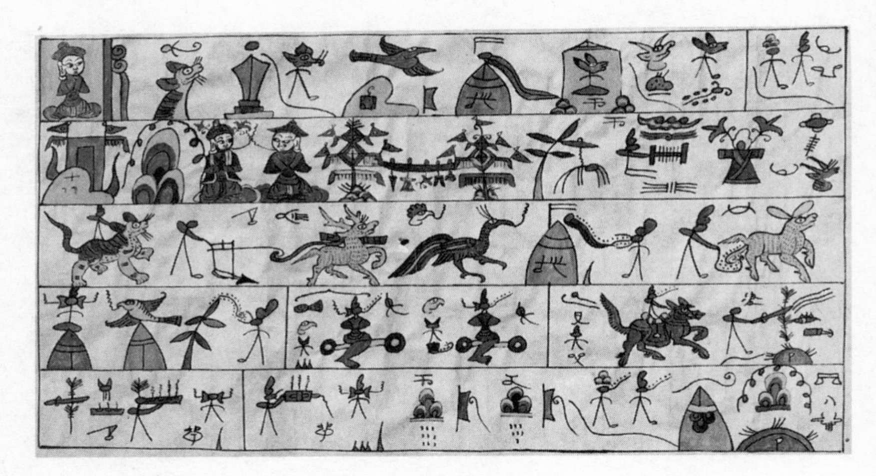

Fig. 5. The legend of Love-Suicide Meadow. This contemporary Naxi pictograph recounts the legend associated with a subalpine meadow in the Naxi homeland in Lijiang, Yunnan, where young Naxi lovers committed suicide in protest against the spread of the Han custom of arranged marriage. Photograph by Jack D. Ives. Reprinted courtesy of Professor Ives.

FIVE

"The Customs of Various Barbarians" by Li Jing (1251–?)

Translated by Jacqueline M. Armijo-Hussein

TRANSLATOR'S PREFACE

I first encountered this text while carrying out research for my dissertation on Sayyid 'Ajall Shams al-Din (1210?–1279; Ch. Saidianchi), a Muslim official who served the Mongol Yuan dynasty. Although numerous official documents describe his policies towards the indigenous peoples of Yunnan and the various institutions he created to improve their lives, descriptions of the people themselves have proved difficult to find. This dearth of information on local "barbarians" was not surprising, given the priorities of court record-keepers, but it was frustrating. I finally located this text, which although written shortly after Sayyid 'Ajall's death, is close enough in time to give us some idea of the peoples he encountered and worked with closely during his governance in Yunnan.

I translated this text while living in Yunnan, and one of the most interesting aspects of working on it there was the extent to which I could recognize in the present-day population of that region of southwest China the descendants of many of the groups described in the text. As a consequence, when it came to translating some of the more derogatory descriptions of these peoples, I found myself wanting to use less offensive synonyms. My impulse here was clearly misguided, as one of the goals of translation is to convey the attitudes and meanings intended by the author. Another aspect of the text that I found intriguing was its similarity to the account of the indigenous peoples of Yunnan attributed to Marco Polo, who traveled through this region at the same time as the author of this text, Li Jing. Marco Polo, like his Han Chinese counterpart, seems to have focused on the sexual practices, clothing or lack thereof, as well as the eating habits of these peoples. Apparently, at least in this case, a Han Chinese

Confucian official and an Italian Catholic shared common views of the "other."

INTRODUCTION

What is now known as Yunnan province in southwest China was once a fiercely independent region inhabited by a variety of indigenous peoples ruled by several autonomous kingdoms. For centuries Chinese emperors sought to conquer and subjugate this area in order to colonize it and exploit its extensive natural resources. Ironically, it was during the rule of the "barbarian" Mongols in China that this territory was finally conquered and incorporated into China proper. The Mongols arrived in Yunnan in 1253, and during the first twenty years of their rule military strategies predominated. In 1274, however, the emperor Qubilai decided to change the nature of his Yunnan administration and to that end appointed Sayyid 'Ajall Shams al-Din, one of his most experienced civilian administrators, to be Director of Political Affairs of the Regional Secretarial Council of Yunnan. The arrival of Sayyid 'Ajall signified the end of military rule and the beginning of what can best be described as a "civilizing project."[1] Unlike all other colonizing/civilizing projects in China, however, this one was led by a Muslim from Central Asia.

Whereas earlier Chinese officials had used force, violence, and even terror to subjugate indigenous peoples,[2] Sayyid 'Ajall's approach to governing depended on diplomacy and on convincing the local population of the benefits of being members of the state. In addition to introducing agricultural technology from the heartland, Sayyid 'Ajall also set about introducing traditional Chinese values and customs. Buddhist, Daoist, and Confucian temples were built, and schools were established on the grounds of the Confucian temples. While the writings of some Han Chinese officials reveal that many viewed the state's efforts to "civilize" the local people as a means to "humanize" them, the historical records that survive portray Sayyid 'Ajall as a man who sought to improve the quality of life of the indigenous peoples and who treated them with consideration and respect. According to He Hongzuo, the contemporary Superintendent of Confucian Studies for all the counties of Yunnan, when the peoples of Yunnan were convinced of the sincerity of Sayyid 'Ajall, they set off to welcome him:

> From the edges of the world people came, climbing over mountains and sailing over seas, and through a myriad of languages, they offered tribute and paid their respects [to Sayyid 'Ajall]. At this time he established temple schools and invited teachers. The exteriors of the temple schools were elaborately decorated, and inside there were images of the great sages, so that the local people could behold them and pay their respects. During the spring and autumn they performed the rituals and music to honor the memory of the sages of old.[3] And thus the orang-

utans and butcherbirds were transformed into unicorns and phoenixes, and their felts and furs were exchanged for gowns and caps.[4]

The choice of the orangutan and butcherbird is highly evocative and reflects common literary and popular perceptions of the time. From earliest recorded history in China, apes and monkeys have been depicted as both magical and diabolical[5] —on the one hand admired for their anthropomorphic qualities, but also used as a trope to dehumanize the non-Han peoples encountered by the Han Chinese. The choice of butcherbird *(jue),* although a less common image, may nevertheless be a more powerful one, as it denotes a species of bird renowned for its clamorous calls and its brutal rapacity.[6] The imagery of transforming the local people of Yunnan into unicorns and phoenixes—creatures that symbolized all that was precious and rare—dramatized the impact of the civilizing process for readers of this text.

In addition to using the imagery of the animal kingdom, the Han Chinese also used a scale based on gradations from "raw" to "cooked" to denote the status of "barbarians." Those whose customs were most different from what was considered "civilized" were labeled "raw" *(sheng)* and were often compared to animals, whereas those who had adopted some of the customs and outward appearances of the Han Chinese, were considered "cooked" *(shu)* and well on their way to becoming civilized/human.

The *Yunnan zhilüe,* written by Li Jing (style name Jingshan) at the beginning of the fourteenth century, has survived as a fairly comprehensive description of the peoples of Yunnan during this period. This text reveals a great deal not only about its subject but also about its author and the values of his culture and society. As the first gazetteer written after the establishment of Yunnan as a province of China, the *Yunnan zhilüe* formed the basis of all later gazetteers written in the Ming and Qing periods. It also represents the earliest as well as the most comprehensive and reliable description of the indigenous peoples of Yunnan and has been the foundation for much of the later research on the history of the different ethnic groups of Yunnan.

Li Jing, a native of Hebei, was appointed Deputy Pacification Commissioner of Wusa and Wumeng (the far northeast corner of Yunnan and the northwest corner of Guizhou) in 1301. According to his own introduction, Li Jing arrived in Yunnan in the midst of the Mongol campaign in Burma. His responsibilities included traveling throughout the province in search of supplies and funding for the military campaign. *Yunnan zhilüe* is believed to have been originally written in 1303 in the form of a report of the author's findings during his two years of travel. It was edited and revised in 1331. In his introduction Li Jing explains that he decided to compile information about Yunnan because so little had been written about that region, and what had been written was not accurate: "Early on I discovered that what had been written before was full of mistakes—for you can hear all sorts of fanciful tales along the road—and that what had been written about were not things the writers had experienced themselves. And because of all that I have seen, I have interviewed many people and have compiled *Yunnan zhilüe* in four *juan.*"[7]

In the chapter from *Yunnan zhiüe* translated here, Li Jing begins with a description of the Bai people, whom he clearly believes are the most "cooked" and to whom he devotes the most comprehensive description, and ends with a rather cursory account of the Pu Barbarians. The Bai, who are the only ones honored with the appellation "people" *(ren),* are described in detail and with respect.[8] His descriptions of the Bai introduce to the reader what it was about these "others" that the Han Chinese found most intriguing and noteworthy.[9] As one proceeds down his list toward the rawest of the raw, characteristics associated with violence receive more emphasis. This may in part be the result of progressively less evidence and thus more reliance on hearsay.

Li's preoccupation with the sexual practices of the peoples he describes borders on obsession.[10] Apparently, from the point of view of the Han Chinese, sexual practices served as a measure of civilization or barbarism.[11] Clothing (or lack thereof) and hairstyles are also emphasized in his account, as are courting, marriage, and burial rituals; these, according to James Watson, are the means by which Han Chinese defined themselves and differentiated themselves from others.[12]

In the translation that follows, present-day equivalents, or the closest approximation thereof, of place names and ethnic group identifications are noted in square brackets.

ORIGINAL TEXT[13]

The Bai People

The Bai people have both surnames and clan names. Han Wudi opened the Bo Road, going through the Southwest Barbarian Road in today's Xuzhou county. As a result, Zhongqing [Kunming], Weichu [Chuxiong], Dali, and Yongchang [Baoshan], formerly all Bo areas, have now become Bai areas. During the Tang reign period of Taihe [827–836], the Meng clan captured the three prefects of Qiong, Rong, and Sui [all in present-day Sichuan] and then entered Chengdu. They captured children, women, and craftsmen numbering several tens of thousands and brought them back south. From that time onward Yunnan started producing embroidered silk. In Bai language, the phrase for "donning clothes" is "garbing." The term for eating a meal, which in Chinese would refer to eating rice, is "drink soup-and-vegetable." The phrase for "gathering fuel" in Chinese is "collecting grasses," whereas in Bai language they speak of "cutting tinder." They call silk "coverlets" and refer to liquor by the name of the vessel, "goblet." Their term for "saddle" is "fear of mud," and all walls in Bai language are "brick battlements." There are countless similar examples. Such linguistic similarities make it plain that the Bai people were formerly Bo people.[14]

Both men and women wear hats *[cigong]*, which are similar to the bamboo hats worn by the fishermen of the heartland, except that they are bigger. They weave bamboo to make them and then cover them with black felt. When relatives and old friends see each other, even after a long separation, they do not *kowtow;* they only take off their hats in greeting. Men wear felt and put their hair up. The women do not wear any makeup. They put a type of oily substance in their hair; then they take blue threads and braid them into the hair, then wrap it up around the head making a coil, then gather it in under a black turban. They wear gold earrings and ivory bracelets. Their clothes are embroidered with squares of cloth, and they use a fine felt to cover the upper body. Unmarried girls and widows can come and go as they please without restraint; the young men, who are known as "splendid ones" *[miaozi]*, roam about at night, either playing their multi-reed pipes or singing ballads, the harmonies of which express their affections. When their affection is mutual, they then go off in pairs to have sex, and only afterwards do they get married. The roof beams in their rooms are curved eaves, like those found in temples and palaces. Food is preferred raw; for example, pork, beef, chicken, and fish are all minced raw, mixed with garlic paste, and then eaten.

Every year on the twenty-fourth day of the twelfth month, they offer sacrifices to their ancestors, like the "going to the grave mound" ceremony in the heartland.[15] On the twenty-fourth day of the sixth month, throughout the night, they lift up on poles blazing torches that light up the sky. All the children play with the burning pine torches. This is known as the "sacrifice to drive away evil spirits."[16]

Buddhism is flourishing greatly among them, and those who have a spirit of strict discipline are known as the ones of the "virtuous path." Laypeople greatly respect them. The monks who are married are known as teacher monks *[shiseng]* and are responsible for teaching the children. They mainly read Buddhist texts, but few know the Six Classics. After the Duan clan came to power, they selected officials from among these monks. According to local tradition every household, regardless if it is poor or rich, has a Buddhist altar; every morning and evening families strike the drum and come together to pray, and both the young and old never let go of their prayer beads. Every year they fast [refrain from meat and certain other foods] almost half the year.

All the other barbarians are pig-headed and even enjoy killing. When a slight disagreement arises among close relatives, they always use knives against each other. They do not know how to serve the Buddhist spirit; they are like the unfilial "mother-eating owl and father-eating muntjac tiger." Only the Bai deeply revere the Buddha, and few have the stomach for murder. It can thus be concluded that the establishment of Buddhism has had a beneficial effect on some of the most bizarre customs.

Their refined gentlemen are quite good at calligraphy, and they follow the style of the Jin period. Their own history states,[17] "During the reign of Baohe,[18] the king of Nanzhao sent Zhang Zhicheng [a Bai scholar or official] to study at the Tang imperial court." For this reason the people of Yunnan respect Wang Xizhi[19] even though they do not even know to respect Confucius or Mencius. After our [Yuan] dynasty conquered this area, it [Yunnan] was divided up into administrative units, and Confucian temples were ordered built in every county. The local barbarians regarded Confucius and Mencius as Buddhas of the Han Chinese.

The marketplace is called "the street." It is packed until noon, and everyone leaves by dusk. Cowry shells are used as currency in trading. They are commonly called *ba:* one *ba* makes a *zhuang,* four *zhuang* make a *shou,* four *shou* make a *miao,* and five *miao* make a *suo.*

When a person dies, the body is washed and bound up in a sitting position. The coffin is shaped like a square wooden chest. They beat a copper drum to start the funeral and cut off their hair as a sign of filial piety in mourning. When they cry, it sounds more like singing than wailing. They then burn the corpse and save the bones to inter.

In winter and summer it is neither too cold nor too hot, and in all four seasons there are flowers and trees in bloom. There are many paddies, and they call five *mou* [of land] a *shuang.* The landscape is beautiful, but still inferior to that of Jiangnan. Their hemp, wheat, vegetables, and fruit are much like that of the heartland.

Their king is known as the *piaoxin* and the heir apparent is called the *tanchuo.* The princes are called *xinju,* the premier is the *buxie,* and the literate among those who govern are known as the Pure and Peaceful Officials. Their noblemen wear clothes that are similar to those of the Han Chinese of recent years, and their other customs are also similar.

The Luoluo

The Luoluo [Yi] are also known as the Wu Man, or Black Barbarians.

The men put their hair up in a coil and pluck their facial hair, or shave their heads. They carry two knives, one at each side, and enjoy fighting and killing. When a disagreement arises among fathers and sons and among brothers, they are known to attack each other with military weapons. Killing is taken lightly, and they consider it a sign of valor. They prize horses with cropped tails, their saddles have no trappings, and their stirrups are carved from wood in the shape of a fish's mouth to accommodate the toes.

The women wear their hair down and wear cotton clothing, and the wealthy wear jewelry and embroidered clothes; the humble are garbed in sheepskin. They ride horses side-saddle. Unmarried girls wear large earrings and cut their hair level with their eyebrows, and their skirts do not even cover their knees. Men and women, rich and poor, all wear felt wraps and go barefoot, and they can go as long as one year without washing face or hands.

It is the custom of husbands and wives not to see each other during the day, but only to sleep together at night. Children as old as ten *sui* most likely have never seen their father. Wives and concubines are not jealous of each other. Even the well-to-do do not use padding on their beds, but just spread pine needles on the ground with only a layer of felt and mat. Marriages are arranged with the maternal uncle's family, but if a suitable partner cannot be found they can look elsewhere for a match. When someone falls ill they do not use medicine, but instead call in a male shaman, who is known as the *daxipo*. He uses chicken bones to divine good and evil fortunes. The tribal leader always has the shaman at his side, and he must consult the shaman to make a final decision in all matters great and small.

A woman who is about to get married must first have relations with the shaman, and then "dance" with all the groom's brothers. This custom is known as "making harmony." Only after that can she be married to her husband. If any one of the brothers refuses to go along with this custom, he will be regarded as unrighteous and everyone will be disgusted with him.[20]

The first wife is known as the *naide,* and it is only her children who can inherit their father's position. If the *naide* has a son who dies before marrying, she will go ahead and arrange a wife for him anyway. Anyone can then have relations with the deceased son's wife, and any child born is considered the child of the deceased. If the tribal leader does not leave a male heir, his wife's [the *naide*'s] daughter then becomes the leader. However, she then has no female attendants—only ten or more young male attendants, with whom she can have relations.[21]

When the tribal leader dies, they wrap his body in a leopard skin, cremate him, and then bury his bones on a mountain at a location known only to his closest relatives. After the burial they take images of the Seven Precious Things[22] and place them on a high platform. They then go steal the head of a neighboring nobleman and offer it as a sacrifice. If they are not able to obtain one, they cannot make the sacrifice. At the time of the sacrificial ceremony all the relatives arrive, and they sacrifice more than a thousand cattle and sheep, or at least several hundred. Every year when they celebrate the spring festival during the twelfth month, they take a long vertical pole and a horizontal piece of wood, [and arranging a seesaw] with one person on each side, they go up and down together playing.

They support many soldiers, who are called *juke,* and they generously provide for them. When they go off to battle they view death as "returning home." They expertly craft armor and swords that are worth dozens of horses. On their javelins and crossbow arrow tips they put a poison that kills instantly.

They are found in Shunyuan [near Guiyang, Guizhou], Qujing, Wumeng [Zhaotong], Wusa [near Weining, Guizhou], and Yuexi [north of Xichang, Sichuan].

The Gilded-Teeth "Bai" Barbarians

The Gilded-Teeth "Bai" Barbarians [Jinchi Baiyi (a Dai people)] do not use characters to keep records, but instead use carved pieces of wood as contracts.

When their tribal leader dies, if someone who is not his son or grandson tries to usurp the position, everyone will attack him.

Men are tattooed, and all their facial hair [mustache, beard, hair on temples, eyebrows, and eyelashes] is removed. They put red or white makeup on their faces, tie up their hair with pieces of colored silk, wear red and black clothes and embroidered shoes, carry a mirror, say *a ye wei* when they are hurt, and look just like actors from the heartland. They look askance at farm work and stay home to look after the children. During the Tianbao reign period [742–756], they sent someone with [the Nanzhao ruler] King Cuan Gui to the Tang imperial court, and our present-day drama called *cuan nong*[23] originates from this time.

The women pluck their eyebrows and eyelashes, do not wear makeup, put their hair up in two coils, and wear embroidered clothes, which they adorn by sewing on small shells. They work very hard at farming, never even stopping to take a break. Right up until delivering a baby they hardly ever rest. When they give birth, they immediately take the baby up in their arms, wash it in the river, and then hand it over to the care of the father and return to work as usual.[24] Their chickens do the same: after the hen lays the eggs, the rooster then incubates them.

The topography is such that at lower levels it is very humid and at higher levels it is very hot, so most people put up bamboo houses [on stilts]. They live by the banks of the river and every day bathe up to ten times. Mothers and fathers, older and younger brothers, everyone bathes together without any embarrassment.[25] When they are sick they do not take medicine; they only put a mixture of ginger and salt in the nose. Betel palm, powdered clam, and China root leaves are offered to guests.[26] Their horses are few, but sheep are many.

They have too many leaders and consequently no absolute authority or discipline, so whenever a minor feud erupts, they fight each other violently. When they defeat an enemy, they behead him and put the head at the bottom of a platform. Their military leaders then gather together, and when they have finished fighting, with great bravado they stick the tail feathers of ringed pheasants in their hair coils, grasp their spears, and dance around their captives. They also sacrifice a chicken and have the shaman invoke its spirit saying, "Oh tribal chieftain [of the enemy], you and your people should quickly come surrender to me." When the sacrifice is finished, they recount what happened in battle, mete out rewards and punishments, and then drink wine, make music, and disperse. When they attack a town or destroy a fortified palisade, they do not kill its ruler, but cast out his entire family. Or else, they imprison them until they die.

In marriage they do not make distinctions between close relatives [i.e., they are allowed to marry close relatives]. There is not much importance attached to virginity, and they are as profligate as dogs and swine. Young women wear red headdresses and let their hair down. If a woman dies before marrying, all the men who had relations with her must hold up a banner to see her off, and if the banners number a hundred it is considered the most beautiful. Her parents cry and lament: "How could we have known that a woman with so many lovers could have died so young!"

They gather together to trade once every five days; in the morning the women go, and in the middle of the day the men go to barter for felt, cloth, tea, and salt. This land has many mulberry trees and orange trees, and they raise silkworms year-round.

The ones who cover their two front teeth with gold are known as the Gilded-Teeth Barbarians, the ones who stain their teeth are known as the Stained-Teeth Barbarians, the ones who tattoo their faces are known as the Embroidered-Face Barbarians, the ones who tattoo their feet are known as the Flowery-Feet Barbarians, and the ones who put pieces of colored silk in their hair are known as the Flowery-Topknot Barbarians. Of the barbarians of the southwest, the Gilded-Teeth "Bai" Barbarians are the most powerful. To the north they border Tibet [Tufan], and in the south they reach Cochin-China [Jiaochi], and their customs are probably mostly the same.[27]

The Moxie Barbarians

The Moxie Barbarians [Moxie Man, or Mosuo/Naxi] live north of Dali, near the border with Tibet [Tufan], along the Jinsha River. This region is cold, and there are many sheep, horses, and musk oxen, as well as the famous iron. They live along the river in places that are strategically located and difficult to access. Their villages are scattered like stars in the sky and are independent of one another.

The men are expert fighters, enjoy hunting, carry daggers, and adorn themselves with pieces of giant clam. When there is any dissatisfaction, they strike a gong, and the men who are a party to it attack each other. The women from the two families must then get in between them to pull them apart, whereupon they disperse. The women wear felt wraps, black clothes, go barefoot, and put their hair up. Women cut their hair level with their eyebrows, wear wool yarn as a skirt, and are otherwise practically naked without being ashamed. After they marry they change their style of dress and have no prohibitions regarding licentious behavior. They do not worship Buddha or other spirits, but only ascend the mountain on the fifteenth day of the first month to offer sacrifices to heaven. This is a very serious and grand affair in which more than a hundred men and women take part. Everyone holds hands, and they dance in a circle and have a wonderful time.

Their customs are very frugal, and the food they eat is coarse and of poor quality. A year's worth of food might half consist of turnips. The poor families know no other seasoning but salt. The men, who are especially strong, respect their leader. Every year in the eleventh month they slaughter cows and sheep and then compete with each other in inviting guests. They host banquets every single day, and if even one guest does not attend, it is considered a great insult.

When someone dies, they carry the body up the mountainside wrapped in a bamboo mat. There is no outer or inner coffin, and everyone is cremated at the same place regardless of their status. They do not save the bones. A person who dies from unnatural causes is cremated separately. Except for this, their other customs are similar to those of the Wu Man [Black Barbarians, or Yizu].

The Tulao Barbarians

The Tulao Barbarians [Tulao Man, or Zhuang] are found throughout the region extending from the south of Xuzhou [Yibin, Sichuan] to the north of Wumeng [Zhaotong].

At the age of fourteen or fifteen boys have their two front teeth knocked out,[28] and then they get married, living with their pigs and sheep in the same room. They do not use spoons or chopsticks, but instead roll their food up into balls and eat it with their hands. They walk on stilts, going up and down the hillsides like deer running away. Women go barefoot, wear their hair in a high bun, use birch bark as a head covering, and wear large earrings, black cotton clothing, and a lock-like amulet around the neck. As they go in and out of the forest, from a distance they look like gibbons.[29] When someone dies, the body is placed in a wooden coffin, which is then perched on a ledge built into an eight-thousand-foot cliff. The first to fall is considered blessed.

The hillside land is limited and of very poor quality. They use the slash-and-burn method of agriculture. All the grain they harvest is hung up in a bamboo shed, and then they grind it as needed day to day. They often gather litchis and supplement their living by trading in tea.

The Savages

The Savages [Ye Man, or Jingpo] are located to the west of Xunchuan, scattered among the valleys. They do not wear clothes but instead use bark to cover their bodies, and they are repulsive in appearance. The men are few and the women many, so every man has more than ten wives. They arm themselves with wooden arrows for protection from invasion and attack. They do not farm, but rather enter the mountains and forests to collect plants, trees, and animals to eat. They do not have any utensils and wrap their food in banana leaves.

The Woni Barbarians

The Woni Barbarians [Woni Man, or Hani] are located five hundred *li* to the southwest of Lin'an [north of Tonghai] and dwell in the mountains and forests. They live very frugal lives, but hoard cowry shells in their homes, burying them underground in caches of 120. When someone is about to die, they entreat their children: "I have buried a certain amount; you can take some of it, but do not touch the rest, for I will use it when I am reborn." Such is the extent of their stupidity.

The Pu Barbarians

The Pu Barbarians [Pu Man], also known as the Puzi Man, are located to the west of the Lancang River. They are brave and strong, are expert robbers and thieves, and can ride horses bareback. They go barefoot and wear short armor, which leaves their knees and shins exposed. They are masters of the spear and crossbow. They stick ringed pheasant tail feathers on their heads, and when they ride they can fly like the wind.

NOTES

I would like to thank Professor Fang Hui of Yunnan University and her father, Fang Linggui, Professor Emeritus of Yunnan Normal University, for their extensive assistance in the translation of this text. I would also like to thank Stevan Harrell for reviewing the final draft. I alone am responsible for errors that remain.

1. I use this term as defined in the following manner: "A civilizing project . . . is a kind of interaction between peoples, in which one group, the civilizing center, interacts with other groups (the peripheral peoples) in terms of a particular kind of inequality . . . [and it] draws its ideological rationale from the belief that the process of domination is one of helping the dominated to attain or at least approach the superior cultural, religious, and moral qualities characteristic of the center itself" (Harrell, "Introduction: Civilizing Projects and the Reaction to Them," 4).

2. Von Glahn, *The Country of Streams and Grottoes: Expansion, Settlement, and the Civilizing of the Sichuan Frontier in Song Times.* See also an account of subsequent Ming campaigns in this region in the biography of the early Ming general Fu Youde (d. 1394) in Goodrich and Fang, *Dictionary of Ming Biography 1368–1644,* 1:468–69.

3. During the second month of spring (the second month in the Chinese lunar calendar) and the second month of autumn (the eighth month of the lunar calendar) special offerings were made to honor Confucius and the sages.

4. He Hongzuo, "Zhongqinglu xue liyueji," a stele composed in 1341.

5. The earliest reference to apes and monkeys can be found in the Shang (sixteenth to eleventh centuries, B.C.E.) oracle bone inscriptions. For a comprehensive

description of the etymology of the major characters used to denote monkeys and apes, see Van Gulik, *The Gibbon in China: An Essay in Chinese Animal Lore,* 18–43. This classic work by the great Sinologist includes extensive descriptions of both literary and pictorial depictions of monkeys, gibbons, and other apes over three thousand years of Chinese cultural history.

6. "Butcherbird" is the popular name given to shrikes, "known throughout the world on account of their merciless habits in destruction of life, and their methods of impaling insects and small rodents upon thorn and barbed wire," according to ornithologists Harry R. Caldwell and John C. Caldwell (*South China Birds,* 175). The other unusual trait of the butcherbird is its highly varied warbling song, which is especially evident in duets. This characteristic could explain the Chinese term *jueshe* (butcherbird tongue), which dates back to the second century B.C.E. and refers to the incomprehensible "languages of the barbarians."

7. Wang Shuwu, *Dali xingji [jiaozhu]; Yunnan zhilüe [jijiao],* 66.

8. The imperial Chinese practice of describing and documenting the appearance, cultures, and geographic spaces of the "barbarians" encountered and often subjugated by imperial authorities resembles practices common in the British Empire during its period of colonial expansion. In his work on the British Raj, Bernard Cohn observes: "A large colonial bureaucracy occupied itself, especially from the 1860s, with classifying people and their attributes, with censuses, surveys, and ethnographies, with recording transactions, marking space, establishing routines, and standardizing practices. The total effect exceeded the sum of each appropriation of information: colonial regimes were trying to *define* the constituents of a certain civil society, even as they hid the act of creation beneath the idea that society was a natural occurrence and the state a neutral observer and regulator" (cited in Cooper and Stoler, "Tensions of Empire: Colonial Control and Visions of Rule," 611). On the invention of an Oriental "other" by scholars and the subsequent historical consequences when these inventions are taken as facts and incorporated into political policies, see Edward Said, *Orientalism.*

9. As mentioned in the translator's preface, one of the most interesting aspects of working on this text while living in Yunnan was the opportunity to see the present-day social conditions of the descendants of many of these indigenous peoples. To this day the Bai are held in high regard by the Han Chinese as the most "civilized" of the minorities, whereas the adjective most commonly used to describe the other minorities is *luohou* (backward). Not surprisingly, after centuries of the dominant culture defining what it means to be civilized, many of the minority groups in Yunnan today describe themselves as "backward." By the same token, today many Bai proudly announce that they are the "most civilized of the minorities."

10. Marco Polo, who visited this region at the same time, was equally obsessed with the sexual habits of the indigenous peoples. However, unlike Li Jing, his preoccupations reflected the values of the Catholic church. For a startlingly similar view of this region, see the account in *The Travels of Marco Polo: The Complete Yule-Cordier Edition,* 2:44–123. A detailed comparison of the two accounts appears in Armijo-Hussein, "Sayyid 'Ajall Shams al-Din: A Muslim from Central Asia, Serving the Mongols in China, and Bringing 'Civilization' to Yunnan."

11. For centuries Yunnan, more than any other place in China, has represented to the Han Chinese majority a place of exotic, promiscuous women and an imagined sexual licentiousness not found elsewhere. Local entrepreneurs are currently taking full advantage of these misconceptions, recruiting poor minority women from the

countryside and offering them jobs in the cities, where they are sold into brothels. Another way in which the exoticization of minority women is capitalized upon is a ruse perpetuated by some of the sex workers themselves. In Xishuangbanna, a Dai region of Yunnan, there are many Han Chinese women from other parts of China who have migrated there to work in the sex industry. Many of them, in order to attract their overwhelmingly Han Chinese customers, dress in the distinctive traditional clothing of the Dai minority group. For an analysis of the social consequences of these essentialized views, see Armijo-Hussein, "Young People and Social Change in China: A Survey on Risk Factors for HIV/AIDS in Yunnan Province." Other scholars who have examined the popular perception of ethnic minority women throughout China include Stevan Harrell ("Introduction: Civilizing Projects and the Reaction to Them"), Dru Gladney ("Representing Nationality in China: Refiguring Majority/Minority Identities"), and Rey Chow ("Ethnic Minorities in Chinese Films: Cinema and the Exotic"). On contemporary sex tourism, see Hyde, "Sex Tourism Practices on the Periphery: Eroticizing Ethnicity on the Lancang." See also Schein, *Minority Rules: The Miao and the Feminine in China's Cultural Politics.*

12. See Watson, "The Structure of Chinese Funerary Rites: Elementary Forms, Ritual Sequence, and the Primacy of Performance."

13. Source: Wang Shuwu, *Dali xingji [jiaozhu]; Yunnan zhilüe [jijiao],* 86–96.

14. Here the author of the text seems to be illustrating a linguistic affinity between the Bai and the Bo. To illustrate the terms from Bai language he must transliterate Bai sounds using Chinese characters. Therefore it is worth noting that the characters he selects call attention to the ecological and cultural differences between the Han Chinese and the Bai. For instance, the term he uses to translate "eating a meal" drops the Han Chinese reference to cooked rice, and the phrase for gathering fuel connotes the ready availability of wood for kindling.

15. Probably refers to the Qingming Festival and the early spring "sweeping of the graves."

16. This practice refers to the Torch Festival, an annual celebration held every year down to this day throughout Yunnan province by several indigenous peoples. For more detailed information on the history of this ritual, see Deng Qiyao and Zhang Liu, *The Festivals in the Mysterious Land of Yunnan,* 167.

17. The title of this text is unknown, but presumably refers to a very early work written in Bai.

18. Baohe is a reign period of the Nanzhao Kingdom ruler Quan Fengyou (824–?).

19. Wang Xizhi (321–371) (style name Yishao) is widely regarded as the greatest artist in the history of Chinese calligraphy.

20. This custom of guaranteeing that a new bride is not a virgin when she first sleeps with her husband was apparently widespread throughout what is now southern China. Needless to say, it runs counter to more traditional Chinese values regarding chastity, the paternity of the first child, and the custom of primogeniture. In *The Local Cultures of South and East China,* Wolfram Eberhard identifies a series of "chains" that are in essence cultural traditions found among different groups of peoples in south and eastern China. His description of one of these chains offers a potential explanation for the above mentioned custom: "This chain showed the existence of beliefs and customs characteristic of a folktale type which is based on the idea that a girl to-be-married should not be a virgin because virgins carry a poison and contaminate the first lover" (139).

21. And her children will be considered the rightful heirs.

22. This list was originally Buddhist but evolved over time. There are several different versions of what these seven precious things are, but the most common version includes gold, silver, colored glaze, the giant clam, agate, pearl, and rose quartz.

23. Regarding the genre of drama called *cuan nong,* see West, "Mongol Influence on the Development of Northern Drama," 450–51.

24. For a fascinating and extensive discussion of this practice, which is known as *couvade,* in societies in many different parts of the world, see the scholarly commentary in *The Travels of Marco Polo,* 2:91–95 n. 4, and 596.

25. On a research trip to Xishuangbanna in 1997, I joined a tour group organized specifically for local tourists and made up primarily of Han Chinese from other parts of China. At one stop a local entrepreneur boarded the bus and handed out leaflets advertising his special tour to hidden sites along the riverbank to watch the local Dai women bathing.

26. The use of betel nut in this region has continued down to this day. Eberhard has the following to say about the practice: "All Southerners chew betel. They have silver or tin boxes with three compartments, containing the nut, the necessary lime, and the leaves for wrapping . . . The lime is a shell lime or ordinary lime, which is wrapped in the leaf together with the betel" (Eberhard, *The Local Cultures of South and East China,* 288).

27. *The Universal History (Kitab Jami' al-Tawarikh)* by Rashid al-Din also includes a brief description of these people. Written at the same time as both the Chinese and Italian accounts, his descriptions are similar to theirs. Nineteenth-century scholar Colonel Henry Yule noted: "There is another passage of Rashid among Elliot's extracts in which this people is mentioned . . . 'Beyond that is the country of *Katban,* then *Úman* [Wuman], then Zardandan, so called because the people have gold in their teeth. They puncture their hands and color them with indigo. They eradicate their beards so that they have not a sign of hair on their faces. They are all subject to the Kaan. Thence you arrive at the borders of *Tibet,* where they eat raw meat and worship images, and have no shame respecting their wives. The air is so impure that if they ate their dinner after noon they would all die. They boil tea and eat winnowed barley'" (Yule, *Cathay and the Way Thither: Being a Collection of Medieval Notices of China,* 2:274–75, n. 1).

28. This practice is also discussed by Eberhard, who offers the following explanation: "Knocking out teeth is customary among the Liao peoples, mostly as a form of initiation rite. Usually one upper molar and one incisor are knocked out. The reason usually given is that it is an embellishment. The better reason, more rarely given, is that it is intended to prevent a transformation into an evil creature that can bite" (*The Local Cultures of South and East China,* 451).

29. As mentioned earlier, when describing "barbarians," Chinese would often make comparisons with monkeys and apes. The gibbon was an especially favorite example, due to its popularity as a subject of Chinese poets: "The graceful movements of the gibbon and his saddening calls are referred to by nearly every poet who wrote from the 3d to the 7th century," notes Van Gulik (*The Gibbon in China,* 51). The following excerpt from an essay written by Fu Xuan (217–278 C.E.) reflects both the common comparisons made between monkeys, apes, and "barbarians," and several of the captivating attributes of the gibbon and the other primate common in China, the macaque: "When I am merry with wine, and my happy face has not yet been composed, I play with my macaques and let my gibbons have their way. Their admirable features are really staggering. I give them scarlet turbans for hats, and red

cloth for leggings. First they make faces, with their cinnabar lips, lifting their eyebrows and creasing their foreheads. Now they look sad, then they glare angrily. Others just look ahead restraining themselves, others again start bawling and wrangling. Others, assuming a dignified air seem to hesitate what to do, others wail sadly and moan and sigh. Thus they now resemble an elderly gentleman, then a barbarian dancing girl. Now they look down and groom their fur, then they clap their hands and jump about in confusion" (Van Gulik, *The Gibbon in China,* 27).

The tendency to liken non-Han peoples to nonhuman primates was so common that not only were "barbarians" compared with monkeys, but monkeys were also compared with "barbarians." For example, the macaque was known by the appellation *husun* or "grandson of a barbarian" (Van Gulik, *The Gibbon in China,* 35). These types of analogies have remained popular down to this day in China. In his work *The Discourse of Race in Modern China,* Frank Dikötter documents both early Chinese descriptions, dating back to the eighth century C.E., comparing Europeans with macaques (13–14), as well as more recent ones. In an interesting conflation of Darwinian theories of evolution and Chinese concepts of racial nationalism, a popular zoology textbook printed in Shanghai in 1916 made the following assertion regarding racial origins: "The 'black slave' was classified in the gorilla branch, and the Malays were descendants of the orangu-tan" (quoted in Dikötter, *The Discourse of Race in Modern China,* 147). Another Chinese scholar even offered a theory of de-evolution when he stated, "People who are indolent in the use of their intelligence will waste away and become macaques and long-tailed monkeys" (Zhang Binglin [1869–1936], quoted in Dikötter, *The Discourse of Race in Modern China,* 122).

Fig. 6. Portrait of Luo Rufang.
Source: *Luo Mingde gong wenji* (1632).

SIX

Selected Writings by Luo Rufang (1515–1588)

Translated by Yu-Yin Cheng

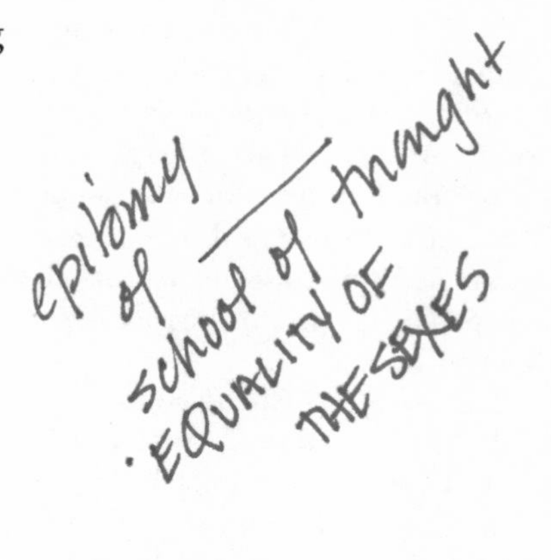

TRANSLATOR'S PREFACE

My interest in Luo Rufang's (1515–1588) writings on women began when I discovered that his view of cosmology stresses the interchangeable positions of *qian* and *kun* (the first two hexagrams in the *Book of Changes [Yijing]),* and the mutually encompassing forces of yin and yang.[1] Because Luo's unusual view places *qian* and *kun*—and so also yang and yin—in reciprocal relationship to one another, it also points implicitly to the equal status of both elements in each pair. Since yin and yang also symbolize female and male, I became interested in such issues as how Luo Rufang perceived the women of his time, what kinds of gender issues his writings might raise, and how these issues might figure in his philosophical system. I read through Luo's collected works *(Luo Mingde gong wenji)* and found that his writings about women celebrate and indeed praise women, both old and young, who pursued intellectual and philosophical interests. He also championed the virtue of motherly nurturance and love *(ci),* which he considered as important as the central Confucian virtues of filial piety *(xiao)* and brotherly respect *(ti).* Luo further suggested that *ci* constituted the source of filial piety. No Confucian scholar before Luo's time had ever written of motherly love in this way; *ci* is not even mentioned in Mencius's Five Human Relationships, which are the foundation of most neo-Confucian teachings on the subject of virtue. From Luo's writings about women, one sees how women helped to shape Confucian values, especially Confucian social ethics.

INTRODUCTION

Luo Rufang's ideas and his popular appeal represent the culmination of the influence of the Taizhou school of thought, which is widely regarded as the most liberal interpretation of Confucianism in late imperial times.[2] Scholars of the Taizhou school believed that all people, regardless of their social background, are endowed with the same innate knowledge *(liangzhi),* and that once made aware of this innate knowledge, any person can achieve moral autonomy. The principal concern of Taizhou scholars like Luo was not personal attainment of sagehood, nor philosophical accomplishment. What marked them as different from other neo-Confucian scholars of their time, in addition to the belief that common people could become sages, was their personal sense of mission—to go out and teach the common people about this potential.

A native of Nancheng county in eastern Jiangxi, hundreds of miles from Taizhou, Luo Rufang played a key role in the expansion of the Taizhou networks, while synthesizing the ideas of earlier Taizhou scholars. Luo explained the philosophical term "innate knowledge" *(liangzhi)* by talking about inborn goodness of heart (*liangxin,* or conscience), a notion more accessible to his commoner audience. He was greatly inspired by his observations of a mother's intuitive love for a child, which he viewed as a direct expression of *liangxin.* He therefore emphasized that *ci* is a cardinal Confucian virtue, regarding it as the source of filial piety and brotherly respect, thus making the obligation between parents and children reciprocal, instead of one-sided and authoritarian. Luo's deep humanitarianism led him to believe in the equality of all individuals—implicitly, both men and women. In his far-flung travels in several provinces, Luo lectured and conducted seminars in all sorts of places, from private academies, guild halls, jails, and lineage shrines to Buddhist or Daoist temples. He made skillful use of proverbs, songs, music, and the printing press to make his lectures accessible to commoners. Delivering inspiring and emotional lectures, he eventually developed a dinstinct evangelical style.[3]

The five essays translated here comprise two epitaphs: one for Luo Rufang's mother, Lady Ning, and one for Lady Guan, the mother of Luo's friend; one family letter addressed to his wife, sisters-in-law, and daughters-in-law; a biography of Wang Danxuan, the mother of one of Luo's own pupils; and a commemorative essay honoring Lady Dong, who personified Luo's idea of *ci.* Together these writings present two important perceptions of women. The first is a belief in and admiration for women's pursuit of their own intellectual and philosophical interests. The second is an appreciation for women's virtue, especially *ci,* in Confucian social ethics.

Luo's high regard for women's intellectual efforts can be found in the epitaph in memory of his mother, in the biography he wrote for Wang Danxuan, and in his family letter. Luo's mother, née Ning (1491–1569), was a devotee of philosophical Daoism, but she introduced her son to the Confucian classics at the age of five *sui,* using the *Book of Filial Piety,* the *Analects,* and the *Mencius,* and then guiding him through the biographies of leading figures in the dynastic histories. She remained skeptical of the civil service examinations, however, and her husband gave up his pursuit of a civil service degree on her advice.[4] This makes it less surprising that her son Rufang, having successfully passed the metropolitan examination, procrastinated for ten years before sitting for the palace test. While neighbors and friends gossiped, Lady Ning defended her son with the argument that he was simply showing respect for public office by earnestly trying to improve his level of education before becoming an official.[5] Still later, in 1565, after his father died, he returned home from his prefectural post to fulfill his mourning obligations. At this juncture his mother urged him to give up his official career for good, and he did so.[6] From very early on, Lady Ning had immersed herself in the Great Void *(taixu),* and she seems to have understood philosophical Daoism so thoroughly that her heart-mind became "completely empty and clear" *(kongkong dongdong).* Lady Ning was an exemplary woman, at least in the eyes of Luo. As a mother, she displayed what a kindly mother could do by giving her children freedom to choose whatever career they liked and encouraging them to cherish their goals without regard for family name or material success. As a woman, Lady Ning demonstrated that women were capable of pursuing philosophical interests—in her case, philosophical Daoism.

Luo's admiration for women's quest for intellectual fulfillment can also be found in his "Biography of Wang Danxuan." This essay was written by Luo in 1574 during a trip to Mount Huagai in Chongren county, Fuzhou prefecture, Jiangxi, where he met Wang Danxuan, the mother of one of Luo's own disciples, Wang Wanshan. Because Danxuan's husband and all three of her sons were enrolled in the county school, she had time to herself, which she used to pursue her own interests. She built a pavilion on the large pond in the family garden where she could sit and watch the reflection of Mount Huagai, enjoying the beautiful scenery surrounding her home and in this way achieving an inner tranquillity. When visitors like Luo Rufang came by, she would talk with them about her communion with nature and her insights into the universe. Here we see a striking similarity between Danxuan and Lady Ning: both were interested in philosophical Daoism, and each had reached a certain level of understanding. Luo's emphasis on these women's intellectual interests, especially philosophy, shows how he was drawn to women whose philosophical bent has thus far received little attention from historians.

We thus are not surprised to find that his letter to the female members of his family addresses the importance of pursuing philosophical interests.

In 1576, when Luo was serving as Vice-Commissioner of Government Farms in Yunnan, he received a letter from his wife, Lady Wu, recounting her absorption in "reciting sutras and pursuing the Way" *(nianjing xiangdao)*. Luo's letter encourages his wife to persist in her devotions, and he exhorts his female relatives, including his sisters-in-law and even his daughters-in-law, to eschew the pursuit of wealth and high status. Believing as he did that the ultimate concern of every living human was the pursuit of philosophical or religious questions, Luo did not hesitate to encourage women to pursue their quest for intellectual or religious fulfillment. His underlying assumptions are clear: the true goal of a woman's education is her own religious and philosophical fulfillment, and gender difference should not intrude into this vital human endeavor.

Luo's emphasis on the contribution of *ci* to Confucian social ethics can be found in the two remaining texts translated here: the epitaph for Mother Fu, the Lady Guan, written in 1568; and the commemorative "Essay on the Hall of Motherly Nurturance and Chaste Widowhood at Linchuan, Jiangxi," written in 1584. Lady Guan was the mother of Fu Shijing, a friend of Luo and a scholar of the Jiangyou (eastern) branch of the Wang Yangming school. She was taught by her father as a young girl. Her lessons included Zhu Xi's *Xiaoxue* (Elementary learning) and *Ershisi xiao shi* (Poems about the twenty-four stories of filial piety). When her husband died while traveling in Guangdong on business, she was only twenty-one and Fu Shijing was just nine months old. She took over the responsibility of educating him. Luo's epitaph sketches Lady Guan as a great raconteur, with a lively colloquial style of teaching classics to her son and a permissive attitude toward his scholarly training. Although she encouraged her son to study, she never required him to make strenuous efforts in pursuit of a career. Her son grew up to become a great lecturer, pursuing *jiangxue* (lecture and discussion) and enlightening many persons, and Luo Rufang attributed the son's success to Lady Guan's good influence.

The biography "Essay on the Hall of Motherly Nurturance and Chaste Widowhood at Linchuan, Jiangxi" celebrates a widow who, like many faithful widows publicly honored in late imperial times, is known only by her natal family's surname, Dong. Lady Dong was both a devoted mother and a faithful widow who had lost her husband soon after the birth of her son, Chen Shiwei, but never remarried. She overcame many difficulties, including pressure to remarry from her husband's family, in order to bring up her son, who became a successful scholar. A Ming prince bestowed upon her an honorific tablet naming her residence the Hall of Motherly Nurturance and Chaste Widowhood. In the beginning of this essay, Luo gives a brief summary of his distinctive views on the emotional content of human relationships, especially motherly nurturance *(ci)*, filial piety *(xiao)*, and love *(qing)*. Luo believed that both parental nurturance and filial piety are innate and bestowed by Heaven *(tianyi)*; they are "deeply rooted in the heart-mind" *(xin)* and are intrinsic to human nature. Both *ci* and *xiao* in this sense are among the normal capacities *(changfen)* bestowed on humans by Heaven. Therefore, these virtues come naturally to mothers and children, and it should not be difficult for a mother to love her child. Moreover, as Luo says, "A mother's affection, the natural outpouring of her heart-mind's feelings, invokes her child's filiality, and the child repays her affection with filial piety." For Luo, *ci* is the source of filial piety.

Although this essay is about motherly nurturance and chastity, he is clearly less interested in the issue of women's chastity. In Luo's view, when a mother becomes a widow, she has to retain her maternal devotion to her child while holding a steadfast resolve to remain chaste and faithful *(jie)* to her deceased husband. Luo stresses that this abnormal *(bian)* condition, which he contrasts with the normal *(chang)* state of human beings, poses enormous difficulties. Of course to Luo, sages are not different from ordinary people, because all share an inborn goodness of heart *(liangzhi* or *liangxin)*. But he maintains here that the extraordinary moral virtue displayed in a widow's chastity surpasses what even a sage could reach.

ORIGINAL TEXTS

"Tomb Inscription for My Deceased Mother, the Honorable Lady Ning"[7]

On the eleventh day of the twelfth month of the third year of the Longqing emperor's reign, the year *jisi* [1570], this unworthy son Luo Rufang, prefect of Ningguo prefecture in Anhui province, and his two younger brothers, Rushun and Ruchu, respectfully buried their mother, née Ning, who was granted the posthumous title of Honorable Lady, along the eastern side of Cong'gu Mountain, south of the Nancheng county seat. Weeping blood,[8] Rufang writes this eulogy.

Ah! How great was my mother's virtue, pure and complete it was! From the time when I first walked beside her as a child until this moment, I have never dared forget her every word and deed, preserving them in memory to be transmitted forever.

My mother was intelligent by nature, a trait displayed early in her youth. From her childhood, she was able to comprehend completely the profound meanings of the *Elementary Learning [Xiaoxue]*, the *Biographies of Exemplary Women [Lienü zhuan]*, and other classics, without any teacher's instructions. After she was married to my father, the honorable Master Qianfeng, who is now deceased, my mother always assured him firmly that the sages and worthies of antiquity offered models of sagehood to which we all can aspire. [Thanks to her influence,] the people of Xu [Nancheng county] first began hearing scholarly lectures and expositions of the Way from my father.

Mother was well-known for her filial service to my deceased grandfather, Sir Lianggang; to my grandmother, Madame Jiang; and to my grandfather's concubine, Madame Huang. She reared the orphaned son of my father's younger cousin until the child could establish his own career. With Mother's assistance my father was able to organize the lineage members to build a new lineage hall, contribute grain to the community granaries, and establish a charitable school—activities that can be compared indisputably with those of earlier men of learning like Fan Zhongyan and Wen Tianxiang [of the Song dynasty]. After my father went to study at the prefectural school and encountered minor failures in his examinations, Mother immediately persuaded him to return home to instruct us, his unworthy sons. Day and night until that point, our study of the classics and histories had mainly been guided by Mother herself. Whenever we read about models of extraordinary deeds and virtues, Mother would point to them and ask: "Can you boys be like that?"

After passing the metropolitan examinations [in 1543], I waited for ten years before I took office. Yet my mother was not at all uncomfortable about this. Later, after I had served as the magistrate of Taihu county and prefect of Ningguo prefecture, I decided to relinquish my official responsibilities and returned home to care for my parents. Although I reached home impoverished, my mother was not concerned. She even ordered me to resign permanently from officialdom not long after my father passed away!

Mother also exhausted all her resources to help the poor. Whenever there was need for community projects, such as constructing bridges across local waterways, Mother contributed her dowry jewelry to help. She used to tell our family: "Until my trunk is empty of every length of silk cloth and every bit of silver, I will not feel at peace and free of care." By the time Mother was making this statement, she had long been exploring the meaning of the Great Void *[taixu]* and had thoroughly comprehended the essence of human nature. Each day she concentrated on closing her eyes to practice quiet sitting. She would say nothing to me even when I waited beside her for hours. Occasionally, when I would ask her a question, she would reply: "I have arrived at the point where my mind is empty. I grasp everything completely *[kongkong dongdong]*." She went on like this for three years. Then one day after a meal, she suddenly gathered all the women in the family and told them: "Human beings have always suffered from desiring long life. But living for even a thousand years is no different from facing the coming of this day."[9] She then called her maid to prepare her bath. After bathing, she had her hairpins, combs, and keys put up in a high place. When the maid asked, "Won't it be a bother to take them down in the morning?" Mother smiled and said to her, "I won't be needing them any more."

In the middle of that night, she grew ill. She sat straight up, fluid poured from her nostrils, her tendons loosened, and she died. The time was the *yin* hour of the morning [3 to 5 A.M.] on the twenty-fifth day of the sixth month in the same lunar year [that I am writing this eulogy, i.e., 1569].

My mother's father was the honorable Master Ning Zheng, the sixteenth in line in his family in Youqi. Throughout his life he concealed his virtue from others. He married a woman née Rao, who bore my mother at the *chen* hour [7 to 9 A.M.] on the twenty-sixth day of the seventh month of the fourth year of the Hongzhi emperor's reign [1491]. At the time of her death, my mother had lived for seventy-nine years. In the year *gengshen* [the thirty-ninth year] of the Jiajing emperor's reign [1560], owing to my excellent performance as a secretary in a bureau of the Ministry of Punishment, Mother was awarded the title Honorable Lady. She bore three sons and a daughter, who married Huang Wei, a student of the [Nancheng] county school. By her sons, Mother had six grandsons and fifteen great-grandsons.

Letter to the Family (Number 8) from Yunnan[10]

I earlier received from the hand of my worthy lady [he calls his wife "worthy lady" using the intimate word for wife—*xian nainai*].[11] Your letter telling me that you are reciting the sutras and pursuing the Way *[nianjing xiangdao]* at home, and that your mind is letting go of all attachments *[yiqie fangxia]*. My heart rejoiced at this news . . .

Everything in life can be put off—except the destiny we hope to achieve by the time we die. This is the critical thing. I have charged my two younger brothers to help you in your devotion to doing good and to understanding the paramount significance of life and death. You should feel free and easy in your mind, such that whenever you encounter other people's affection or resentment or praise or slander, your mind will be peaceful and tranquil, free of turmoil and unencumbered. At the present time, even if you believe you have comprehended this completely, you will only be able to grasp a minor portion of the truth at moments of crisis. Even the tiniest hindrance, though it may seem like a minute particle in your mind, will become as weighty as an iron or copper wall when you face crises in the future. I hope that you, my worthy lady, can give your full attention to this and persist in your pursuit of your goals with more effort than ever and with increasingly refined results. I will also exert myself here to work in concert with you toward these goals.

Regarding family matters, since I have you, my worthy lady, to make decisions for me, and since my two younger brothers are also at home, I have nothing to worry about. My only wish is that my two sisters-in-law and my many grandsons and my daughters-in-law will also become clear-headed. They must not think only about wealth and high rank, and they must not seek gratification through dishonest means. You must know that the more wealth and the higher the rank one seeks, the more evil karma one produces. Wealth and rank one day disappear, but evil karma follows us forever. As long as we have food to eat, clothes to wear, and are not being beaten and scolded by others, we can carry on our lives and concentrate on our efforts to pursue our ultimate destiny *[ziji qiancheng]*. Each one of you, heed my words! Whether or not you reach this goal, and how quickly, depends on your own ability! . . .

"*Biography of Wang Danxuan*"[12]

Danxuan's surname is Wang, her given name is Xi, and her adult name is Zhongbao. For generations her family has lived in Chong village in Chongren county. The village is about one hundred *li* away from the county seat, surrounded by mountains, whose tall trees and dense forests when observed from afar penetrate to the sky and enfold the entire village, as if there were no roads leading in. Once one enters the village itself, however, one finds more than ten ponds situated at its center, their water deep and bright, fresh and spring-fed. The dwellings of the Wang family are lined up along the ponds, standing tall and close together and totaling nearly one hundred rooms.

In the year *jiaxu* [1570], I visited Mount Huagai and stopped halfway there, at noon, at the Wang compound. My disciple Wang Wanshan had respectfully provided food and drink for me, and therefore I had an opportunity to meet his mother, Danxuan.

Danxuan's age [at the time] was close to seventy, but in mind and bearing she appeared pure and simple [like a much younger woman]. Her every word and deed was detached and solitary, untouched by vulgar worldly customs. With her husband and three sons all enrolled at the county school, she had leisure time, during which she indulged in metaphysical pursuits. She ordered a small pavilion built above the water of the pond. There she would often sit alone, reciting poems. Sometimes she would look downward, other times she would gaze upward, as if she were fully enlightened. When guests came and asked her questions, she merely smiled without replying. Often she would take her wine cup and lean on the banister of the pavilion to gaze upon the lofty Mount Huagai, its many layers of green and its upside-down reflections clear in the water and as bright as the blue sky. She would point to this and ask her guests: "Is this not how we realize love? Is this not where love comes from?[13] Things have ten thousand forms, and yet water reflects them all. Water is a single substance, yet the many faces of this world appear on its surface. Over the pavilion the light of the pond, the colors of the mountain glow and refract, catching our eyes and touching our hearts—yet shall we be burdened by such external things? I draw tranquillity from the water into my pavilion, and tranquillity from my pavilion into my mind-and-heart. Liberated, I lift my spirit up to rest in the Not-Even-Anything Village *[heyou zhi xiang]*;[14] floating, I return to my true state in the land of the Daoist immortals *[kongdong zhi yu]*."[15]

Hearing her words, we all can understand that [the name of] Danxuan's pavilion is more than simply a word meaning "tranquil," and that the tranquillity Danxuan achieved did not come easily. I have therefore recorded in detail what she said to me so as to convey her words to my disciple, her son Wang Wanshan, in the hope that the Wang brothers and their descendants will keep these records to be praised by the world.

"Tomb Inscription for Mother Fu, the Lady Guan, at Linchuan, Jiangxi"[16]

In my youth I heard of the name [and the deeds] of Fu Shijing of Linchuan, which made me anxious to meet him. Finally, in 1546, when Master Fu came to Nancheng to take a prefectural examination, I had a chance to visit him. Sitting there discussing the Dao, Master Fu expressed his ideas so clearly[17] that we listeners forgot our weariness. Another person who was present at the meeting said, laughing, "Wouldn't Master Fu make a fine matchmaker for the Dao?" After that Master Fu traveled far away to take up an official appointment; I also assumed an office, and we did not see one another again for over twelve years.

In the year *bingyin* [1566], when I returned home to mourn my father's death, Master Fu came to my residence at Cong'gu Mountain to offer his condolences. Soon after that, I returned the favor by visiting him to pay my respects to his mother, Lady Guan. Although she was already eighty-three years old, she walked easily, without visible difficulty. Her face was full of mirth and she spoke merrily—truly, mother and son were well matched. So I remarked to her admiringly: "The reason why Master Fu is so unpretentious is because of your upbringing." Master Fu responded: "This is my mother's inborn nature, it is not something she acquired as she grew up." Privately, he said to me, "It will not be difficult for my mother to live a hundred years." Yet two years later I received word that she had died. When I arrived to offer my sympathy, she had already been buried on an auspicious day. Still weeping, Master Fu brought her seal and a copy of her biography and asked me if I would compose an epitaph.

According to the biography, Lady Guan was the daughter of Guan Shengliang of Qitang, which is in the southern part of Linchuan county. From birth, she was gentle and intelligent. Her understanding of the essence of Confucianism began under her father's instruction, using books such as the *Elementary Learning*. Later, when she was taught to read the *Poems about the Twenty-Four Stories of Filial Piety,* she would recite them endlessly from morning until night. At fifteen, having reached marriageable age, she was betrothed to Master Fu Xu. She carefully attended to her wifely duties *[fu dao],* serving her husband's grandmother and mother with utter devotion. Although her mother-in-law was stern, Lady Guan could always delight them both and win their favor. On her deathbed, Lady Guan's mother-in-law thanked her and made a wish for her newly married daughter-in-law: "May your children and grandchildren attain honors and glory."

The Fu family had been merchants for several generations. Yet Lady Guan tried to convince her husband, Fu Xu, to pursue a scholarly career and attain an official position. When Fu Xu's grandfather became ill in Guangdong while attending to the family's business interests there, he summoned Fu Xu to come and care for him. At the time, Fu Xu's son, Fu Shijing, was only three months old. Six months later, after he had arrived in Guangdong, Fu Xu himself failed to adapt to the climate there, became seriously ill, and died. At the time Lady Guan was only twenty-one. When she heard the news of her husband's death, she cried, but quickly dried her tears. Taking her son in her arms, she declared, "Relying on you, I can have no fear." She then quickly searched for a carriage and drivers and sent them hastily to bring back her husband's coffin. By selling the remainder of her dowry jewelry she was soon able to retrieve the coffin and to see to the burial.

Throughout her days Lady Guan never sighed. She never mentioned any strenuous effort and never alluded to her long years of faithful chastity. She did often caress her son and tell him interesting stories. While she was teaching her son books for young children, she would from time to time interpret the classics for him, using popular sayings. Before Master Fu Shijing went off to study at school, therefore, he was already familiar with the deeds of the ancient sages and worthies. He was always ahead of his class in the examinations for prefectural school. Later on, hearing that the teachings of Wang Yangming were being transmitted by Master Chen Mingshui, Fu Shijing traveled enthusiastically to Zhejiang to meet the famous scholars there. In so doing, he also inspired his comrades and the talented youth of his own hometown. That is why local wags often said of him: "Matchmaker for the Dao! Matchmaker for the Dao!" But none of this was simply due to his inborn nature—much was the result of Lady Guan's guidance.

When Master Fu subsequently was nominated for government office and appointed as an Assistant Instructor in Jian'an county, Fujian, Lady Guan accompanied him to his new post. Every day she admonished him to make himself a model teacher so that he would not dishonor the hometown of Zhu Xi. But soon after, when he was promoted to the position of Instructor in Datong prefecture, Shanxi, she ordered him to resign his post and return home.

Whenever she was introduced to a woman in her neighborhood or in her lineage, no matter how close or how distant the relationship, she would take out a handkerchief or a kerchief from her collection and present it as a gift. Often, she would sign a copy of the *Poems about the Twenty-Four Stories of Filial Piety* and give that as an encouragement for learning.

She moved into the central district of the city of Linchuan to escape the threat of looting, yet she remained sympathetic to people in need. Whenever she heard a beggar's voice, she would hasten to provide him with food or money, her anxiety that she might be too late showing on her face. This compassion and sympathy arose out of her inborn nature.

Master Fu married a Miss Huang, who bore two grandsons to Lady Guan: Yuanhe passed the provincial examination in the year *wuwu* of the reign of the Jiaqing emperor [1558], and Yuanshun won the *jinshi* degree in the year *wuchen* of the reign of the Longqing emperor [1568]. That these two grandsons could accomplish so much so soon, inspiring to reach sagehood and acquiring knowledge to fulfill their father's ambitions, is also largely owing to the instruction and nurture they received from Lady Guan.

Lady Guan lived for eighty-five years. All her sons and grandsons were worthy, honorable, and glorious. Even so, their demeanor was easy and tranquil. When they were praised by others, they raised their hands and head to show their debt to Heaven. When they heard people acclaim their moral integrity, they sternly rejected the accolades, saying, "These are only our duties. How can they be difficult to achieve?"

Ah! There are many examples of chaste widows and worthy mothers in other biographies, but those exemplary women exhausted their energy holding firm to their chastity and vowing their fidelity. Lady Guan was different—at peace and of good cheer, although she had to struggle at first to support her son, and her responsibilities as the mother of an orphan went on for years. There is no hint of pretense or pride in her life's record. Examples like hers cannot even be found in ancient times. Could it be Heaven's intent to glorify the Fu lineage and sustain the celebrations of the family for all time?

"*Essay on the Hall of Motherly Nurturance and Chaste Widowhood at Linchuan, Jiangxi*"[18]

A mother nurtures her child with affection *[ci]* and a child serves his mother with filiality *[xiao]*. This is the normal capacity of every human being. Such normal capacities are bestowed by Heaven *[tianyi]*. They are rooted in the heart-mind *[xin]* and given expression in emotions, and will never stop. A mother's affection, the natural outpouring of her heart-mind's feelings, invokes her child's filiality, and the child repays her affection with filial piety. If we recognize that a mother's affection is "normal," we must also acknowledge that when great hardship befalls her and she must sustain her affection for her child while preserving her fidelity to her husband *[jie]*, her actions have exceeded the norm and become extraordinary *[bian]*.

From ancient times to the present, there has never been a woman who has not reared a child after she becomes a mother. When times are normal, her affection toward her child is easy to sustain. But in extraordinary circumstances, it may prove difficult. In times of hardship a mother may suffer greatly even while she tries to sustain her affection for her child, which will in turn invoke the child's filiality. But by the same token, hardship will make it difficult for a child to behave in a filial manner to repay his mother's nurturance *[ci]*. A case in point is what happened to the student Chen Shiwei.

Shiwei's father died soon after he was born. At the time his mother, Lady Dong, had just passed her sixteenth year, yet she vowed resolutely to rear her infant son. So desolate was her life that she had only her own form and shadow for consolation. Yet in order to bring glory to her husband's family, she wished her son to grow into a dignified man of spirit and serve as an official with ritual duties. The extraordinary hardship she suffered, as difficult as climbing a ladder to reach Heaven, fills us with admiration and also with sadness. And now His Highness, Prince Yi, has specially composed the following tribute, inscribing the words "Motherly Nurturance and Chaste Widowhood" on the tablet of the hall in his own hand; and the tablet has been duly presented by Prefect Gu of Jianchang and Magistrate Zhu of Nancheng. This is not simply to praise Madame Dong's virtue, but also to manifest clearly the hardships and difficulties she suffered!

Facing the conditions of her life, Madame Dong exhausted her energies to overcome hardship, remaining faithful and chaste for years, just exactly as it has been recorded in the detailed records of her deeds, which are so unbearably painful to read that one closes the book without finishing. Having passed decades in this manner, she now claims the accolades of the present.

Reflecting on his mother's suffering, her son Shiwei is easily moved within his heart; reading the tablet inscribed in her memory, he also easily expresses his heart outwardly. And isn't this just as it should be, when filial piety responds to parental nurturance, flowing out naturally from one's Heaven-bestowed heart, and love is aroused spontaneously, without encumbrance?

Mencius wrote: "There is a way to please one's parents. If one examines himself and finds himself to be insincere, he cannot please his parents."[19] Our heart-minds and our love are innately endowed by Heaven. What we sense and what we touch stimulate them and arouse them spontaneously. Can this happen in the absence of sincerity? I have never known a person who was sincere who failed to please his parents; nor have I ever known a child who pleased his parents who failed to be loyal . . . Shiwei, who has learned about innate knowledge under the tutelage of his uncle, Chen Mingshui, is striving to fulfill his ambition to become a sage. Surely he will achieve his aim gradually over time without worries . . .

In ancient times there was a saying: "Filial piety—extend it to spread over the four seas! Array it to fill Heaven and earth! Continue it day and night from the past into the present!" These are hardly empty words. What is to prevent our Shiwei from achieving everything he is capable of?

NOTES

1. Luo Rufang, *Mingdao lu,* 2:9b–10a.

2. See Ching, "Lo Ju-fang"; Tang Junyi, *Zhongguo zhexue yuanlun: Yuan jiao pian* 2:440; Mou, *Xinti yu xingti* 2:117–35, especially 122–27; Handlin, *Action in Late Ming Thought,* 36–57; Araki Kengo, *Mindai shisō kenkyū,* chapter 5; Cheng, "Pursuing Sagehood without Boundary: The T'ai-chou School's Message and Lo Ju-fang's Intellectual Development, 1515–53"; Cheng, "Sagehood and the Common Man: T'ai-chou Confucianism in Late Ming Society," chapter 4; Cheng, *Wan Ming bei yiwang de sixiangjia: Luo Rufang shiwen shiji biannian.*

3. Cheng, "Sagehood and the Common Man," chapter 4; Cheng, *Wan Ming bei yiwang de sixiangjia.*

4. Luo Rufang, *Luo Mingde gong wenji,* 4:53b–54a.

5. Luo Rufang, *Xutan zhiquan,* 2:39b.

6. Luo Rufang, *Luo Mingde gong wenji,* 4:54a. On mother-son relationships in the late imperial period, see Hsiung Ping-chen, "Constructed Emotions: The Bond between Mothers and Sons in Late Imperial China."

7. Source: Luo Rufang, "Xianmu Ning Tai'anren muzhiming," in *Luo Mingde gong wenji,* 4:53a–54b.

8. A filial son sheds blood, rather than tears, at the death of a parent.

9. Lady Ning's view of life and death here is close to Zhuang zi's. For relevant English translations, see Watson, *The Complete Works of Chuang Tzu,* esp. 47, 84, 190, 235, 257.

10. Source: Luo Rufang, *Luo Mingde gong wenji,* 5:36b–38a.

11. It was not uncommon in this period for a man to refer to his wife by the intimate term used by children for their grandmothers. See a joke about this from Feng Menglong's collection of jokes *(Xiao fu),* cited in Wang Liqi, *Lidai xiaohua ji,* 3:304.

12. Source: Luo Rufang, "Wang Danxuan zhuan," in *Luo Mingde gong wenji,* 4:40b–41b.

13. Wang Danxuan uses the word *ai* (love) in the Daoist sense found in the fifth chapter of *Zhuang zi,* titled "The Sign of Virtue Complete": "In loving their mother, they loved not her body but the thing that moved her body." Zhuang zi views love as the apprehension of the essence that underlies physical form or substance. See Watson, *The Complete Works of Chuang Tzu,* 73.

14. The Chinese phrase *heyou zhi xiang* comes from the chapter in the writings of Zhuang zi titled "Free and Easy Wandering," translated in Watson, *The Complete Works of Chuang Tzu,* 35.

15. *Kongdong zhi yu,* the region mentioned here, is the home of the Daoist immortal Guangchengzi.

16. Source: Luo Rufang, "Linchuan Fumu Guan ruren muzhiming," in *Luo Mingde gong wenji,* 4:55a–57a.

17. The term Luo uses here to describe Fu's style is taken from a description of Confucius speaking at the court. See *Analects* 10:2. The term, *kankan,* means "freely and in a straightforward manner," i.e., unpretentiously, engagingly.

18. Source: Luo Rufang, "Linchuan Cijie tangji," in *Luo Mingde gong wenji,* 3:42a–44a.

19. Translation of *Mencius* 4A:12 from Chan, *A Source Book in Chinese Philosophy,* 74.

Fig. 7. Portrait of Yang Jisheng. From a Qing morality book. Yang is depicted here composing his famous memorial denouncing a powerful prime minister, a bold act of loyalty to the throne for which he was ultimately executed. His wife assists him by bringing a candle. Source: *"Guandi bao xun" xiang zhu* (1731; reprinted 1882), 1:5. Courtesy of the East Asian Library, University of California, Berkeley.

SEVEN

Final Instructions by Yang Jisheng (1516–1555)

Translated by Beverly Bossler

TRANSLATOR'S PREFACE

I chanced to come upon this text as I was searching the library shelves for other, better-known admonitory texts for women. As a historian of a much earlier period of Chinese history, I had never heard of Yang Jisheng; but the fact that several different editions of his *Final Instructions* (*Yang Zhongmin gong yibi*) were shelved next to the more standard works of the genre suggested to me that his text must have circulated fairly widely in the late Ming and Qing. I opened it with curiosity and was immediately struck by the colloquial style of the writing, as well as by the fact that it was addressed to Yang's wife. When I sat down and actually worked through the text, I was stunned: here was a famous official writing about the tensions and problems of family life with a frankness and specificity I was accustomed to seeing in contemporary ethnographic literature, but not in historical sources. That this text was circulated as a model for managing family life suggests that the problems Yang describes were all too familiar to its upper-class readers in the later imperial period.

INTRODUCTION

The text here is a translation of the final instructions of Yang Jisheng (1516–1555) of the Ming dynasty. The instructions, directed to Yang's wife and sons, were composed while Yang was in prison, awaiting sentencing for having written a memorial excoriating the evils of the Grand Secretary Yan Song (1480–1565).

Yang was a promising young official during the reign of the Jiajing emperor.[1] He passed the *jinshi* examinations in 1547 at the age of 31 and held positions in important ministries in the capital. He is remembered today, however, not for his political accomplishments but for his extraordinary courage in daring to speak out against powerful officials at court. Yang wrote his first famous memorial in 1551, protesting the establishment of horse-trading markets set up to appease the Mongols.[2] His reward for this audacity was to be thrown in prison, tortured, beaten, and finally demoted to the ignominious position of District Jailer in a remote corner of the empire. He had served in that position less than a year when, the winds having shifted at court, he was rehabilitated and appointed District Magistrate in Shandong. By the end of 1552 he had received three successive promotions, the last to Vice Director of a bureau within the Ministry of War. At this point, by his own account, Yang began to feel that he must find a way of repaying the state for the extraordinary favor that had been shown him. As he sat up late one night meditating on how to proceed, his wife questioned him. In the course of the ensuing conversation, she pointed out that with corrupt officials in charge of the court, the only course open to him was withdrawal from office. On hearing this, Yang tells us, he suddenly knew what he must do, and he began to plan his memorial attacking Yan Song.[3]

The memorial was submitted on the eighteenth day of the first month of 1553. This time Yang was tortured and beaten far more brutally and came close to dying.[4] He survived, but remained in prison until the fifteenth day of the tenth month of 1555, when he was sentenced to death. Although his wife, Zhang Zhen, memorialized the emperor herself, begging to be allowed to die in Yang's stead,[5] the execution was carried out in the eleventh month of 1555.

The *Final Instructions* translated here was composed in prison, as Yang was awaiting the final disposition of his case. In contrast to the formal classical prose used in Yang's memorials and even in his autobiographical "Yearly Record" ("Nianpu"), the language in the *Final Instructions* is quite strikingly colloquial. Presumably, the simpler style reflects Yang's desire to be clearly understood by his wife and sons, who did not necessarily share his classical education. More important, however, Yang's instructions show us a very different side of this man who is otherwise known only in his official persona. To be sure, in the *Final Instructions,* as in Yang's other writings, we see a man overwhelmingly concerned with fulfilling the demands of moral integrity. But the arena here is the family rather than the state, and in the process of exhorting his wife and their descendants on their proper roles, Yang reveals just how complicated family morality could be. He seems particularly anxious on three counts: that the family not become the subject of ridicule, that his sons get along with one another, and that his wife not commit suicide.

The experiences of his own youth gave Yang ample reason to be concerned about the first two issues. As he reports in his "Yearly Record,"[6] he was but four years old when his mother was replaced in his father's affections by a concubine. The household situation became so untenable that the mother's brother reported the matter to the local officials. The consensus of the relatives was that continuing to live together would only cause Yang's mother more difficulty, so it was arranged that Yang, his mother, his older brother, and his older sister should live in a separate household from Yang's father, the concubine, and the concubine's son. The household property was divided into three parts, with the father's household receiving two parts and the mother's household, one. Only a year later, Yang's older brother, who was already married,[7] decided to live separately from his mother, and the property was once again divided in two. Yang, his mother, and his sister were left in such straits that all three were forced to engage in farm labor. Within another year, Yang's mother was dead. Yang's father and the concubine, fearing a lawsuit, fled temporarily to another place, until relatives eventually persuaded them to return. Obviously, Yang knew what it was to be the butt of village gossip.

His mother dead, the seven-year-old Yang became the charge of his elder brother. Their relationship was clearly strained from the beginning. Although the "Yearly Record" shows that Yang's brother interceded with their father to enable Yang to begin attending school, in general Yang depicts his brother in a distinctly negative light. The "Yearly Record" portrays the brother as repeatedly making life difficult for the young Yang, even though the brother was frequently bested by the latter's cleverness. The *Final Instructions* reveals quite explicitly that the relationship remained problematic throughout Yang's life (though it is worth noting that some editions of the text excise the passages in which Yang makes disparaging comments about his brother). Thus Yang harbored no illusions about how difficult it could be for brothers—even brothers born of the same mother—to remain on good terms with one another. Where half-siblings (i.e., the children of concubines) were concerned, he had no greater aspirations than that they not be treated "like strangers on the road."

Other than what he himself says in the *Final Instructions,* our sources provide no hints as to why Yang was so worried about his wife committing suicide. It may be simply that the Ming social milieu so encouraged widow suicide that he feared this would be the logical choice for her.[8] Certainly he had reason to worry about the future of his household: in the face of his long-strained relationship with his brother, he could hardly expect his children to receive much help from their uncle. Or it may be simply that as he indicates in the *Final Instructions,* he knew her to be impetuous. In any event, he was right to be worried, and all his exhortations were to no avail: on the same day that Yang was executed in the marketplace his wife, Zhang Zhen, committed suicide by hanging.[9]

ORIGINAL TEXT[10]

The stupid husband instructs his virtuous wife Zhang Zhen:

The ancients said, "Death can be as weighty as Mt. Tai, or death can be as trifling as swan's down."[11] If one dies when one ought to die, then death will be even more weighty than Mt. Tai. If one ought not to die and one dies, then it is of no value to the situation and will be even more inconsequential than swan's down. The circumstances of life and death must be evaluated in accord with the Dao. If I should suddenly die before you, you have such an impetuous personality that I fear that you will not understand this principle of death being lighter than swan's down. I am terribly worried about this, and so have prepared these words to exhort you.

Among women, there are those who die with their husbands. This is because the husband is [the wife's] master, and there are no children to maintain: there would be no purpose in living. Only [in this situation] can those who follow their husbands in death be said to die when they ought, and their deaths [be regarded as] weightier than Mt. Tai. Only this do we call "chaste fidelity" *[zhen jie]*. But even if the husband and master dies, if there are still young daughters and orphaned sons with no one but the wife to rear them, then the husband's ancestral sacrifices, the bloodlines, and his life's work are all bound up with [her]. If she dies, then she is abandoning her husband and master's ancestral sacrifices, letting his work degenerate, turning her back on the important affairs with which her husband and master has entrusted her, causing him endless posthumous distress. In this case not only is her death more trivial than swan's down, it will also be cursed by the multitude. Such a woman does not understand Principle *[li]!*

[Previously,] I was beaten 140 strokes and did not die: this was due to Heaven's protection. If I did not die then, why would I be likely to die this time [lit., how could there be a Principle of me dying this time]? If by some chance I do die, my death will be heavier than Mt. Tai. My only regret will be that my two sons are both young.[12] In studying they have both made progress, and in the future they will both succeed. I only fear that [my death will] adversely affect their [future]. My one daughter is not yet married; without someone to teach, guide, and take care of her, I am afraid she will be ridiculed. If I should happen to die, I leave you behind to teach and guide my sons and daughter into adulthood. If each is able to complete their household and establish their objectives, then it will be as if I am still alive. Under the Nine Springs, I will be able to be at peace and joyful, and I will be grateful to you. In the present circumstances, whether our family does or does not have me does not matter. [But] if it does not have you, then nothing will be accomplished: the people will die and the family be destroyed. It will fulfill some people's [i.e., Yang's enemies] desires and cause some people to smile. You are someone most clever and understanding of Principle: what need is there for me to speak? Above all, if only you would restrain your impulsive tendencies and regard my children as the important thing, then everything will be all right.

[My concubine] Erzhen is still young and moreover has no children.[13] After I have died, see that she marries someone else. Give her an allotment of clothing and jewelry. During these three years that I have been in prison, she has expended her energy in maintaining a vegetarian diet and reciting the [Buddhist] scriptures. In this she has repaid my favor. You must not have her stay at home and maintain widowhood. Although our older brother is unreasonable *[wu dao li]*, he has no ulterior motive—it is only that he is the kind of person who likes to take advantage. Whatever the issue, just give in to him a bit, let him have the advantage, and he will be happy. You must not fight with him. As for second elder sister and fourth elder sister, I'd like you always to look after them. As for fifth elder sister and sixth elder sister, when our father's concubine dies you should also become close to them.[14] As for Yingmin, ever since he was young I have taken care of him—you should also give him a bit of land.[15] The remaining household affairs I am sure you will deal with well. I will also say more below, so there is no need to go on at length here.

Written by Master of Pepperwood Mountain [Jiaoshanzi][16] at Futang, on the twenty-sixth day of the tenth month in the thirty-fourth year of the Jiajing reign [1555].

The father "Pepperwood Mountain" instructs his two sons, Yingwei and Yingji:

It is necessary for human beings to establish their intent.[17] Among those who when young set their will on becoming a gentleman *[junzi]*, there are many who later change and act as inferior persons. If in the beginning you do not first establish a set intent, then in your heart [*zhong*—lit., center] you will not have a set direction. In that case there will be nothing you will not do, and thus you will become an inferior person in the world, and the multitude will disdain and dislike you. If you take great care and establish your intent to become a gentleman, then whether or not you become an official, everyone will respect and admire you. Thus I want you before all else to establish your intent.

The heart-mind *[xin]* is the master of a person's body. It is like the root of a tree, like the stem of a fruit. It is most important first not to destroy one's heart-mind. If in one's heart Heavenly Principle *[tian li]* and public-spiritedness *[gong dao]* abide, then one's actions will all be good works and one is close to being a gentleman. If what abides [in one's heart] is human desire and selfishness, then even if one wants to do good works, there will be beginnings but no completion. Even if one wants to be a good person on the outside, people will see through you, as when the root deteriorates and the tree becomes withered, or the stalk rots and the fruit falls. Thus I want you to stop your heart from going bad.

Thought is the vocation of the heart-mind. When you are sitting alone, or in the deep of the night, when a thought arises you should think to yourself, "Is this a good thought; or is this a bad thought?" If it is a good thought, then expand it, and you will certainly manifest it in action. If it is a bad thought, then stifle it and do not think [further] of it. Each time you are about to do something, you should consider whether or not it is in accord with Heavenly Principle. If it is not in accord with Heavenly Principle, then stop it and do not put it into action. If it is in accord with Heavenly Principle, then carry it out. You must not do even the tiniest act that goes against your heart and injures Principle: then Heaven above will certainly protect you and the ghosts and spirits will aid you. If not, then Heaven and Earth, the ghosts and spirits will give you no quarter. You are studying: if you pass the local examinations or become a *jinshi,* considering my bitter [experiences] it is best if you do not become an official. If you do become an official, you must be upright and honest, loyal and trustworthy, wholeheartedly serving the country to the best of your ability. You absolutely must not imitate my wild stupidity. [But] in addition you must not—because I have encountered disaster as a result of my loyalty—therefore alter your heart and change your behavior, slacken your ethical intentions, and cause people to ridicule us as "virtuous father with unworthy sons."

If I am not around, your mother is an extremely honest, upright, and fair person. You two must be filial to her. In all things rely on her. You must not say that your mother prefers that son, or does not prefer that son; prefers that daughter-in-law or does not prefer that daughter-in-law. If you cause her to become [even] a bit angry, this is unfilial. Not only will Heaven punish you: from where I am below the Nine Springs I will also deal with you.

You two are brothers born of the same mother: as brothers, you ought to be close all your lives. You must not individually accumulate private assets and give rise to cause for disputes. You must not get angry and red-faced over small lapses in speech or affairs. Yingji's personality tends to be somewhat more temperamental. Yingwei, from the time you were small you have known about his temper. Have some regard for his[18] "face." If he offends you in some way, be magnanimous about it. Yingji, respect your older brother. You must be exceedingly careful: you really should treat him with the same respect you accord me. If your elder brother takes issue with you, you should take the initiative in kneeling down to beg his forgiveness. If he is absolutely furious and unwilling to forgive you, you should entreat your elder brother's good friends to exhort him. It must not be that when he gets angry you don't give in. Your senior uncle has been heartless and has given me a hard time, yet I still respect him.[19] You have seen this with your own eyes. In your behavior toward your older brother, you must do as I have.

Yingwei's betrothed is from a scholarly family. Yingji's betrothed is the daughter of an official family. This is an extremely difficult situation to deal with.[20] Yingwei, you must instruct your wife to love your younger brother's wife as her own younger sister. Just because the other is the daughter of some official, she must not get angry and give way to jealous feelings. Yingji, you must instruct your wife to respect her elder sister-in-law as her own elder sister. [Have her] refrain from wearing the very best clothing and hair ornaments: if your older sister-in-law sees them, even if she says nothing, in her heart she will feel somewhat frustrated. Dislike and rifts are born of this. As for seasonal clothing, at each social occasion [lit., incoming and outgoing], the two daughters-in-law should be the same, and the two brothers should also be the same. At each meal, you two should eat in the same place as your mother, and the two daughters-in-law should eat together elsewhere. You may not each eat with your wife in your own apartments. Over time, this would give rise to hatred.

You two, even if there is a great vexation from Heaven, must privately ask the assembled relatives to help reconcile you. You must remember never to sue in court. If one first goes to court, the other should take this scroll and present it to the officials: the one who first goes to court is unfilial, and the officials must deal with him severely. I entreat you two, no matter what happens, for my sake you must be resolute.[21] I would also like to address in advance the presiding officials: if you see this scroll, I would be most fortunate if you would pity my bitter distress and instruct my two sons, repeatedly exhorting and leading them, turning conflict once again into amicability. Thereupon under the Nine Springs, I will certainly amply repay your kindness.

Your paternal cousins Yanxiong, Yanhao, Yanjie, and Yanxian are all people who understand [the distinction between] good and evil. Although they have been cool and distant toward me, it actually has nothing to do with them. As the saying goes, "In good times they are outsiders, in bad times they are family." You two must respect them and give way to them. The division of ancestral property has unequal aspects: if they want to take advantage, simply let them. You absolutely must remember not to dispute with them. Others will certainly remark on [their actions].[22]

You two are young in years. I fear that if you come to the notice of slick, sleazy people, they will try to tempt and defraud you. Some will ask you to dinner, some will tempt you to gamble, some will present you with objects you desire, some will tempt you with beautiful women. As soon as you enter their snare, you will suffer losses to them. Not only will the patrimony be completely dissipated, they'll also keep you from becoming a proper person. If this type of person coaxes you, just think about what I have said, recognize that his being friendly with you is for an evil purpose, and distance yourself from him. Choose a person who is experienced, loyal, and trustworthy, willing to read books, and willing to study the good, and develop an intimate and trusting friendship with him. Interact with him on a daily basis and you will naturally become a good person and not enter the ranks of the inferior.

When you read books and see a good action, then think to yourself, "In the future I must certainly put this into practice." When you see a bad action, then think to yourself, "In the future I must eschew [such action]." When you see a good person, then think, "In the future I must be like him." When you see someone who is not good, then think, "In the future I must certainly refrain from imitating him." In this way the ground of your heart-mind will naturally be brilliant and just, and your actions naturally ethical. And thus you will become the very best sort of person under Heaven.

Preparing for the examinations is simply a matter of memorizing a great deal and composing a great deal. From the basic classics of the *Four Books,*[23] memorize one thousand selections and read one hundred essays, one hundred policy inquiries, fifty declarations, and eighty judgments. If you have extra energy, read one hundred selections from the Five Classics, and one hundred sections of better ancient prose. Every day compose one section of text, and every month write three essays and two policy inquiries. It is crucial to remember that you must not pass a single day without a teacher. If you have no teacher, then you have no strictness and no fear. Without tests and corrections, even if you are completely diligent, in the end [your efforts] will be diffuse, as you are too comfortable. Also, you must select a good teacher. If you are unsatisfied with a teacher, then leave and seek another. You must not procrastinate and thereby impair your studies. You must also choose good friends. Each day meet with them to discuss and sharpen [your ideas]. Then you need not worry about your studies coming to naught.

As for day-to-day life at home, the most important thing is that the boundaries between inner and outer must be kept with strictness and vigilance. Girls above the age of ten *sui* must not be allowed to pass out of the central door. Boys above the age of ten must not be allowed to enter the central door. Women from outside [the family], even the closest relatives, must not be allowed to be visiting all the time. Partly this is to avoid gossip that leads to disharmony in the family; partly it is to avoid having them become the go-betweens for licentiousness and thievery. If you simply carry on as I have done, it will be fine. The walls of the yard should be extremely high, and on the top you should have a dense border of barbs and prickles. If there are the slightest losses or problems, you must thoroughly investigate the circumstances. If under the heavy rains of summer the walls of the yard collapse, you must repair and reconstruct them immediately. If the rain makes this inconvenient, you must [at least] immediately construct a stockade and screens. Don't procrastinate for days or months, and you will generally be able to avoid giving rise to licentiousness and thievery. Wine, meat, flour, and fruit, as well as oil, salt, sauces, and vegetables should all be stored in a warehouse. The five grains and other starches should be stored in a granary. The family head should have control of the keys, so that members of the family will not be able to pilfer supplies. Clothing should be simple, and living spaces should not be lofty and grand. Meals should be frugal. Do not see someone wearing fine clothes and decide to have some made, or [see someone] living in a fine house and decide to build one yourself, or [see someone] using fine utensils and decide to buy some. This is the path to extreme poverty. If you do not have quite enough to meet your expenses, then calculate how much you can afford to spend and sell land to make up the difference. Remember that you must never take on debt. If you take on debt, the interest accumulates daily: your debts pile up ever deeper, and you become poor all the faster. Don't do it! Don't do it!

As for paddy land, there is slightly more than four *qing*:[24] it is sufficient for you two to cultivate. You mustn't view good paddy land with a greedy heart and buy more. If you have a great deal of land, your household necessarily becomes grander, and your agricultural corvée [responsibilities] greater. I fear it will come to be a burden, and you will suffer the anger of the county officials.

In relations with other people, the most important thing is to be humble and sincere. When working with others, don't shun the hardest tasks; when dining with others, do not be greedy for the best morsels; when walking with others, do not choose the best path; when sleeping with others, do not hog the bedding. It is always preferable to give in to others; don't have them give in to you. It is better to tolerate other people and not make them tolerate [you]; better to let people take advantage and not take advantage of other people; better to suffer others' anger and not have them suffer your anger. If someone has shown you favor, do not forget it your entire life. If someone has shown you enmity, then immediately disregard the offense. When you see a good point in someone, unceasingly praise him to others. If you hear about a person's faults, then close your mouth and say nothing of it to others. If someone tells you that "so-and-so is extremely grateful to you," then say, "He has been very good to me; I've done nothing for him." When the person who is beholden to you hears this, his feelings [of gratitude] will be even greater. If someone says to you, "So-and-so is angry with you and is slandering you," then say, "He and I have always been the best of friends; how could he possibly be angry with me and slander me?!" [lit., how could there be a principle of him being angry with me and slandering me?]. Then when the one who is angry with you hears it, his anger will dissipate. If someone is superior to you, then respect and value him: you mustn't have an arrogant or jealous attitude. If someone is inferior to you, then be modest in your dealings with him: don't act disparagingly. The more you interact with people and over time become increasingly intimate [with these principles], then when you put this into practice [in service to] the country, you will have no regrets.

My mother gave birth to four children who are still living: your eldest uncle, second aunt, fourth aunt, and myself. Your uncle has four good sons, and in addition his family finances are prosperous. You needn't be concerned for him. Your second aunt and fourth aunt are both poor: you must always look after them, and respect them as you would me. As for your fifth aunt and sixth aunt,[25] you also must not regard them as strangers on the road. If among the kinsmen there are people who are hungry or cold, who can't bury their dead, or who cannot get married, you ought to help them as your resources permit. You mustn't forget that you come from the same roots and be totally indifferent to [their troubles].

Our family is a scholarly family: capping ceremonies [coming-of-age rites for boys], weddings, funerals, and sacrifices should be carried out in accord with the *Family Rituals*.[26] If you don't know them, you should consult with other people. You mustn't follow popular customs and be careless: that way the various sons and grandsons will have a model to follow.

Your older sister is your sister by the same mother; if in later years she is wealthy, then that's the end of it, [but] if she is poor, you two must sincerely provide for and look after her. If your mother wants to give her things, you two must not stand in the way. Not only would you thereby forsake the affection between siblings, but you would make your mother angry. It would be both unloving and unfilial. Remember this! Remember this!

As for Yang Yingmin, we have reared him since he was young. In future you should give him a dwelling in the village, and give him fifty *mou* of nearby land to the left of the [ancestral] graves. If he is reasonable and fair, then give these to him. If he is the slightest bit selfish and privately accumulates money and wealth, then you don't need to give him the house or the land. As for Qu Yue, if he keeps to his place,[27] when the time comes give him 20 *mou* of land and a small village dwelling. If he makes a disturbance and in his heart wishes to return, you should discuss it with your two fathers-in-law. Tell them that originally he was purchased for four taels of silver. For each year, each tael earns interest of six cash. Ask him for payment in accordance with the number of years [he spent with us]. You mustn't let him off, for fear the petty servile households will imitate his behavior and it will become difficult for you to manage them. Little Fushou, Jiashou, and Yang Ai all served me when I was in prison: in future you should give each of them 20 *mou* of land and a small dwelling. All of the above people should be given nearby land to the left of the [ancestral] graves. Have them watch over the tombs and allow them to cultivate the land, but do not permit them to sell it.[28]

My second memorial has already been submitted to the emperor, and I fear that the reply will be swift. In haste, I have written this in the lamplight, and it is really very disorganized. Still, the basic principles of family management and proper behavior are all here. After you have taken it and shown it to your mother, make a cloth bag to contain it and place it on the altar in front of my spirit[-tablet]. Each month on the first and the fifteenth, the whole family, young and old, should worship and sacrifice before my spirit. Take this handscroll and read it out loud from beginning to end, the whole family listening. Even if there are urgent matters, do not abandon this practice.

NOTES

1. For an English-language account of Yang Jisheng's official career, see his biography in Goodrich and Fang, *Dictionary of Ming Biography,* 2:1503–5.

2. For the background to this incident, see Mote and Twitchett, *The Cambridge History of China,* 7:471–76.

3. Yang Jisheng, "Nianpu," in *Yang Jiaoshan xiansheng yan xing lu,* 26.

4. Yang's autobiographical "Yearly Record" ("Nianpu") records in gory detail the tortures and their gruesome physical aftereffects. See Yang Jisheng, "Nianpu," in *Yang Jiaoshan xiansheng yan xing lu,* 27–32.

5. According to Yang's biography in the *Dictionary of Ming Biography* (Goodrich and Fang, 2:1504), the memorial was actually written by the famed scholar Wang Shizhen.

6. The account of Yang's childhood here is drawn from his "Yearly Record." See Yang Jisheng, "Nianpu," in *Yang Jiaoshan xiansheng yan xing lu,* 10–13.

7. Yang suggests that his brother was led astray by his wife, who had herself been led astray by their father's concubine.

8. There is an expanding literature in English on the development of the cult of widow chastity in the Yuan dynasty and after, as well as on the operation of the cult in the Ming and Qing dynasties. For the seminal article on this topic, see Holmgren, "The Economic Foundations of Virtue: Widow-Remarriage in Early and Modern China." See also Mann, "Widows in the Kinship, Class, and Community Structures of Qing Dynasty China"; Leung, "To Chasten Society: The Development of Widow Homes in the Ch'ing, 1773–1911"; Birge, "Levirate Marriage and the Revival of Widow Chastity in Yuan China"; and Carlitz, "Shrines, Governing-Class Identity, and the Cult of Widow Fidelity in Mid-Ming Jiangnan."

9. See Yang's biography in *Mingren zhuanji ziliao suoyin,* 719–20.

10. Source: Yang Jisheng, *Yang Zhongmin gong yibi.*

11. The original source of this quotation is Sima Qian, the author of *Records of the Historian (Shi ji),* one of China's earliest historical texts. Sima Qian used this analogy in a famous letter to a friend ("Bao Ren Shaoqing shu"), in which he explains that he has chosen to undergo the dishonor of castration (and thereby survive to finish his historical work) rather than taking the more honorable route of suicide. For an English translation of the letter, see Birch, *Anthology of Chinese Literature,* 95–102 (the quoted passage appears on page 99).

12. From the "Yearly Record" we learn that Yang's daughter was born in 1542, his eldest surviving son in 1545, and his second son in 1549, so they were respectively 13, 10, and 6 when their father died. Yang's first son had been born in 1540, but died in 1546.

13. This passage presumably refers to Yang's second concubine, surnamed Huai, whom he purchased early in 1551. Yang had purchased his first concubine, surnamed Liu, in 1547, just after he became a *jinshi* and received his first official appointment. Liu died in 1549, shortly before Yang's wife gave birth to their third son.

14. From these two lines, it appears that the second and fourth sisters were children of Yang Jisheng's own (deceased) mother, while the fifth and sixth sisters were children of a still-living concubine.

15. I have been unable to pinpoint the precise identity or origins of this "Yingmin." In Yang's instructions to his sons that follow, he is referred to as "Yang Yingmin," and the fact that the characters of his name share the pattern of Yang's sons'

names suggests that he might originally have been an indigent or orphaned relative (though it should be pointed out that other cousins mentioned do not share this naming pattern). He may also have been an adopted son, but if so he clearly did not enjoy the same status as the two surviving natural sons.

16. "Master of Pepperwood Mountain" was a literary name that Yang Jisheng had adopted for himself, following the custom common among men of his class.

17. The idea of "establishing the intent" (*li zhi,* often translated as "establishing the will") was a central tenet of neo-Confucian thought and implies establishing the intent/will to become a moral person. The instructions that follow give a good sense of the sort of effort Yang Jisheng had in mind.

18. Here and at several other points in the text, Yang phrases his hypothetical examples in terms of "me" or "I." Since this tends to read awkwardly in English, I have rendered the "I" as "him" or "you" as the context warrants.

19. This and the remaining lines of this paragraph are left out of some versions of the text.

20. The "Yearly Record" reveals something of the circumstances of these betrothals. The older son (Yingwei) was betrothed in 1551 (at age six) to the niece of a man with whom Yang had been a classmate in his youth. Yang explains that although there had been prominent officials interested in allying with him, he felt that the disparities in wealth were too great, and moreover he was not particularly close with any of them. See Yang Jisheng, "Nianpu," in *Yang Jiaoshan xiansheng yan xing lu,* 21. The betrothal of the younger son was first broached in a conversation with his friend and colleague Wang Lin (style name Jijin) just after Yang had submitted his memorial criticizing Yan Song. Yang, knowing that he had embarked on a dangerous course, asked Wang to look after his family, and Wang responded by offering to betroth his young daughter to Yang's son. The betrothal ceremonies were carried out in the fourth month of 1555, at which time the second son would also have been six years old. See Yang Jisheng, "Nianpu," in *Yang Jiaoshan xiansheng yan xing lu,* 27–28, 32.

21. "Resolute" is a not entirely satisfactory translation for the very colloquial Chinese term *zhiqi,* which can be rendered as "determination" or "courage" but has the more general sense of establishing the moral will to get ahead or make a name for oneself in the world. Here Yang asks his sons to "expand" their *zhiqi* somewhat *(zhang xie zhiqi);* in other words, to have the courage to look beyond their differences.

22. In other words, the cousins' unfairness will be the subject of gossip, and they will thereby lose face.

23. Zhu Xi, who more than any other individual was responsible for the synthesis of neo-Confucian ideas in the late Song period, isolated four sections of the larger classical canon as essential for education. These *Four Books* (the *Analects,* the *Mencius,* the *Great Learning,* and the *Doctrine of the Mean*), with Zhu Xi's commentaries, became the basis of the examination curriculum from the mid-Yuan period on.

24. The "Yearly Record" reveals that in the winter of 1554 a number of Yang's friends pooled funds amounting to over 200 taels in order to purchase three *qing* of land for his family. See Yang Jisheng, "Nianpu,"in *Yang Jiaoshan xiansheng yan xing lu,* 32. A *qing* was equivalent to 100 *mou,* or roughly fifteen acres.

25. As noted earlier, these were apparently the author's half-sisters, children of his father's concubine.

26. The *Family Rituals* was a handbook of ritual etiquette compiled by Zhu Xi

in the Song dynasty, and reprinted and revised frequently thereafter. The compilation and evolution of the text are described in Patricia Ebrey's *Confucianism and Family Rituals in Imperial China: A Social History of Writing about Rites.* Ebrey has also translated the text into English (Ebrey, *Chu Hsi's Family Rituals*).

27. In the sense of "knowing one's place" in a social hierarchy or being content with one's lot. Judging from the discussion that follows, Qu Yue was an indentured servant of some type. Here as elsewhere Yang Jisheng seems very concerned lest generosity to social inferiors leads them to become presumptuous or insolent.

28. This entire paragraph is excised from some editions of the text.

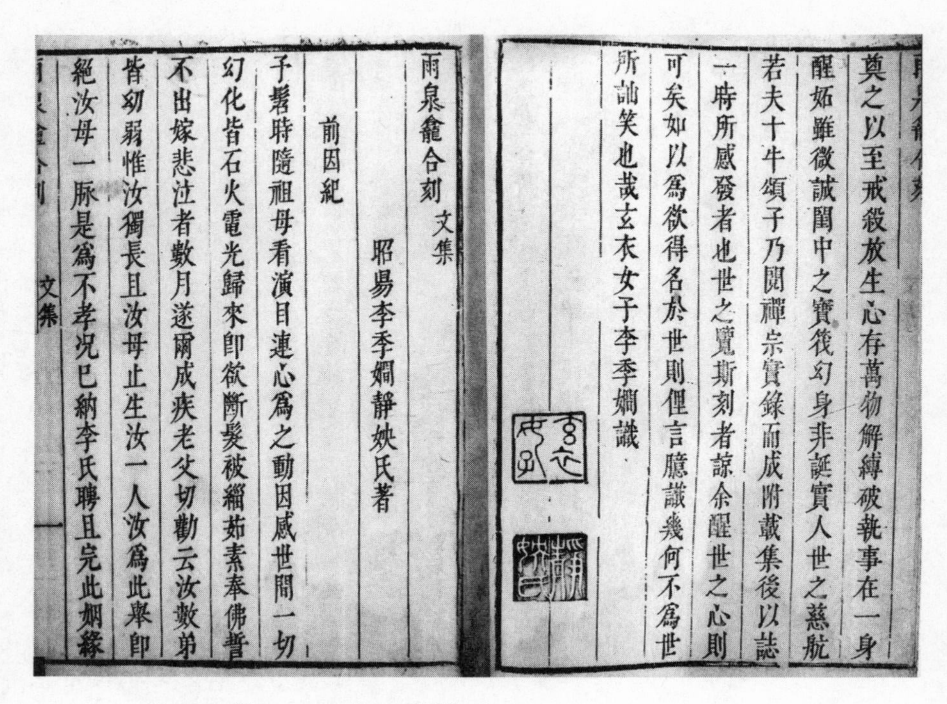
奠之以至戒殺放生心存萬物解縛破執事在一身
醒姤雖微誠閨中之寶筏幻身非誕實人世之慈航
若夫十牛頌予乃閱禪宗實錄而成附載集後以誌
一時所感發者也世之覽斯刻者諒余醒世之心則
可矣如以爲欲得名於世則俚言臆識幾何不爲世
所訕笑也哉玄衣女子李季嫻識

雨泉龕合刻 文集

昭易李季嫻靜婉氏著

前因紀

予髫時隨祖母看演目連心爲之動因感世間一切
幻化皆石火電光歸來卽欲斷髮被緇茹素奉佛誓
不出嫁悲泣者數月遂爾成疾老父切勸云汝數弟
皆幼弱惟汝獨長且汝母止生汝一人汝爲此舉卽
絕汝母一脈是爲不孝况已納李氏聘且完此姻緣

Fig. 8. Two pages from Ji Xian's prose collection in the *Combined Printing of Rain Fountain Shrine (Yuquankan heke)*. The right-hand page is the end of her "Self-Preface," with her seals "Woman in a Dark Robe" and "Jingyang." The left-hand page is the beginning of the text "Record of Past Karma." Source: Rare book collection, Beijing Library.

EIGHT

"Record of Past Karma" by Ji Xian (1614–1683)

Translated by Grace S. Fong

TRANSLATOR'S PREFACE

During my search for late imperial women's writings locked away in rare book archives in libraries in China, I discovered an undreamed-of multitude of voices in handwritten manuscripts and printed collections of poetry and prose. In volume after volume, whether relatively well preserved or in various conditions of decay—water-stained, dust-covered, with worm holes meandering through the pages—Chinese women's voices, inscribed through the medium of the brush and print on paper, spoke to me across the centuries. I feel it is my task as a woman scholar today to render these rich and moving voices audible across national, cultural, and linguistic boundaries. In short, I would like to make it possible for these women to be heard, through the medium of translation, by a new readership in a cross-cultural context. For there is much that we can learn from these writings, which often offer fresh, gendered perspectives and dimensions of experience from within the context of Confucian patriarchy. These women wrote because they wanted to record their thoughts, emotions, and experiences, and because they desired to be heard and understood in their own time and place, as well as by future generations. These women understood well the literary "immortality" accorded to the person through writing in the Chinese tradition. Textual production was the one means that women of the gentry class could appropriate for self-reproduction and broader cultural participation—processes commonly denied them in the patriarchal family and social structures.

Ji Xian's *Combined Printing of Rain Fountain Shrine* (*Yuquankan heke;* preface dated 1657) is one of the most exceptional collections I came across in my search. The only extant copy is housed in the Beijing Library. Her work is exceptional—among other reasons—for the prose collection it includes along with her poetry collection, as women were not encouraged to practice prose writing, and examples of their prose are thus rare. To my knowledge, the first essay in the collection, the "Record of Past Karma" ("Qianyin ji"), translated here, is the only example of an autobiographical essay written by a woman that focuses on her religious experience.[1] It is written in a simple literary style with a high incidence of dialogue reminiscent of narrative fiction and in a first-person voice distinctly marked by the frequent use of the first-person pronoun *yu*. These characteristics of the original text fortunately enable Ji Xian's voice to come across readily in translation. To allow the reader to hear Ji Xian's own voice framing her essays, I have also translated the sole self-preface *(zixu)* she wrote, which was composed for her prose collection.

INTRODUCTION

As the "Record of Past Karma" is itself a highly personal and selective autobiographical account, framing a period of serious illness in the context of Ji Xian's lifelong Buddhist aspirations, my introduction does not focus on her story but aims to provide additional information on her literary achievements and biographical background that situates her life in its broader social and historical context. Ji Xian (style names Jingyang, Xuanyi nüzi [lit., woman in a dark robe]) came from a reputable scholar-official family in Taixing county in central Jiangsu province—a part of the larger Lower Yangzi region known for its high concentration of educated women in the Ming and Qing period. Her father, Ji Yuyong, attained the prestigious Metropolitan Graduate *(jinshi)* degree in 1622 in the late Ming and served as magistrate in several counties in Zhejiang before he retired to look after his father.[2] Apparently hers was not a family of Ming loyalists. Shortly after the Manchu conquest, two of her seven younger brothers (Ji Zhenyi and Ji Kaisheng) attained the Metropolitan Graduate degree (in 1647 and 1649) and served in high positions in the Qing bureaucracy. Ji Xian's writings contain not a hint of the change of dynasties that she lived through. Her brother Ji Kaisheng, who died in 1659 at the age of thirty-three, already merited a biography in the local history, *Yangzhou fu zhi,* compiled a few years later, in 1664. All of the other brothers also received mention by name in the nineteenth-century gazetteer of Taixing county.[3] Significantly, in the section on women *(lienü),* Ji Xian's name appears as one of four in the category "Talented Women" *(caiyuan);* another is her daughter, Li Yan.[4] Though her husband, Li Chang'ang (style name Weizhang), did not attain any office, his father, Li Sicheng, was a minister in the central bureaucracy in the late Ming.[5] Her son, Li Weilin, obtained the prestigious post of Junior Compiler in the Hanlin Academy after he became a Metropolitan Graduate in 1659, an event Ji Xian celebrated in her poetry. That is the public side of the family—the official and literary achievements of its members recognized in local gazetteers.

From Ji Xian's own writings and from prefaces for her poetry and prose collections written by relatives and family friends, we learn more details concerning the private side of the family and about Ji Xian herself. She states in the "Record of Past Karma" that when she was six or seven she became so traumatized after seeing a performance of the popular Buddhist drama about Mulian saving his mother from hell that she wanted to become a Buddhist nun.[6] Her father then told her that she had been betrothed to a son of the Li family in Xinghua county further north. He counseled her, appealing to her sense of filial piety, and persuaded her to go through with the marriage at some point. Filial piety in particular and feminine virtue in general became the sites of her textualization by her male relatives—brothers, cousin, nephew, and husband. In the prefaces to her literary collections they called attention to her virtue, as though not to let it be overshadowed by her talent.[7] They reiterated the fact that Ji Xian had twice performed *gegu*—the practice of slicing off a piece of one's flesh, usually from the arm or thigh, to use as medicine for one's parents—once to save her younger brother's life (for her mother's sake) and a second time to save her mother's. Ji Xian herself was naturally silent in her writings about these self-sacrifices. For her acts of filial piety she might have merited a mention in the local gazetteer, as performers of *gegu* often were. Instead, she is recognized for her literary accomplishments, which speaks to her literary reputation.

From references given in the prefaces to both extant editions of her poetry, it appears that Ji Xian's poetry had been put to print three times already—once before 1648 and again in 1648 and 1653—before *Combined Printing of Rain Fountain Shrine* was printed in 1659 or shortly after. As befitted a seemingly modest and retiring woman, her brother and cousin initiated the printing of the 1648 collection, and her husband claimed editorship for the subsequent collections of her poetry, but not for her prose collection. This raises the interesting question of "censorship," particularly in the case of her husband, for the reader can see expressions of Ji Xian's dissatisfaction with her husband's philandering in the "Record of Past Karma," but only idealized portraits of marital harmony in her poems.

Combined Printing of Rain Fountain Shrine, as the title indicates, is a joint printing of one volume of poetry and one volume of prose. There are 224 poems in several *shi* genres with a predominance of regulated verse in the former, and eight essays in the latter. This is a relatively substantial collection for a woman writer; the most prolific women writers have over a thousand poems in their collections. Ji Xian's fame as a woman poet in her own lifetime is evidenced by references to her poetry in the writings of her eminent contemporaries, the scholar-official poets Wang Shizhen (1634–

1711) and Chen Weisong (1626–1682).[8] Her poems were included in at least two important contemporary anthologies of women's poetry: the *Anthology of Eight Famous Women Poets* (*Shiyuan bamingjia ji*, preface 1655) compiled by Zou Siyi, and the *Poetry Classics by Famous Women* (*Mingyuan shiwei*, 1667) by the woman poet Wang Duanshu (see chapter 12). Ji Xian herself also compiled an anthology of women's poetry from the Ming dynasty; however it is no longer extant.[9]

While liberating as a mode of lyrical expression, poetry could paradoxically be circumscribing, given its well-established generic conventions. There was a horizon of expectation within which one learned to write about certain themes and not others, in certain styles and not others, and according to certain rules and models. Prose was the dominant genre for public and formal discourse both in examinations and in intellectual scholarship—male domains from which women were excluded, except in fictional instances concerning the former, when cross-dressed women were depicted as taking the examinations with great success. In the domain of scholarship, those few women who wrote prose commentaries on classical works and on subjects such as science and mathematics were exceptional cases.[10] Moreover, their intellectual scholarship was marginalized. There was little effort to preserve and transmit women's prose. Most writings were lost over time, and only a fraction of the titles of women's prose collections survive in catalogues and bibliographies. Thus, while a significant number of women from gentry families were allowed or even encouraged to learn to write poetry as an art for self-expression, they were discouraged from engaging in serious prose writing, whether in the ancient style or in the current, eight-legged style required in the civil service examinations. Relatively few women were trained in the requirements for prose composition, which may be another reason—in addition to the authority and legitimation conveyed by men's words—why men rather than women generally wrote prefaces to women's works.

Ji Xian is unusual among women writers in having an extant collection of prose essays. All except one of her eight essays are Buddhist in theme and content, with titles such as "Discourse on Giving Alms" ("Shiji shuo"), "Essay on Avoidance of Killing" ("Jiesha wen"), "Essay on Freeing Living Creatures" ("Fangsheng wen"). While Ji Xian did not compose a preface to her poetry collection, she felt the need to justify her prose by writing a self-preface *(zixu)*. She begins her self-preface by distinguishing between two types of prose—Confucian and Buddhist—and also acknowledging what was no doubt the commonly held view that writing prose is not the business of women. As she sees herself crossing gender and genre boundaries by writing prose, she turns to past female models and her religious motivation to legitimize her apparent act of transgression. Significantly, the precedents she draws on—Ban Zhao (ca. 49–ca. 120) and Cai Yan (ca. 200)—are famous women scholars from the hallowed antiquity of the Han dynasty. She makes the point that women can speak out in writing and that, furthermore, her motivation for setting words to paper is altruistic and not self-serving. She ends the preface in a self-conscious declaration of disinterest in the fame obtained through writing. As she was already a famous woman poet, her statements highlight the ambiguous status of women's prose in traditional China.

As I mentioned earlier, the first essay in her prose collection, "Record of Past Karma," is an extraordinary autobiographical narrative, telling her life story from the perspective of her religious experience. Underneath the self-narrative, she weaves in a subtext of marital disharmony and discloses untold efforts on her part to control her jealousy. The essay records her psychosomatic response to the strain and stress of living in a polygynous household from childhood to middle age. She falls seriously ill, and the cause of her illness is projected onto the ghost of a male friend whom she had murdered when she herself was a young male scholar in a past life. This ghost becomes her nemesis in her present life. For several months at the most acute stage of her illness, she has psychic encounters, visions, or what nowadays might be called hallucinations—both visual and auditory. She also records two fantastic dreams in which she meets the deity Lord Guan, who ultimately removes her tainted heart and replaces it with a pure one in the shape of a lotus pod.[11] One sees in her vivid account not only the physical and psychological crises in her life, but also the intersection of gentry life with popular culture and religion.

ORIGINAL TEXT[12]

"Self-Preface"

In the universe there are various kinds of writings. There are writings that make a reputation in the world, and there are writings that awaken the world. The words of famous writings are intelligent; their goal is far-reaching. These are the writings of the Confucians. The words of writings that awaken the world are also intelligent, but their goal is close at hand. These are the writings of the Buddhists. Neither concern the affairs of women. Yet when I consider that in former times both Lady Ban and Lady Cai[13] produced writings well-known in the world, I feel that though I am not clever, I cannot be silent. I am emboldened to take what I have experienced, seen, heard, and come into contact with in my life and variously make them into a few essays to awaken the world. This I do in order to assist the purpose of Buddhism. By recording the unusual, one can document the karma of the past.[14] By practicing devoutly, one can fulfill one's vows.

If one is concerned about the poverty of others, one makes a point of giving alms. If one grieves another's death, one offers an elegy in sacrifice. In avoiding killing and in freeing living creatures, one holds in one's mind the myriad beings. As for the release from bondage and breaking the hold of one's opinions, such matters depend entirely on oneself. Though to awaken from jealousy is a trifling matter, it is truly a precious raft[15] in the inner quarters. When the illusory self is not born, that too is a compassionate vessel in the human world. As for the ten cowherd songs, they come about from my reading the True Records of the Chan School.[16] I have appended them to the end of the collection to record my momentary inspirations.[17] It will be fine if those who peruse this volume understand my desire to awaken the world. But if readers believe I wrote this to gain a name for myself, how will my vulgar words and opinions escape their mockery and revulsion?

Recorded by the Woman in a Dark Robe, Li Ji Xian.

"Record of Past Karma"

When I was a child, I went with my grandmother to see a performance of Mulian. I was quite shaken up by it.[18] It made me feel that everything in the world was illusory, like sparks from a flint or lightning. When I came home I wanted to cut off my hair and don the Buddhist habit, follow a vegetarian diet, and serve the Buddha. I swore that I would never marry. After weeping in sorrow for several months I became sick. My father counseled me earnestly, "Your brothers are all small and weak; only you are grown. Moreover, your mother gave birth only to you. If you take this step, you would be ending your mother's only bloodline,[19] and that would be unfilial. Another thing is, you've already been betrothed to the Li family. You must go through with this destined match. After you have established a family, you can devote yourself to cultivation according to your wish." Though at the time I forced myself to follow my parents' orders, I felt depressed about it all the same.

One night I dreamt that a divine being carrying a bell on the left and a pan on the right came to me and said, "In the west we are opening a place of worship. If you can charge through to it, you'll get a bell, otherwise you'll get a pan."[20] When I awoke I knew that I had fallen into the demon's realm. Since I could not hold on to the Way, and being afraid that my nature would easily get confused, I vowed to the Buddha that beyond three dozen years I would cut off all false ties. I would take a separate room from my husband to seek escape from the sea of suffering. From then on I recited the Buddha's name day and night without interruption.

When I married, my mother-in-law loved me like a daughter. My husband Weizhang also treated me with courtesy. I thought to myself that life and death were grave matters; it felt like sitting on a mat made of needles. I no longer cared about mundane affairs or family matters, except that my longing for my parents and kin persisted in disquieting me. Weizhang was an unrestrained and free-spirited person who did not concern himself with family business. I thought that since I am now someone's wife, I should help to make things perfect in his family. Thus, not shrinking from the worries of worldly burdens, I became quite bound up in the vulgar realm, and my old illness acted up frequently. For years it was incurable.

At the end of the winter of 1654, my illness suddenly got much worse. I sincerely repented to the Buddha. There was in town[21] an eminent monk by the name of Lazy Stone. I told my son Lin'er to go to him and tell him about my condition and to engage him to chant the Diamond Sutra and the Great Compassion Incantation.[22] This was on the twenty-ninth day. The next night was New Year's Eve. Weizhang and the children set out wine in front of my bed. I was then reclining on my pillow. As Weizhang encouraged me to sit up, I forced myself to do so. After everyone left, when I was about to go to sleep, I suddenly heard someone speaking into my ear: "Thanks to your practicing Buddhism, I have obtained transcendence."

Startled, I asked who it was. He said, "In my previous life I was a scholar; you were also a scholar, and we were very good friends. Since I was poor, I pawned my wife's jewelry to hire a boat with you. When we reached the river, you coveted my money and so pushed me into the middle of the current. Then you took everything and went home. Later you estimated how great your evil was and took refuge in Buddhism to seek release from your transgression. I hastened to tell the officer of the underworld. But he said that you had already repented and embraced Buddhism, that your practice of the Way was firm, and I had to wait for the next life to bring this case to a conclusion. Now that you have been born as a woman, I have come to seek retribution."

I said, "Since I have carried my sins for several decades, why didn't you come to take my life?"

He replied, "Though your debt of karma is heavy, your blessings are also abundant. Furthermore, you have not forgotten your past karma, so I've been tarrying on my part. As I sup on your vital energy every day, your illness gets worse by the day. Moreover, I make you drink lots of medicinal brew to repay me for drinking the river water in the past. Now since Chan Master Lazy Stone has achieved great merit for you by reciting the sutras, I think carrying on one wrong for another is endless. So I'd rather we give each other release from now on and cultivate fruits of merit forever in the Western Paradise."[23]

Full of shame, I thanked him. "The debt of my crime is fathomless, but now you have graciously forgiven me. How can I repay your kindness once you are gone?"

He said, "As you have developed a capacity for truth from your past life, you will attain the Way in the future. When you take a vow, if you would be willing to pray for me also to enter the Way, that would be repaying me."

He was still chatting away when Weizhang arrived. But when Lin'er came to wish me good night, he suddenly became quiet. I asked him why he talked when Weizhang came and why he didn't when Lin'er arrived. He said, "This child will have great achievements in the future;[24] therefore I avoid him." From then on he often spoke into my ears. Sometimes he would appear with a form and then disappear; sometimes servants also saw him. On the third day of the first month, he went away to listen to the sutras and then was back at night. Quite frightened, I asked him anxiously, "Since you talked of release, why did you come back?"

He replied, "The temple is a place of purity with the Guardians protecting the Law, so I don't dare dwell there. Just let me take shelter under the thatched eaves until the end of the sutra recitation, then I'll go away permanently." Then he said, "In all cases, people are stirred because of one single thought. When a thought arises, the demon arrives. If a thought does not have anything to adhere to, then the demons will not be born, and I will not come."

When he came again on the night of the twelfth, in alarm I asked him the reason. He said, "I am about to go away for good."

I said, "The sutra recitations are just halfway through; why are you leaving all of a sudden?"

He replied, "The eminent monk has great power: Buddha has sent down a decree. The officer of the underworld has already granted me a male body so that I may be reborn in Shandong.[25] The sutras that have not yet been recited can be recited sincerely in order to help in my being reborn."

When I implored him to show me what to do afterwards, he said, "You've always had a good foundation. You don't need to fret over things. When the heart is settled, life and death are settled." With that he left and never came again. As the grip of my illness gradually let up, I also stopped taking medicine.

Several months later I dreamt that while walking on an embankment I saw the god Lord Guan sitting solemnly in a pavilion facing the water.[26] He was fiery and awe-inspiring in his stern majesty. I dared not look at him close up. After a while, the god descended from his seat and called to me, "You must get rid of your afflicted heart and change it for a pure heart. Then your illness will be cured."

Weeping in grief I held onto his robe and asked how my deceased mother was doing.

"Your mother still has unfinished karma."

Sobbing loudly, I woke up with a start without having said all I wanted to say. I regretted deeply not having been able to beg to have this heart changed. After ten days, I dreamt again that someone announced, "The venerable god Lord Guan is coming." Before I was able to make him welcome, he had already arrived at my bed. There were more than ten people, all in strange shapes and weird forms, crowding around. Zhou Cang was holding the crescent-moon saber.[27] On it was hung a heart in flesh and blood. It was shaped like a lotus pod, glittering like gold and gems. He wanted to change my heart for me. I was just wondering how the heart inside could come out and how the heart outside could go in. When I looked down, a hole had opened up in my diaphragm. He had already changed my heart and hung it on the knife. He ordered me to look at it. I felt that it was incredibly filthy. I thought that this must be what the Sixth Patriarch called the hearts of delusion, of covetousness, and of anger.[28] Waking up, I still felt a slight pain in my heart. Only after three days did it calm down.

I related this to my father at the time. He was quite glad about it. "When the ancients dreamt about changing the head, bones, the brain, and beard, there was always prosperity coming. The fact that you had this unusual dream means that you have good foundations. What's more, the heart was lotus-shaped; it is truly a thing of purity. In the future it will bear witness to good fruit." I was quite happy about it. I then said to my father, "Some of my younger brothers are filial sons serving you at home, and some have brought fame to the family's name abroad. As I am a daughter, I have parted from you for a long time and have not repaid your hard labor. If by any chance I could bear witness to the Way, I will take a golden lotus to set up a seat for you, my parents, to repay your kindness in giving me birth. This is merely one ten-thousandth of what I owe you."

After that I felt everything was wrapped up. Accordingly, Weizhang and

I took separate beds. Weizhang at first set up two concubines. Since neither of them were agreeable, they were sent away. Then he secretly kept a mistress surnamed Fan. For a long time she was hidden outside the home. I only found out about it in the spring of 1657. I said, "I originally wanted to set up another person for you. Since you have this one now, why don't you bring her home?" But Weizhang stubbornly refused to do so.[29] I thought that since I am often ill and Weizhang is often deluded by feelings, why should I thus be deluded along with him? So I asked a favor of our relatives to discuss with Weizhang the idea of setting up two residences to allow me to practice Buddhism in a pure and tranquil manner.[30] I would rely on this to repay my parents and be done with life and death. My thoughts of the Way grew firmer by the day. I felt that everything I had experienced before was like an illusory dream. Relying on my own Buddha-strength, I was able to achieve transcendence. My heart burst forth in joy. Only then did I realize Weizhang was my good friend, and Miss Fan was also my good friend. They were the ones who helped me to realize my Buddha seed.

The intention in my childhood to follow the Way finally reached its fulfillment. I am thus very fortunate. Therefore I record this from beginning to end in so many words to tell all people in the world to cultivate the Buddha fruit, to bear witness together to the Great Way, and to make Weizhang turn around to repent in the future so that he can leave the destinies of the dusty world. We will ride the precious raft together to reach the other shore.

NOTES

I wish to express my sincere gratitude to the Chiang Ching-Kuo Foundation for Scholarly Exchange, whose generous support made the research for this translation possible.

1. Though autobiographical writings by women in premodern China are not so common, women did manipulate the expressive function of the poetic genre, the self-representational potentials of self-prefaces, and the form and organization of their collections of poetry and other writings to effect autobiographical inscriptions. See Fong, "Writing Self and Writing Lives: Shen Shanbao's (1808–1862) Gendered Auto/Biographical Practices." The famous "Postscript to the *Catalogue of Inscriptions on Metal and Stone*" written by Li Qingzhao (b. 1084) focuses on the author's relationship with her husband through their common literary and aesthetic interests and pursuits. See Owen, *Remembrances: The Experience of the Past in Classical Chinese Popular Culture,* 80–98, for a sensitive reading and translation. Wu's *The Confucian's Progress: Autobiographical Writings in Traditional China* is limited by a narrow, Western-derived conception of autobiography, but it remains a pioneering study of Chinese autobiographical writings by male authors.

2. *Guangxu Taixing xian zhi,* 20:21b–22a.

3. *Yangzhou fu zhi,* 17:58b–59a; *Guangxu Taixing xian zhi,* 21:1a–4b.

4. *Guangxu Taixing xian zhi,* 26:10b.

5. The name and official title for Ji Xian's father-in-law is given in the biographical note on Ji Xian by Wang Duanshu in her anthology of women poets, *Mingyuan shiwei* 18:1a. He was a Metropolitan Graduate during the Wanli period (1573–1619).

6. Mulian was a disciple of Buddha who descended into hell to save his mother. This great Buddhist drama was very much a part of popular culture in late imperial China. It is still regularly performed at temple festivals and funerals in Taiwan and China. It can be a terrifying experience, especially for a child, to see the theatrical representation of hell. See the excellent collection of papers on this religious drama in Johnson, *Ritual Opera, Operatic Ritual: "Mu-lien Rescues His Mother" in Chinese Popular Culture.*

7. There are a total of seven prefaces to her poetry included in the *Combined Printing* edition. The first two and last two were written for the printing of this edition; the three middle ones are taken from earlier printings of her poetry, of which a small volume, *Selected Poems of the Rain Fountain Shrine* (*Yuquankan shixuan,* preface 1653), is still extant in the Beijing Library.

8. Chen Weisong writes in the *Furen ji:* "[Ji Xian's] heart-mind roams in primal emptiness, [and] she lodges her feelings in the Dao. She does not compose a great deal of poetry, but that makes one appreciate it even more. Her poems are virtuous utterances" (18a).

9. Hu Wenkai, *Lidai funü zhuzuo kao,* 900–901. See entry in *Heyin Siku quanshu zongmu tiyao, zongjilei cunmu,* 5:4348. For discussion of the scope and selection criteria of Wang Duanshu's and Zou Siyi's anthologies, see Chang, "Ming and Qing Anthologies of Women's Poetry and Their Selection Strategies," 156–59.

10. For the lost prose works of two well-known women scholars, see the entries on Gu Ruopu and Wang Zhenyi in Hu Wenkai, *Lidai funü zhuzuo kao,* 206–9 and 236. Ironically, of Gu Ruopu's prose writings, only her self-preface is extant (see also chapter 9 of this volume). Similarly, while Wang Zhenyi's various works on mathematics and astronomy are lost, her self-prefaces to them are included in her prose collection *(wenji).* See also Zurndorfer's seminal discussion of the woman scholar Wang Zhaoyuan (1763–1851), who wrote annotations to Liu Xiang's (79–8 B.C.E.) *Biographies of Women* (Zurndorfer, "The 'Constant World' of Wang Chao-yuan: Women, Education, and Orthodoxy in Eighteenth Century China").

11. Lord Guan, that is, Guan Yu, is one of the chief heroes of the Three Kingdoms period popularized in drama and fiction. A cult developed around Lord Guan, who turned into both the god of war and the guardian of Buddhist temples. See Brook, *Praying for Power: Buddhism and the Formation of Gentry Society in Late-Ming China,* 288–93, for a discussion of the development of his cult in Dangyang county, Hubei. The lotus is a symbol of purity in Buddhism.

12. Source: Ji Xian, "Qianyin ji."

13. Ban Zhao (ca. 49–ca. 120) and Cai Yan (ca. 200) were famous women scholars of the Latter Han period. Ban Zhao was author of a book of instructions for upper-class women; she also completed portions of the official history of the Han dynasty. See Swann, *Pan Chao: Foremost Woman Scholar of China.* Cai Yan enjoyed a reputation as a brilliant poet. Scholars have questioned the authenticity of the three extant poems attributed to her, but obviously Ji Xian considered these poems authentic. See Frankel, "Cai Yan and the Poems Attributed to Her."

14. From this point on, Ji Xian weaves the titles of her essays into the passage: "Record of Past Karma," "Taking a Vow," "Giving Alms," "Elegy for the Immolated

Girl," "Avoidance of Killing," "Freeing Living Creatures," "Release from Bondage," and "Breaking the Hold of One's Opinions." Curiously, the last two titles in her collection—"Awakening from Jealousy" and "The Illusory Self"—have no accompanying text.

15. The raft is a metaphor for the teachings of Buddha, which carry the faithful to the shore of enlightenment.

16. The True Records *(shilu)* are records of the teachings of the Chan Buddhist masters.

17. These songs do not appear in the text.

18. See note 6.

19. Ji Xian's mother, the principal wife, gave birth only to her. The other children were all born of concubines.

20. The bell and pan appear to symbolize respectively religious practice and domesticity.

21. Literally, "in Xingyi" or "district city of Xing." It probably refers to the county seat of Xinghua, where her husband's family lived.

22. A scripture related to Guanyin, the Bodhisattva of Compassion. It is another name for the Thousand Hands Sutra *(Qianshou jing)*, which contains a spell against lust (Soothill, *A Dictionary of Chinese Buddhist Terms*, 88).

23. The paradise of Amida, the Buddha of the popular Pure Land sect, where good souls are reborn.

24. Her son obtained the Metropolitan Graduate degree in 1659 and became an official. We do not know whether this essay was proleptic or whether it was written after the fact.

25. Shandong is the province to the north of Ji Xian's native Jiangsu.

26. See note 11.

27. In the historical romance *Three Kingdoms (Sanguo yanyi)*, Lord Guan's faithful subordinate Zhou Cang committed suicide to follow him after he learned of Lord Guan's execution by Sun Quan in the state of Wu. See Roberts, *Three Kingdoms: A Historical Novel*, chapter 77. The saber in the shape of a crescent moon, known as the Green Dragon Saber, is Lord Guan's famous weapon and has become part of his iconography.

28. The Sixth Patriarch of the Chan Buddhist sect is Huineng (638–713), whose hagiography and teachings are recorded in the Platform Sutra *(Tan jing)*. It was no doubt among Ji Xian's spiritual readings. For a translation, see Yampolsky, *The Platform Sutra of the Sixth Patriarch*.

29. Since Ji Xian is the principal wife, any concubine brought into the household would be under her authority. Hence her insistence on her husband bringing Miss Fan home. But the dismissal of two previous concubines and her husband's stubborn refusal to bring his present mistress home are indicative of her power to control the women in the household. Her husband seems wary of re-submitting his sexual interests to her surveillance or interference.

30. To involve relatives in her negotiation to maintain a separate household seems to be an unusually radical measure. Ji Xian chooses this tactic to make her displeasure known.

Fig. 9. Mencius's mother cuts the web of her loom. As retold in the illustrated *Gui fan* (Regulations for the inner quarters), a popular didactic book of Gu Ruopu's era, Mencius's mother moved three times to shield her son from bad influences. When he still would not apply himself to his books, she took a knife and cut the web of her loom. Having thus learned his lesson, Mencius grew up to become a Confucian sage. Besides the power of motherhood and the virtue of perseverance, this tale also teaches a gender division of labor: he studies; she weaves. Source: Lü Kun, *Gui fan*, in *Zhongguo gudian wenxue banhua xuanji,* comp. Fu Xihua, 343.

NINE

"Letter to My Sons" by Gu Ruopu (1592–ca. 1681)

Translated by Dorothy Ko

TRANSLATOR'S PREFACE

My first reaction upon reading this letter was disbelief. Its tone is so vivid and authoritative that it seemed as though the forty-year-old matriarch Gu were sitting in front of me, lecturing her two sons. Opening with the personal pronoun "I," the letter is unusually direct with its frequent use of "I" and "you" in colloquial forms of address.[1] Ostensibly Gu speaks mostly of her sufferings, but her pride and awareness of her own power are palpable between the lines. I do not know of any seventeenth-century writing that better conveys the emotional contours of elite family life from a mother's perspective.

The emotional poignancy of Gu's letter is astonishing, even tantalizing, for it evokes the immediacy of everyday speech. Indeed, with her sons in daily attendance, why did Gu have to write a letter? She might have wanted to add weight to her words, or she might have been compelled to convince other family members. All we know for sure is that Gu bestowed her letter on posterity by including it in her collected works. The commercial publisher Wang Qi (fl. 1620–1668) later selected it for a popular anthology of model letters, a copy of which is housed in a Japanese library.[2] Through the initiative first of Gu herself, then a commercial publisher and Japanese collectors, and now, scholars in the United States, Gu Ruopu still speaks. I hope that her authority and immediacy have not diminished in the process of bringing her words to a broader audience.

INTRODUCTION

Gu Ruopu (1592–ca. 1681) was a poet, teacher, virtuous widow, and matriarch of the Huang family. Daughter of a notable gentry family in Hangzhou, she married Huang Maowu, an examination candidate from a comparable local family, in 1606. They shared some tender moments during their thirteen years together, which produced two sons and two daughters. In 1619, Huang passed away after a long illness. For the rest of her long and prolific life Gu stayed the course of a virtuous widow.[3]

As was typical of gentry daughters in the region, Gu received a literary education in her youth. Upon her widowhood, her father-in-law decided to give her a classical education so that Gu could take her dead husband's place in preparing her two sons for the civil service examinations. Over the next six decades Gu educated not only her sons but also numerous women from the Gu and Huang families. Her niece emerged as the founder of a famed female poetry club, the Banana Garden Five, which was later expanded to include seven formal members.[4]

After her father-in-law passed away, Gu became the matriarch of the family. Local histories remembered her as a public-minded elder who sought to establish "sacrificial fields" to finance rituals honoring the entire family. Her leadership and vision were felt in other ways. Having seen to it that both sons married capable and learned wives, Gu decided to divide the family property and establish separate households ("stoves") for them. In the letter translated here, dated 1632, Gu outlines her support for the Confucian ideal of familism and its principle of patrilineal descent, but admonishes her sons to recognize women's indispensable roles in the male-centered kinship system.[5]

This letter is a rare example of a woman's candid reflections on her multiple roles in the Confucian family.[6] It demonstrates the efficacy of the moral education that Gu was brought up with—she was a diligent bride and chaste widow. At the same time, this letter suggests that gentrywomen like Gu had strong reasons to be compliant, for the family offered mothers and mothers-in-law not only emotional satisfaction but also economic power and moral authority.

This letter was written at a critical juncture for the Huang family: the family stove was to be split and Gu's sons were to set up separate households. Even though we do not have further information on the conflicts that Gu had to mediate, family division was always controversial and emotionally trying in a property-owning family. Standard didactic texts reiterated the Confucian ideal of five generations under one roof. Yet for economic and other reasons, in practice the nuclear family remained the norm for the majority of people. Gu Ruopu's discourse on human fickleness allows us into the thought process whereby family heads negotiated the dubious terrain between ideal and reality.

ORIGINAL TEXT[7]

Ever since I married your father in 1606, I have been involved in the affairs of our family. For twenty-six years I tasted all sufferings and experienced every tribulation. In fear and caution I rose early to toil and retired late to ponder the day. My only thought was to avoid any mistake, so that my ancestors' law will not be violated and my parents' concerned care will not be in vain. Do you suppose that I endured all the hardship because I enjoyed it?

Barely ten months after your father was born your grandmother passed away. By the time I married into the family, poverty and illness had taken their toll [on your father]. Many obstacles stood in his way, and troubles assaulted him from more than one direction. On his deathbed, he merely instructed me to be frugal with his funeral, to teach you well so that you can inherent his family's scholastic tradition, and to serve your grandfather with devotion to make up for his own untimely departure. Abiding by his will, I strove to be even more cautious in everything than in the previous thirteen years. As if treading on the edge of an abyss or on a sheet of thin ice, I was constantly wary that one misstep would ruin the bygone elders' enterprise. After your grandfather passed away, more tribulations befell a widow and her bereaved sons; it is not easy to recount them one by one in public.

I gave birth to my son Can in 1612 and to son Wei in 1614. You two only know that you were born into a scholar-official family. You have grown up in comfortable quarters, enjoyed adequate food and clothing, and scarcely tasted distress or pain. Little did you know that your mother had to battle poverty, illness, and fatigue to keep the family from going adrift. For twenty-six years I persevered as if it were one single day.

Fortunately, my children are now grown-up and duly married. Finally able to pass on my heavy responsibilities, I feel slightly relieved. Intent on achieving unity through division, I am separating you—my two sons—(into two branches) so that you can each tend to your family affairs. I would have been happy to keep shouldering the burden alone so that you can relax and so that our ancestors' deeds can be emulated. But what I have observed has led me to think otherwise.

People have often preached the propriety of housing nine generations under one roof. It is also true that both brothers are filial and equally known for their virtue. But even those who are one in sentiments often part ways in their handling of practical matters. Some are generous, others frugal;

some prefer abundance, others meagerness: people have incompatible likes and dislikes. The similarities and differences in human feelings can take many forms; how can I expect to always get what I want? Moreover, it is human nature that when people have been together for a long time, they tend to slacken in behavior, which easily breeds disdain. Hence when people are apart they want to be united; when they are together they want to go separate ways. One has to discern the forces that draw distant people together and the forces that tear intimate people apart.

I am glad that both my daughters-in-law are virtuous and wise. Frugal and restrained, they abide by the teachings of the ancestors. Before I advance in years and run out of energy, I wish to clearly divide up every item [of family property]. You will now know just how difficult it has been to provide for this family and how taxing the ways of the world have been. You will establish yourselves on your own, so that each of you will gradually ascend to the gateways of propriety and righteousness. Then the family will not be weakened by internal strifes, nor will it be threatened by permanent extinction. Why should unity be held up as the only desirable goal?

Every fiber and every grain that this family owns are the fruits of my industry and hardship over several decades. Preserve and magnify them. These are the high hopes I have for my two sons.

NOTES

1. Ming-Qing women were avid letter writers. For the importance of letters to their social networks, see Widmer, "The Epistolary World of Female Talent in Seventeenth-Century China."

2. The publisher Wang Qi also edited this three-volume anthology of letters, *Chidu xinyu.* Ellen Widmer's research has shown that the collection was an remarkable market success. Besides the copy I consulted in the Naikaku bunko, Widmer has located other extant copies in the People's Republic of China. For a study of Wang's publishing house and the reading public he both catered to and shaped, see Widmer, "The Huanduzhai of Hangzhou and Suzhou: A Study in Seventeenth-Century Publishing."

3. Maureen Robertson has translated Gu's mourning poems for her husband and discussed her poetic innovations in "Voicing the Feminine: Constructions of the Gendered Subject," 90–95. For Gu's self-representations as virtuous wife and intellectual, see Robertson, "Changing the Subject: Gender and Self-Inscription in Authors' Prefaces and *Shi* Poetry," 186–87.

4. For Gu and the Banana Garden poetry club, see Ko, *Teachers of the Inner Chambers: Women and Culture in Seventeenth-Century China,* 234–46. Marsha Weidner has discussed the members' accomplishments as poets and painters in *Views from Jade Terrace: Chinese Women Artists, 1300–1912,* 108–9.

5. For a succinct discussion of Confucian familism, see Eastman, *Family, Fields, and Ancestors: Constancy and Change in China's Social and Economic History, 1550–1949*, 15–40. Patricia Ebrey has described the three characteristics of the Confucian family—patrilineal descent, patriarchy, filial piety—in her "Women, Marriage, and the Family in Chinese History."

6. Women assumed different kinship roles as they journeyed through stages of their life cycle. These changing kinship roles and ties are often salient themes in women's poetry. Ann Waltner and Pi-ching Hsu have studied the poetry of two young late-Ming gentrywomen who were sisters-in-law. See their "Lingering Fragrance: The Poetry of Tu Yaose and Shen Tiansun." For an intimate description of how eighteenth-century women negotiated progressive stages of their life course, see Mann, *Precious Records: Women in China's Long Eighteenth Century*, 45–75.

7. Source: Wang Qi, *Chidu xinyu chubian.*

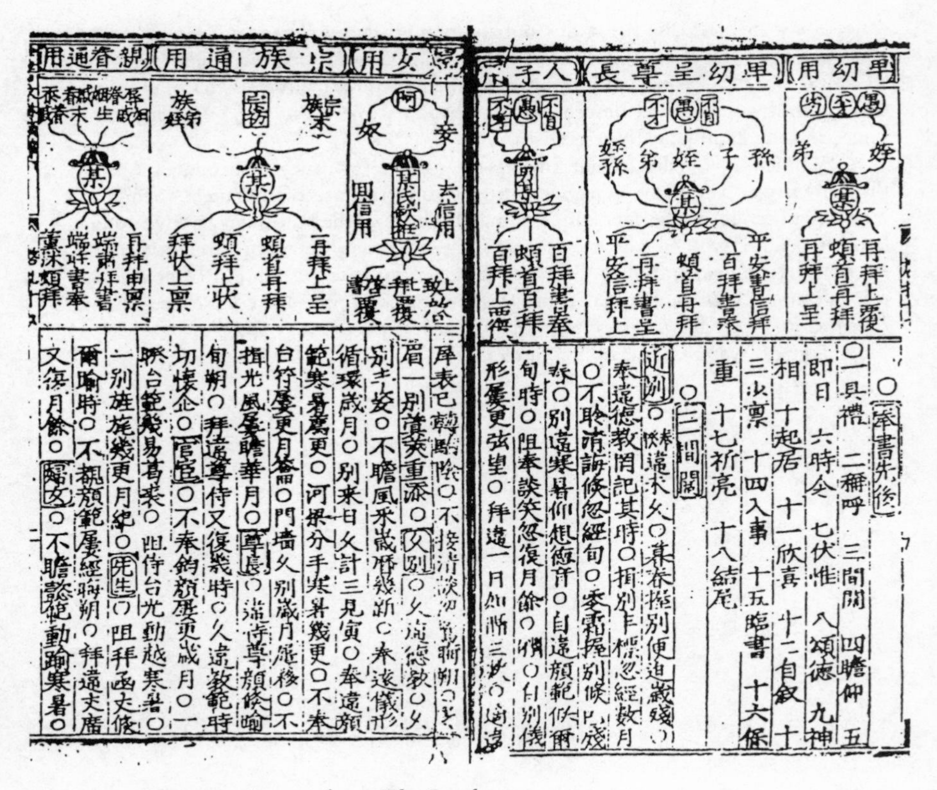

Fig. 10. A page from *The Book of Myriad Treasures (Wanbao quanshu),* 13:1b–2a. The bottom half of the page provides the template for writing a proper letter. The top register diagrams forms of appellation prescribed by the relationship between writer and recipient, using a graphic format built around the image of the lotus. Reproduced with permission of the Harvard-Yenching Library.

TEN

Personal Letters in Seventeenth-Century Epistolary Guides

Translated by Kathryn Lowry

TRANSLATOR'S PREFACE

My foray into seventeenth-century letters is part of a project to gauge the nature and implications of the expanding scope of late-Ming letter-writing manuals—first, to understand how print circulated materials for use in daily life, and second, to explore the question everyone has: who were the audiences for popular publications? Personal letters were collected for their calligraphy, crossing the boundary from private life into the public realm, as early as the Han.[1] Love letters are the most interesting in this regard, since publications of this genre blur distinctions both between private and public realms and between pragmatic letter-writing guides and fiction that was read for pleasure.

I first became interested in letter-writing guides through the discovery of a number of anonymous song texts from the late Ming (late sixteenth century to early seventeenth century) that describe the occasion of reading a letter. These songs depict the feelings of frustration experienced by someone awaiting a letter or receiving a letter that is illegible or even blank.[2] When I found that household encyclopedias *(riyong leishu)* from the late Ming include detailed practical guides to composing personal letters, invitations, and announcements of social rituals, as well as contracts, I decided to look at them for an explanation of the seemingly new, close depiction of the use of letters in popular song.[3] By a strange coincidence, I found a pair of love letters cobbled together out of popular tune names—a fantastic illustration of how letter writers recycled materials from the realm of print. An example of this kind of letter, exchanged by a man from a Suzhou merchant family and a Nanjing courtesan, Fan Caiyun, is translated here under the title "Memorable Words to a Beloved Courtesan." On one level, the way the tune names are strung together is simply word play, similar to that which shows up in the many popular song texts composed of tune names, flower names, or names of medicines. On another level, these love letters are pastiches of elements found in commercial publications, drawing on print sources at the level of the individual phrase. In this respect, the composition of the letters mirrors the way letter manuals break down the conventional elements of letters into their components, phrase by phrase.[4]

INTRODUCTION

A huge number of letter-writing guides were published and reprinted from the late-Yuan dynasty through the Ming dynasty. Most were volumes devoted entirely to letters, such as the late-Yuan work *Forms of Correspondence As Good As Ready Cash (Qizha qingqian),* the early-Ming *Complete Book [of Writings] in Pen and Ink (Hanmo quanshu),* and the late-Ming collection *Plum Sprig Letters (Zhemei jian),* from which I have drawn here. Letter-writing guides were also printed as sections of larger works, such as the household encyclopedia *The Complete Book of Myriad Treasures (Wanbao quanshu),* which went through at least five or six editions. Such works were extensively rewritten, reprinted, and pirated during the Ming. As Timothy Brook has noted, their popularity attests to the circulation of letters among a growing literate population and to the increasing reliance of social practice on texts that literacy made possible, but it also suggests that people needed a primer to tell them how to express themselves in writing.[5] Few books are marked with their price, but two household encyclopedias survive with the bookseller's imprimatur and the remarkably low price of "one and two-tenths taels of silver."[6]

A section on letters addressed to family members *(jiashu)* is a fixture in Ming household encyclopedias. It invariably includes paired letters from husband to wife and wife to husband, placed toward the rear of the section. Such letters address regulative concerns, counseling each partner to keep family matters in order. The husband writes to his wife at home that he is surprised at the swift passage of time, that he misses her, and that he regrets that the burden of care for his parents and children rests on her shoulders alone, but he expects his "good wife" *(xianqi)* to behave in an exemplary fashion. Model letters from the wife to her husband who is away, in turn, assure him that she can maintain the household but lament the passing months or years, asking him to return as soon as possible and warning him to avoid other women's company. This agenda varies only in minor details from one compilation to another. There are slight changes in vocabulary and in the degree of elaboration of the pretense for writing. The most obvious distinction among the letters translated here is that some include glosses explaining particular phrases, which may be a clue to the literacy level of their intended readers.

Two sets of letters between a husband and a wife are translated here. The first, "A Husband Who Is Away Writes to His Wife" and "A Wife at Home Presents a Letter to Her Husband," is from an unusually detailed guide to letters addressed to family members: a slim early-seventeenth-century work titled *Valley of Flowers (Wanhua gu)*. This is the only letter-writing manual I have found that is designed for people of a single region—natives of Huizhou prefecture in Anhui province. *Valley of Flowers* offers simple models of letters for a broad range of occasions and also serves as a guide to composition from the ground up, beginning at the level of the individual phrase. It includes a group of models for "letters home on standard occasions" *(xunchang jiaxin shi)* offering phrases one should know (*zhuju zhaiyu*, or literally, "piecemeal expressions and selected phrases"), including vocabulary for New Year's greetings, phrases of congratulation, words of praise, and ways to express foreknowledge and delight. The guide also gives composite phrases to wish family members well, to comfort them, to say one has received a letter, to tell them one is well or delighted, to resolve a matter, or to alert them that one is sending money home. Ellen Widmer has suggested that the nature of merchant activity in the late sixteenth century had an important part in expanding the scope and refining the practice of personal letter-writing between family members and colleagues.[7] This epistolary guide, intended for natives of the region most famed for its merchants, bears out her observation. The high ratio of phrase-oriented materials to model letters suggests that those who used the manual were able to compose with some facility rather than merely copy.

The second set of letters between husband and wife comes from *Plum Sprig Letters (Zhemei jian)*, a work attributed to the impresario of vernacular literature Feng Menglong.[8] This guide includes a slightly more refined version of the same messages between husband and wife. The body of one letter, for example, includes an interlinear note to explain that the phrase "looking down at the ground . . . to see the shimmering frost" means the season is winter. This sort of seasonal referent, underscoring the passage of time, would be familiar to anyone with a rudimentary knowledge of poetry, but this could not be taken for granted among the readership of letter-writing guides. *Plum Sprig Letters* itself covers a wide range of topics, beginning with a list of forms for letter-writing *(shujian huotao tishi)* that outlines the eleven essential elements in a letter. A step-by-step guide begins by explaining how to greet the addressee and works up to "bringing up the reason for writing" somewhere around step six.

The core of the Ming letter-writing manual is devoted to life rituals such as capping ceremonies, weddings, funerals, and memorials. Yet it extends the scope of earlier etiquette manuals to systematically present models and ready-made phrases for letters on every imaginable occasion in private and public life.[9] The topics covered in letter manuals include requests to borrow a book, a zither, or a garden space for a party; requests to procure or deliver objects; and notes to accompany or acknowledge gifts. We find page upon page of ready-made phrases for use in invitations to visit, to banquet, to see a theatrical performance, or to go wandering in the hills *(qingzhao youshang)*. There are also extensive lists of vocabulary for referring to a gift that is given, as distinguished from the term for the same object when it is received. These invaluable guides to social intercourse are expressly intended for people of all classes. They open up the social universe, not only to readers during the Ming but also to modern scholars, by displaying the array of appropriate linguistic forms to address various people. For example, guides to how to write a greeting at the start of a letter present a hypothetical set of all those people who were literate to some degree and might have needed help with drafting a letter. The list of people to whom one might write a letter includes family members, teachers, fellow students and examination candidates, doctors, apprentices, Buddhist and Daoist monks, prognosticators, woodworkers, women of high status, and ordinary women. The top register of the page shown in figure 10 lays out forms of appellation and closing salutations around the image of the lotus. The lower half-page indexes phrases by topic. Even models of perfunctory letters home from merchants or students are accompanied by lists of ready-made phrases indexed to the general structure of the letter.

The genre of love letters *(qingshu)* is rarely included in Ming letter-writing guides. Instead, most love letters appear in household encyclopedias under the topic of romance *(fengyue men)*, together with instructions for how to conduct oneself in brothels and recipes for aphrodisiacs *(dongfang chunyi miaofang)*. Love letters are also found in published literary anthologies on romance. Under the rubric of "love letters" are included letters conveying a broad range of feelings or passions *(qing)*, from conjugal or sexual love to admiration and brotherly loyalty and attachment. They read like short epistolary fiction, not like models for letter writers. No explicit rules are given for how to compose love letters; there are no step-by-step forms or model phrases. Nor are love letters presented in a deliberative style like the model letters between husband and wife offered in conventional letter-writing guides. In fact, the love letters of the Ming dynasty most resemble the letters of consolation and declarations of love or mutual admiration that began to appear in France in the late sixteenth century.[10]

The examples of love letters in *Plum Sprig Letters* lend themselves to being read as epistolary fiction. Each set of letters is preceded by a short narrative frame that contextualizes the exchange. These narratives identify the writers and relate their feelings to concrete objects, places, and events, rather than to abstract forms. Such a strategy might be seen as an antidote to the explosion of rules and appropriate phrases suggested for use in private social interactions by late-Ming letter-writing manuals.[11] These same narratives can also be viewed as a mode of fiction that plays on the reader's understanding that a flair for letter writing is a type of illusionism. That is, the scenes, objects, and love tokens described in a love letter are material expressions of the writer's emotion, while the letter itself is literally a physical trace of the writer. The pleasure of reading a letter, then, lies in part in the reader's appreciation for its artifice and for its power to sway and thereby to change the course of events.

In *Plum Sprig Letters* the love letters, which constitute the last *juan* of the work, entitled "Memorable Love Letters" *(Fengyun qingshu),* far outnumber the model letters addressed to family members *(jiashu)* noted earlier. There are twenty-one sets of love letters in all. With one exception,[12] each of the forty-four letters is read as part of a pair. Each pair of letters is given a title ("So-and-so and so-and-so are fond of one another") listing the two surnames *(mou* and *mou qinghao).* The letters fall into four groups: (1) memorable words exchanged between husband and wife *(fuqi fengyun),* (2) words shared with one secluded in the women's quarters *(yougui fengyun),* (3) words shared by (male) friends *(pengyou fengyun),* and (4) memorable words shared with a beloved courtesan *(qingji fengyun).*

The love letters incorporate various literary genres, from art song and song lyric to regulated verse, presenting an alternative to the highly formalized, relatively abstract forms of letters appropriate for other kinds of social relationships. Some of the conventional phrases used in letters between husband and wife appear here as well, such as "the paper is not long enough to say all I have to say" *(zhi duan yi chang bujin)* and "words cannot express my feelings" *(ci bujin yi).* However, the letters focus on fantastic literary motifs, such as a wife's dream of persuading the emperor to recall her husband from his post by weaving a pattern poem in brocade to impress and sway him.[13] In one pair of letters a wife in Zhejiang writes to her husband, a merchant who has been away for three years. Her letter describes her loneliness in terms of the song "Crow Cries at Night" ("Wu ye ti"), and then scolds him for neglecting her—and unthinkably neglecting his parents. She appends to her reproachful monologue a vulgar poem *(bi shi).* To his apologetic response he appends a regulated quatrain "to express his regret at making her suffer this way."[14] In another letter, Dong Hui'e writes to her husband, whose father has sent him away to study after he failed the prefectural examinations. She describes her longing for him by copying out passages that she found underlined in his copy of the play *The Story of the Western Wing.*[15]

These examples locate the emotion the writer wishes to convey in some other narrative. Incorporating, as they do, poetry and snatches of novels, the letters inadvertently reveal what people were reading at the time. By the same token, these letters seem to have had the appeal of literature. The short prefaces to the letters make it possible to read them as fiction set in a particular place and time. In that sense, the genre of love letters is the exception to the rule that proves the rule. Letter-writing manuals provide forms to "substitute for" or "embody" *(dai)* emotions and convey them across time and space. The correspondence between husband and wife illustrates the use of letter manuals to standardize social practice and to articulate the sentiments appropriate to conjugal relations. In contrast, the love letters derive their aesthetic appeal from inventive renderings of the emotions of separation, striking diverse chords in a broad reading public. Consideration of the two types of models for personal letter writing published in seventeenth-century China shows us how an increasingly literate population imagined and defined gender roles from the inside out. Print disseminated models for regulating domestic relationships and enforcing social orthodoxy, on the one hand. On the other hand, commercial epistolary manuals blurred the line between fiction and practical guides and explored the means to fulfill individual desire, providing forms for expressing the emotions appropriate to companionate marriage, romantic entanglement, and even homoerotic love.

In the translations that follow, the interlinear notes that appear in small clerical script in the letter-writing guides are rendered in italics, without parentheses or brackets, to indicate that they are part of the original text, not the translator's interpolation. Blanks for letter writers to fill in are indicated by lines, written *mou* in the original text. The term *shi* is an honorific added to the surname, a rough equivalent of "Madame" or "Mister." Readers will find that some interlinear notes appear mid-sentence.

ORIGINAL TEXTS

"A Husband Who Is Away Writes to His Wife"[16]

Journeying to distant regions for profit, I suddenly find *many months / several years* have passed.[17] I think of my family with such longing that my mind feels as if drunk and my spirit takes flight. The many odd matters of our household all rely upon my virtuous wife. *My parents preside over the central room of the family home / Our children lie in your arms* and look to you in countless ways *to serve them / to protect them.* Don't make *our parents complain that you are unfilial / our children suffer for lack of instruction.* Thus my good wife will show great favor [to my family]. I am sending a considerable sum of silver now to cover expenses for the time being. Later, when it is convenient for someone to carry it, I will send more. There is much more I want to say. Forgive me, I must stop here.

My good wife ______ *shi,* my darling, in your chaste quarters
______ month ______ day   your clumsy husband sends a letter
to tell you that all is well.

"A Wife at Home Presents a Letter to Her Husband"[18]

A man's thoughts naturally are of travels to distant parts of the realm. This is nothing untoward. I only hope that *your profits fulfill your wishes / your trade satisfies your desires.* That would be your wife's good fortune. Your wife can manage the many chores of the household; *serving your parents / nurturing your children* is *best suited to / as it should be for* your wife. You need not take the trouble to advise and counsel me over such a distance. But the time goes so quickly, and our youth can never be renewed. If you can earn a bit more in your business dealings, you should return home to care for your parents and to raise your son. Don't make your parents stand at the gate watching for your return, nor make me, your humble wife, lament that you might not remain faithful to me into our old age. While you are staying there, make sure to take care of yourself. When I touch pen to paper, my spirit races away and I cannot express everything I want to say.

Kneeling *before the desk / at the feet* of my fine husband   your
wife[19] *worthless concubine / lowly wife* ______ *shi*   pulls the
lapels of her clothes together respectfully to greet you.

"A Husband's Letter to His Wife"[20]

I have traveled a great distance to this faraway place. In no time at all more than a year has passed. My thoughts linger on matters in our household, my heart and spirit as if drunk. For the duration of the night my dreaming spirit roams five hundred miles away, and then when dawn arrives I sit alone in sadness. Our elders are at home, and our young child rests in your embrace. They all rely on my good wife's constant care of them, which must not waver from the beginning to the end. Don't give my parents occasion to complain that I am not filial, or let our children lack formal instruction. In this way, my good wife will show great favor [to my family]. As soon as my business in the area where I'm traveling is better, I will take up my riding whip to start the journey homeward. I take advantage of the wind, which is stirred by my longing to return, to send my feeling to you. I am enclosing a small amount of silver to help with household expenses for the time being. Later on, when it is convenient for someone traveling that way, I will send some other things. Forgive me for the hardship you bear because of our being parted.

Dutiful wife ______ *shi,* my darling   in your chaste quarters
______ month ______ day
Your clumsy husband sends a letter to tell you that all is well

"A Wife Sends a Letter to Her Husband"[21]

Since your departure, the hibiscus has bloomed twice. Your exhortations when we parted I, your lowly wife, always bear in mind and dare not transgress. I, your lowly wife, am responsible for feeding your parents, and I must raise our young children. I personally make sure the many details of the household are in order, and you need not worry about us while you are far away. However, the light of dawn quickly fades into darkness and small rivulets quickly disappear. *These two phrases mean time passes quickly.* When you calculate that you have garnered a seemly profit, please come home as early as you can to serve our parents and nurture our youngsters, so that we who are of the same flesh and bones can be united and speak together happily in the same hall. Do not make our parents stand by the door watching for their son's return. Your worthless wife has written a "Lament of White Hair."[22] Our bedchamber is before my eyes, while you are far away. My thoughts are a thousand miles away, and as I write, I have to wipe away the tears and I find myself unable to control the words I want to say. In this period, the frost's sheen covers the ground. *The phrase "In this period . . ." means the present tense; "the frost's sheen covers the ground" tells the reader it is winter.* Make sure you eat, and watch after yourself.

My fine husband   at your knees   your lowly wife ______ *shi*
pulls the lapels of her clothes together respectfully to greet you.

"*Memorable Words to a Woman of Good Family*"[23]

WU AND SHEN WERE FOND OF ONE ANOTHER. Wu Zhizhuo was a native of the Suzhou region. Shen Suqiong was a talented woman of the area outlying the city. One evening as she was watching the sunset from a tower, Wu happened to pass by on his way home from his studies. Shen had just eaten a green olive and by accident let fall the pit, which landed on the student's chest. Looking upwards, he saw her and gasped in surprise. Seeing that she had mistakenly dropped the pit on him, Shen also gave a little gasp, leading the student to believe she had done this on purpose. After this, he often passed by her dwelling, and each time he passed he spoke out loud, "Such a thing bothers a man." Shen thought he was trying to make trouble for her. What was done unintentionally was taken as a purposeful act. Wu had a neighbor Old Mrs. Ma, who was a skillful matchmaker. He paid her a generous sum for her troubles, asking her to deliver a letter and to raise the question of marriage. The two first made a private agreement, and later married.

"Student Wu's Letter to Shen Suqiong"

The unworthy student Wu Zhizhuo touches his head to the floor in respectful greeting.

May the Jade One [Miss] Shen receive this in her chaste quarters.

Some time ago, I was returning home from my studies in the evening and passed outside [your] tower. Unwittingly, the Jade One let a green olive pit fall. My countenance is not that of Master Pan *Pan Yue was so handsome that whenever he left the city [of Loyang] women found him attractive and presented him with fruit by the cartload*[24] and yet I have been favored with a piece of fruit from someone who admires me. Further, I have been favored with a sign that to me is worth a fortune of more than a thousand in gold. From that time, I have secretly longed for the Jade One. My capacity for drink is diminished, and my face has grown pale. Regret adds to my heart's cares and furrows my brow. I have no interest in cultivating historical and classical studies but want to compose poetry about nature and the seasons. Layer upon layer of clouds mirror the feelings pent up in my breast. The whistling wind is transformed into sighs in my mouth. Whether it comes from the resident of an influential house or a beauty in the labyrinth,[25] the green fruit is the fruit of bitterness.[26] Alas! The flowers of Mt. Tiantai were beautiful and yet Young Ruan could not find a way to approach them.[27] Thick clouds covered the Wu River Gorges, yet Song Yu composed only a rhapsody on the emptiness of passion. *Song Yu composed the "Rhapsody on Gaotang."* My spirit is depleted, as if it has been wounded. My mind is clouded, as it is wracked by pain. Today I present a [letter on a] measure of silk to express a small part of my feeling. I beg you to condescend to think of my humble person and save my life. In the romantic story of [the play] *Western Chamber* a small coincidence opened up the Milky Way and the Bridge of Magpies to Student Zhang. I look forward to the pleasure of meeting the Weaving Maid.[28] I long unbearably for a word in reply to comfort me. I will say no more of my melancholy. Wu Zhizhuo once more sends his greetings.

"Suqiong's Letter in Reply to Student Wu"

Your humble concubine Shen Suqiong pulls the lapels of her clothes together respectfully to greet you in reply.

To the young man Wu who studies at the feet of the historian.

A month ago I climbed the tower to watch the sunset and let a green olive pit fall. Certainly I did not toss fruit to show favor to Pan Yue. You, sir, insist on confusing Hangzhou with Bianzhou.[29] You represent my chaste quarters as a pavilion of rain and clouds,[30] and you point to a green olive pit as the catalyst for a predestined meeting [of man and woman]. This is a mistake! A mistake! This incident came about by accident, although it seems as if it was intentional. I was favored to receive your letter [and so on]. I am aware that you long deeply for me. When the moon is intent upon coming in through the window, who could prevent it? When the white clouds emerge unbidden from the mountain peaks, the wind draws them forward. You cannot compare yourself to [Sima] Xiangru taking Zhuo Wenjun[31] for his wife. However,

"Spring colors fill the garden and cannot be contained."[32]

"When separated by the wall, the flowers' shadows [show that] The Jade One is coming."[33]

Sincerely in reply,

"Memorable Words to a Beloved Courtesan"[34]

SU AND FAN WERE FOND OF ONE ANOTHER. Su Shangmin, of the Wu region, formed a bond with the famous Jinling courtesan Fan Caiyun.[35] After Su parted from Fan, he could not control his longing for her, and he joined together the names of tune-types to write a letter, which he sent to Fan. Fan also wrote a letter composed of the names of tune-types in reply to his, making their fondness for one another even more evident.

"Student Su's Letter to Caiyun" *names of tune-types*

It was when the chrysanthemums had just opened that I thoughtlessly stopped 'Delighting in the Beauty.' Now 'The Little Peaches—are already—Ripening,' and not a day passes that I am not 'Longing for the Southland.' Each time 'I Remember Her Many Charms,' teardrops fall, forming 'A River of Water.' I wonder if 'My Good Sister' has ever 'Struggled to Forget Her Cares' on account of 'A Man of Talent.' Yesterday 'I Climbed the Low-Storied Building' and saw 'The Geese Descending.' I have not received 'A Single Letter' and cannot keep my regrets from 'Increasing with Each Moment.' When may I 'Loosen—my darling's—Fragrant Sash,' and 'Take Off Your Blouse,' fully 'Taking Delight in the Three Pleasures' once more 'Locked Inside the Golden Canopy' until the 'Fifth Watch Comes Around'? I wish to ply the oars 'Against the Stream's Flow,' waiting until 'The Lovers [Cross] the Bridge of Magpies' and are united. Then I will 'Watch the Golden Oars at the Riverhead' with you, my dearest, once again.

"Caiyun's Reply to Student Su's Letter" *names of tune-types*

Since I stood where 'The Golden Banana Leaf was Falling' [i.e., in Nanjing] to send you off toward 'Lesser Liangzhou,' 'Nanjing's Peonies' are already blooming. Your humble concubine watches 'The Colored Butterflies' circling and flitting. 'The Yellow Oriole' cries *"Guan, guan."* How badly I want to 'Upbraid My Fine Lover' for not making a 'Prelude to "Thoughts of Returning"'! In the past few days your concubine's 'Broidered Sash' grows loose. I no longer 'Sit beside the Dressing Table,' and am 'Too Weary to Paint My Brow.' 'Overturning the Silver Lamp,' I sit at night and helplessly 'Cry for Longing.' If only my love could catch 'The Wind on the River' and row 'A Night Boat' to return home, we could stay there to compose 'A Verse to Make One Smile,' watching the 'Moon over the Splendid Hall'! I fear and 'Worry I Grow Thin and Peaked' and that 'A Single Flower' shall fall neglected by 'The Third-Placed Degree Candidate.'

Respectfully in reply,

NOTES

1. Some of the earliest examples of private letters were published as works for aesthetic appreciation. See Bai, "Chinese Letters: Private Words Made Public." David Pattinson has studied the formal and stylistic development of the epistolary form called *chidu,* as distinct from formal letters, or *shu.* See Pattinson, "The Chidu in Late Ming and Early Qing China." A special issue of *Renditions* devoted to classical letters includes correspondence between husband and wife from the Han and Republican periods. See *Renditions* 41/42 (Spring and Autumn 1994): 1–3, 153–64.

2. See Lowry, "The Transmission of Popular Song in Late-Ming China," 179–83.

3. I examine the particular forms, format, and duplication of materials in letter-writing guides in "Writing and Reading Letters in Late-Ming China."

4. In translating the love letters and correspondence between husband and wife, I try to preserve the word order of the original text in order to show where people using the manual would fill in or vary the wording to personalize a conventional message.

5. Brook, *The Confusions of Pleasure: Commerce and Culture in Ming China,* 56–62.

6. The range of book prices is discussed in Lowry, "Transmission of Popular Song," 33–41. See also Oki Yasushi, "Minmatsu Kōnan ni okeru shuppan bunka no kenkyū"; Shen Jin, "Mingdai fangke tushu zhi liutong yu jiage."

7. Widmer, "The Epistolary World of Female Talent in Seventeenth-Century China," 6–7.

8. The anthology *Plum Sprig Letters* is identical to the letter-writing guide *Phoenix from Cinnabar Mountain (Danshan feng),* of which *Plum Sprig Letters* was either the third revised edition or a pirated copy.

9. These sorts of materials cite Sima Guang's *Shuyi* (Verbal etiquette) and use it as a model. See Ebrey, "Tang Guides to Verbal Etiquette."

10. Roger Chartier refers to two writing styles, deliberative and epideictic, in characterizing the transition when the "site at which eloquence was practiced" shifted from the courts of law to worldly and courtly society in France of the late sixteenth and early seventeenth centuries. See "Secretaires for the People?" 72.

11. Alain Boreau discusses the emergence of letter-writing guides as a cultural technique in the European Middle Ages (ca. twelfth or thirteenth century) and examines how the need to write letters and to comply with the appropriate rules was interiorized. See "The Letter-Writing Norm: A Medieval Invention," 25.

12. *Zhemei jian,* 8:19b–20b. "Ruan and Du were fond of one another" ("Ruan Du qinghao") is a set of four letters between a man from Jiangling county and a courtesan, Du Shanshan. After they had a misunderstanding, he used part of a song-lyric to break off the relationship, and she remonstrated with him.

13. *Zhemei jian,* 8:2a–3a. "Deng and Xu were fond of one another" ("Deng Xu qinghao") is the only letter that is not contemporary. Deng Chunren is introduced as a gentry man of good moral character who was exiled to Guangxi during the Southern Song.

14. *Zhemei jian,* 8:3b–4a. "Wu and Tao were fond of one another" ("Wu Tao qinghao") involves Wu Zhen of Yuzhang (Zhejiang) and Tao Yucao.

15. *Zhemei jian,* 8:4b–5b. On the use of *The Story of the Western Wing* as a reference for lovers, see West and Idema's introduction to *The Moon and the Zither: The Story of the Western Wing,* 96–97.

16. Source: *Wanhua gu,* 6:9a–b.

17. The two phrases are printed in small script and presented in two registers within the text of the letter, so that the reader can choose the appropriate phrase.

18. Source: *Wanhua gu,* 6:9b–10a.

19. *Jizhou fu,* translated "wife," is literally "dustpan-and-broom wife," or simply *jizhou,* which refers to a wife or concubine.

20. Source: *Zhemei jian,* 5:5a–b. The fifth *juan,* cited here, is titled after the work it is based on, *Sanke zhushi Yasu bianyong caijian* (The third annotated edition of variegated letters for convenient use by the elegant and the common).

21. Source: *Zhemei jian,* 5:5b.

22. "Lament of White Hair" ("Baitou yin") is the title of a *yuefu* (ballad). It gets its name from Zhuo Wenjun's lament that her husband could not stay faithful until both of them were old and white-haired. This lament persuaded him not to take a concubine. See Liu Xin, *Xijing zaji,* 1:18.

23. Source: *Zhemei jian,* 8:8b–9b. The short narrative introduction is entitled "Wu Shen qinghao"; the small capitals in the translation reflect the format of the original book.

24. Pan Yue (style name Anren, d. 300) was recognized for his poetic talent and for his good looks.

25. Emperor Yang of the Sui established his capital in Yangzhou because of its reputation as a city of pleasure, and he built a labyrinth *(milou)* for his palace ladies.

26. The fruit of bitterness, *nieguo.*

27. There is a story that Ruan Zhao and Liu Chen met two women immortals in the mountains and found when they returned to their homes that a century had passed. Young Ruan is a standard figure for losing oneself in a love affair. See Liu Yiqing, *Youming lu,* 1–2.

28. The Cow Herd and the Weaving Maid are legendary lovers who could meet only once a year when they crossed the Bridge of Magpies (or Stars) on the seventh night of the seventh month.

29. Bianzhou probably refers to Bianliang, the capital city of the Northern Song. The character is miswritten as *bian,* "rash" or "excitable," omitting the water radical.

30. "Rain and clouds" is a poetic term for sexual intercourse, based on a description of a fleeting encounter with the goddess in the "Rhapsody on Gaotang" ("Gaotang fu"), attributed to Song Yu (Xiao Tong, *Wen xuan zhu,* 1:250–51). See David Knechtges's translation (*Wen xuan, or, Selections of Refined Literature,* 3: 325–39). A partial translation of this work is also included in Owen, *An Anthology of Chinese Literature,* 189–93.

31. Zhuo Wenjun eloped to marry the Han dynasty writer Sima Xiangru.

32. The third line from Ye Shaoweng's "Youyuan bu zhi" (Going to the garden and not happening to find you)—famous for the startling sexual innuendo of the line that follows it (Qian Zhongshu, *Songshi xuan zhu,* 295–96).

33. This line from Cui Yingying's letter to Zhang Junduan is one of the most renowned from Chinese love letters, and was interpreted by him as an invitation to come to her. Here it is slightly misquoted. See Wang Shifu, *Xixiang ji,* book 3, act 2, 137; and West and Idema, *The Moon and the Zither,* 205.

34. Source: *Zhemei jian,* 8:20b–21a. Shen Suqiong's letter also appears in Chen Shao, *Mingyuan chidu,* 2:37a–b, with some emendations and without preface. The small capital letters in the translation reflects the format of the original book.

35. There is no evidence that these people actually existed. Li Yunxiang's anthology *Jinling baimei* includes biographies and writings by and about courtesans, but does not mention a courtesan Fan Caiyun. Five courtesans with the surname Fan appear in this work.

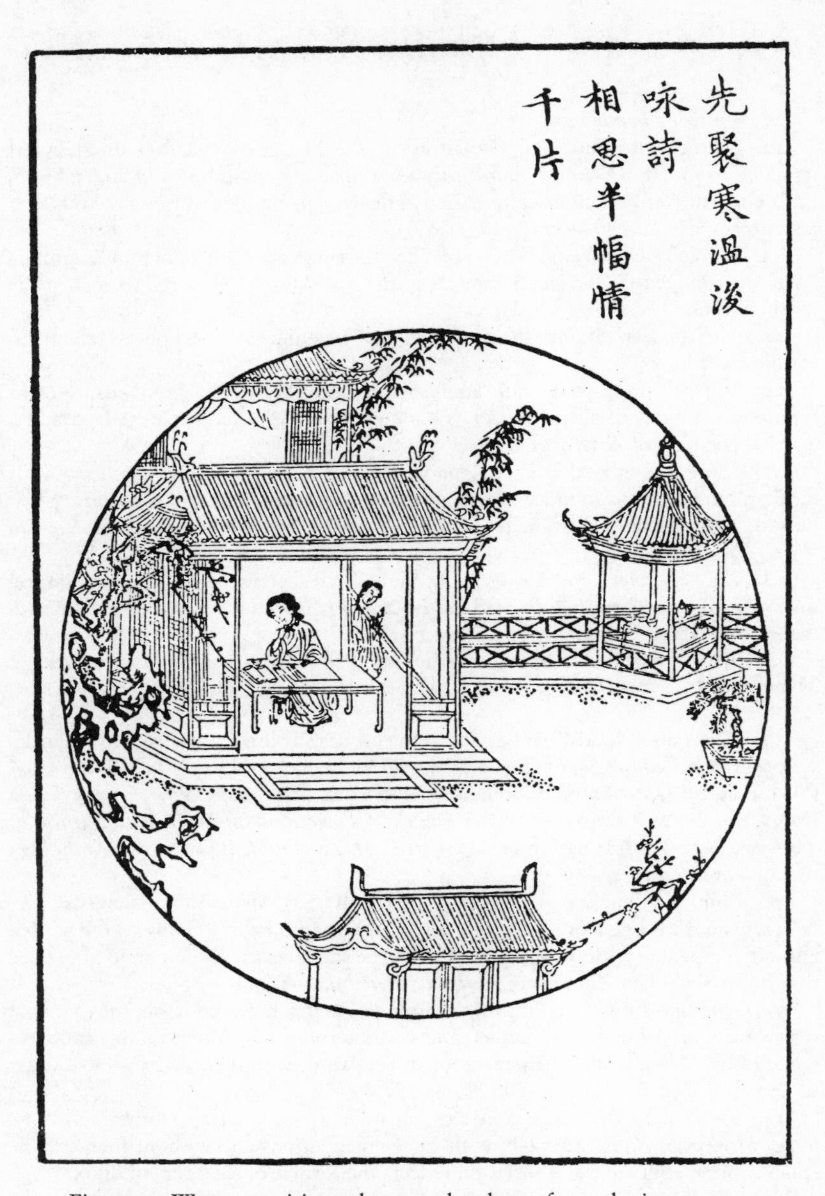

Fig. 11. Woman writing a letter to her lover from the inner quarters. This scene illustrating a short story is captioned "drafting a letter" *(caojian)* and is accompanied by a couplet: "I first inquire after your well-being, and then recite you my poems. Although words of love cover only half the paper, my feelings for you would fill a thousand pages." Source: *Yuanyang meng* (ca. 1644–1661; reprinted in Fu Xihua, *Zhongguo gudian wenxue banhua xuanji,* 872).

ELEVEN

Letters by Women of the Ming-Qing Period

Translated by Yu-Yin Cheng

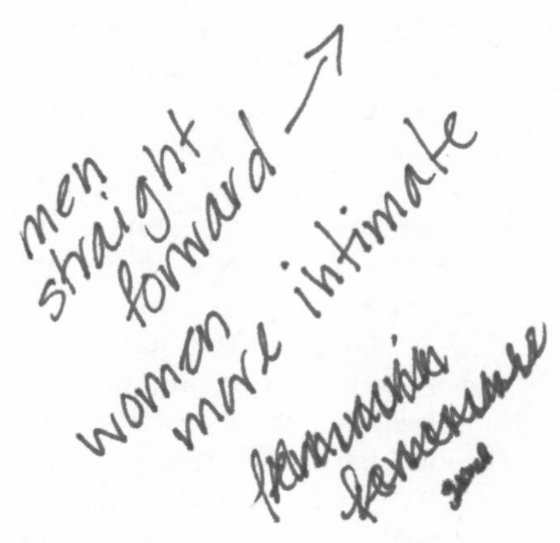

TRANSLATOR'S PREFACE

I chose to translate these letters because despite the great number of letters by women from the Ming and Qing periods that survive, they remain largely uncharted territory for gender study.[1] The letters also interest me because their contents give us a "live," sophisticated picture of how women's lives, thoughts, and activities were woven together. Although household management and duties dominated most women's lives, letters tell us that Ming and Qing women in elite families shared other concerns, including study, writing, and the development of intellectual interests. In addition to writing poetry, they also enjoyed reading and commenting on historical works and classical literature; they were skilled in calligraphy and painting—on which they did not hesitate to offer comments to each other; and like most Confucian scholars, they were also concerned with moral cultivation and the pursuit of the Way. Their scholastic interests helped them bridge the gaps of seniority and age difference within their families, while shortening the distance among one another as peers. As we see in their letters, they visited and wrote to each other, and they organized literary clubs of their own.

INTRODUCTION

The seven letters that follow, all written by women from scholar-gentry families, represent the two most common types of women's letters: family letters and social letters.[2] The family letters chosen here include one from a mother-in-law to her daughters-in-law, two from a wife to her husband, and one to a sister-in-law. There are two striking differences between family letters by women and those by men. One is a difference in style. Letters by men to family members, being more or less private letters, tend to be relatively straightforward in their ideas and their language, as we see in the letters by Luo Rufang and Yang Jisheng translated in chapters 6 and 7. Women's family letters, although similarly straightforward in their ideas, are written in a more elegant, less colloquial style.

Another striking difference is in the issues that concerned men and women. As head of the family, a man wrote family letters focused on domestic affairs, including family relationships, communications with neighbors, family members' responsibilities, male descendants' study programs, and sometimes, family financial situations.[3] Women's family letters seldom touched upon domestic affairs, unless special conditions required them to do so, as we see in Gu Ruopu's letter translated in chapter 9. Instead, many women's family letters show an interest in intellectual pursuits, such as improving writing skills, critiquing historical and literary works, and practicing moral self-cultivation. This is perhaps because household management and family obligations were so routine in women's daily lives that they preferred, when writing, to speak of higher aspirations. One senses that each family member actually played dual roles in the eyes of these women, one as a family member and the other as an intellectual companion.

Actual family letters exchanged between husband and wife also reveal an interesting gender difference, compared with the model letters between husband and wife translated in chapter 10. However else they may differ, all letters from husbands—whether model or not—share a common focus on Confucian family obligations. But the wives' letters vary. Confucian family obligations remain the center of model family letters for wives; however, the actual letters written by women to their husbands show little interest in family obligations. Instead, intellectual, literary, and artistic interests predominate.[4] The letter in fact becomes a vehicle for expressing a woman's individual creativity. One thus wonders whether model family letters for women were actually written by men with didactic aims, and how much influence these letters actually had on highly educated women.

The social letters translated here comprise two letters exchanged between friends and a letter to the members of a literary club. Unlike family letters, which are always straightforward and intimate, social letters display a range of intimacy and formality, depending on the writer and the addressee. For instance, the letters exchanged between two female friends are written in a style filled with intimate feeling and straightforward language, very much in the style of private family letters. The letter to the members of a female literary club, by contrast, is clearly a "public" letter, in that the author uses ornate allusions to express her ideas more formally and politely and with less emotion. In terms of content, women's social letters clearly reveal the women's intellectual interests as they support each other in their efforts to improve literary and artistic skills and religious pursuits and offer each other spiritual comfort.[5] In this respect, women's social letters are similar to letters to a spouse or to relatives of the same generation. Communications beyond the family, however, expand women's social and spiritual space.[6] Women's social letters, in other words, identify their own *zhiji* (friends who know me best). A circle of friends like this, even if it is small, is a most precious asset in the eyes of Confucian scholars.[7]

The first of the letters that follow was written by Shang Jinglan (1603–ca. 1667), the widow of the Ming loyalist Qi Biaojia (1602–1645). Like Gu Ruopu, she was the matriarch and mother-teacher of her deceased husband's family. But as a mother, Shang suffered more than Gu, having lost both sons when they participated in a loyalist plot during the Ming-Qing transition.[8] Ironically, it is because of Shang's tragic life that we have a chance to read this rare letter addressed directly to her daughters-in-law, Zhang Dehui and Zhu Derong. More commonly, an upper-class woman wrote letters to her son, with a brief instruction to his wife appended. (An example is Gu Ruopu's letter translated in chapter 9.) Shang's letter pays the apparently obligatory attention to moral values, but its true focus is fulfillment of the promise of one's talent in literary work. Shang sees talent and virtue as complementary qualities in a woman.[9] Her instructions to her daughters-in-law echo what Confucius said: "When accomplishments and character are equally matched, we then have a person of virtue."[10] At the same time, Shang's voice in the letter carries the power of a mother-in-law's authority: admonishing her sons' wives to do better and holding them to ever-higher standards of performance.

Zhou Geng, the author of the next set of letters, was a native of Putian, Fujian, during the mid–seventeenth century. The Zhous were a reputable scholar-gentry family whose ranks included several learned ladies, among them Zhou Geng herself, her father's concubine, and her sisters-in-law.[11] Zhou Geng studied Chinese classics and poetry writing under the tutelage of her second sister-in-law, née Fang.[12] After Zhou Geng was married to Chen Chengkuang, a student and likewise a resident of Putian, her writings came to the attention of Chengkuan's teacher, Zhou Lianggong (1612–1672), a renowned scholar-official and artist. Greatly impressed by Zhou Geng's ingenious commentaries on Chinese literature and history, which she copied into her family letters, Zhou Lianggong decided to incorporate them into his *Mingxian chidu xinchao* (Letters by renowned worthies, new edition). In Zhou Lianggong's view, the letters of only two women— Gu Ruopu and Zhou Geng—are worthy of collecting, because Gu Ruopu's letters demonstrate the "model of a great house" *(dajia guifan)* and Zhou Geng's letters "embody the essence of the Way with elegant style" *(dao yun yafeng)*.[13] Since then, Zhou Geng's works have frequently been included, cited, and discussed in scholars' collections of women's letters and in their miscellaneous notes.[14] Contemporary Taiwan publishers even incorporate Zhou's works in their published model letters of Chinese worthies.[15] The three selections translated here are among the best known of Zhou Geng's many published letters. The "Letter to My Second Sister-in-Law" reveals not only the two women's shared interest in history, but also their superb mastery of classical Chinese. Since traditional Chinese texts are unpunctuated and unparagraphed, settling the meaning of a historical work by proper punctuation and commentary required a long period of training in classical Chinese language as well as a thorough understanding of the Confucian classics and the dynastic histories. That Zhou Geng and her sister-in-law were able to punctuate and comment upon Chen Shou's *History of the Three Kingdoms* is proof of the high level of their scholarship. Zhou Geng's comment on Liu Bei, for example, is a cryptic way of displaying her moral understanding of political history, since Liu Bei—as the ruler of the Shu kingdom—was considered the legitimate heir to the Han throne during an age of disorder in which usurpers Cao Cao and Sun Quan were his leading opponents. The letter to her husband about praying to Guanyin for a son, though purposely wry and amusing, points obliquely to the pressures borne by all women of child-bearing age. Zhou Geng shows here her own resolution of these distressing demands. Zhou Geng's last letter, her commentary on Qu Yuan's "Encountering Sorrow," displays her insight into Qu Yuan's emotions as he composed his masterpiece. This commentary has been highly praised by Confucian scholars, one of whom wrote: "[She is] not only able to grasp the wondrous insights of "Encountering Sorrow"; she is also capable of the subtlety required to read it properly."[16]

The authors of the last set of letters translated here are Qian Feng Xian (style name Youling), Lin Yining (style name Yaqing), and Li Shuzhao (style name Duanming). All were members of the Banana Garden group, a gentrywomen's poetry club whose members lived in and around the city of Hangzhou during the mid–seventeenth century. Qian Feng Xian, the wife of Hangzhou scholar Qian Tingmei, shared many similarities with Lin Yining.[17] Lin and Qian Feng were the core members of the Banana Garden poetry club, expert in poetry and other literary writing, and skilled in painting and calligraphy.[18] Qian Feng Xian's photographic memory made her unusually knowledgeable in the fields of classics and philosophy. From an early age she had immersed herself in Daoist philosophy, and she was said to enjoy a reclusive lifestyle in which she cultivated "tranquillity of the heart-mind."[19] Her letter to members of the Banana Garden poetry club, accordingly, is redolent with Daoist allusions, tastes, and sensibilities. For the third Banana Garden poet, Li Shuzhao, there is no extant biography. She left only letters—more letters, in fact, than any of the other members of the Banana Garden group. Li's letters show that she once belonged to the group, but that for some reason—perhaps marriage—she became separated from the others. After more than sixteen years she returned to Hangzhou to live with her mother in the northern part of the city, bringing her sons, daughters-in-law, and grandsons with her. Thus she was able to rejoin her poet friends.[20] Together, the letters by Qian Feng, Lin, and Li offer us an intimate glimpse of the Banana Garden poets' social, literary, and intellectual life. They seem to have visited freely and gathered together without difficulty, except for the occasional intrusion of family responsibilities. The contents of the letters also demonstrate their undying concern with improving their writing style and their calligraphy, and with intellectual pursuit of the Dao.

ORIGINAL TEXTS

"Letter to My Daughters-in-Law" by Shang Jinglan[21]

After burning my pens and discarding my inkstones for nearly thirty years, I happened to see on my son's desk a copy of the *Combined Manuscripts of the Zither Tower [Qinlou hegao],* written by Zhang Chayun of Wuling, Zhejiang. Chayun was a talented lady and a filial daughter. Therefore her poetry is honest and tranquil and comes straight from her nature and her feelings *[xingqing],* in the tradition of the *Book of Odes.* I explored her poems over and over again. I could not bear to let them out of my hands.

When I think of Chayun's talent, I know that you may be able to match it. When I think of her filiality, I know you can equal that too. But to reach Chayun's state of perfection, you will still need to admonish each other.

Three Letters by Zhou Geng[22]

"Letter to My Second Sister-in-Law"

You have punctuated the entire *History of the Three Kingdoms [Sanguo zhi]* and settled the meanings. I should exhaust myself to add my commentaries on [the work]. But one thing I cannot understand—how did the ancients decide whom to praise and whom to blame? Myself, I'm biased toward Liu [Bei].

"Letter to My Husband"

People who worship the White-Robed Guanyin believe that is one way to conceive a male child. I worshipped her for three years, but all I got were more daughters. Finally I realized that making offerings to the bodhisattva in order to ensure good fortune is ignorant. The way to ensure good fortune is simply not to violate her virtuous teachings. We can worship Guanyin, but we do not need to ask her for anything.

"Letter to My Husband"

The subtlety of the great epic poem "Li Sao" [Encountering sorrow] lies in its unsystematic *[luan]* language and its lack of any starting point. The more unsystematic the work is, the deeper the sorrow it conveys and the more profound and complex its meaning. Even the ancients could not fully understand it by themselves. Therefore the reader should position herself in a dignified pose with a sincere and upright mind before seeking why and how the work was written. When illumination suddenly comes while she is in this position, she will no longer feel it is unusually obscure and difficult to understand.

Three Letters from the "Banana Garden" Poets

"Letter to the Ladies in My Literary Club" by Qian Feng Xian[23]

This morning the mail courier brought me your letter[24] inviting me to join you to pluck wild sesame[25] and dine on the herbs of the immortals[26] to satisfy the hunger of the spirit. How can I bear to decline! But alas! I have been bound by mundane problems and from the spring until the autumn, I have not once picked up my pen[27] to write you. Please understand that my mind was cluttered with distractions.

On the Day of Double Nine[28] I was delighted to see all the chrysanthemums under the fence, their yellow petals reaching out into the bright sunlight. I wanted to pick up the rhyme of Tao Qian's poem[29] and compose a new one, but up until now I still have not completed one line! Recall the barbs about how even a genius like Jiang Yan[30] ran out of talent—what can one say about people like us?

And on top of all of that, my husband is traveling far away and my mother-in-law is sick in bed, which keeps me from leaving her. So all I can do is gaze at the distant pavilion where you will gather, and when I see colorful clouds gathering there, I will know that the moment has arrived and the white phoenix words[31] are issuing from your mouths. Then I will solemnly pull up my sleeves and raise my wine cup to salute your precious work.

"Letter to Li Duanming" by Lin Yining[32]

Yesterday when I received my esteemed sister's letter, I dashed off a reply without taking time to compose it carefully. It was really impolite. But in spite of that, you thought my running-hand calligraphy worthy of praise. Are you really praising me, or are you making fun of me? If I start practicing my calligraphy because of your praise and I transform it from something false into something true, it will all be due to your encouragement.

"Know each other with our hearts; admonish each other with the Dao." Let us strive together, guided by these words!

"Letter to Lin Yaqing" by Li Shuzhao[33]

My humble house is in the northern part of the city. It's like living in the countryside. Very often it happens that an entire day will pass without any visitors at all. Yesterday though, surprisingly, beauties surpassing all the generations came hand in hand to see me. This was a heaven-sent opportunity that had never before presented itself.

I picked up my humble manuscripts and asked for your gracious instruction. In my lifetime I never want my writings to enter this mundane world as something to read before wine-drinking.

NOTES

1. The one study in this area is Widmer, "The Epistolary World of Female Talent in Seventeenth-Century China."

2. In general, these letters are not long, ranging from 29 to 130 characters, which is not unusual. Although length is not a standard for distinguishing between men's and women's letters (see Widmer, "The Epistolary World of Female Talent," 3), women tended to write short letters. For example, among the thirty-seven Ming-Qing women's letters collected by Chen Shao in *Lichao mingyuan chidu,* only eight are longer than 150 characters and only two are longer than 300 characters. Among these eight letters, almost all are love letters, except those written by Gu Ruopu. See Chen Shao, *Lichao mingyuan chidu,* 2:1a–18b. Men's letters, however, vary greatly: theirs can be as short as women's, but letters longer than 500 characters are not uncommon for all Confucian scholars. Tang Xianzu (1550–1617), for example, was a scholar whose letters seem to usually be short. See Tang Xianzu, *Yuming tang chidu.* The terms for letter in Chinese are various, including *chidu, shudu, jian* (lit., fine paper for writing poetry or letter), *jian* (lit., simple), *zha, chishu, shuqi.* Some of them, such as *jian*-style letters, are usually short, very much a note-like letter.

3. Yang Jisheng's letter translated in chapter 7 is an example. As for Luo Rufang's family letters, among the ten letters extant, nine are about domestic affairs, excepting the one translated in chapter 6. See also Xu Yitang, *Lidai mingxian chushi jiashu,* 1–11, 13–14.

4. Zhou Geng's five letters to her husband, which are still extant, range from her comments about Qu Yuan's *Encountering Sorrow* and about a painting titled "A Lady Standing by Rocks in a Pine Forest" to her interest in seeking seclusion in the mountains. See Zhou Lianggong, *Mingxian chidu xinchao,* in *Congshu jicheng chubian,* 2978:236–37.

5. On the importance of women's social letters, see Widmer, "The Epistolary World of Female Talent."

6. Ko, *Teachers of the Inner Chambers: Women and Culture in Seventeenth-Century China,* 226–42.

7. For a discussion of friendship in late imperial China, see McDermott, "Friendship and Its Friends in the Late Ming."

8. On Shang Jinglan and her daughters-in-law, see Ko, *Teachers of the Inner Chambers,* 226–32.

9. On the relationship between women's talent and moral virtue, see Ko, "Pursuing Talent and Virtue: Education and Women's Culture in Seventeenth- and Eighteenth-Century China"; and Chang, "Ming-Qing Women Poets and the Notions of 'Talent' and 'Morality.'"

10. *Analects* 6:16. Translation adapted from Legge, *The Chinese Classics,* 1:190.

11. See a letter to the second sister-in-law, "Yu zhongsao tie," in Wang Xiuqin and Hu Wenkai, *Lidai mingyuan shujian,* 3:68.

12. *Fujian tongzhi,* compiled by Shen Yuqing and Chen Yan, 45:12. Unfortunately, the woman née Fang burned all of her writings after the death of her husband, Zhou Wen.

13. For Zhou Lianggong's interest in Zhou Geng's letters, see Zhou Lianggong, *Min xiaoji,* 4:78. For his commentary on Gu Ruopu's and Zhou Geng's letters, see Zhou Lianggong's preface to *Mingxian chidu xinchao,* 4.

14. See, for example, Shi Hongbao (d. 1871), *Min zaji,* 4:60; Chen Weisong, *Furen ji,* in *Xiangyan congshu,* vol. 1, no. 2:32b; and Wang Xiuqin and Hu Wenkai, *Lidai mingyuan shujian,* 3:67–70.

15. Xu Yitang, *Lidai mingxian chushi jiashu,* 11–12, 141.

16. Shi Hongbao, *Min zaji,* 4:60. Qu Yuan's poem expresses his despair that his ruler has rejected his sage counsel. See also chapter 16.

17. For Lin Yining, see Ko, *Teachers of the Inner Chambers,* 240–48.

18. Shi Shuyi, *Qingdai guige shiren zhenglüe,* 2:25b.

19. Shi Shuyi, *Qingdai guige shiren zhenglüe,* 2:25b.

20. Wang Xiuqin and Hu Wenkai, *Lidai mingyuan shujian,* 3:79–81.

21. Source: Chen Shao, *Lichao mingyuan chidu,* 2:35a–b.

22. Source: Chen Shao, *Lichao mingyuan chidu,* 2:23a–b.

23. Source: Chen Shao, *Lichao mingyuan chidu,* 2:16b–17a.

24. The word for letter here, *qingniao,* is an allusion to the bird messenger of the Queen Mother of the West. By convention in Qian Feng Xian's day it had come to mean simply "mail courier." However, her use of a Daoist term here is purposely echoed in other Daoist allusions that follow. See *Shanhai jing, juan* 16, in Yuan Ke, *Shanhai jing jiaoyi,* 271.

25. Wild sesame *(huma)* is an allusion to plucking medicinal herbs in the mountains and meeting Daoist adepts. The allusion comes from a story set in the Eastern Han period, when Ruan Zhao and Liu Chen went to Tiantai in Zhejiang to gather medicinal herbs. While lost on the mountain, they met two female immortals who invited them to their abode and fed them wild sesame. Ruan and Liu stayed with the

immortals for six months, only to find on returning home that ten generations had passed. See Li Fang, *Taiping guangji, juan* 61.

26. *Yuxie,* translated here as "herbs of the immortals," is another Daoist allusion to elixirs of immortality, or possibly to food that prevents illness. Chinese poets and writers also used the phrase to describe elegant writing. See Zhang Qiyun, *Zhongwen da cidian,* 21:392.

27. The term she uses here for pen, *tongguan,* comes from the *Shi jing,* where it means a red reed or tube sent by a girl to a man. See Legge, *The Chinese Classics,* 4:69.

28. The ninth day of the ninth lunar month is the holiday when chrysanthemums are at the peak of their bloom and friends and families gather to admire them. The author perhaps has in mind here the poem by Meng Haoran titled "At an Old Friend's," in which the last two lines read: "Just wait until the Double Nine / I'll come again for the chrysanthemums" (translation is from Chang, *Chinese Poetic Writing,* 44).

29. The author alludes here to the fifth stanza in Tao Qian's "Drinking Wine," especially the fifth and sixth lines: "I pick chrysanthemums by the eastern hedge / See the southern mountain, calm and still." For an English translation, see Watson, *The Columbia Book of Chinese Poetry: From Early Times to the Thirteenth Century,* 135. Tao Qian's love of chrysanthemums and his hermetic lifestyle have made chrysanthemums the "flower of the hermit" in China. The author's allusion to Tao's work may again indicate her Daoist interests, in this case, her interest in philosophical Daoism.

30. Jiang Yan was regarded as a writer of genius in the Six Dynasties period. However, the quality of his writing declined as he aged. Legend thus has it that he dreamed one night that the immortal Guo Pu asked him to return the five-colored pen he had earlier lent to Jiang. Once the pen was returned, Jiang could no longer write well. See Xin Yi, *Zhongguo diangu da cidian,* 313–14.

31. *Baifeng* (white phoenix) is a Daoist term describing precious birds seen only in the land of the immortals. The author here refers to the precious works created by her poet friends. See Zhang Qiyun, *Zhongwen da cidian,* 6:416.

32. Source: Chen Shao, *Lichao mingyuan chidu,* 2:38a.

33. Source: Chen Shao, *Lichao mingyuan chidu,* 2:32a. *Lichao mingyuan chidu* here prints Li Duanming's first name as "Maozhao," yet other records, such as *Lidai mingyuan shujian,* would print her first name as "Shuzhao." Since the former contains numerous errors, I rely here on *Lidai mingyuan shujian* (compiled by Wang Xiuqin and Hu Wenkai).

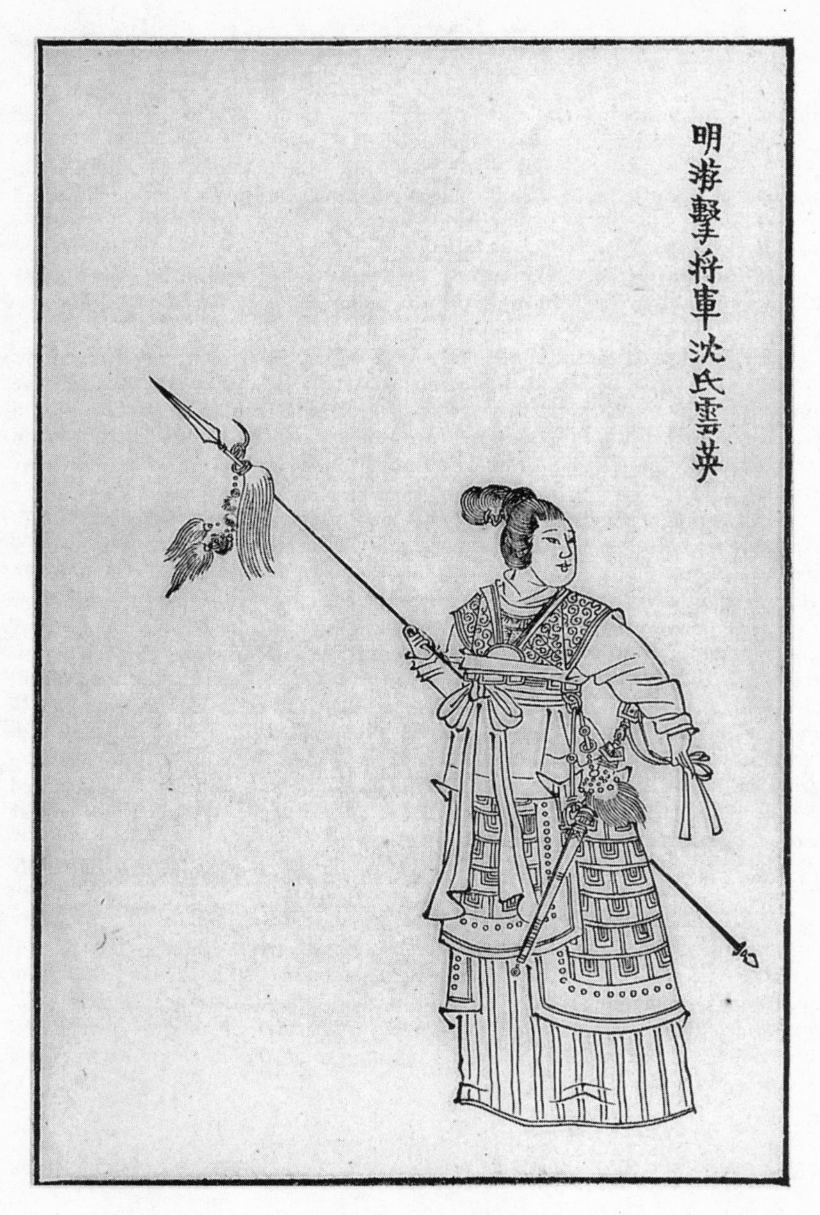

Fig. 12. Portrait of the Ming-loyalist woman fighter Shen Yunying. Like Wang Duanshu, Shen was from the Kuaiji (Shaoxing) area. Wang's own military ambitions never took her to war, but she was an ardent Ming loyalist and is known to have drilled maids and family members in military maneuvers when she was a child. Source: Ren Xiong, *Yu Yue xianxian zhuan* (1856). Reproduced with permission of the Harvard-Yenching Library.

TWELVE

Selected Short Works by Wang Duanshu (1621–after 1701)

Translated by Ellen Widmer

TRANSLATOR'S PREFACE

I find Wang Duanshu's blend of talent and unconventionality intriguing. From the first she manifested unusual ability at writing, and she turned out to be an excellent painter. Her substandard skills at normal female accomplishments like embroidery seem not to have worked against her, and they may have been one reason that she could devote years on end to her scholarly pursuits. In other ways as well she seems to have defied the conventional definition of modesty and submissiveness that one normally associates with women of the Qing.

Wang's chief surviving editorial endeavor, *Mingyuan shiwei* (Classic poetry of famous women; completed 1664, published 1667) is especially impressive because of its vast size and conscientious scholarship. It must also have been slightly iconoclastic, in that it includes the works of singing girls alongside those of more respectable women, albeit in separate chapters. I admire *Mingyuan shiwei* as an accomplishment, but I also value its revelations of Wang's thoughts and standards. This one source in particular, along with Wang's surviving poems, means that she lends herself to biographical inquiry more readily than most women of her day.

Wang is also intriguing because of her wide social network, which included many leading Ming loyalists, male and female, but also non-loyalists like Li Yu (1610–1680). Along with her husband, Ding Shengzhao, she was well known for her hospitality, but she could also be retiring and shy. Other details about her life, such as her tendency to dress extravagantly at parties and her unusual relationship with the concubine who bore her daughter, suggest a complex individual who adroitly negotiated numerous social shoals.

INTRODUCTION

Wang Duanshu was born in 1621 and died over eighty years later, some time after 1701.[1] She was the second daughter of Wang Siren (1575–1646) of Shaoxing, who judged her a better reader than any of his eight sons and was so impressed with her that he sent her out for tutoring with her brothers.[2] Her elder sister, Wang Jingshu, though less strikingly talented, was also a poet.[3] A younger sister, Wang Zhenshu, was literate but was better known for her skill at embroidery.[4] Wang Duanshu appears to have been rather tomboyish as a child, and she enjoyed drilling her mother, sisters, and maids in military formations. At the same time, she was often ill. Her beloved mother, a concubine, once led her on a perilous pilgrimage to Zhoushan Island (off the coast of Ningbo) to avert a smallpox scare.[5]

Wang Duanshu married Ding Shengzhao, to whom she had been betrothed as a child. Her husband's family had ties in both the Beijing and the Shaoxing areas. Throughout her life Wang was scrupulously attentive to filial obligations—to her own father and mother as well as to Ding's parents and relatives. For the most part, she divided her time between Beijing and Shaoxing.

Before the fall of the Ming and perhaps again thereafter, Duanshu lived near Beijing with her husband, but in the years just after 1644, the couple returned to Shaoxing and kept company with a group of Ming loyalists that included Zhang Dai (1597–1684?) and the painter Zeng Yi.[6] During their stay in Shaoxing, they rented a house that had once belonged to the dramatist Xu Wei (1521–1593) and was later the home of the painter Chen Hongshou (1599–1652).[7] After that, Duanshu lived in Hangzhou, where she became acquainted with celebrities from all over.[8]

According to one account, Duanshu was a very sociable and engaging person who did not hesitate to exchange poems with all who came to see her, thus flouting the convention that normally separated women from men.[9] Another account maintains that she would dress to the hilt for guests to the point of resembling the moon goddess; but her feathers, jewels, and other finery masked an underlying nervousness in social situations.[10] Her acquaintances with the writer Li Yu and with such well-known female loyalist-poets as Huang Yuanjie and Wu Shan almost certainly date from her stay in Hangzhou.[11] Wang was on good terms with other celebrated loyalist women as well, including Shang Jinglan from Shaoxing, the wife of Qi Biaojia (1602–1645), and Liu Rushi (1618–1664), the concubine of Qian Qianyi (1582–1664).[12]

Yinhong ji (Writings of the fall), a collection of Wang Duanshu's prose and poetry, was published sometime between 1651 and 1655, probably in Shaoxing.[13] Except for the final *juan* of *Mingyuan shiwei,* which consists of Wang's own writings, it is the only set of her own poems that survives. Its publication was financed by her husband, Zeng Yi, Zhang Dai, and the other members of their poetry group. *Yinhong ji* was well received by the literary establishment.[14] It was said to be different from other writings by women in its emphasis on loyalism rather than love.[15] Despite her loyalist sentiments, Wang was summoned around the same time to become a tutor of women in the Qing court, an assignment she vigorously refused.[16]

Wang Duanshu's next datable publication is her preface to Li Yu's drama *Bimu yu* (Sole mates)[17] of 1661. This short preface is interesting in the connection it makes between Li's work and the dramas of Xu Wei. Duanshu's *Mingyuan shiwei* is a far more substantial endeavor. Containing approximately fifteen hundred poems by over one thousand women, it may have been the largest collection of women's poems of its day. Wang worked with her husband and other family members on this collection, which she began in 1639 and completed in 1664;[18] but she took sole editorial responsibility for it. Like *Yinhong ji, Mingyuan shiwei* was privately financed, again by subscriptions from friends, and it was probably published in Hangzhou.[19] Copies were hard to come by within only a year of its publication, but the collection attracted considerable interest among male and female writers, even after it became difficult to buy.[20] Other datable writings by Wang Duanshu include four letters in the collection *Chidu xinyu guang bian* (Modern letters, enlarged edition), 1668, and a short commentary on another drama, *Qinlou yue* (Moon at Qin Pavilion) by Zhu He (Suchen), which came out sometime between 1669 and 1680.[21]

Wang Duanshu's other writings and anthologies are apparently no longer extant, though their titles survive. These include the edited volumes *Mingyuan wenwei* (Classics of prose by famous women) and *Lidai diwang houfei kao* (Research on imperial princes and concubines through the ages), as well as Wang's own writings, including *Yuying tang ji* (Writings of Yuying tang [Wang Duanshu]), *Shiyu* (Historical stupidities), *Hengxinji* (Writings of a constant heart), *Yilou ji* (Writings of Yi Tower), *Wucai ji* (Writing without talent), and *Liuqie ji* (Works left in a writing chest).[22] Of these, the two anthologies plus *Wucai ji* and *Liuqie ji* are mentioned in the preface to *Mingyuan shiwei,* which means that they were completed by 1667.

In addition to her writing, Wang Duanshu was widely known and praised for her artistic talent. She was accomplished at both painting and calligraphy. One of her landscape screens bears the date 1664.[23] Another work, a painted fan, was listed in a recent auction catalog for Christie's.[24]

Biographies always mention the extraordinary range of Wang's reading, which included classics and history as well as popular fiction. This may help to explain Wang's pronounced interest—unusual in a woman—in prose as well as poetry. Her interest in prose is demonstrated by her edited volume *Mingyuan wenwei,* which was an anthology of prose writings, and the collection *Yinhong ji,* which contains several chapters of prose.

Wang Duanshu's literary and artistic activities in the years between *Mingyuan shiwei*'s publication in 1667 and her death some time after 1701 remain a mystery. With the exception of the one brief comment on *Qinlou yue* and the letters published in 1668, no traces of her work from these more than thirty years survive.

Throughout her career as writer and publisher Wang received considerable encouragement from her husband, Ding Shengzhao. Ding thought of his wife as a literary companion and seemed not to mind her total indifference to housework, though he mentions it in his preface to *Yinhong ji.* Without his strong support, it appears certain that *Yinhong ji* would never have been published. Ding was also instrumental in the publication of *Mingyuan shiwei,* for which he wrote one of the prefaces, another being by Qian Qianyi. In addition, Ding helped to gather at least one *juan* of its materials. This was a collection of poems by singing girls that became *juan* 25.[25] For her part, Wang Duanshu was her husband's mainstay during his several years of severe depression after the fall of the Ming. She used her own jewelry to put up the bride price for a concubine,[26] and her reading and writing constituted one of his chief joys. The concubine, Chen Suxia, provided the couple with a daughter, whom Wang Duanshu adopted. Ding had other children, but as they are not mentioned in Wang's biographies, it may be that she had no children of her own.[27]

Wang's two major surviving works were both under way by the time she was thirty years old. *Yinhong ji* deserves attention for the wide range of genres it encompasses, as well as for its Ming loyalism. *Mingyuan shiwei* is one of the earliest and most ambitious anthologies of women's writings. Not until Yun Zhu's *Guochao guixiu zhengshi ji* of 1831 would another work of comparable scope edited by a woman emerge. Despite the loss of most of Wang Duanshu's writings and paintings in the three hundred years since her death, these two collections establish her as one of the most accomplished women of the Qing.

ORIGINAL TEXTS

Ming-Loyalist Writings[28]

"Lament"[29]

Before 1644 people were prosperous.
I remember the days when my own life was still opulent.
Orioles twittered outside the curtains as the day's shadows lengthened.
I would slowly arise in the women's quarters with traces of last night's
makeup still on my face.

Then soldiers on horseback crossed from Hangzhou,
Books flew in all directions, and hordes of cash were abandoned.
We undid our elegant hairstyles and donned plain garb.
In disarray, our clan elders retreated to the countryside.
The Wuning [Xuzhou] army issued strict orders.
The divisional soldiers would not allow us to sleep in private homes.
With this change, my heart became overwhelmed with grief.
The wind of the river chafed my face, but I dared not cry.
At midnight the river tide roared in like thunder.
I called my child, who could not be roused; the situation was precarious.
We slept by the river bank and water reached our bodies.
Our light clothing was completely drenched.
We heard the military order: we had to march in rows.
Cold dew penetrated our thin bodies, the cock had not yet crowed.
Following one another, we knew not where we would stop.
A horse neighed, reminding me of military music.
Sweat poured down drenching my clothes; my tears were like blood.
Heaven brought us more difficulty: the bridge at the river was out.
How can sick people endure such circumstances?
The heels of my shoes were split open, my skin was cracked.
At Dinghai waves bombarded the shores like thunder.
Clinging to life, we reached this point but could no longer hope.
Beset by thoughts of our parents, our hearts were burning.
We were willing to be stabbed by sharp knives and brave death to return.
As I walked, I was surprised to discover that sunset was upon us.
A dilapidated boat had been abandoned at the Qiang family crossing.
We were robbed of our travel funds, our food was not enough.
The driving wind and rain left us overwhelmed by the road ahead.
Secretly we gloated that our lives had been saved.
But we were shamefaced and embarrassed to have no means of support.
Our walls were overrun by tendriled plants, our doors were half ajar.
My younger sister had become a nun, my old father had died.
From this moment I became estranged from my blood relations.
For the time being we would live east of the pond.
Fortunately we had poems and books to enrich our simple hut.
Being on a remote pathway, we did not strive to accommodate the carts
of famous people.
At dawn, rain from the pear tree washes the dark window.

At sunset the stars in the sky fill in between the broken tiles;
I happen to hear the cry of a swan as it lands out of the blue
And grieve that its pain is just like ours.

"Biography of an Idle Tippler"[30]

The identity of the Idle Tippler shall remain anonymous. Since the dynastic change of 1644 he has been living in the eastern corner of my home district, Kuaiji. Though I complete poems with him day and night, drink wine with him, and call him my best friend, I still am not sure where he comes from. As a person he is addicted to self-respect and enjoys his poverty; he is carefree and brooks no restrictions, therefore he takes "The Idle Tippler" as his style name. He often says of himself: "We have enjoyed the state's favor and held public office. They can cut off my head, but they cannot change my ideas. If I am not dead, it is because I have not yet buried my father properly." So he took his wife and children and moved to the east of the pond. His roof is in a remote location, his walls are crumbling, and his path is grown over. He lives amidst disorderly tombs and desiccated trees. Whenever the wind is harsh or it rains violently, tiles and gravel fly everywhere. Strange birds call out in grief, hungry snakes slither around him. The cold of winter penetrates his bones, and no furniture nestles against his walls. Sometimes cold moonbeams penetrate the windows; sometimes he wraps himself in a worn comforter. People from the village feel sad when they think about him; passersby look at him and start to cry; relatives are embarrassed by him and friends feel compassion, but the Idle Tippler is not concerned. He considers wealth and status as transient things and thinks back to the coldness of people [who liked him only when he was successful]. Daily, he pawns his clothes to buy wine. At night he holds his *qin* [zither] and sings drunkenly. When his clothes run out and he has nothing more to sell, he substitutes tea for wine and goes on singing without stopping.

Nowadays he has the monk Fanlin as his Buddhist friend; Shikui sheng [Zhang Dai] as his friend for discussing history; Echi zi as his wine friend; Shuihe zi, Qinghuai zi, and me as his poetry friends. Whenever we meet, we stay up all night, forgetting to return home. Anyone in or outside the walls of Yue who has a modicum of talent flocks to him. Someone said, "The ancients contend: 'The gentleman should select his friends.' Now the Idle Tippler has friends in abundance. Why is this?" The Idle Tippler says, "Bo Juyi once wrote a biography of the Man Who Chants Poetry While Drunk. Someone once satirized him. The Man responded, 'Few people achieve perfection in their natures. Everyone has some idiosyncrasy.' I am like this myself, in not having achieved perfection. As for running a business and reaching calamity, taking a risk and thus destroying my family, seeking immortality and failing to achieve it, these all bring harm rather than benefit. Fortunately, I do not have such faults but content myself with drinking wine and chanting poetry. If you think this is reckless, so be it. What is the harm in this?" On the other hand, the Idle Tippler is good-natured and sincere. In matters however trifling, he avoids immorality and never says what ought not to be said. He increasingly enjoys entertaining, to the point that his wife and children have insufficient food and clothing, but he still maintains his good spirits. He has many friends and relatives at court, so that it would be easy for him to abandon his principles and [ride the political tide]. If he did so, he could easily become well known. Moreover the Idle Tippler has land in the Beijing area. His houses are comparable in magnificence to those of a prince. For him to have relinquished all of this and brought only a few close relatives and a few shabby books to this dilapidated house and these shabby walls—can one really maintain that this is not a political statement?

Two Biographies[31]

"Guan Shaoning"[32]

Guan Shaoning's courtesy name was Chengzhai; his literary name was Taijie. He was from Dantu, Nan zhili, and was registered in Wujin. He placed third on the palace examination of 1628 and was appointed a compiler. Shortly thereafter he was promoted to Vice Director of Studies [in the Directorate of Education]. He became the Left Adviser of the heir apparent. He also took charge of the Hanlin Academy in the Southern Capital. Then he was promoted to be Vice Supervisor of the Household of the Heir Apparent. He had not yet taken up this position when the events of 1644 occurred. After the Hongguang emperor [of the Southern Ming] took the throne, Guan was selected as Right Vice Minister of the Ministry of Rites. With Minister Gu Xichou he was in charge of all the major ceremonies, and he restored the posthumous names of the Jianwen [1399–1402] and Jingtai [1450–1457] emperors, and also gave posthumous titles to all the officials of the old regime. This period was promptly touted as a renaissance and seemed like a turn for the better. But when the Qing soldiers crossed the Huai River, Shaoning went back home [to Changzhou]. At that time, the order [of the Qing that all males] cut their hair was very strict. A certain *jinshi* from Yangzhou had already surrendered to the Qing and changed his name. He was made an official of Changzhou. He put out a false summons calling for righteous revolt and ordered all the gentry to come to the prefecture for public discussions. If they did not come by a certain time, it would be assumed they had surrendered to the [Qing]. Shaoning believed the order; but on the day [he went to the prefecture], its two corridors were filled with soldiers in ambush, numbering several hundred. Inside were several tens of people whose foreheads had already been shaved. The gentry were bound and their hair was promptly cut. Only Shaoning cursed loudly and did not submit. He was executed outside the prefectural office. The matter reached the ears of the [Prince of Lu], who appointed him Minister of Rites, with the posthumous name of Wenzhong. He was given a state funeral and other rites, and his son inherited his rank.

In his years of living in his hometown, [Guan Shaoning] was upright and deferential. He never treated people arrogantly just because he was rich and famous. On the day of his death, people of all descriptions shed tears. That same Changzhou official was in my husband's examination class and was most highly praised for his integrity. This just goes to show that before the lid is put on the coffin one cannot assume that one really knows another person. What a pity!

"The Beggar of Nanking"[33]

I don't know what the Beggar of Nanking's name was, but he begged in the Southern Capital [Nanjing]. In the fourth month of 1644 we first heard the news of the change of dynasty in the Northern Capital [Beijing]. The beggar inquired around but could not get the true facts. One day he was begging at Peach Leaf Ford. He met a scholar and tugged at his clothes, asking the news, "Do you happen to know what happened in the Northern Capital?" The scholar said, "Yes. It is bad news. The sad proclamation has already arrived. The Chongzhen emperor has hanged himself." When the beggar heard this he sighed repeatedly, then went to buy a beaker of wine in the market. The usual price was two *fen*. The beggar dug in his pocket and only had seven *li* [one *li* = one-tenth of a *fen*]. He said, "If you are willing to give me the whole beaker for free, you will have done a good deed. If you're unwilling, then just give me my money's worth." The merchant generously gave him the whole amount. The beggar drank it all in one swig. He then walked around to the river. The merchant thought he was drunk and suspected nothing. The beggar then let out a loud wail and said, "The Chongzhen emperor is really dead." He beat his breast a number of times, faced north, and kowtowed repeatedly, then he stepped into the river and died. The merchant reported this to the local official, who conducted a funeral ceremony for him and buried him. Someone said [the beggar] puts all the people who served two dynasties to shame. I do not know who this person was.

"Postface to the Biographies"

Wang Duanshu comments: The six biographies from Guan [Shaoning] to the Beggar of Nanjing were written off and on in 1648 and 1649. Our finances were in ruins following the collapse of the Ming. We were temporarily dwelling at Plum Mountain, but I had no inclination to take up household duties. I managed to find pen and ink and to set down my depressed thoughts. I am ashamed to say these pieces are not polished; even so, I can be criticized for showing off my talent before experts. But the six biographies are all based on what I myself saw and heard and contain no exaggeration, even though they are coarsely written and do not give every detail. As for whether these people had worthy lives or not, they naturally have epitaphs and family biographies, and there is no need for me to go into this further. My husband's fellow poetry society member Zhang Dai planned to write a book entitled *Shigui shu* [Stone chest writings], and he wanted to include these six biographies. He came and asked for them many times. I believed they were too badly written and did not want to part with them, so I refused him very vehemently. But the more I refused, the more he asked. So I finally copied them and gave them to him. Now they are recorded in his *Shigui shu.*[34] He did not change a word. How embarrassing that he respects me so! I record this to document that these pieces were merely written to express my own humble thoughts.

Writings on or to Women: Poems[35]

"On Reading a Poem by Huang Yuanjie of Jiaxing"[36]

Bamboo flowers come to life in the shadings of your ink.
Elegant paper preserves your great composition.
The bold strokes of your moon make me think of Huang Tingjian.
Your brush work on the unfurling clouds reminds me of Wang Xizhi.
A clap of sound reaches me amidst the loneliness of fall waters.
The empty echo is picked up by the mist far away.

Your inborn nature is highly unusual.
Its hidden qualities find expression on the page.

"Following Wu Yanzi (Wu Shan)'s Rhyme"[37]

You draw distant mountains like slender eyebrows, and you paint
a green lake.
Yuan Haowen's poem enters your landscape of fishermen.
Recently I have heard that when you come up with a simple rhyme
scheme, many people respond.
I wonder what will happen with your more difficult compositions.
No matter how you bedeck yourself, you are always elegant.
As long as I have your poems and other writings, I will never be lonely.
How could such an immortal have descended to earth?
Like Sima Xiangru, you express your poetic feelings to the wine jar.

Writings to Women: Letters

"To Madame Feng"[38]

After illness my energy seems insufficient. I close my books, my inkstand is idle; dejectedly, I store my writing table. Each day ten and more people come, wanting writings from me. I force myself to get up to accommodate them, but I still cannot do many. If I overdo, I get a headache. Occasionally I chant poems, but I do not finish them easily. Sometimes I cogitate about them all night long. The next day I look in the mirror and see I've gained a few more white hairs. I have painted a figure of a female character from a drama on the fan you sent, for your inspection.

"Presented to Madame Yun"[39]

The other day I received your draft collection *Haozhan shi* [Artemisia anvil poems] from my husband and read through it. Then I sang its praises to him. The splendor of the words is as lush as the embroidered robes of a mountain dragon. The marvelous meaning of the poems is as profound as an immortal island crane's singing. The words remind me of beautiful garments and their sounds are like the most subtle music. Your work is certainly outstanding among today's poems and will stand the test of time. I wonder: how is it that we have never before exchanged poems? The first collection of my [*Mingyuan*] *Shiwei* has already been published, but I hope you will be good enough to let me publish your works in a new supplemental volume of poetry.

Selected Writings from Mingyuan Shiwei[40]

"Organizing Principles" for *Mingyuan Shiwei*

1. Editing follows certain conventions. Gentlemen past and present have edited many writings by women. I have always wanted to be an editor, but I was afraid that for a woman to critique the works of men would not be elegant. Wouldn't it be better for a woman to point out what is correct in women's poems? Fang Zhongxian of Tongxian's *Gonggui shishi* [A history of poems of palace women], Ji [Xian] of Bangshang's *Guixiu chuji* [First collection of writings by women], and Shen [Yixiu] of Songling's *Yiren si* [Thoughts of women] are my predecessors. After these, not many such collections are seen. I am emboldened to wield my pen in order to demonstrate the wealth of material that there is.

2. Women's poems from Han . . . to Song were widely collected and broadly gathered. Old and new, ancient and modern—the best of these have been completely culled. For some time there have been numerous editions, and set critical views about them have developed, so that there is no need to evaluate them further.

3. There is no complete, printed edition of the poetry of contemporary palace ladies. This includes both the Ming and the current dynasty. Social customs are gradually improving, but gems of literature remain uncollected, and there is still no literary judgment on them. So I take the occasion to gather these up in a comprehensive way. This should be viewed as the sequel to Fang Zhongnian's *Gonggui shishi* [A history of poems by palace women].

4. This project began in the tenth month [winter] of 1639 and continued through the ninth month [fall] of 1664—in all, twenty-six years. It is the product of one person's selections, drawn from a myriad of materials, all arranged systematically, with evaluations. It is neither artificial nor excessive; it might be called an overview.

5. Every entry has my commentary; whether I comment on the person or the poems, I focus on what ought to be. With people, I have tried to give details about their lives and families, but when I could not do so completely, I left a blank to be investigated later.

6. Poems are preserved around people. For example, if a person has her

own collection, then I have selected the best poems from it. If only one poem or half a poem of an individual's work survives, even if it is defective, I have still recorded it in order to preserve something of that individual.

7. If a poem was very high minded or very old, I preserved it. If it was very mysterious or showy, I preserved it. If it was very beautiful but vulgar, or wanton but absurd, I also preserved it. Is this going too far? I say not. When Confucius edited the classic of poetry he did not completely omit the poems of Zheng and Wei. Instead he limited himself to one poem from each. You can see this for yourselves.

8. This collection is drawn from anthologies edited by famous men, as well as compendia and collections of great scholars. Other sources, like novels and joke books, were not recorded here but will go into this work's "catch-all" chapter.

9. Every edited volume supplies criticism that reflects the editor's readings. My criticism leaves nothing out. I have consulted the criticisms of other anthologies, making use of whatever in them suits the purposes of this volume.

10. The poems I have edited consist mostly of the original words. In cases where I have made small changes, I have always followed the regulations respectfully. When "fish-eyes" were confused with "night-shining pearls," the author of "fish-eyes" would have felt very sorry, so in such cases I decided to restore the original meaning.

11. This anthology's poems, from the palace chapter to the miscellaneous chapter, comprise thirty-four chapters *[juan]*. There are also two chapters of *ci,* two of *sanqu,* one of miscellaneous writings, and one of the names of painters—in all, forty chapters. This is what is known as water running its course and mountains reaching completion. That is to say, the ancients always enjoyed it when things came to an end and something new appeared. Poems and essays are similar, in that when one has finished with correctness, along comes elegance to succeed it. This is why we have poems first, then *ci,* then *sanqu,* then songs collected from the streets and folksongs in a chapter on miscellaneous writings. By including them, I have provided readers with a complete view.

12. To bring order into something is necessarily to pick firsts and lasts. I have spent years completing this collection and have gone through hardships in collecting and editing it. This means that the works I obtained first were printed first and the ones that came in later were given to the printer later, so the sequence is untidy. It is not that I deliberately made it chaotic.

13. Many women have superior literary talent. My limitations as an editor mean that I have missed many gems. This is a pity. If there are other outstanding writings, please mail them to the Linyun Ge Bookshop of Hangzhou, so that we can add them later on.

14. I had several old poems of my own, which my husband edited into a volume. These appear at the end in a separate chapter called the "Houji." I have only limited insight and feel especially embarrassed about them.

Preface to "Omitted Poems"[41]

My *Mingyuan shiwei* includes a chapter on omitted poems. What is the reason? It is that I cannot bear to think that there are famous women writers who will not otherwise be recorded. Someone may ask, "You know they can write and you know their names, why not record their poems?" I answer, "Their works are buried without a trace, so I could not obtain them. Thus I only transmitted their names. Women live deep within the inner chamber and occupy themselves exclusively with womanly duties and household management. They're not allowed to discuss family matters on the outside. They may have two or three poems secretly tucked away in their writing boxes, but how can an outsider gain access to them and see their profundity? Additionally, poems get lost in war, they are burned by censors, they are suppressed by old-fashioned fathers and brothers, they are destroyed by unfilial sons and grandsons—too many obstacles for me to enumerate them all. In the end, the pleasant picture of [women writing in the women's quarters] can turn into a desolate scene and provoke resentment. This is the reason my chapter 'Omitted Poems' seeks to fill in what is missing."

Preface to "Painting Chapter"[42]

Duanshu comments: I had all but finished the *Shiwei,* when I realized I regretted not transmitting the names of painters. I felt this to be a defect, so I took what other books had recorded, from Xu Jingfen on down. I present names only and call this the "Painting Chapter." I am a woman. I have not gathered materials widely, and there are surely many omissions. I hope that famous lords and rich officials and others in the know will not hesitate to make suggestions, so that I may go on adding to the list in subsequent printings and together we can finish this great enterprise.

NOTES

1. Wang Youding's biography of Wang Duanshu, a preface to *Mingyuan shiwei,* states that she was born in this year. On the length of her life, see Yu Jianhua, *Zhongguo meishujia renming cidian,* 121. See also Zhong Huiling, "Qingdai nü shiren yanjiu," 279–95. For a study of Wang's literary standards, see Lin Meiyi, "Wang Duanshu shilun zhi pingxi—jian lun qi xuan shi biaozhun." Wang also comes up for comment in Kang-i Sun Chang's "Ming and Qing Anthologies of Women's Poetry and Their Selection Strategies." Other translations of her work, with biographical data, appear in Chang and Saussy, *Women Writers of Traditional China: An Anthology of Poetry and Criticism,* 363–66, 691–94.

2. Wang Youding biography. See also Deng Hanyi, *Shiguan chuji,* preface, 12: 37a.

3. Hu Wenkai, *Lidai funü zhuzuo kao,* 255.

4. Wang Duanshu, *Mingyuan shiwei,* 17:3a–b.

5. Wang Youding biography.

6. Hu Wenkai (*Lidai funü zhuzuo kao,* 249) notes that she lived at some unspecified time in Beijing. The poem entitled "Lament" and the "Biography of an Idle Tippler," translated here, invoke the family's flight south after the fall of the Ming. See these and the preface to *Yinhong ji* for evidence of the couple's connection to Zhang Dai. Ding Shengzhao, Zhang Dai, and a number of other loyalists, including Zeng Yi (on whom see Yu Jianhua, *Zhongguo meishujia renming cidian,* 1079) were members of a society (*Qiu she*—Autumn society) that sponsored the publication of *Yinhong ji.*

7. See Meng Chengshun's biography of Wang Duanshu, which appears after Wang Youding's at the beginning of *Mingyuan shiwei.*

8. Deng Hanyi, *Shiguan chuji* 12:37a.

9. Deng Hanyi, *Shiguan chuji* 12:37a.

10. See the biography of Ding Shengzhao's concubine Chen Suxia at the beginning of *Mingyuan shiwei.*

11. Li Yu is known to have lived in Hangzhou during the early 1650s. See Hanan, *The Invention of Li Yu,* 12. Huang Yuanjie, originally from Jiaxing, attended a party given by Wang Ruqian in Hangzhou. See Hanan, *The Invention of Li Yu,* 217. Wu Shan, from Dangtu, in modern Anhui province, spent time at West Lake (on which see Wang's poem to Wu to this effect in *Yinhong ji,* "Seven-Word Regulated Verse," 1).

12. Qian Qianyi, on behalf of Liu Rushi, summoned Wang to write a poem for an elderly aunt. See Wang Duanshu, *Mingyuan shiwei* 42:2a. And during Huang Yuanjie's celebrated visit to Shang Jinglan in Shaoxing, Wang Duanshu came to visit. See Wang Duanshu, *Mingyuan shiwei* 9:3a–b.

13. The last date mentioned in the collection is 1651. An edition of Zou Siyi's *Shiyuan ba mingjia ji,* with preface dated 1655, refers to this collection. The translation of the title is based on the biography of Wang by Meng Chengshun. It establishes a link between the color red, autumn, and Wang's doleful thoughts brought on by the fall of the Ming.

14. Deng Hanyi, *Shiguan chuji.*

15. See Wu Guofu's preface to *Yinhong ji.*

16. Yu Jianhua, *Zhongguo meishujia renming cidian,* 121. The summons took place at an unspecified time during the Shunzhi reign (1644–1661).

17. This translation, following Hanan, *The Invention of Li Yu,* puns in English on the Chinese phrase *bimu* (lit., paired eyes), which is used to refer to flatfish such as flounder and sole. Devoted spouses are likened to the eyes of the flatfish, drawn inexorably together for the duration of life.

18. "Fanli," *Mingyuan shiwei.*

19. See Wang's note in the prefatory materials to *Mingyuan shiwei,* which alludes to funding sources. See also the second-to-last passage in the "Fanli," translated here, which asks readers to submit future entries to a Hangzhou bookstore.

20. Several letters in section 24 of the enlarged or third edition of *Chidu xinyu* (preface 1668) discuss *Mingyuan shiwei.* This collection was edited by Wang Qi and Xu Shijun. The third edition is held in the Nanjing Library. On *Mingyuan shiwei* being hard to come by, see a letter by Zhu Kuangding, 3:24:9a–b.

21. The year 1669 is the date when the episode described in the play ended, on which see Xu Fuming, *Yuan Ming Qing xiqu tansuo,* 213. The drama has marginal notes by Li Yu, who died in 1680. I am indebted to David Rolston for drawing this source to my attention.

22. Hu Wenkai, *Lidai funü zhuzuo kao,* 248.

23. Yu Jianhua, *Zhongguo meishujia renming cidian,* 121.

24. Weidner, *Views from Jade Terrace: Chinese Women Artists, 1300–1912,* 184.

25. See Wang's introduction to this section.

26. See the biography of the concubine Chen Suxia in the prefatory materials to *Mingyuan shiwei;* also Wang's note on Chen in *Mingyuan shiwei,* 17:9a.

27. Wang's relationship with Chen's daughter is described in the biography of Chen in the prefatory materials to *Mingyuan shiwei.* See also Wang's note on Chen in *Mingyuan shiwei* 17:9a. Ding Junwang is identified as Wang's daughter in *juan* 17:5b–6a of *Mingyuan shiwei,* but the entry on Chen makes it clear that Chen was her natural mother. An entry in the character description section, "Xingzhuang," in *Yinhong ji* about a female ancestor of Wang Duanshu's husband, mentions that Ding had three daughters. Yet nowhere is it suggested that any of these children were Wang's own.

28. The Ming-Qing transition is one of the prominent themes in Wang's writings, especially in *Yinhong ji.* The poem "Lament" may reflect Wang's own experiences, or it may voice a more generalized retrospective. The prose sketches are all about loyalists Wang knew of personally.

29. Source: Wang Duanshu, "Ku'nan," in "Songs," *Yinhong ji,* 3:2a–3a.

30. Source: Wang Duanshu, "Jiupi sanren zhuan," in "Biographies," *Yinhong ji,* 20:9a–11b. From the poet's familiarity with the subject and from evidence elsewhere in *Yinhong ji,* it is clear that this is a biography of her husband.

31. These two biographies are from a set of six in the biography chapter of *Yinhong ji;* see Wang's postface included here.

32. Source: Wang Duanshu, "Guan wenzhong gong Shaoning zhuan," in "Biographies," *Yinhong ji,* 20:1a–2a.

33. Source: Wang Duanshu, "Jinling qigai zhuan," in "Biographies," *Yinhong ji,* 20:8a–9b.

34. For example, see Zhang Dai, *Shigui houji,* 315, for the biography of the Beggar of Nanjing.

35. To an extent, Wang Duanshu's writings about women are also writings about the Ming. The poems to Huang Yuanjie and Wu Shan are indirectly imbued with loyalist feeling, as Huang and Wu were fellow female loyalists; but they also chronicle real relationships between good friends.

36. Source: Wang Duanshu, "Du Yuanhu Huang Yuanjjie shi," in "Five-Word Regulated Verse," *Yinhong ji,* 8:12b. A slightly different translation appears in Chang and Saussy, *Women Writers of Traditional China,* 364.

37. Source: Wang Duanshu, "Ci Wu Yanzi yun," in "Seven-Word Regulated Verse," *Yinhong ji,* 7:2a–b.

38. Source: Wang Duanshu, "Jian Feng furen," in *Chidu xinyu,* ed. Wang Qi and Xu Shijun, 3:24:9b. The identity of Madame Feng is unknown.

39. Source: Wang Duanshu, "Yu Yun furen," in *Chidu xinyu,* ed. Wang Qi and Xu Shijun, 3:24:11a. According to the editorial note, Madame Yun is the wife of the painter Yun Shouping (1633–1690). This makes her an ancestress of the nineteenth-century female anthologist Yun Zhu.

40. The philosophy behind the collection *Mingyuan shiwei* is conveyed in the "Fanli," or "Organizing Principles," as well as in the prefaces to various chapters. Chapter 32, entitled "Yiji," or "Omitted Poems," consists of only the names of writers who have left no works behind. Wang's statement on why this chapter is necessary establishes the strength of her commitment to preservation generally and her sense of the reasons women's writings often do not survive. Finally, the preface to chapter 40 on painters illustrates her interest in painting in addition to writing and hints at the difficulties of being a woman editor.

41. Source: Wang Duanshu, "Yiji," in *Mingyuan shiwei,* 32.

42. Source: Wang Duanshu, "Huiji," in *Mingyuan shiwei,* 40.

Fig. 13. The most dramatic moment in the story of Liansuo. Military man Wang has just shot the monstrous underworld clerk with an arrow; the ghost Liansuo stands half hidden in the doorway, shielding herself with her sleeve; her lover, Yang, holds his wrist in pain, his dagger and the rock that dashed it from his hand on the ground before him. The wispy clouds suggest that the scene is taking place in a dream. The poem inscribed on the picture reads: "Weeping poplars in barren grassland, / dark is the night sky. / She chants her poem so sadly, / no trace of moonlight. / Waking from an underworld dream / ten years long— / Why must she wait for real incense / to revive her soul?" ("Real incense" refers to a legendary incense *[fanhun xiang]* said to evoke visions of dead souls and also to a magic herb said to bring the dead back to life.) Source: 1981 facsimile reprint of Pu Songling, *Xiangzhu Liaozhai zhiyi tuyong* (1887).

THIRTEEN

Two Ghost Stories from *Liaozhai's Records of the Strange* by Pu Songling (1640–1715)

Translated by Judith T. Zeitlin

TRANSLATOR'S PREFACE

Pu Songling's (1640–1715) masterpiece, *Liaozhai's Records of the Strange (Liaozhai zhiyi)* consists of nearly five hundred tales and anecdotes written in literary Chinese. Unfortunately, there is as yet no complete translation of this marvelous work in English. I have chosen to translate the tales below for this volume because they so wonderfully realize cultural fantasies about gender and sexuality in seventeenth-century China. The difficulty one faces in translating Pu Songling into English is how to capture his concise, chiseled cadences without making his prose sound like Hemingway, since for the English reader short, abrupt sentences connote a muscular, modern style rather than classical elegance. A related problem is that literary Chinese routinely omits transitions and other sorts of information that the English reader requires to make sense of a narrative. In my translations, I prefer to incorporate any necessary fillers directly rather than setting them off with brackets and disturbing the flow. I have always liked the Reverend Herbert Giles's translations of Pu Songling's tales because to my ear the wordy, old-fashioned ring of Giles's Edwardian English so nicely evokes the faintly archaic flavor of Pu's prose. The same Edwardian sensibilities coupled with his missionary background, however, compelled Giles to ignore many of the most interesting stories in the collection and to expurgate or take terrible liberties with many of the ones he did include. Giles dedicated his volume to his six grandchildren; the two bawdy and somewhat disturbing tales I translate here are precisely the sort that Giles found most unsuitable and left out.[1]

INTRODUCTION

Scholars now generally agree that Pu Songling composed his collection of tales over a period of about thirty years, between roughly 1670 and 1700.[2] The son of a merchant of modest means with scholarly leanings, Pu Songling's career got off to a brilliant start when he passed the first set of civil examinations at the precocious age of eighteen and earned a local literary reputation. Thereafter, like so many aspiring scholars of the period, he floundered badly, repeatedly failing to pass the higher examinations, which would have qualified him for an official post. In 1679, when his fortunes reached their nadir, he penned the preface to *Liaozhai;* its dark mood fully reflects the frustration and bitterness of this period in his life.[3] Things improved later that year after he took up the post of resident tutor and literary factotum in the Bi household, a local gentry family with whom he enjoyed cordial relations. The bulk of his stories, which combine sharp social critique with fantasy and wish-fulfillment, were most probably composed during the thirty years he spent there in relative stability and obscurity. Although the manuscript of *Liaozhai* circulated among friends, family, and others in the district, it was not published until 1766, more than half a century after Pu's death.[4] The book was an immediate success, inspiring any number of imitations and adaptations into other forms and becoming one of the most famous works in Chinese literature.

With the exception of a single year in Jiangnan (1670–1671), Pu Songling spent his entire life in Zichuan, a county near Jinan, the provincial capital of Shandong.[5] *Liaozhai* is often justly praised for its pronounced regional flavor, and indeed the majority of the stories in the collection are set in Pu Songling's native northeast.[6] The two tales I translate here are somewhat atypical in being set in the south, particularly "Ingenia," the second of the two, which transpires in the exotic locale of Hainan Island, at the southernmost border of the Qing empire.

In terms of theme, however, both tales are quite typical of the romantic orientation of many *Liaozhai* stories, particularly those from the earlier phase of the collection's composition.[7] Erotic liaisons between elite men and supernatural women (fox spirits, goddesses, immortals, and especially ghosts) are a staple in Chinese tales of the strange; accounts of such relationships appear from the beginning of this literary tradition, which can be traced back to the fourth century C.E., and continued up through the twentieth century.[8] The subject remains an abiding interest of Chinese folklore and popular culture, particularly Hong Kong cinema. But it is also important to recognize the particular seventeenth-century spin that Pu Songling put on such tales.

Pu Songling was heir to the rich late-Ming cult of *qing,* which glorified individual love and passion as a cardinal value. Throughout much of his work we can detect the strong influence of *The Peony Pavilion (Mudanting)* (1598), Tang Xianzu's famous southern drama about a woman who dies from unfulfilled love, returns as a ghost to consummate her passion with her human lover, and is finally resurrected through it and happily married. Like Tang Xianzu, who borrowed the scholar-ghost romance to situate *qing* on the borders of life and death in his play, so too in the tales translated here Pu Songling reshapes the traditional ghost story to emphasize the redemptive power of love and the cosmic generativity of male sexuality.[9]

One of Pu Songling's innovations was to incorporate the conventional happy ending of the drama into the structure of the tale. Before him, accounts of sexual relations between a man and a supernatural woman usually concluded with the separation of the lovers and the reinstatement of the boundaries that had been transgressed. In *Liaozhai,* as Wai-yee Li has pointed out, the strange is instead "domesticated."[10] As we see in the tales translated here, liaisons between man and ghost or man and fox are frequently allowed to become permanent: the supernatural woman may be incorporated into the human protagonist's household as a legitimate wife, and she may even be enlisted to fulfill the social mission of the family by reproducing the patriline.

ORIGINAL TEXTS

"*Liansuo*"[11]

There was a man named Yang Yuwei who moved his residence to the banks of the Si River.[12] His study looked onto a vast expanse of wasteland, and outside his window were many ancient graves. At night he could hear the wind whistling in the white poplar trees—the sound like stormy waves. Sitting up past midnight, candle in hand, he was overcome with desolation. Suddenly outside his window a voice chanted two lines of verse:

> In darkest night, a dismal wind
> blows queerly backward.
> Flitting fireflies tickle the grass,
> then stick to my skirt.[13]

The lines were repeated over and over; to his ear, the mournful voice sounded faint and delicate like a girl's. He wondered about this. The next day when he looked outside the window, there was no trace of footprints; only a purple ribbon had been left behind in the brambles. This he picked up and took home, placing it on the windowsill. Around the second watch of the night, the chanting came again, as it had the previous night. Yang moved a stool over and climbed upon it to take a look, but all at once the chanting ceased. He realized it had to be a ghost, but his heart went out to her. The next night, he lay in wait on top of the wall. The first watch was nearly over when a girl came daintily through the grass, grasping a small tree for support, and chanting mournfully with her head bent. Yang coughed softly. The girl instantly plunged back into the weeds and disappeared.

From then on Yang waited for her at the foot of the wall. When he heard her finish chanting, from the other side of the wall he recited a couplet of his own to continue the poem:

> What mortal glimpses this hidden desire
> and inner sadness?
> Kingfisher sleeves are thin against the cold
> at moonrise.

For a long time there was silence, and so Yang went back into his room. Just as he sat down, he suddenly saw a beautiful girl come in. She adjusted her garments to show her respect and spoke: "Sir, you are undoubtedly a literary man of taste and refinement. It's just that I'm filled with so many fears and apprehensions." Yang was delighted and tugged at her sleeve. Slender and chilled, she shrank back as though she could not bear the weight of her clothes.

"Where is your home? Have you been sojourning here long?" he asked.

"I'm from the northwestern province of Gansu," she replied, "but I followed my father and took up residence here. At thirteen, before my time, I died of a sudden illness.[14] That was already over twenty years ago. In the desolate wastes of the underworld I've been as lonely as a wild duck in the marshes. The lines I've been chanting I composed myself to express my hidden anguish. I've thought long and hard, but couldn't come up with another couplet. Now you've kindly continued the poem for me; joy welled up in me, even in the underworld."

Yang wanted to enjoy the pleasures of love with her. Frowning, she said: "These moldering bones from the grave are no match for the living. A liaison with a ghost only hastens a man's death; I could not bear to harm a gentleman like you." Yang then desisted, but he playfully put his hand inside her bodice; the tips of her breasts were tender as newly shelled nutmeats; clearly she was a virgin. He also tried to inspect the twin hooks of her tiny slippers beneath her skirt. The girl lowered her head and giggled: "You lunatic! What a bother you are!" As he was toying with her slippers, he noticed that one of her silver brocade stockings was tied with a strand of multicolored string; he took another look and saw that the other was fastened with a purple ribbon.

"Why aren't there ribbons on both of them?" he asked.

"Last night as I was fleeing you in fear, I must have lost it somewhere."

"I will replace it for you." And he went over to the window to get the ribbon and handed it to her. Surprised, she asked where he had found it, and he told her the whole story. She removed the string and fastened her shoe with the ribbon.

After that, she began flipping through the books on his desk. All at once, she caught sight of "Ballad of Lianchang Palace."[15] Sighing passionately, she said: "When I was alive this was my favorite poem. Seeing this now, I feel it was almost a dream!"[16] He began to discuss literature with her and found her clever and charming. Trimming the lamp at the west window, he felt as though he had found a dear friend. From then on, every night he had only to hear the strains of her chanting and before long she would appear. Every time she would caution him: "You must keep my existence a secret and tell no one. From my youth, I have been timid and fearful. I'm afraid some dreadful stranger might make trouble." Yang promised to do as she asked. They were as happy together as fish are in water. And though they never consummated the relationship, their intimacy surpassed that of the most devoted husband and wife.

The girl would often copy texts for Yang by the light of the lamp. Her characters were well-formed and bewitching. She also selected one hundred palace-style poems, which she copied and chanted for him. She had Yang set up a chessboard and purchase a *pipa* mandolin. Every evening she instructed Yang in the game of chess, or else she plucked the strings of the mandolin. When she played "Raindrops on the Plantain Window," the tune stabbed one's heart to the quick. Yang couldn't bear to hear it to the end, so she changed to "Orioles Warbling in the Morning Garden," and at once, a sense of well-being and ease flooded his breast. Trimming the lamp and amusing themselves, they were so happy they would forget the coming of daybreak. But as soon as she noticed the glimmering of dawn at the window she would hurry away.

One day, a certain Mr. Xue came to pay a visit and found Yang asleep during the day. He looked around the room and noticed the mandolin and the chessboard, which he knew Yang had no expertise in. He then flipped through Yang's books and came across the palace-style verse. He noticed the calligraphy was fine and pretty, which aroused his suspicions even more. When Yang awoke, Xue asked where the gaming board and musical instrument had come from. Yang replied that he wanted to study these things. Xue then asked him about the volume of poems, and he made the excuse that he had borrowed it from a friend. Xue turned it over and over, inspecting it carefully. He saw that on the very last page was a column of tiny characters that read: "Written by Liansuo on such and such a day in such and such a month." He laughed. "This is a girl's personal name. Why are you going to such lengths to deceive me?" Yang was in a very difficult spot and couldn't think what to say. Xue questioned him with increasing intensity, but Yang could make no reply. Xue tucked the volume of poems under his arm, and Yang, feeling under even more pressure, blurted out the truth. Xue begged for a single glimpse of her. Yang then told him about the girl's instructions to keep her existence secret, and Xue's desire to see her became even more ardent. Yang had no way out but to agree.

That night, when the girl arrived, Yang broached the subject with her on Xue's behalf. The girl grew angry and cried: "What did I tell you? And now you've gone and blabbed about me to someone else!" Yang explained himself by describing what had really happened, but the girl said: "My destiny with you is over!" Yang tried to comfort her and smooth things over in every possible way, but in the end she was still displeased and got up to leave, saying: "For the time being I'll just avoid him." The next morning when Xue came, Yang conveyed the message that seeing her would be impossible. Suspecting he was making up excuses, Xue arrived that evening with two school friends and refused to leave. They deliberately kicked up a ruckus and kept making a racket all night long, which annoyed him greatly, but there was nothing he could do. After several nights of this, having seen not a glimmer, the group gradually decided to leave, and as they did so, little by little the hubbub ceased. Suddenly the sound of chanting became audible. As they listened, the voice was so sad and delicate it took their breath away. Xue was just straining his ears in total concentration when a military man named Wang picked up a large stone and threw it, shouting: "Putting on airs and refusing to see visitors! What kind of poetry is this, moaning and wailing and making people feel unbearably depressed!" The chanting abruptly ceased. The rest of the group was extremely angry. Yang's rage and indignation were apparent on his face and in his words. The next day they finally left for good.

Yang slept alone in his empty study, hoping the girl would come back, but there was no trace of her. Two days later, she suddenly arrived in tears:

"Those wicked strangers you brought almost frightened me out of my wits!" Yang apologized over and over without stopping. The girl stormed out, saying, "I told you our destiny together was finished. From now on we will go our separate ways." He tried to hold her back, but she had already vanished.

After that, for more than a month she did not return again. Yang longed for her till his flesh was wasted and his bones protruded, but there was no way he could pursue her and bring her back. One night, he was in the midst of drinking alone, when the girl suddenly pushed open the curtains and came in. Yang was overjoyed. "Have you forgiven me?" he asked. With tears streaming down, the girl was unable to utter a single word. He urgently asked her what was the matter. She was about to speak, then checked herself: "I left in a huff and now I've come to seek your help in a crisis. It's hard not to feel ashamed." Yang repeatedly begged her to tell him.

"I don't know where this ogre of a clerk came from, but now he is trying to force me to become his concubine. As the descendant of a good family, how could I stoop so low as to marry a ghost of a clerk in the underworld? But how can I resist him with this weak frame of mine? If you still have regard for the love allotted to us, you mustn't leave me to deal with this alone."

Yang flew into a rage so hot he vowed to fight to the death. But then he worried that men and ghosts walk different paths and he would be powerless. However the girl told him: "Tonight sleep early and I'll simply intercept you in a dream." After that they once again sat lost in conversation till dawn. As the girl was about to leave, she warned him not to take a nap that day to prepare for his nocturnal assignation. Yang promised to do as she asked. So in the late afternoon he drank a little wine and took advantage of his wooziness to climb into bed, where he lay fully dressed. Suddenly he saw the girl, who handed him a dagger and led him away by the hand. They came into a compound and had just closed the door and were talking when they heard someone throw a stone at the door. Startled, the girl cried out: "My enemy is here! "

Yang opened the door and charged forth. He saw a man clad in a red hat and a black robe, with curly hair around an upturned snout. Yang roared at him in rage. The clerk's blazing eyes were full of enmity, and he shouted vicious insults. In a fury, Yang flew at him. The clerk grabbed rocks and pelted him with them like rain. A rock struck Yang's wrist and he could no longer hold onto his dagger. Just at this most dangerous moment, he caught sight of a man in the distance hunting with a quiver of arrows at his waist.

When he got a better look, it turned out to be the military man Wang [who had earlier thrown the stone at Liansuo]. He shouted loudly for help. Stretching his bowstring, Wang raced over and shot the clerk in the thigh. The next arrow struck him dead.

Overjoyed, Yang thanked him gratefully. Wang asked him to explain, and Yang told him everything. For his part, Wang was glad that this could atone for his former misdeed. They then went together into the girl's chamber. Trembling and recoiling in fear and shyness, the girl stood her distance and did not utter a word. On the table lay a small dagger. It was only a little over a foot long, but it was decorated with gold and jade and flashed with a mirror's gleam when taken out of its scabbard. Wang sighed in praise and could not put it down. He chatted a bit with Yang, but seeing how pitiful the girl was in her fright and shame, he left and went upon his way.

Yang also went home. He climbed over the wall and fell, whereupon he awakened to hear the village roosters already crowing lustily. But his wrist still ached terribly. When he examined it in the morning light, the flesh was red and swollen. At midday, Wang arrived and mentioned the extraordinary dream he had had the night before. "You didn't dream about shooting any arrows, did you?" asked Yang. Wang was amazed at his prescience. Yang showed his hand to Wang and explained the reason for it. Wang recalled the girl's beauty in the dream and regretted he could not see her for real. He rejoiced that he had done a good deed for the girl and requested permission to see her again.

That night, the girl came to express her thanks. Yang chalked up the credit to Wang and then communicated Wang's sincere wishes to see her. "I could never forget my savior's assistance. But he is too warrior-like, and truly I fear him." She went on: "He loved my dagger, which was actually purchased by my father for a hundred taels when he was on a mission to Canton. I loved it, and so it became mine. I had it inlaid with gold threads and encrusted it with pearls. My father pitied me for dying young and buried the dagger with me. Now I am willing to surrender what I love to present it as a gift to your friend. Seeing the dagger will be like seeing me." The next day Yang conveyed this message. Wang was thrilled. That night, the girl indeed brought the dagger. "Warn him to treasure it," she said, "for this is not a Chinese object." From then on, she came and went as before.

Several months later when they were sitting by the lamp, she suddenly smiled at Yang as though she had something to tell him, but she blushed and broke off several times. He took her in his arms and asked her what it was. "Having been favored so long with your love, I've absorbed the breath *(qi)* of the living. Dining daily on cooked food, these bare bones of mine have suddenly conceived the intention to live. All I need is the essence and blood of a living man and it will be possible to come back to life." Yang laughed. "You were the one who was unwilling. When would I ever withhold myself from you voluntarily?"

The girl said: "After our union, you will fall seriously ill for some twelve days, but medicine can cure you." He then made love to her. Afterwards she dressed and rose. "I still require a drop of blood from the living," she said. "Are you willing to suffer pain for the sake of our love?" The scholar took a sharp blade and stabbed his arm until the blood flowed; the girl lay on the couch and he let the blood drip into her navel.[17] Then she rose and said: "I won't come to you anymore. Remember that one hundred days from now, when you see bluebirds singing from the top of the tree by my grave, you must immediately exhume my remains." Yang listened attentively to her instructions. As she left she warned him: "Remember exactly what I've said and don't forget! Neither late nor early will do!" And she departed.

Over ten days later, Yang fell sick as predicted, and his belly swelled up so painfully he wanted to die. After taking a remedy prescribed by the doctor, he excreted a foul substance something like mud. Within twelve days he had recovered. When he calculated the hundred days were up, he had servants bring along spades and wait there. As day turned to night, he saw a pair of bluebirds singing as foretold. Overjoyed, Yang said: "Now!" And so they hacked at the brush and opened the tomb. He saw that the coffin had completely rotted away, but the girl looked as though she were alive and seemed slightly warm to his touch. Covering her with clothes, he had her carried home in a sedan chair and placed her in a warm place. Her breath came in and out, finer than a silken thread. He gradually got her to take some thin gruel, and at midnight she revived. She would always tell him: "Those twenty-odd years just seem like a dream!"

"Ingenia" ("Qiaoniang")[18]

There lived in Canton a member of the Fu lineage who belonged to the local gentry and was already past sixty. He had only a single son by the name of Lian, who was extremely clever but a eunuch by birth. At the age of sixteen, his penis was only the size of a silkworm. His condition was known far and wide, so no family would betroth their daughter to him. The father deemed that his ancestral line would be severed; day and night he worried over it, but there was nothing he could do.

Lian was studying for the examinations with a tutor. One day the tutor had to go out for some reason, and an entertainer with a trained monkey happened to pass by the gate. Lian went out to watch and played hooky. When he calculated it was time for his tutor to get back, he took fright and ran away. He was not more than a mile[19] or two from home when he saw a young lady dressed in white walking ahead of a little maidservant. The girl turned her head for a moment: she was preternaturally beautiful, beyond compare. With her bound feet she could only hobble along, and Lian swiftly overtook her. The girl glanced back at her maid and said: "Would you ask the young gentleman if by any chance he might be going to Hainan Island?" The maid did as she was told, and Lian asked why she wanted to know. "If you're going there, I have a letter I would trouble you to deliver to my village gate on your way. My aged mother is at home, and she could offer you hospitality." Lian had left home with no fixed destination in mind. Figuring he might as well sail across the sea, he agreed to go. The girl took out the letter and handed it to her maid, who in turn handed it to the young man. He asked her name and address. "My family's name is Hua. They live in Daughter of Qin village;[20] it's about one or two miles north of the Haikou city wall."

Lian boarded a boat and sailed away. When he reached the northern wall of Haikou city, it was already dusk. He asked how to get to Daughter of Qin village, but nobody knew, so he headed north about one or two miles. The moon and stars glittered in the sky; the expanse of sweet-smelling grasses blurred his gaze. This was an uninhabited region without any inns, so he found himself in terrible straits. Just then he saw a tomb by the side of the road. He thought of stopping for the night alongside the grave, but he was mortally afraid of tigers and wolves. So he shimmied up a tree as nimbly as a monkey and crouched in the branches above. As he listened to the wind blowing in the pine trees and the mournful chirping of the night-time insects, his heart thudded in fear and he burned with regret at having come. Suddenly he heard someone talking below. When he peered down to look, a courtyard was now visible. A beauty was sitting on a rock, and two maids, one on the left and one on the right, were holding painted candles and waiting upon her. The beauty looked over to her left and said: "Tonight the moon is silvery bright and stars are few; let's brew a cup of tea from the round cake Aunt Hua gave us to enjoy this fine night." The boy thought they must be ghosts or demons; his hair stood on end and he dared not even breathe.

Suddenly the maid looked up and cried: "There's someone in the tree!"

The girl jumped up in alarm: "Where did such a bold fellow come from, peeping at people in the dark!" The boy was petrified, but there was nowhere to hide; so he climbed down and knelt on the ground, begging their forgiveness. When the girl got a close look at him, however, her anger turned to joy, and she pulled him up to sit beside her. He cast a sidelong glance at her: she was between sixteen and seventeen years old, dazzling in looks and bearing. Listening to her speech, he found they spoke the same local dialect. "Where are you going?" she asked. "I'm serving as a postman for someone," he replied. "There are many violent bandits in these wilds," she said, "and sleeping out in the open is worrisome. If you don't mind a rustic cottage, I would like you to be my guest." And she invited the boy in. There was only a single bed in the room, and she told the maid to unroll two quilts on top of it. Ashamed at his body's foulness, he offered to sleep at the foot of the bed.

She smiled. "Meeting with such a fine guest, how could I presume to be a female Yuanlong and take the loftier sleeping place for myself?"[21] The boy had no choice but to join her on the bed, but he was so scared and nervous that he kept himself rolled up in a ball. Before long, as they lay in the darkness, the girl's slender fingers reached inside the quilt and lightly stroked his thigh. The boy pretended he was asleep and unaware of what was going on. A little while later, she opened the covers and came in. She shook him, but he didn't move. The girl then reached down to explore his private parts. Her hand paused in disappointment; then she stealthily climbed out of the covers and left. Soon the sound of crying was audible.

The boy was mortified. How he hated Heaven for having made him deficient! The girl called her maid to put a lamp in a bamboo basket. The maid saw her tear stains and asked in surprise what was troubling her. The girl shook her head. "I'm just sighing over my fate, that's all." Her maid stood at the head of the bed and closely watched her mistress's expression. "You can wake the boy up now and turn him out," she instructed. Hearing this, the boy felt twice as humiliated; he was also scared at having nowhere else to go in the middle of the night.

Just as he was pondering what to do, a woman pushed her way through the door. "Aunt Hua is here," exclaimed the maid. A furtive glance revealed that the aunt was somewhere in her fifties, but still rather stylish. When she saw the girl was still up, she began questioning her. Before the girl could reply, the woman noticed there was someone lying in the bed, and so she asked her who was sharing her couch. The maid replied for her: "Oh, it's just some young man who was staying here for the night." The woman laughed. "I didn't know Ingenia was lighting wedding candles tonight!" Then she saw the tears glistening on the girl's face. "Crying isn't normal on one's wedding night—could the young gentleman have been too rough?" she asked in alarm. The girl kept silent but she looked even sadder.

The woman wanted to take a look at the boy so she pulled at his clothes, but as soon as she shook them, the letter fell out onto the bed. She picked up the letter and looked at it. In amazement, she cried: "This is my daughter's handwriting!" She tore the letter open and read it, sighing with surprise. The girl asked what was in it.

"It's a letter home from Tertia," said the woman. "She says her husband, Mr. Wu, has died. She has no one to support her and doesn't know what to do."

"He did say that he was delivering a letter for someone," said the girl. "Luckily we hadn't driven him away yet."

The woman called to the boy to get up and questioned him how he came to have the letter. The boy told her everything. "You've gone so far and taken so much trouble to deliver this letter, how can we ever repay you?" Then she looked carefully at the boy, and asked with a smile: "How *did* you cross Ingenia?" "I don't know how I offended her," he replied. So she asked the girl, who sighed. "I'm pitying myself because during my lifetime I was married to a eunuch; now that I'm dead I take a lover and he turns out to be a castrato too. That's the reason I'm so sad."

The woman glanced back at the boy: "Oh, my clever lad, are you really female though male? But you are my guest now; it wouldn't do to stay here any longer, bothering other people." Then she led him into the eastern wing of the house, where she thrust her hand inside his pants to examine him. She smiled. "No wonder Ingenia shed tears! But fortunately you do have a stem there, so there's still something we can work with." She trimmed the lamp and presently rummaged through a chest, where she found a black pill. She gave it to the boy and told him to swallow it. Then giving him strict instructions to lie motionless, she left. The boy lay down, brooding in his solitude; he wondered what ailment the medicine was supposed to cure. Sometime around three in the morning, before the fifth watch, he awoke. He felt a filament of hot vital energy from below his navel shoot straight into his genital region; then he felt a wriggling sensation as though something were dangling on his thigh. He reached down to explore, and lo and behold, he now had the body of a powerful man. He was astonished and thrilled, as though he had suddenly received the nine ancient insignias of imperial favor. When he could just make out the color of the window frame because it was growing light, the woman came in to leave some steamed bread in his room. She told him to sit there patiently, and then refastened his door.

She went out and said to the girl: "For his service of delivering the letter, I'm going to keep him here and summon Tertia home so they can become sworn brother and sister. I'm going to keep him shut up in here not to vex you." Then she went out the door.

The boy circled the room in boredom. From time to time he went near the crack in the door, like a bird peering through its cage. Whenever he caught sight of Ingenia from a distance, he wanted to call her over and present himself, but embarrassment made him tongue-tied and he always stopped. This went on until nightfall, when the woman arrived home with her daughter in tow. She opened the doors, saying: "You must have been bored to death! Tertia has come to pay her respects and thank you."

The woman he had met on the road entered calmly and gestured politely in greeting. The woman told them to address each other as older brother and younger sister. "Older sister and younger sister would be fine too," tittered Ingenia. They all went out together into the main hall and sat in a circle with drinks set out. While they were drinking, Ingenia teased him: "Does a eunuch like yourself still get excited at a beautiful woman?" "A lame man does not forget what shoes are like, nor does a blind man forget his sight," retorted the boy. Everyone burst out laughing. Considering that Tertia must be exhausted, Ingenia urged her to retire. The woman glanced meaningfully at Tertia and told her to take the boy with her. Tertia flushed scarlet and did not budge. "This fellow is really a damsel—what's there to be afraid of?" said her mother, pressuring them to go off together. She whispered to the boy: "You may be my son-in-law in secret, my son in public."

The boy was pleased, and taking Tertia's arm, climbed into bed with her. The sharpness of a blade fresh from the whetstone can be imagined. Later, lying beside her on the pillow, he asked Tertia who Ingenia was. "She's a ghost. In talent and beauty she has no equal, but fate has gone against her. She was married to the young master of the Mao family, but illness made him a eunuch. At the age of seventeen he was still incapable of performing a husband's duties. She fell into deep depression and died, entering the underworld full of resentment." The boy was taken aback and suspected that Tertia was a ghost too. "I'll tell you the truth," she said. "I'm not a ghost but a fox. Ingenia was living all alone with no companions; my mother and I were homeless, and so we're putting up in this tomb for the time being." Now the boy was truly astonished. "Don't be scared," said Tertia. "Even though we're really ghost and fox, we're not the type to hurt you."

From then on, they spent every day chatting and drinking together. Even though he knew Ingenia was not human, he still fancied her loveliness, only regretting that he had no window of opportunity to present himself. The boy was a cultivated and refined sort of person, good at witty repartee, and Ingenia began to feel rather tenderly toward him. One day Mrs. Hua and her daughter were going to go off some place, and so they shut the boy up again in his room. The boy was terribly bored, and he circled the room calling to Ingenia through the door to let him out. Ingenia gave orders to her maid, who tried several keys in succession until the door finally opened. The boy whispered in her ear to grant him a private interview. Ingenia sent her maid away, and the boy hoisted her up on the bed and leaned intimately beside her. She playfully grabbed his crotch, saying: "Too bad an adorable boy like you is so lacking here." Before the words were completely out of her mouth, something brushed against her hand and filled her fist. In amazement she asked: "How is it that something so tiny before has become so thick and heavy?"[22] The boy laughed. "Before he was shy at meeting a stranger, so he shrank back; now finding this ridicule and slander unbearable, he has puffed up with rage." And so the two made love.

Afterwards she grew angry: "Now I realize there was a reason they kept locking the door. Some time ago Mrs. Hua and her daughter were wandering about with no place to live, so I let them stay here. When Tertia studied embroidery from me, I never kept any of my techniques secret. And to think she could be as jealous as this!" The boy tried assiduously to comfort her and also told her what had happened. The girl remained resentful. "I had to keep it a secret," said the boy. "Aunt Hua gave me strict instructions." Before the words were out of his mouth, Aunt Hua entered, shutting the door behind her. Flustered, the two of them leaped to their feet. Aunt Hua glared at Ingenia. "Who opened the door?" Ingenia laughed and confessed. Aunt Hua grew even angrier, and gave her a long tongue-lashing. "My aged aunt is just making fun of me," said Ingenia with a deliberate sneer. "This fellow is really a damsel—what mischief could he do?" Tertia, seeing her mother and Ingenia bitterly attacking each other, felt guilty to be uninvolved and interposed her own body between them to make peace; only then did they suppress their anger and look happier. Ingenia said that even though she was furious about it, she would henceforth make a special concession and defer to Tertia. But Aunt Hua was vigilant day and night, so the boy and Ingenia were unable to express their feelings for each other; all they could do was to exchange smoldering glances.

One day Aunt Hua said to the boy: "Both my daughter and my foster daughter have dutifully attended to your comfort. But I've been thinking it over, and living here is not a viable long-term plan. You should return home and tell your parents to let you exchange wedding vows as soon as possible." With that, she packed his bags and hurried him on his way. The two girls looked at each other with woebegone faces. Ingenia in particular couldn't bear it. The tears rolled down her face like a broken strand of pearls, and there was no end to her sobbing. Aunt Hua cut short their farewells and then pulled the boy out the door. Once he reached the other side of the gate, the house and yard vanished; all he could make out was a desolate tomb. Aunt Hua accompanied him to the boat. "After you leave, I will bring my two girls to rent lodgings in your fair city. If you still recollect your former happiness, you may go in person to the Li family's abandoned garden to welcome your bride."[23]

And so the boy returned home. During his disappearance, his father had hunted everywhere for him in vain and was consumed with worry. Now seeing his son again, he was overjoyed at this unexpected homecoming. The boy gave his parents a rough outline of the story from beginning to end, and also brought up the matter of becoming betrothed to Miss Hua. "Why should we pay any heed to the words of a demon?" snorted his father. "The only reason you managed to escape death at their hands is simply because you're a eunuch!"

"Although she is an alien being, her feelings are still human," said the boy. "Furthermore she is clever and beautiful, and if I marry her, no one from our lineage will laugh at us." His father refused his consent and simply ridiculed him. The boy then retreated, but itching to show off his new skills, he misbehaved and seduced the maids. Gradually, it got to the point where he was broadcasting his lechery in broad daylight, with the hope that his parents would hear of his antics. One day, he was glimpsed in the act by a young maid, who ran and reported it to his mother. She didn't believe it until she drew near enough to observe them. It was a great shock to her. She called the maid to make a thorough investigation and so obtained a full report of his condition. Then she was beside herself with happiness and broadcast the affair to everyone she met to advertise that her son was eunuch no longer. She intended to discuss matrimonial prospects with a prominent local clan. But the boy secretly told his mother: "I won't marry anyone but Miss Hua."

"There is no shortage of beautiful women in this world; why must you insist on a monster?"

"If it weren't for Mrs. Hua, I would never have learned the way of mankind. It would be inauspicious to turn our backs on her."

His father finally acceded to his wishes, and sent a manservant and an old serving woman to go and reconnoiter. About two or three miles after leaving the eastern city wall, they soon came to the Li family garden. Amid the crumbling walls and the thicket of bamboo they saw a thread of cooking smoke. The old woman dismounted and went straight to the door. She saw mother and daughter wiping the table and scouring the place as though they were already expecting someone. The old woman paid her respects and conveyed her master's orders. When she saw Tertia she exclaimed in surprise: "Is this going to be our young master's wife? Seeing her even I feel tender feelings; no wonder the young gentleman can't get her off his mind and out of his dreams!" Then she asked about Tertia's older sister. Aunt Hua sighed: "Oh, you mean my foster daughter. She died suddenly, just three days ago." And then she set out food and drink for the old woman and the manservant.

When the old woman returned she described Tertia's demeanor in detail, to the delight of the boy's parents. At the end when she told how Ingenia had died, the boy looked stricken and on the verge of tears. On his wedding night, he personally asked Aunt Hua about Ingenia, who replied: "She has already been reborn as somebody else up north." The boy sobbed for some time. Even after he brought Tertia home as his bride, he could never forget Ingenia. Whenever anyone came from Hainan Island, he would always summon the person to make inquiries about her. Eventually someone told him that ghostly weeping could be heard at night coming from a tomb in Daughter of Qin village. The boy was amazed at this extraordinary news, and went in to report it to Tertia, who brooded for a good while and then burst into tears: "I have double-crossed my sister!" In response to his questioning she told him: "When my mother and I came here, we never actually let her know we were leaving. That sound of resentful weeping—who else but Ingenia could it be? I wanted to tell you earlier but I was afraid of airing my mother's dirty linen."

When the boy heard this, his grief turned to happiness. He immediately ordered a carriage and traveled day and night at breakneck speed to her tomb. He knocked on one of the trees planted by the grave and called out: "Ingenia! Ingenia! I'm here!" Suddenly he saw a young woman with a babe in swaddling clothes emerge from the grave pit. Lifting her head, she cried bitterly, her face filled with boundless resentment. He too wept. Reaching toward the infant in her arms, he asked whose son it was. "This is your wicked legacy, born a good three months ago," said Ingenia.

"I made the mistake of listening to Aunt Hua and caused you and our son to bury your sorrow in the earth below. How can I ever make up for my crime?"

And then he took them in his carriage to a boat, and they sailed across the sea for home. When they arrived, he went in to tell his mother, holding his son in his arms. His mother regarded the child: he was plump and strong and didn't look like a ghostly creature, which increased her joy. Ingenia and Tertia got on extremely well together, and they served their mother-in-law with the utmost filial piety.

Some time later, Mr. Fu fell ill and they sent for the doctor. "This sickness is incurable," said Ingenia. "His soul has already left home." And she supervised the preparations for the funeral. Once these were complete, Mr. Fu died.

When their son grew up, he looked the spitting image of his father. He was exceedingly clever, and at the age of thirteen passed the first set of civil service examinations and qualified as an imperial student.

Gao Heng[24] heard this story when he was sojourning in Canton. Some of the place names were missing; nor did he ever find out how it ended.

NOTES

1. See Giles, *Strange Stories from a Chinese Studio*. Other sizable translations into English include Mair and Mair, *Strange Tales from Make-Do Studio*.

2. For the argument about not taking 1679 as the year *Liaozhai* was completed, see Zhang Peiheng, "Xinxu"; and Barr, "The Textual Transmission of *Liaozhai zhiyi.*"

3. For an excellent account of the relationship between Pu Songling's life and *Liaozhai*'s thematic concerns, see Barr, "Pu Songling and *Liaozhai zhiyi:* A Study of Textual Transmission, Biographical Background and Literary Antecedents."

4. Half of a manuscript of *Liaozhai* in Pu Songling's hand is still extant and has been published in facsimile.

5. Zichuan, one of the counties comprising Jinan prefecture during the Qing, is now the modern city of Zibo.

6. For an innovative example of using *Liaozhai* for a study of Shandong local history, see Jonathan Spence's *Death of Woman Wang*.

7. I follow Allan Barr's reconstruction of *Liaozhai*'s original order here, which

would place "Liansuo" and "Ingenia" as stories written toward the earlier years of the collection's composition. Barr argues that earlier stories tend to focus more on love and sex and later stories on social satire. See Barr, "A Comparative Study of Early and Late Tales in *Liaozhai zhiyi.*"

8. See Zeitlin, *Historian of the Strange: Pu Songling and the Chinese Classical Tale.*

9. For a fuller exposition of these ideas, see Zeitlin, "Embodying the Disembodied: Representations of Ghosts and the Feminine."

10. See Li, *Enchantment and Disenchantment: Love and Illusion in Chinese Literature.*

11. Source: Pu Songling, *Liaozhai zhiyi [huijiao huizhu huiping ben],* 331–37. For an analysis of this tale, see Zeitlin, "Embodying the Disembodied."

12. In today's Pei county, Jiangsu province.

13. At Karl Kao's suggestion, I translate *wei* here as "the front panel of a skirt," rather than the more common meaning of "bed curtains."

14. Fourteen *sui* in the original. Throughout my translations, I have converted all ages to the Western reckoning.

15. Yuan Zhen's (775–831) "Ballad of Lianchang Palace" ("Lianchanggong ci") is a poetic response to the An Lushan rebellion (755–763), a civil war that almost toppled the Tang dynasty. During the Emperor Xuanzong's flight from the capital, a mutiny of his soldiers forced him to condone the execution of his beloved concubine, Yang Guifei; soon after, he was obliged to abdicate the throne in favor of his son. Yuan Zhen's ballad is not a romantic narrative of these historical events but a rumination on the causes and aftermath of the rebellion filtered through the nostalgic topos of a visit to the ruined palace. Pu Songling could presume his readers' familiarity with this famous poem. The opening couplet of the ballad contributes to the story's ghostly atmosphere because it suggests both ruins and the underworld: "Lianchang Palace was planted with princely bamboo; deserted for years, the place is dark as a thicket."

16. Here, and at the end of the story, we detect strong echoes of a line from Yuan Zhen's "Ballad of Lianchang Palace": "Returning is like a dream, like madness."

17. The navel is the seat of generative vitalities in Chinese medical conceptions of the body and hence an appropriate spot to absorb the blood necessary for her rebirth.

18. Source: Pu Songling, *Liaozhai zhiyi [huijiao huizhu huiping ben],* 256–64.

19. I convert Chinese *li* into English miles throughout my translations.

20. Daughter of Qin village *(Qinnü cun). Qinnü* may refer to Nongyu—legendary daughter of King Mu of Qin, who supposedly became an immortal—but I am unaware of any particular connection between this mythical figure and Hainan Island.

21. Chen Yuanlong was a hero from the Three Kingdoms period (third century C.E.), who refused to observe the normal protocol for a host in sleeping arrangements, taking the superior position in the front of the bed for himself and relegating his guest to the inferior position at the foot of the bed.

22. The compound *leiran* is usually descriptive of thick clusters of fruit.

23. It was part of wedding ritual for the groom to go to the bride's house to escort her back to his home. This was called "welcoming the bride" *(yingqin).*

24. Gao Heng (1612–1697) was one of the most noted scholar-officials and literary men from Shandong in his day. A friend and patron of Pu Songling's, he authored the first preface for *Liaozhai.*

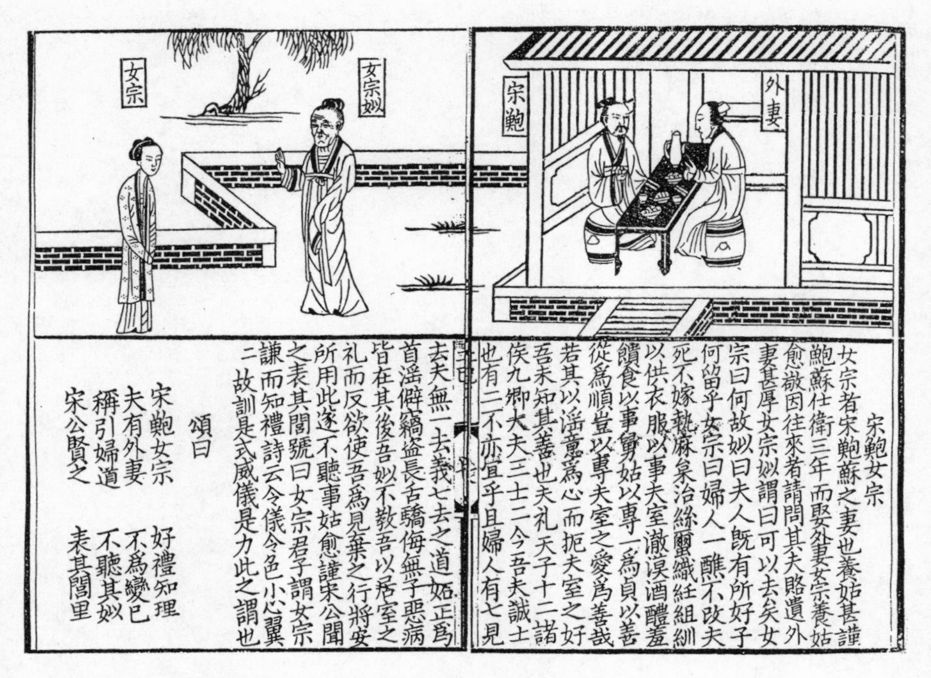

宋鮑女宗

女宗者宋鮑蘇之妻也養姑甚謹
鮑蘇仕衛三年而娶外妻女宗養姑
愈敬因往來者請問其夫賂遺外
妻甚厚女宗姒謂曰可以去矣女
宗曰何故姒曰夫人既有所好子
何留乎女宗曰婦人一醮不改夫
死不嫁執麻枲治絲繭織紝組紃
以供衣服以事夫室澈漠酒醴羞
饋食以事舅姑以專一爲貞以善
從爲順豈以專夫室之愛爲善哉
若其以淫意爲心而扼夫室之好
吾未知其善也夫礼天子十二諸
侯九卿大夫三士二今吾夫誠士
也有二不亦宜乎且婦人有七見
去夫無一去義七去之道妒正爲
首淫僻竊盜長舌驕侮無子惡病
皆在其後吾姒不教吾以居室之
礼而反欲使吾爲見棄之行將安
所用此遂不聽事姑愈謹宋公聞
之表其閭號曰女宗君子謂女宗
謙而知禮詩云令儀令色小心翼
二故訓是式威儀是力此之謂也

頌曰

宋鮑女宗　好禮知理
夫有外妻　不爲變已
稱引婦道　不聽其姒
宋公賢之　表其閭里

Fig. 14. Nüzong, wife of Bao Su, was given the title "model woman" by the Duke of Song for her faithful care of her mother-in-law even though she knew that her husband, posted elsewhere, had taken a mistress. She is shown rejecting her husband's sister's advice to seek a divorce, while the overleaf shows her husband enjoying himself with his new partner. Her words, often repeated in later texts, are: "A woman once having drunk of the marriage cup does not change, and if her husband dies, she does not marry again" (Liu Xiang, *Gu lienü zhuan* 2:7a–b). Stories from this text would have been well known to Zhang Xuecheng and his contemporaries, male and female alike. Woodcut from *Biographies of Exemplary Women (Lienü zhuan),* originally compiled by Liu Xiang, reprinted in 1825 by Ruan Fu.

FOURTEEN

Two Biographies by Zhang Xuecheng (1738–1801)

Translated by Susan Mann

TRANSLATOR'S PREFACE

As a graduate student I studied Zhang Xuecheng's philosophy of history with David Nivison, who was completing his book on Zhang's life and thought at the time. I barely noticed then that Zhang had taken an interest in women's learning, and it was not until years later that I discovered his intimate and unabashedly affectionate portraits of women. Most striking of all to me was the realization that Zhang's views of women, based on his own relationships with women, shaped his philosophy of history. As I reconsidered Zhang's philosophical and literary treatises after studying his biographies of women, I was struck by how much better I could understand what he was talking about. Some of his most complex notions, such as the idea that the historian's words must be "everyone's"—that the historian articulates the Dao without regard to personal fame or achievement, but simply based on an understanding of what is right or true at the time—were clearly inspired by the examples of women he knew. Zhang especially appreciated the fact that women were uncorrupted by the competitive race for fame and glory that engaged all men who strove for success in the civil service examinations. His descriptions of women he loved also reveal deep feelings and an empathic sensitivity that his more formal writings mask. Understanding this personal and emotional side of a philosophical and cerebral male writer made me realize how much an understanding of Chinese thought and the Confucian scholarly tradition depends upon an understanding of gender relations in historical context. Without seeing the women in the life of a male scholar whose work had shaped my understanding of Confucian China, I had failed to grasp not only the full power of his ideas but also the breadth of his emotional experience and humanity.

INTRODUCTION

Zhang Xuecheng has long been recognized as one of China's leading philosophers of history. Ironically though, among his contemporaries Zhang was best known not for his writings on the philosophy of history, but for a lengthy essay titled "Women's Learning" ("Fu xue"), in which he attacked other prominent scholars of his day for their interest in and patronage of women writers. The essay, which traces the presence of learned women through China's historical record, is now an invaluable aid to students of Chinese women's history.[1]

Zhang himself was not much interested in women writers or in the poetry that was their métier. Instead he seems to have focused on women's moral commitments and on their ritual authority as mothers and wives. In many of his writings about women he suggests that women were the models for his own moral philosophy.[2] The women in Zhang's own life, one of whose biographies appears here, were probably his closest confidants. Among his rather boisterous circle of male comrades he was a misfit—difficult to get along with and awkward in social groups. A bookish and homely child, he grew up in a household surrounded by women, including a solicitous aunt and an elder sister who doted on him. With no brothers and no paternal uncles, Zhang's most influential male role model was his father, Biao. Zhang Biao appears briefly in Zhang's biography of Lady Xun, translated here, when he invites Lady Xun's husband (Zhang's ne'er-do-well cousin Yuanye) to join him at his first official post as magistrate of Yingcheng, Hubei. This appointment was to prove disastrous for Zhang's father, who was dismissed in 1756 in a scandal from which he never recovered politically or financially. The disaster is foretold, as we see in the biography, by Lady Xun's dream. Zhang Biao's misfortune may have soured Zhang Xuecheng permanently on service in the imperial bureaucracy. He never accepted an official post, and he made no secret of his scorn for the "quest for fame" that dominated the lives of his male friends.[3]

The two biographies translated here are different genres. The first, dated 1768, is a *xingshi,* that is, a "factual record of the life" of Zhang's elder cousin's late wife. The second is a *lienü zhuan,* that is, "biography of an exemplary woman," written by Zhang when he was compiling an officially commissioned provincial history. The "factual record" is an intimate biographical form that could be written only by someone personally acquainted with the subject and/or her family. In contrast, the "exemplary woman" biography is what a scholar of the time might have considered a routine, even formulaic, writing assignment. In Zhang's hands, both genres are transformed.

The "factual record" of Lady Xun's life—anecdotal and full of homely detail, laced with wit and sharply observant, at once empathic and didactic—is unusually long. Covering several full pages of Chinese text, it portrays a woman who obviously meant the world to Zhang. As an astonishing example of the power of classical Chinese to convey the most delicate nuance in human relationships, the biography also packs a heavy-handed historical judgment. No reader will miss Zhang's utter disdain for his cousin, Lady Xun's husband, whom we readily come to despise as Zhang's sketch unfolds.

Zhang was interested in his subjects' bodies as well as their minds, and part of the facticity of the *xingshi* in his hands is its realistic detail. He leaves nothing to our imagination when he tells us what Lady Xun had to put up with when her father-in-law's aging concubine became incontinent, or how it felt to be in charge of the ancestral sacrifices when she herself could barely stand upright. Zhang is tickled to point out the contradiction between Lady Xun's own dismissive views of Buddhism and the rich religious imagery that filled her dreams. He selects a single anecdote to show how she worked her psychological power over her daughters. And he even hints that her overbearing moralism did not come without a price by deftly quoting an uncle's humorous aside. Notice that all of this is done by innuendo and insinuation. Zhang never tells us what to think about his subjects. He inserts his voice as a historian only when he talks about his sources. He tells you what they are, he tells you how he got them, and he gives you a sense of their authenticity and reliability.

Zhang was known as a master of the human interest story. But this is only to be expected, because he believed that the deeds and words of living people display the moral models everyone needs to live by.[4] This sensibility is evident not only in the *xingshi,* but also in Zhang's expansive rendition of the conventional form for a *lienü zhuan.* Zhang went out of his way, as we see in his "exemplary woman biography" of Jiang Lan, to expand the range of exemplary conduct considered appropriate for local histories. Whereas the majority of women's biographies in the Qing period focus on martyrs (especially the faithful widow who remains devoted to her husband's family throughout her long and lonely life, or the young woman who commits suicide when threatened by rape or by forced remarriage), Zhang took care to include in his own chapters on exemplary women those with talent in art and literature. In an essay on the genre of women's biography he ridiculed the subjects commonly treated in the standard histories, which singled out women who had won imperial commendations for chaste widowhood. In Qing times, commendations were awarded only after certification that a woman had been widowed before the age of thirty and that she had remained faithful to her deceased husband past the age of fifty. "As if," Zhang scoffed, "you could measure a woman's virtue in years!"[5]

His story of Jiang Lan is a fine example of his determination to free the "exemplary woman biography" from its conventional strictures. Like

Zhang's more intimate account of Lady Xun, his biography of Jiang Lan brings her to life, quoting from her letters and her conversations to reveal her personality as well as her talent and wit. Readers cannot fail to notice that Jiang Lan, like Lady Xun, is a living reproach to her spouse. On every front, as we see so clearly—and as Zhang so plainly wants us to see—women are the superior sex. They are smarter, they work harder, they have higher moral standards, and they are more interesting than the men with whom they must pass their lives.

ORIGINAL TEXTS

"*A Biographical Sketch of My Elder Cousin's Wife, Goodwife Xun*"[6]

Lady Xun, titled Goodwife, was the daughter of Xun Chenglong. Her late father came from Shanxi and later made his home in the capital. He had three sons and four daughters, of whom she was the youngest. Her family was very well-to-do. She was the most intelligent of the daughters, especially beloved by her parents, and so they gave her everything she wanted—clothing, food, playthings.

After she married my elder cousin Yuanye, she had to serve her mother-in-law, Lady Chen, who was known for her strictness and her simplicity. Her new husband's family was also very poor. The Goodwife accepted this with equanimity, embracing a frugal life as if she had been born to it. In meeting all the daily needs of the household, she never failed to please her mother-in-law.

Of the four generations of Zhangs born since my elder cousin's family moved to the capital, every single one has come to stay with him when they come to Beijing. He must plan to house and feed all of them. The Goodwife paid special attention to these kinsmen. She would wash and mend their clothes, cook for them, make them comfortable in her home. Even though she was very short of money, she would go to any lengths, so that people who stayed with her always forgot they were far from home. Whenever [my nephews or grandnephews] . . . talked about her, they were always moved to tears.

From 1737, when my father first sat for the *jinshi* examinations, until recently, when I became an Academy Student, I always stayed at her home. Because we were close relatives, she treated me especially well and continued to do so for more than thirty years. As a result, I knew her better than anyone else.

When she was first married, she knew nothing about the world outside the women's quarters. When she saw grain growing in bunches between the tiles on the roof of her new husband's family home [a sign of poverty], she was delighted and said to her mother-in-law: "Sorghum! Sorghum is extremely good! I never saw it before in my own family!" This made even her stern mother-in-law relax her face in a smile. But before long she got used to hardship. She was frugal with respect to her own needs; she forgot herself and attended personally to every household task. Whatever her mother-in-law needed she would always provide, and so her mother-in-law loved her.

In no time, however, her husband's family grew poorer still. She would have to cook the same grains over and over again until they were dried out, then add water to soften them up. She could not always obtain meat to offer her mother-in-law, so she left a standing order with the butcher to cut fresh meat, which she boiled and stored against the time when it would not be available. After a time her credit was exhausted and she could not pay her bills, so she sold her dowry jewelry bit by bit to keep the account open. She herself ate coarse food as if it were fine wheat. She never took a stitch of clothing for herself, and she was so fastidious that although she wore the same garments for decades, they retained their original texture and color. Even now when her body lies in a coffin, she is wearing the clothes she brought with her dowry.

In her final years, Lady Xun's mother-in-law was afflicted with an illness of the mouth and teeth that grew increasingly severe, so that whenever she ate, she would clench her teeth and press her lips together. Lady Xun would rise at dawn, kneel down and hold her and feed her, tilting the spoon between her lips. Each mouthful took a long time to swallow. She would calculate how long she needed to cook each meal of steamed beans and grains [so that her mother-in-law could eat it easily] and only afterward would she unbend her knees. For half a year thus, she was unfailingly respectful. When her mother-in-law was on the verge of death, she comforted her daughter-in-law, saying: "You have suffered a lot caring for me. I have no way to repay you. But after I die, I hope my son's circumstances will improve and you will be able to relax for many years in exchange for the way you have labored for me."

Lady Xun's father-in-law took a concubine named Chen. The mother-in-law, seeing that the concubine had no children and had adopted a life of chastity after their husband died, suffered together with her. Lady Xun was especially respectful of this concubine. But as the concubine aged, she became an alcoholic, cursing whenever she was drunk. Lady Xun treated her with respect as before. Later the concubine became ill and unable to control her bladder and bowels. Lady Xun wiped her body clean of urine and feces and never pleaded weariness. Earlier the concubine had been a Buddhist and had taken vegetarian vows, but after she got sick she began to indulge in both wine and meat. Lady Xun gave her what she wanted to eat and then began to abstain from meat herself, saying, "When you start something, you must finish it. I am only taking her place to make amends for her profligate behavior." Lady Xun herself did not believe in Buddhism. Even though her family was poor and they had no meat to eat, she never once referred to herself as a vegetarian.

In the year 1751 my father was appointed magistrate of Yingcheng, and he invited my elder cousin to accompany him on his journey to his new post. At the time Lady Xun had two daughters. The elder was just a few years old, the younger barely five months. There were six or seven mouths to feed in the household, but no other able-bodied helpers. Nearby kinsmen never came to inquire after them, and so even though my elder cousin was in fact terribly shiftless, there was no one to turn to. Somehow she found five thousand cash for him to pay for his expenses on the journey. Each time he was about to leave, however, he could not bring himself to part. Finally he sighed and said, "How sad that I am fated to starve to death." So saying he left, unable to look back.

Lady Xun took her dowry jewelry and pawned it. She exchanged her jewelry for fuel and rice, continuing to save whenever she could so that they could survive in an emergency. At that time her middle elder brother, Xun Yuxiu, was holding office as a tax official in Tongzhou, Jiangnan, and he was able to give her some assistance. Also, her niece had married a man named Ren Zhaoyuan, who was a secretary in Tanzhou, and he too supplied some of her needs. In this way she was able to set aside one or two dowry items and deposit them to earn compound interest that could sustain the family. And so, it is said, they passed years and months of bitter hardship.

Lady Xun always considered it shameful to borrow money. Every year when her female relatives gathered, whenever they talked about household budgets and financial transactions, she would distance herself as if she were fleeing from a stench. When she first came to my elder cousin's house, she realized how poor he was. But when she paid her visit home to her natal family, she said not a word about it. For that reason more than ten years passed before the Xuns knew about the Zhangs' financial straits. Then later the maids from the two families got to talking, and gradually the truth came out. When Lady Xun's own family members heard about it, they began to worry. However, they themselves were slowly losing their fortune. As siblings, she and her elder brother had been very close, and now it was his turn to rely on her for help.

My elder cousin traveled for three years. When he returned, she held out to him a small account book. Inside she had recorded every cent of income and expenditure, from the assistance she had received from her brother and her niece, to the gifts received from the six kinsmen, to the seasonal entertainment and even gifts of wine and food they had given and received, as well as minuscule expenses outside the home. You could follow it line by line, day by day. Even though the certificates from the pawnshop had long since been ruined or lost, each one was clearly recorded. Debits and assets matched exactly. During those three years she had augmented the budget with income from her weaving and sewing. In the home she had neglected nothing, and outside the home she had borrowed nothing. The toll of all this showed on her careworn face.

From the time I met Lady Xun at their rented home in the south city when I came to the capital in 1760, she talked with me candidly. Once she even took out that old account book and showed it to me. She was a person of few words who rarely smiled, and she never intended to show off her good character. She would talk only with me. She felt that as long as she had handled things well she should be able to confide in someone.

When my elder cousin was about to leave on his journey, he took out several kinds of old and rare books in famous imprints of which he was terribly proud and entrusted them to her, saying: "If worse comes to worst, you can sell these." Lady Xun took them and stored them. Before long they had nothing left to pawn and the fire in the stove had gone out. Yet she would not consider pawning those books. When my elder cousin returned to face her, his bags empty, he didn't dare ask what had happened while he was gone. Instead he chatted about other things. But he kept looking around for those books. Lady Xun, dissembling, said: "I sold all your books to buy food." My elder cousin nodded and looked terribly distressed. He went out and asked his relatives and friends what had happened. They all told him about Lady Xun. When he came back, he searched the containers, and every volume was still there, with the seals untouched. For the first time, he felt joy and delight, but also guilt and pain.

Lady Xun was resolute and rarely disheartened, believing as she did that those who live in poverty cannot allow their determination to flag. Even in the direst straits, she refused to yield to the twists and turns of fortune. For that reason, during the entire three-year period that her husband was away, she met every request and gave generously to all of her lineage relatives, close or distant. From time to time when the demands became too much for her, she would grow lofty and aloof, while the others stood back in awe and dread, thinking their words could not affect her. Yet when giving, she always measured out grain and cloth freely to aid poor relatives—even those she had never heard of before who later became needy she would help as much as she could.

All her life Lady Xun paid special attention to rituals and sacrifices. For instance, when her mother-in-law went back to her natal home to care for a younger brother who was ill, as she did from time to time, she could not herself attend to the death-day rituals in the family, so she asked Lady Xun to assume responsibility for them in her absence. For the next several decades, on every sacred ancestral death day, Lady Xun would prepare in advance a funerary text and the vessels for sacrifice. To these she always attended in person. This year she suffered from the growth of a tumor that had grown increasingly severe, so on the day of a sacrifice she would have to drag herself around to make the preparations. When she kneeled to prostrate herself, she would speak hoarsely and gasp for breath from asthma, and several people would have to support her while she regained her composure. Still she carried on, upholding the instructions of her mother-in-law.

She reared her two daughters in the best family traditions. When they were just children, they once saw a neighbor eating fruits and dumplings, and they began pulling on their mother's garments and begging her to get them some. Lady Xun was angry at them for envying what other people had, and she gave them each a beating. Then she said to them, "You girls ought to pay more attention to your own moral standards." Whereupon she took out their zither and the table on which it rested, sold them for several strings of cash, and the next day bought some treats for them with the money. Her lesson to them was: don't covet things you don't have.

When I first met the girls, the elder was past ten *sui* and her younger sister was ten. Their every movement was proper and measured. When they heard anyone speak of common things such as influence or profit, they would turn their backs. That was ten years ago. You could pass the women's quarters in their home and never hear a sound. Their uncle, Jian, always praised them, though he sighed and said, "When you're in their house it's too strict—like monastery. The loneliness I feel is deeply touching; it's not really like a home should be." So both of the girls had their mother's way about them. The elder married into the Hu family; within three years of her marriage, she died. The Hu lineage is large and very contentious, but since her death they have all agreed on one thing—her unusual sagacity. The younger daughter remained at home. She was very bright and precocious and she understood moral principles. While she was in mourning for her mother, her grief was extreme, but when she heard that I was writing an account of her mother's life, she spoke to me and gave me her detailed memories of words and deeds she knew of from every period of her mother's life. Her account was extremely complex and complete. The relationships she described were portrayed with great eloquence and emotion, but she was at her best talking about her mother.

Alas! Such a family! How worthy of this record, which follows.

The Goodwife was born in Kangxi 54, the year *yiwei* (1715) and died in Qianlong 33, the year *wuzi* (1768) at the age of fifty-four *sui*. At twenty-two she married my elder cousin, and ten years later she was in mourning for her mother-in-law. Five years after that came my cousin's three-year sojourn in the south. After his return, over a period of a decade or more, the family sank into poverty and she did not enjoy a single day of peace. So when she died, my cousin wailed, saying "How I failed you! How I failed you!"

Her first child was a son, Jisheng, who died as an infant. She bore four daughters after that, but none survived. Finally she had the two daughters I spoke of. The elder married Hu Wenxian, a *jiansheng* degree holder from Daxing. She predeceased him. The younger was betrothed to Zhao Guotai, a *shengyuan* degree holder from Zhuozhou, but she also died. My cousin adopted my third son, Huashou, as his heir, following the wishes of his late wife.

When Lady Xun was born, her mother, née Zhang, dreamed that a nun entered her chamber. Lady Xun herself did not like Buddhist beliefs, and she dismissed ghosts, spirits, and dreams as things without any substance or reality. Nevertheless, her dreams sometimes came true. When in 1751 my elder cousin was going to Yingcheng with my father, my father wanted the whole family to go along, but she refused. She had a dream in which her mother-in-law put an arm around her shoulders and said, "You look out for yourself." In fact, as it turned out, my father's journey did result in disappointment. On another occasion, when she was waiting for a letter from my cousin while he was away, she had a dream about her father-in-law, the Lord of Red Mountain, who appeared and said to her: "It will come on a certain day in the fourth month." It was already the second half of the fifth month, but when the letter came and she opened the envelope, she discovered that it had been sent on exactly the day he had mentioned.

One final example: in the spring of the preceding year, my cousin reburied his parents and grandparents at Shiliuzhuang. When he finished, Lady Xun was anxious and distressed. She told me: "A long time ago I had a dream. The gate of the tomb swung open to reveal a bedchamber. I went in and saw a lamp burning, and in the glow three pillows and quilts. My mother-in-law appeared and spoke to me and said: 'This is where I live with the concubine Chen. We are saving a place for you.' I looked and said nothing. Suddenly she donned a yellow garment and departed. How ominous it was!" I immediately changed the subject and rattled on about other things, but after I withdrew, my heart ached for her.

Her second daughter recalled: "On the fifteenth day of the eighth month my mother's illness grew very painful. The next day she said to me, 'Yesterday I dreamed my body was light and I was sitting in the hall of a Buddhist temple. I felt that all my sickness was completely gone, and my body floated free and untrammeled into the shadows of the afterlife. How auspicious!'" Alas—those were her very words!

In composing this sketch of my cousin's late wife, I have used what I heard and saw, what my cousin told me, and what her daughter recounted from her memories. There remain some fragments that I have arranged in the form of an afterword.

Lady Xun was a learned woman, but she loved to recite popular novels. From the time she was an unmarried girl, whenever she heard the blind storytellers drumming and plucking to accompany their tales—of extreme loyalty or bitter chastity or steadfast courage in the face of harrowing danger—she was always moved to sighs and cries as if she were an eyewitness to the events. Her family members all thought she was silly.

My cousin had a maternal uncle who was senior in rank and old in age but very unruly, so much so that he ran afoul of the law wherever he went. He stayed in my cousin's house for several months. Lady Xun received him with irreproachable good manners, both in word and in deed. No matter how hard he tried to find fault with her, he could not. She was always by nature so upright that she never spoke improperly to him. Although this annoyed him greatly, he had no way to get around it. He would say to people: "The Goodwife Xun is truly wise and intelligent—truly she is!"

My cousin reached middle age and still had no son. Lady Xun wanted to present him with a concubine, but my cousin put her off, saying they were too poor. She said to me: "I would like you to reason with your cousin." Later he purchased the concubine née Hu. Lady Xun looked after her for five or six years without ever a harsh word. In fact, once when my cousin scolded the concubine for a slip of the tongue, Lady Xun came vigorously to her defense and when she was unable to protect her, she comforted her afterward. When Lady Xun passed away, the concubine wailed for her pitifully until she lost her voice, as if she had lost her own parents.

"Biography of Jiang Lan"[7]

Jiang Lan's adult name *(zi)* was Shuzhen; she was also known by the *zi* Huicong. She was the daughter of a noted Hanyang family and the wife of the Huizhou prefect Zhang Shuting. Both the Zhangs and the Jiangs had produced important government officials for generations, and this marriage of talent was hailed as an auspicious match.

When Lan was young she lost both her father and her mother, and she was reared in her elder brother's family, studying along with her male cousins in the family school. There she mastered the Mao *Odes,* the Dai edition of the *Li ji,* and the *Lienü zhuan.* She was skilled in composing poetry. After she married Shuting, she ably served her parents-in-law, she was respectful toward all the members of Shuting's household, and she got along well with her sisters-in-law. Shuting had a number of concubines, whom she looked after and loved with deep sincerity. With those among them who could read and write she would exchange poems, like a teacher with friends. Sometimes she would even address them as "beautiful girl!"

In those days the ladies from the great families—the Lius, the Wus, the Jis, and the Wangs—were all related by marriage and went visiting back and forth, exchanging poems and matching rhymes. They had quite a reputation. Among them, Lan stood apart in her goodness and her purity. When her female companions complained, for example, that they resented being shut up in the women's apartments where they knew nothing of government policy-making, she would reply at once: "In fact, I fear that women are by no means absent from court policy-making. But when we speak of the women's quarters, we mean that filial respect and collegial relations extend from there to those who govern. What place then do women not govern?"[8]

During the rebellion in 1688, the entire family fled to safety in a cave, with Jiang Lan personally waiting upon and guiding her elderly mother-in-law during the long climb into the mountains. After enduring much hardship, they returned home when the disturbance had subsided. Lan wrote a record of her experiences, which though full of the chaos and emotion of the event, was not forgetful of filial obligation.

When Shuting sat once again for the examinations in Beijing and failed, Lan wrote him the following letter:

> When a man leaves home and goes into the outside world, he cannot worry about his domestic or personal affairs. If you run short of money, I have two elder brothers holding office in the capital, and they will surely assist you. If you become depressed staying alone in your lodging, why not enjoy the beautiful women in the pleasure quarters? My brothers won't begrudge you their money, and I myself long ago cast aside my dreams of growing old together with you. These are the only things I can offer you. Serving wise men and befriending humane persons, succeeding in your studies, conducting yourself in accordance with the Way, spreading your fame to bring glory to your ancestors—all of those are your tasks; I cannot arrange them for you. It is up to you to strive with all your might.

When Shuting received this letter, he felt very ashamed.

Jiang Lan died in 1696 at the age of twenty-nine *sui.* She was extremely filial. Shuting was the son of a concubine, but his birth mother had died when he was very young and he had been reared by his father's wife, née Liu, as her own son. When Liu fell gravely ill, Lan wrote out a vow to Heaven pleading to die in her place. The vow went something like this: "The first reason I can die is that I lost my parents early. A second reason I can die is that I never saw the mother-in-law who gave birth to my husband. If this living body that can die takes the place of my saintly mother-in-law, it will be a fortunate thing for the Zhang family."

Her words and their meaning were deeply moving. No one who saw this vow could refrain from sighing deeply. She left a collection of prose and poetry called *Leaning on the Cloud Tower.*

NOTES

1. The essay is translated in full in Mann, "'Fu xue: Women's Learning,' by Zhang Xuecheng."
2. See Mann, "Women in the Life and Thought of Zhang Xuecheng."
3. For these and other details of Zhang's life, see Nivison, *The Life and Thought of Chang Hsüeh-ch'eng,* esp. 20–37, 96, 127–33.
4. David S. Nivison, Zhang's own biographer, observed that Zhang "paid special attention to biographies of living women; those who were selected for the honor of inclusion in his history he interviewed personally, often sending carriages to bring them to the yamen to tell their life stories" (Nivison, *The Life and Thought of Chang Hsüeh-ch'eng,* 83).
5. See Zhang Xuecheng, "Lienü liezhuan," in *Zhang shi yishu, wai* 12:13b.
6. Source: Zhang Xuecheng, *Zhang shi yishu,* 20:28a–32b.

7. Source: "Exemplary Women, Section Four: The Clever and Talented" in "Hubei tong zhi," an unfinished and unpublished work compiled by Zhang Xuecheng. Printed in Zhang Xuecheng, *Zhang shi yishu,* 30:109a–10a.

8. Jiang Lan alludes here to a chapter in the *Analects* (2:21), translated by D. C. Lau as follows: "Someone said to Confucius, 'Why do you not take part in government?' The Master said, '*The Book of History* says, "Oh! Simply by being a good son and friendly to his brothers a man can exert an influence upon government." In so doing a man is, in fact, taking part in government. How can there be any question of his having actively to "take part in government" *(xiao hu, wei xiao you yu xiong di, shi yu you zheng, shi yi wei zheng, xi qi wei wei zheng)?*'" See Lau, *Confucius: The Analects,* 66. Note the subsequent allusion to her own display of filiality and friendship (the domestic virtues), even while writing a record of a political event in the public sphere.

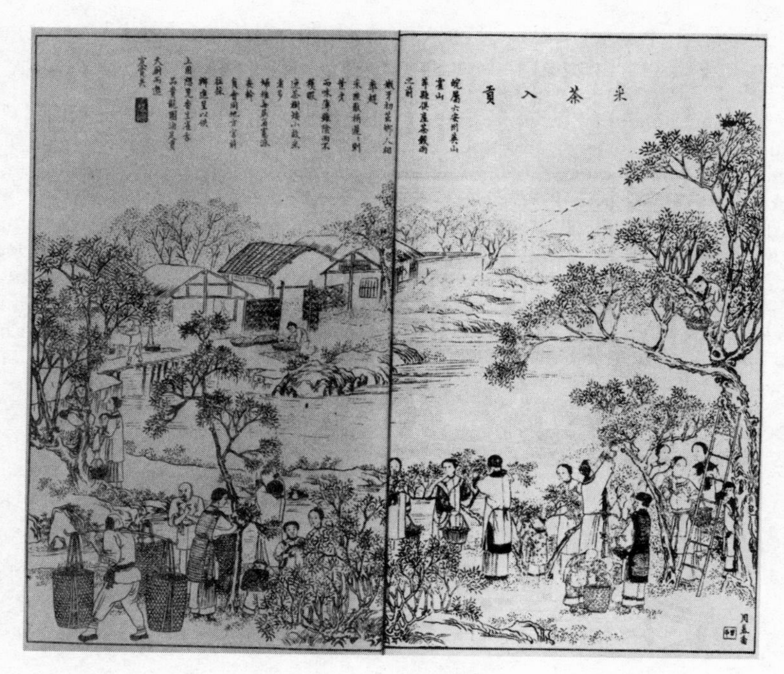

Fig. 15. Picking tea leaves for the emperor. The artist plays on the traditional theme of female labor and state exactions with an inscription describing the urgency of picking the tea leaves just as they open, before they become dry and lose their delicate flavor. Since the tea is destined for the imperial palace itself (the caption tells us that it is "tribute tea"), pressure on the pickers is intense. A local official has turned out to supervise the job, which is performed by women from designated "tea households." Source: *Dianshizhai huabao*, vol. 1, no. 3, 73.

FIFTEEN

Poems on Tea-Picking

Translated by Weijing Lu

TRANSLATOR'S PREFACE

In imperial China, as in many other cultures, women from lower social classes rarely appeared in formal historical writings. I was reminded of this during an exhaustive search of the historical record for evidence of women's work in tea-picking. I could find nothing. To my surprise, on the other hand, I discovered that tea-picking women appear prominently in poetry from the Tang dynasty onward. In poetry Chinese literati indulged themselves in descriptions of tea harvesting, admiring the tea pickers' feminine gestures and movement, praising women's industry, and criticizing social injustice done to the tea-growers. To be sure, the poems seldom reveal village women's real lives; rather, they reflect the gaze of the literati upon the work of these women. However, what I found most illuminating about the tea-picking poems is that they reveal many levels of meaning concerning women, women's work, and rural life. Underlying the imagery of tea-picking women are not only Confucian moral and social messages, but also cultural tastes, aesthetic views, and sensitivity about women's class and status that are often obscured in other elite writings, such as didactic texts about female duty and female behavior. Therefore, reading these poems in conjunction with other writings about women enhances one's grasp of the complexity of gender ideas in imperial China.

INTRODUCTION

Tea-picking is one of the few poetic subjects depicting women's work in classical Chinese poetry. The subject emerged in poetry during the eighth century, when tea cultivation and tea drinking grew into an empire-wide custom and tea connoisseurship took hold in Tang literati culture. In the eyes of the Tang elite, tea was more than a kind of beverage; they viewed it as a "divine plant" that displayed many of their own ideal character traits—refinement, purity, and the capacity to achieve spiritual transcendence. Correspondingly, as seen in the poem by Huangfu Zeng (d. 785) translated here, the act of tea-picking symbolized the cultured and leisured lifestyle of the educated. This elite obsession with tea helps to explain why women tea-pickers were chosen over other working women to be portrayed in poetry.

Early tea-picking poems describe elite men picking tea leaves to display their connoisseurship. But the main subjects of tea-picking poetry through later periods are not elite men but village women. Reflecting in part the socioeconomic changes under way from Song times onward, the imagery of tea-picking was increasingly associated with village women, who comprised the main workforce in tea harvesting. Poets took great interest in portraying these women, albeit in a romantic light, working diligently to support their families and to pay government taxes.

Although tea-picking poems are about women, they were mainly written by men. This is partly because, unlike literati men, elite women had few opportunities to travel or even observe rural activities such as tea-picking, due to the restrictions of Confucian gender norms. Wu Lan, the eighteenth-century woman poet whose work is translated here, is one of the few women who wrote about tea-picking. Her poem serves as an example of how women could write with extreme skill and sensitivity on a conventional subject. Educated women of Wu Lan's era participated enthusiastically in the literati culture of writing poetry, and as recent studies have demonstrated, they often brought uniquely feminine perspectives to their poems, even though their topics and images were drawn largely from literary traditions established by men.[1]

Selected here are poems from different historical periods. Some of their male authors, such as Gao Qi (1336–1374) and Wang Fuzhi (1619–1692), enjoyed empire-wide fame as writers or thinkers, while others were important only in their local communities and local poetry clubs. However, all shared the same social values and cultural heritage: all were trained in Confucian classics, and all were attracted by Daoist views of natural harmony. Consequently, tea-picking poems through the centuries display remarkable constancy in themes, metaphors, and symbols.

Confucian social and moral ideas are powerful shapers of tea-picking poetry. Following a long Confucian literary tradition of poetry as social commentary, Chen Zhang (fl. 1736) and Wu Lan focus on the bitter lives of tea-growers. As writers of the Qing period, when tea production boomed with the expansion of domestic and international markets, Chen and Wu cry out against the abusive governmental policy of "tribute tea" and the exploitation of tea households by the upper classes. In their poetry, tea-picking women symbolize social injustice. This theme is anticipated in an earlier poem by the Ming writer Gao Qi, who reveals that the finest tea had to be reserved for the governor and that the tea-growers never tasted their own product. Yet Gao's message is overridden by the romantic central themes of his lyric, that is, the joy of women tea-pickers and the satisfaction of tea-growers with their lives. Other positive themes, as we see, find their way into tea-picking poems. Poets such as Fan Chengda (1126–1193), Shu Yuexiang (1217–1301), and Wang Fuzhi saw in the joyful scenes of women working together an emblem of prosperous and harmonious village life. In fact, local pride was a driving force behind many of the tea-picking poems. Eighteenth-century poets Cao Weijie and Fang Youjiang stressed the diligence, energy, and endurance of the women tea-pickers from their own locality. Here we see Confucian gender values surface: diligence is a critical virtue for a good woman.

However, some metaphors characteristic of the tea-picking poems embody meanings that stand in direct contrast to the Confucian discourse on women's place and desirable female attributes. In Confucian rhetoric, the task of a respectable woman is to stay at home weaving cloth and making clothing.[2] Moreover, a good woman should have self-restraint and should not talk loudly and casually. In tea-picking poetry, these ideas seem to have been completely negated. Poets found women tea-pickers working out in the open hills most appealing. Talking, singing, and laughing were integral parts of the beautiful scenery of the tea harvest. All this suggests that the poetic representation of women and women's work in the tea industry took a different course from the moralist rhetoric familiar in Confucian didactic texts. The aesthetic tastes of the literati overrode their moral concerns.

Although the poetic representation of women's work is often highly romanticized, poets were sensitive enough to capture class differences in women's work. This is dramatized in the last poem translated here, which portrays a woman doing embroidery—another popular poetic theme. Apparently from an upper-class background, she resides alone in an elegant chamber, and she is overcome by lovesickness. Reserved and quiet, she contrasts sharply with the outgoing and unrestrained tea-pickers from the mountain villages.

ORIGINAL TEXT

"Returning Home after Seeing Lu Hongjian Off for Picking Tea"
by Huangfu Zeng[3]

Myriad peaks wait for the recluse;
The fragrant tea grows thick here and there.

In the deep valleys you pick tea;
I envy you—alone, you walk in the clouds and mists.
Far is the mountain temple, where we will meet;
By the lucid stream flowing through rocks we will share our meal.
In remote desolation lights glimmer;
From the temple comes the sound of a *qing*,[4] bringing me thoughts of you.

"Kuizhou Bamboo Branch Song" by Fan Chengda[5]

White-haired old ladies wear red flowers;
Young girls dress their hair in three coils.
Carrying sleepy babies on their backs, they mount the hills;
The season for picking mulberry leaves is over, and it's time for picking tea.

"After Returning to Live on the Farm, upon Seeing Village Women Picking Tea" by Shu Yuexiang[6]

On the near hill a woman is picking tea.
The tea leaves in dewdrops are packed into her basket.
Knowing that the tax is heavy, she works hard.
Singing and smiling, she seems not to worry.
The water reflects her face—who painted her eyebrows?
Wearing a flower, she is not ashamed.
Everyone appreciates a good appearance—
Why shouldn't she comb her hair?

"Tea-Picking Poem" by Gao Qi[7]

The rain has passed over creeks and mountains, and the blue clouds are mild;
In the thick shadows tea leaves are half-sprouted, and shoots are still short.
The girls in silver hairpins sing back and forth;
Looking at each other's baskets, they inquire: "Who has picked the most?"
The fragrance of the tea leaves is still on their hands when they return;
The highest grade tea will be first presented to the governor.
Just cured in the bamboo brazier, the tea is so fresh—but they do not taste it;
Packed into baskets, it will be sold to the Hunan merchants.

The mountain people do not know about growing rice and millet;
Year after year they rely on the tea harvest season for their sustenance.

"Nanyue Tea-Picking Songs" by Wang Fuzhi[8]

Moist clouds conceal the myriad linked peaks;
Amid the clouds I hear the laughing and merry chatting of the tea pickers.
It looks just like a misty moonlit night on Lake Dongting;
The lake's waters are dotted with fishing boats.

"Tea-Picking Song" by Cheng Zhang[9]

The Fenghuang Peak is sweetened with spring dew;
The girls in blue skirts have nimble fingers.
Passing over the streams and crossing the clouds, they go to pick tea;
At noon they return home with baskets still half-empty.
The express edict for "tribute tea" has come down from the capital;
Regardless of the fact that the cold weather has delayed the sprouting
of tea.
After curing, grains of tea appear like seeds of lotus;
Who understands? More bitter than lotus seeds are their hearts.

"Tea-Picking Song" by Wu Lan[10]

The daughter from a mountain family wears her hair in a pair of coils;
She picks the newly opened tea leaves before and after the rain.
The mountain stream is as limpid as a mirror;
Crossing the stream, she sees a reflection of her face, like a flower.
Unable to pick enough to fill the basket, she sighs deeply;
"Whom I can tell about the hardship of spring?"
Carried to the wealthy families to sell, a load of tea is not worth much;
In a cup of spring snow are leaves from thousands of mountains.

"Mount Huangyangjian" by Cao Weijie[11]

Above the poplar trees white clouds lie thickly;
In the *guyu*[12] season the sprouting tea shoots are as thin as pine needles.
Singing songs, village women with lotus feet walk steadily;
Carrying baskets on their backs, they climb the highest peak.

"Xin'an Bamboo Branch Song" by Fang Youjiang[13]

In *qingming*[14] season, the "magic plant" sprouts all over the valley;
Its quality will not be as good when summer comes.

How many are "visiting-home"[15] daughters?
In red dresses, they come out with their mothers to pick tea.

"Summer Poem"[16]

Putting down five-colored threads and the needle, she is tired
of embroidering;
On the jade steps, she sees the pomegranate is freshly blooming.
Nothing else to do in her chamber, where the bed looks like silver, and
the mat like ice;
In the south garden, butterflies grow in number, flying from dawn
till dusk.

NOTES

1. Many studies have been published in recent years about women's poetry in the late imperial period. Maureen Robertson's work in particular offers insight into the emergence of women's poetic voice. See her articles "Voicing the Feminine: Constructions of the Gendered Subject," and "Changing the Subject: Gender and Self-inscription in Authors' Prefaces and *Shi* Poetry."

2. The Chinese imperial state advocated a gender division of labor following the Confucian ideal that "men plow and women weave." Women's work, in this ideology, should be centered on spinning, weaving, making clothing, and embroidery. Susan Mann discusses how the state and the elite during the eighteenth century endeavored to encourage sericulture and textile manufacture as a means to strengthen both the state economy and womanly virtue. See Mann, *Precious Records: Women in China's Long Eighteenth Century,* 148–65. Also see Ebrey, *The Inner Quarters: Marriage and the Lives of Chinese Women in the Sung Period,* 131–51; and Bray, *Technology and Gender: Fabrics of Power in Late Imperial China,* 183–91.

3. Source: Huangfu Zeng, "Song Lu Hongjian shanren caicha hui."

4. *Qing* is a type of musical instrument made of stone.

5. Source: Fan Chengda, "Kuizhou zhuzhi ge."

6. Source: Shu Yuexiang, "Zi gui geng zhuan qi, jian cunfu you zhaicha."

7. Source: Gao Qi, "Caicha ci."

8. Source: Wang Fuzhi, "Nanyue zhaicha ci."

9. Source: Cheng Zhang, "Caicha ge."

10. Source: Wu Lan, "Caicha xing."

11. Source: Cao Weijie, "Huangyangjian shan."

12. *Guyu* (lit., grain rain) is one of the twenty-four solar terms that divide the lunar calendar. It falls normally on April 19, 20, or 21, and it begins the tea harvesting season in many parts of South China, where most tea-growing areas are located.

13. Source: Fang Youjiang, "Xin'an zhuzhi ci."

14. *Qingming* (clear and bright) is another solar term in the lunar calendar. It falls on April 4, 5, or 6.

15. The phrase "visiting home" refers to the customary periodic visits by married women to their natal families. Virilocal marriage, that is, the bride residing with her husband's family, was the norm in imperial China. For a critical discussion, see Judd, "*Niangjia:* Chinese Women and Their Natal Families."

16. Source: "Xia ci." The author of this poem is unknown.

Fig. 16. Portrait of Wu Zao. From *Sixty Famous Women,* attributed to Qiu Ying. Courtesy of the Field Museum of Natural History, Chicago, negative # CSA 48260.

SIXTEEN

Drinking Wine and Reading "Encountering Sorrow": A Reflection in Disguise by Wu Zao (1799–1862)

Translated by Sophie Volpp

TRANSLATOR'S PREFACE

I chose to translate Wu Zao's play *Drinking Wine and Reading "Encountering Sorrow": A Reflection in Disguise (Yinjiu du "Li sao" tu: Qiao ying)* because it is one of the few premodern plays by women that survive in their entirety, none of which have been published in translation.[1] I was also struck by the play's final image: the female poet Xie Xucai merges with her alter ego, a vision of herself crossed-dressed in a man's official robes.[2] The moment recalls a meditation practice in Tibetan Buddhism in which one meditates before the image of a bodhisattva, ultimately imagining the bodhisattva becoming one with oneself. Through the course of the play, Xie Xucai laments that her gifts are not being used and describes the pain of not having her talents recognized. Even as she does so, she moves toward a moment in which the self she has idealized merges with the discontented self she experiences.

INTRODUCTION

Wu Zao (literary pseudonym Pingxiang) was a poet from Renhe in Zhejiang province who was best known for her song lyrics *(ci)*. The biographical traditions surrounding Wu Zao cast her as a latter-day incarnation of the Southern Song poet Zhu Shuzhen. Like Zhu Shuzhen, she was supposedly the daughter of parents who did not understand her literary inclinations, and—like Zhu—she married a merchant who could not appreciate her literary talents. That she never mentions her husband is itself believed to indicate unhappiness in her marriage. We can see here how critics eager to construct a biography have made the very absence of information produce information. The scholarship of theater historian Lu Eting has been invaluable in judging the quality of the evidence on which these various traditions are based.[3]

Wu Zao's play, *Drinking Wine and Reading "Encountering Sorrow,"* is a long soliloquy lamenting the plight of the literary woman of the late imperial period. It has typically been read as an autobiographical work that expresses the frustrations of the author that her own talents were unrecognized. The play's protagonist is Xie Xucai, the name by which the fourth-century woman poet Xie Daoyun was known in later ages. Xie Daoyun's precocious brilliance is celebrated in the *History of the Jin Dynasty (Jin shu)* and in *A New Account of Tales of the World (Shishuo xinyu),* compiled ca. 430 by Liu Yiqing. As a girl, Xie Daoyun won a contest set by her uncle to see who among her siblings and cousins could most poetically describe the falling snow. Her male cousins all submitted pedestrian answers, but she, describing the snow as willow catkins *(xu),* won the contest with effortless brilliance.[4] In Wu Zao's play, Xie Xucai grieves that no one knows her talent and that as a woman, she has no literary disciples to ensure that her name will be known to posterity. "I have a man's ambition and a woman's sorrow and frustration," she declares, bemoaning the fact that she was born in the wrong age.

The performance and subsequent publication of the play brought the author the literary recognition her protagonist so desperately craved. The play was performed in Shanghai by a male actor named Gu Lanzhou; the acclaim that followed the play's performance hastened its printing. A friend of Wu Zao's elder brother Mengjiao brought the play to the attention of its publisher, and it was printed in 1825, when Wu Zao would have been about twenty-seven years old. Lu Eting surmises that the play may have been written three to four years earlier. One year following the publication of the play, Wu Zao was adopted into the circle of Chen Wenshu, a prominent male advocate of women's writing. The next year, in 1827, her collection of song lyrics, *Lyrics of the Flowered Curtain (Hua lian ci)* was published.

The primary conceit of the play is in its staging, which plays on multiple levels with gender crossing. The speaker stands before a self-portrait in which she has depicted herself cross-dressed in official's robes. Wu Zao in fact painted such a portrait of herself, and it was used in the original performance. The self-portrait acts as the on-stage audience for her soliloquy, and she confesses to it that none but the figure in the portrait can be considered her match.

Wu Zao was primarily a lyricist, but it is clear how this long soliloquy, which could have been framed as a suite of song lyrics, benefited from being written as a play. In dramatic form, *Drinking Wine* inscribes a more complicated sequence of gender crossings than might be possible in a song suite.

Wu Zao's stage directions require that the female protagonist Xie Xucai be played by an actor trained to play the male lead. Through this gender crossing, she deliberately problematizes the gender of both actor and character, so that both genders become immanent in both of them.[5] Xie Xucai and her portrait have an inverted and reciprocal relationship. The protagonist is played by the male lead dressed as a woman; the portrait depicts a woman dressed as a man.

Wu Zao's admiration of her cross-dressed self-portrait was one of the most salient features of the play for generations of readers, and even fueled the speculation that she was a lesbian poet.[6] In fact, her cross-dressing both refers to and inverts the gender crossing we find in one of the founding texts of the poetic tradition, Qu Yuan's "Encountering Sorrow" ("Li sao"), which is the very text that Xie Xucai holds as a prop during her soliloquy.[7] In "Encountering Sorrow" Qu Yuan figuratively casts himself as an abandoned woman in order to describe the frustration of a exiled courtier whose desire to serve goes unfulfilled. Wu Zao enacts both terms of Qu Yuan's metaphor. She appears on the stage as an abandoned woman—abandoned by a world that has no use for her literary talents. At the same time, she repeats and reverses Qu Yuan's gesture, presenting herself cross-dressed as an official in the alternate reality of the portrait in order to dramatize Qu Yuan's sentiment of "not being in accord with the times" *(shi bu yu).* Xie Xucai also cross-dresses verbally, casting herself as a succession of male poets through her use of allusion: "I will drink as much as a great whale," she says, referring to the poet Du Fu; "I'll lower a long rainbow into the depths of the sea," alluding to Li Bo; "I will pluck an iron *pipa* lute and sing over the river," posing as Su Shi. The speaker's cross-dressing, both literal and figurative, emblematizes the play's central concern that the talented woman, misunderstood and unappreciated, does not inhabit the time and space proper to her.

Xie Xucai suggests that through her poetry she reaches a state of wholeness and completion in which both genders are present and she, while alone, is completely self-sufficient: "I copy poems in black ink, then chant them accompanying myself with red ivory clappers. Only then am I like a famed man of letters who loves a beauty with total abandon." Only in the presence of the portrait can she shake off the feeling of being out of accord with her time and place. Only the person in the portrait understands her, and only in the presence of that understanding does she feel that the times are not out of joint. Not only is the portrait her witness, it is an externalization of her internal form, an embodiment of her secret and unwitnessed inner qualities that allows her to see and appreciate them.

The play closes with Xie Xucai's words, "I cannot tell the reflection in the portrait from my own form, for they have already become one." Xie Xucai's rhapsody to the portrait leads to her integration with the vision of herself painted in the portrait. Through this process, she internalizes qualities that she has externalized in the portrait. Her depiction of her cross-dressed self in both words and image is a way of "taking charge" of her form, which she had felt to be "shackled," as though she were an "ailing crane shut in a cage." What is most poignant is that Wu Zao's writing of this play represented a similar "taking charge" of her fate and ended in her gaining the recognition she longed for. With the writing of this play, she exerted a kind of agency within the limited confines of her situation by visualizing her unwitnessed self and creating a series of witnesses for it. Not only the portrait but also the implied audience of the play provides a witness for that part of herself—the literary talent—that has not been sufficiently acknowledged.

Xie Xucai suggests that these lyrics form a summons to the soul, an attempt to entice back a departed spirit. In so saying, she continues the allusion to Qu Yuan, referring to the "Summons to the Soul" ("Zhao hun") in the *Songs of the South (Chu ci),* traditionally ascribed to Song Yu.[8] Song Yu was thought to have been a disciple of Qu Yuan, and the "Summons to the Soul" was traditionally read as the disciple's attempt to invoke Qu Yuan's departed spirit. Xie Xucai laments, "Who will summon my poet's frustrated soul? My spirit wants to go and be with Qu Yuan. It labors in dreams dreamt in vain." Lacking a disciple, she concludes that she will have to summon her own soul. "Among the ancients, there were those . . . who wrote eulogies for themselves . . . I sing the 'Summons to the Soul' and drink pine wine." Her rhapsody to the portrait, then, is an attempt to summon her own soul back, an attempt that concludes with the portrait merging with her own body.

Chen Wenshu and the Chinese critics that followed him have read the play as an autobiographical expression of Wu Zao's frustration regarding her inability as a woman to find full use of her talents. Modern readers might hesitate at this identification of author and speaker, and question the long-standing tradition of reading women's writing as inevitably autobiographical—a tradition based on the assumption that women's compass of experience was too narrow to write works about a more "universal" human condition. However, I am persuaded that we ought to read this play as autobiographical. Those members of Chen Wenshu's circle who saw the play knew Wu Zao personally; they read Xie Xucai as Wu Zao's alter ego. As we have observed, Wu Zao's self-portrait was in fact used as the portrait during the performance of the play. Moreover, as the contemporary scholar Hua Wei has noted, there is a strong continuity between the phrasing and sentiments expressed in Wu Zao's play and in her song lyrics; the sentiments expressed by Xie Xucai are not exclusive to this dramatic persona.[9] If the character of Xie Xucai is in effect Wu Zao's self-portrait, the portrait on stage itself reminds us that a self-portrait is not an exact replica but an illustration of the author's hopes, fears, and dreams. The relation between Xie Xucai and her portrait may in fact be analogous to that between Wu Zao and her play. Just as the portrait represents an idealized image that by the end of the play merges with the speaker, so Xie Xucai may have been not merely a reflection of Wu Zao's inner self but a desired other who she became through the writing of this play.

ORIGINAL TEXT[10]

[Actor who plays the male lead enters in turban and robe and sings to the tune "Bei xin shuiling":]

A tree scattered with flowers shelters my study.
All day long I arrange brush holder and tea warmer,
Carrying this jade wine goblet about with me.
I have changed into the green robes that so suit me,
My robes and shoes so stylish,
That I am ashamed to again brush kohl on my brows.

[She sits and speaks:] Steel tempered a hundred times becomes so soft it wraps around your finger. I have a man's ambition and a woman's sorrow and frustration. This morning, I express both in a mournful tune that will wash away the shame of being a woman in this world.

I, Xie Xucai, was raised in the boudoir, but I have always loved books and histories. I am embarrassed to be a woman, for I have no interest in my toilette. My writing, I daresay, could be rewarded with the amethyst pendants of an official. Indeed, I would enjoy being like Huang Shan and talking of swordsmanship.[11] Were I to let loose what is in my heart, I would resemble an egret flying on top of the clouds. But unfortunately I was born in the wrong age, and so I resemble an ailing crane shut in a cage. Alas, I'm shackled in this body, and I can only lament and sigh about it. But when I consider this with care, I realize that even if my form has been given to me by Heaven, it's up to me to take charge of it. For this reason, I recently drew a sketch of myself dressed as a man. I call it "Portrait of Myself Drinking Wine and Reading 'Encountering Sorrow.'" One could say that such a beautiful woman as I may secretly boast of being one of the most dashing of famed literary men. Today I slipped out of my dressing gown and came to my study to enjoy my portrait for a bit, in order to dispel my vexation and anger at the injustice of being a woman.

[She gets up and goes to a corner of the stage and sings to the tune of "Nan bu bu jiao":]

Jesters have always confused the real and the unreal,[12]
Coming up with new and clever ideas.
I water my sorrows and idleness with wine.
I have a chivalrous spirit and the passions of a hero,
But who has heard of me?

[Takes a book out of her sleeve.]

I carry a copy of "Encountering Sorrow."
Bushes of red flowers wind round the steps.

[Attendant moves to the front of the stage and hangs the painting, then sets out a table and chairs, placing wine cups on the table. Xie Xucai looks at the painting and speaks:]

Look at the jade tree before the wind, bright pearl at its side. Lofty brows, long fingers, raven-black hat, green clothes. This portrait is done with such a carefree spirit!

[Sings to the tune of "Bei zhe gui ling":]

You say female scholars lack purpose.
Truly, we are illusory shadows and flowers in the void.
It's as if our due share of good fortune had evaporated.
Look at this mad woman, whom I've painted in a fresh way.
Her luck in this life is truly thin as paper.
I need not add that her thoughts are loftier than the sky.
Her figure is so at ease, hair bound beneath a tilted man's cap.
This is much better than light makeup or some form-fitting sheer gauze.
Why is my powder caked and my fragrance old?
Why have I been ill so long?
Why have I always plenty of sorrow to spare?

I just fear that the cup of rose-red wine in the painting can't possibly sustain the withering of youth reflected in my mirror.

[Drinks wine.]

There is a poem by one of the ancients, Li Bo:

A jug of wine amidst the flowers,
No friends nearby, I drink alone.

I lift my cup to invite the bright moon to drink with me.
Facing my shadow, we become three.[13]

If I were to consider my situation with this poem in mind, I would say that the person in the painting understands me better than anyone in the world.

[Moves to the right to examine the portrait and sings to the tune of "Nan jiang er shui":]

I carefully examine your elegant figure
You've become quite adorable in a new way.
Your rakish features are more comely than those of the lotus flowers.
But I am afraid that this lonely and sad person will be laughed at by
the peach blossoms.[14]
How can my life be as insignificant as that of the small flowers of
the pear?

[Speaks:] Oh, Xucai, Xucai.

[Sings:]

I hold the picture again and cry out madly,
With such a lofty figure as yours,
Who but I could be a match for you?

[Speaks:] Humph. When I think of my disregard for this age, of how my ambitions are loftier than those of the pear flowers, and how my rare ambition is larger than the Yunmeng marsh, I realize that I need not face my shadow and mumble to myself, cutting a foolish figure.[15] Instead I'll take my life's ambitions and ruminate upon them.

[Stands in the middle of the stage, gestures, and sings to the tune of "Bei yan er luo dai de sheng ling":]

I will skim the misty waves with painted oar.
I will ride the winds of heaven, traveling to Penglai.[16]
I will pluck an iron *pipa* lute and sing over the river.[17]
I will look at the Green Duckweed sword[18] and whistle before the lamp.[19]
Ah, I'll lower a long rainbow into the depths of the sea[20] and fish golden
turtles with it.
I will drink as much as a great whale.[21]
I will use a golden sable fur to buy wine on credit.[22]

I will tune my cinnabar strings to play the "secluded orchid tune."[23]
I will wear a court robe and go to ripple the moon in the water.[24]
I'll play the flute; I am even younger than Zijin.[25]
I will use the character for "cake" in a poem, and laugh at Liu Mengde,
who foolishly thought himself a hero.[26]

[Speaks:] Ugh, what a load of nonsense. I am simply a fool interpreting my own dreams. Those who have understood me have always sympathized with my pure and untrammeled nature. Those who don't understand me accuse me of leading a most strange and absurd life. How could they know that my feelings of indignation and frustration are simply innate?

[Sings to the tune of "Nan rao rao ling":]

My whole life I've been proud.
The deeds of a past life must have given sprout to such sorrow.
Don't think me strange if, like Yin Hao, I write in the air: "Tut, tut,
what a strange affair!"[27]
I'm just trying to find an excuse to console myself before those
around me.[28]
Yes, console myself before those around me.

[Speaks:] When I open the wine and bring out the books, I can greatly relieve my sorrow. How can I have once more a few dancers and singers, wind in their skirts, the moon shining on their fans? Wouldn't this be an entertainment fit for a literatus?

[Sings to the tune of "Bei shou Jiangnan":]

Ah, if only I had a red-sleeved companion who would change the
incense while passing a spring evening with me,
The best I can do now is put away my sleeveless jacket and bear
the cold.[29]
And I can certainly forget about the hundred pecks of kohl that I once
mixed to paint my brows.
I copy poems in black ink,
Then chant them accompanying myself with red ivory clappers.
Only then am I like a famed man of letters who loves a beauty with
total abandon.

[Laughs heartily.] It's such fun! We'll penalize you by making you drink a big cup! [Drinks wine and reads book.] Qu Yuan was truly unique. I reckon that in later ages there was no one who could emulate him. I, Xie Xucai, am his equivalent in our times, a lonely figure walking the rivers and marshes chanting poems.

[Sings to the tune of "Nan yuan lin hao":]

On my clothes woven of lotus leaves the scent of fragrant powder floats.
Towards the waters of the distant Xiang River I wander,[30]
Chanting the words of "Encountering Sorrow."
I scratch my head and question the empty azure sky.
I scratch my head and question the empty azure sky.

[Cries in pain.] I know that Qu Yuan's name lingers on earth, even though his soul has returned to heaven. His renown was such that after he died, he even had a disciple who tried to summon his soul by raining tears over Jiangnan.[31] One day, my name will vanish in the mists, and my soul will wander. Who knows what will become of me in the end?

[Sings to the tune of "Bei gu meijiu dai taiping ling":]

Who will summon my poet's frustrated soul?
Who will summon my poet's frustrated soul?
My spirit wants to go and be with Qu Yuan.
It labors in dreams dreamt in vain.

[Speaks:] Among the ancients, there were those who wrote laments for people who were still alive. There were others who wrote eulogies for themselves.

[Sings:]

Now the spring breeze over the paper has come to an end.
I sing the "Summons to the Soul" and drink pine wine.
How many times in one's life can one enjoy sweet grasses in the
setting sun?
How many times can one bear to watch the moon waning in the
morning breeze?
I could have written countless drafts of songs that would break your
heart, adding a portrait that would make anyone grieve.

I am putting away my gold and green-feathered ornaments,[32]
Preparing my poems and wine.

[Speaks:] Ah.
[Sings:]

Standing next to the flowers, I repeatedly mourn my image.

[Takes the portrait down and sings to the tune of "Qing jiang yin":]

Yellow chickens and dawn-white sun hasten me to old age.[33]
When shall I wake from this butterfly's dream?[34]
For a long time to come I will be in the company of the person in
the portrait,
Who will always be like the bird of Jialing, able to rise above the dust
of this world.[35]
I cannot tell the reflection in the portrait from my own form, for they
have already become one.

NOTES

1. "Encountering Sorrow" ("Li sao") is a long poem from the anthology *Songs of the South (Chu ci)* compiled in the second century B.C.E. The poem is attributed to Qu Yuan, who according to legend was a virtuous minister who was doomed to wander in exile because he was misunderstood by his lord and finally drowned himself in despair.

In the subtitle of her play, Wu Zao plays with a number of meanings for the character *qiao,* here translated as "disguise." *Qiao* can also mean "eccentric" or "charming." Readers would have heard more resonances than one can convey in translation; the portrait is not only camouflaged, but charming and eccentric. The word I have translated here as "reflection" *(ying)* also has multiple connotations; it is translated as "sketch," "shadow," and "silhouette" elsewhere.

2. For a discussion of cross-dressing in *Drinking Wine and Reading "Encountering Sorrow,"* see Hua Wei, "Ming Qing funü juzuo zhong zhi 'ninan' biaoxian yu xingbie wenti."

3. Lu Eting, *Qingdai xiqu jia cong kao.*

4. Liu Yiqing, *Shishuo xinyu,* 130; see Richard Mather's translation in *"Shih-shuo Hsin-yü": A New Account of Tales of the World,* 64. For an account of the significance of Xie Daoyun for late imperial women, see Mann, *Precious Records: Women in China's Long Eighteenth Century,* 135.

5. Theoretically, the male lead could be played by either a male or a female actor. The only mention of this play's performance tells of a male actor playing the lead role. Although female actors had been banned from the stage through the Qing, by the time this play was written some female actors were in fact per-

forming on public stages. See Hua Wei, "Ming Qing funü," 601; and Zeng Yongyi, *Shuo xiqu,* 45.

6. See Rexroth and Chung, *Women Poets of China,* 135.

7. See David Hawkes's translation of "Encountering Sorrow" in *The Songs of the South: An Ancient Chinese Anthology of Poems by Qu Yuan and Other Poets,* 67–95.

8. See David Hawkes's translation of "Summons to the Soul" in *The Songs of the South,* 219–32.

9. Hua Wei, "Ming Qing funü," 596

10. Source: The original text can be found in a facsimile edition: Wu Zao, *Yinjiu du "Li sao" tu: Qiao ying,* in *Qingren zaju erji,* ed. Zheng Zhenduo, 287–310. A typeset version with annotation is available in *Qingdai zaju xuan,* edited by Wang Yongkuan, Yang Haizhong, and Yao Shuyi. The text translated here is from the original printing. The play is prefaced with poems by men and women of Chen Wenshu's circle, including the famous woman poet Wang Duan. These poems indicate that the circle of friends did not merely read the play but in fact saw it performed.

11. Huang Shan was the protagonist of the Tang dynasty tale "Huo Xiaoyu zhuan"; here this name invokes a dashing youth.

12. This refers to the story of the court jester Meng in Sima Qian's *Shi ji.* The jester Meng, famed for his verbal wit, dressed as an official in order to gain favor from King Zhuang of Chu for the son of Sun Shu'ao. See Sima Qian, "Huaji liezhuan," in *Shi ji,* 10:3197–3214.

13. Li Bo, "Yexia du zhuo si shou," in *Li Bo ji jiao zhu,* 185.

14. Peach blossoms here signify women who have married and led more conventional lives.

15. Yunmeng marsh is a marsh in present-day Hubei. The Tang poet Meng Haoran spoke of his ambition as being as wide as the Yunmeng marsh. See Meng Haoran's "Wang Dongting hu zeng zhang chang xiang" in Zhang Shuqiong, ed., *Meng Haoran,* 19.

16. Penglai is the mythical island of the immortals.

17. Here the speaker refers to her lyrics as masculine and heroic in the style of Su Shi's lyrics.

18. "Green Duckweed" *(Qingping)* was the name of a famous sword. The phrase "holding the lamp up to regard the sword" was often used by poets to describe their desire to make contributions to the nation.

19. The "whistle" *(xiao)* is something like a long cry; it is associated with spontaneous and unconventional behavior.

20. Here she compares herself to the poet Li Bo, who claimed that he would use the light of the moon as a fishing hook, a rainbow as fishing line, and the unrighteous men of the world as bait to fish giant turtles from the ocean. "Giant turtles" (or "golden turtles") is an epithet for men of worth, and in particular, for successful candidates in the civil service examinations.

21. Du Fu, in his "Song of the Eight Immortals, Written While Drunk" writes of "drinking like a great whale to soak up the hundred rivers" (Du Fu, "Yinjiu baxian ge"; see Chou Zhao'ao, ed., *Du shi xiangzhu,* 1:81).

22. The biography of Ruan Fu in the *History of the Jin Dynasty (Jin shu)* tells us how Ruan Fu used a golden panther fur to buy wine on credit (*Jin shu,* 3:1364).

23. Song Yu was the putative author of the poem "Summoning the Soul" and was traditionally believed to be a disciple of Qu Yuan. Here the speaker refers to Song Yu's "Rhymeprose on the Wind" to characterize her own writing as the re-

freshing "male wind" that Song Yu describes, rather than the pernicious "female wind" that, Song Yu warns, inflicts those it touches with illness. See Xiao Tong, comp., *Wen xuan,* 175–76.

24. A reference to Li Bo's poem on drinking with the moon. See note 13.

25. *The Biography of Immortals (Liexian zhuan)* tells the story of Wang Ziqiao, also known as Zijin, who loved to play the flute and eventually became an immortal, ascending into the heavens on a white crane. See Liu Xiang, *Liexian zhuan,* 10:495. See also Kaltenmark, *Le Lie-sien tschouan,* 109–14.

26. Ji Yun, *Shaoshi jianwen houlu,* 148. Here Wu Zao contrasts her iconoclasm with the pedantry of the poet Liu Mengde, who wanted to use the character for "cake" in a poem, but rejected the word when he realized that the character did not appear in any of the Six Classics.

27. After Yin Hao (the governor of Yang province from 346 to 350) was dismissed from his post by Huan Wen, he went mad and simply wrote the characters "Tut, tut, what a strange affair" *(duoduo guaishi)* in the air from morning till night. In later periods, this phrase was used to describe any strange event. Here the speaker makes an analogy between her painting of the portrait and Yin Hao's eccentric writing in the air. See Liu Yiqing, *Shishuo xinyu,* 1:450. See also Mather, *"Shih-shuo Hsin-yü,"* 451.

28. "Those around me" may refer either to the person in the portrait or the audience.

29. The sleeveless jacket was worn by officials during the Tang dynasty.

30. The Xiang River is a tributary of the Milo River, in which Qu Yuan drowned himself.

31. Here she refers to Sung Yu, the putative author of the poem "Summoning the Soul" in the anthology *Songs of the South (Chu ci).* Written for his teacher, Qu Yuan, "Summoning the Soul" is traditionally read as a lament for Qu Yuan. See notes 1 and 23.

32. A woman's hair ornaments.

33. Here she cites Bo Juyi's "Sung While Drunk" ("Zui ge"). See Bo Juyi, *Bo Juyi ji,* 12:51.

34. "Butterfly dream" refers to an anecdote in Zhuang zi's "Discussion on Making All Things Equal," in which Zhuang zi dreamt he was a butterfly. When he woke up, he was not certain whether he was Zhuang zi dreaming he was a butterfly, or a butterfly dreaming he was Zhuang zi. In other words, he was uncertain which was the more illusory, life or the dream.

35. "The bird of Jialing" is a Buddhist term for a bird with a beautiful voice; the sounds of the Buddhist scriptures are compared to the music of this bird.

Fig. 17. Scenes from life in Taiwan: "Hunting Party" and "Pounding Rice." Source: *Zhuluo xian zhi* (1717).

SEVENTEEN

A Brief Record of the Eastern Ocean by Ding Shaoyi (fl. 1847)

Translated by Emma Jinhua Teng

TRANSLATOR'S PREFACE

The translated passage is a selection from *A Brief Record of the Eastern Ocean (Dongying zhilüe)*, a lengthy travel account of Taiwan written by Ding Shaoyi in the nineteenth century, nearly two hundred years after the Qing first colonized the island. I chose to translate this text because of both the author's treatment of gender and his historicization of the customs of the indigenous people of Taiwan. One noteworthy feature of the text is that the author returns to his own record after a span of several decades and comments upon the historical changes he has observed. I found his views on historical change among the indigenous people to be most interesting.

This text is also a wonderful example of the way in which travel writers situate their own accounts within a larger historical context, relating their own observations to those of earlier travelers or gazetteer compilers. Ding goes one step beyond the typical practice in relating his material to a Jesuit account of North America. I was particularly fascinated by the way Ding used Giulio Aleni's geographic work to draw comparisons between the "native barbarians" *(tuman)* of North America and the "savages" of Taiwan. His comments reveal an awareness of the global dimensions of territorial expansion and "civilizing missions." Ding clearly sees the "civilizing" of the Taiwan indigenes as analogous to the work of European missionaries in North America, with one crucial difference: the Europeans are attempting to transform people by appealing to what he views as an inferior religion, whereas the Chinese will transform people with the superior Confucian doctrine. Ding is speaking here against colonial naysayers who argued that the savages could never be transformed and that it was therefore simply a waste of time to try.

Of particular interest to me is the way in which Ding incorporates gender into his discussion of indigenous customs. He does not separate "women" as a separate category for discussion; rather gender is integral to his account: changes in gender roles serve as an important index of cultural transformation. The story of a woman named Baozhu, related in a number of Qing accounts of Taiwan, is especially intriguing, as it reveals the complex intersections of gender and ethnicity in the colonial context. One telling point of the story is that a Chinese woman serves as the bearer of civilization to the "savages." Yet she also benefits from the notion that women had more power or influence among the "savages" than in patriarchal Chinese culture. The foregrounding of gender in Ding's account is typical of Qing travel writing about Taiwan. This proved to be fortuitous for me as a researcher who is interested in gender studies: reading through the accounts of Taiwan I found I did not need to dig too far to find material that was explicitly about gender. It was a pleasure for me to feel that I was not engaged in a particularly "modern" intellectual enterprise, but rather that I shared certain interests with the Qing writers whose works I was reading for my research on travel accounts of Taiwan.[1]

INTRODUCTION

The island of Taiwan is located about one hundred miles off the coast of mainland China. It was originally populated by indigenous people of Austronesian descent, who were divided into various "tribes" *(she)*. In 1624, the Dutch established an entrepôt on Taiwan and attempted to colonize the island. Chinese laborers were brought in to work on Dutch sugar and rice plantations. In 1661, Ming loyalist Koxinga, who was fighting the establishment of the Manchu Qing regime in China, fled to the island with his rebel forces, expelling the Dutch. The Qing took the island in 1683, defeating the rebels and making Taiwan a part of the Qing empire. Chinese settlers then began to immigrate to the island in significant numbers, attracted by the opportunities this fertile frontier offered. In 1887, Taiwan was officially made a province of China. Less than a decade later, however, in 1895, the island was ceded to the Japanese as a result of the Sino-Japanese War. The indigenous people of Taiwan have thus endured a succession of colonizers.

The colonization of Taiwan was part of a larger process of Qing expansionism on the frontiers. From the mid–seventeenth century to the mid–eighteenth century, the Qing pursued various conquests on the Mongolian, Tibetan, Xinjiang, and southwestern frontiers, doubling the size of its territory. Recent scholarship has sought to compare Qing imperialism with Western imperialism. As Peter Perdue writes, "The Qing empire of China was a colonial empire that ruled over a diverse collection of peoples with separate identities and deserves comparison with other empires."[2]

The indigenous people of Taiwan were dubbed the Eastern Savages *(Dongfan)* by Chen Di, who traveled to the island in 1603, and who was probably the earliest Chinese writer to make a firsthand record of the customs of the natives (*fansu,* or "savage customs"). The term "savage" *(fan)* stuck. Chinese later divided the "savages" into various categories, including "raw savages" *(shengfan),* "cooked savages" *(shufan),* and "tribal savages" *(shefan).* The notion of dividing "barbarians," or "savages" into the "raw" and the "cooked" was a conventional Chinese practice, as described by Jacqueline Armijo-Hussein in chapter 5. In the case of Taiwan, Qing writers offered a wide range of definitions for "raw" and "cooked." But simply put, the term "raw" denoted those savages who were beyond Qing control and who also appeared most "uncivilized" in Chinese eyes. The "raw savages" generally lived in Taiwan's mountainous jungle and were often belligerent toward Chinese who entered their terrain. The term "cooked" denoted those who had submitted to Qing rule, who paid taxes, and who had adopted some Chinese customs, thus appearing more "civilized." The "cooked savages" generally lived on the plains areas of the island. As the Chinese colonization of the island advanced, more and more "tribes" became "cooked." As Ding Shaoyi notes, by the nineteenth century the "cooked savages" had largely assimilated to Chinese ways.

The question of whether or not the Taiwan indigenes could be "civilized" was a matter of great debate among Qing writers—colonial officials, military men, and ordinary travelers alike. Some argued that the indigenes were mere beasts who could not comprehend what it meant to become civilized. Others argued that with education in the Confucian classics, the indigenes would gradually become civilized. Yet others argued that with intermarriage between the Chinese and the native population, ethnic divisions would naturally be erased. Ding's declaration that it would be an injustice to say that the "raw savages" cannot be civilized is made within this context. According to John Shepherd, the official Qing agenda was "to propagate Confucian civic culture and attitudes of submission to constituted authority rather than wholesale sinicization."[3] As a result of this general policy, there was a significant degree of cultural plurality in Qing Taiwan.

The Qing colonial administration had to worry about controlling not only the indigenous population but also the Han settler population, which frequently rebelled against the Qing government. Among the most famous uprisings are the Zhu Yigui rebellion of 1721, the double revolt of the Dajiaxi tribes and Wu Fusheng in 1731–1732, and the Lin Shuangwen rebellion of 1786–1788.[4] Taiwan thus became known as a troublesome frontier.

Qing writers produced numerous accounts of the island. Much of this writing focused on the customs of the indigenous people. As I hinted in my preface, gender was integral to Qing representations of ethnicity. Taking Confucian gender ideology as the norm, Qing travelers interpreted unfamiliar gender roles as an index of a people's "otherness." The subsequent adoption of Chinese gender roles by colonized peoples such as the Taiwan indigenes was taken by Chinese observers as a sign of their becoming "civilized." In both travel literature and ethnographic writing, the discourse of gender became a means of demarcating the "civilized" from the "uncivilized." As I have argued elsewhere, the use of the trope of gender inversion (the reversal of normative sex roles) to represent foreignness has a long history in China.[5] Non-Chinese women, especially from exotic southern regions, were also frequently eroticized by Chinese writers, as Armijo-Hussein also points out. In the case of Taiwan, Chinese travelers repeatedly remarked on what they saw as the dominance of women in indigenous society. They were particularly impressed with the fact that Taiwan had female tribal heads, uxorilocal marriage, and matrilineal inheritance. Moreover, local custom allowed young girls to choose their own marriage partners; divorce and remarriage were also freely permitted. The lack of gender segregation struck Chinese observers as particularly uncivilized, especially when men and women sat around drinking together. In addition, the traditional division of labor in most tribes dictated that women tilled the fields while men hunted, an activity that Chinese saw as idleness. The seemingly anomalous gender roles of the indigenes was one of the most popular topics in Qing travel writing on Taiwan. The claim that the savages "value woman and undervalue man" *(zhongnü qingnan)* became a cliché of ethnographic description. This phrase is a direct inversion of the Confucian maxim "value man and undervalue woman" *(zhongnan qingnü),* and it thus expresses the Chinese idea that Taiwanese society was upside-down, or out of order. Consequently, female gender roles aroused great interest not only because they appeared strange in and of themselves, but also because they served as an index of the strangeness of Taiwan overall. In this way, the discourse of gender was central to Qing representations of Taiwan's "otherness." For example, Qing writers paid little attention to the fact that the indigenous women did not bind their feet. Numerous writers suggested that the women ought to quit farming and take up "feminine" tasks such as weaving and sewing in order to become civilized, but they never mentioned footbinding. As late as the nineteenth century, indigenous women remained barefooted, a fact that drew little comment, whereas bare-breastedness often raised cries of "uncivilized" or "shameless" from travel writers. These are subtle clues that Han Chinese writers viewed Taiwan as a land of strange and exotic sexual practice, not unlike the southwestern province of Yunnan.[6]

What follows is a translation of a passage from *A Brief Record of the Eastern Ocean.* The text, first published by a Fujian publishing house around 1873, is a work in eight *juan,* recording geographical information about nineteenth-century Taiwan. Ding Shaoyi, the author, was a native of Wuxi in Jiangsu. He traveled to Taiwan in the fall of 1847 as an aide to the

Circuit Intendant of Taiwan, in which capacity he served about eight months. It was during this stay that he compiled his account. The account is divided into sixteen topics that include taxes, schools, coastal defense, local products, "savage" villages, "savage" customs, and marvels. Ding traveled again to Taiwan in 1871 and appended material to each item of his original account. The translated passage is Ding's 1871 supplement to his entry on "savage" customs.

In his account Ding appears to subscribe to a notion of social evolution, seeing the changes in "savage" customs as a measure of increasing civilization. At the end of the piece he expresses full confidence that the savages can be transformed into civilized human beings. Yet at other times Ding sees aspects of indigenous culture that are admirable and perhaps ought to be preserved. He quotes a number of earlier texts that idealized indigenous culture and then declares that "one can imagine that this is the world of Lord No-Cares and Getian" (mythical rulers of an idyllic primeval age). His piece thus conveys the ambivalence expressed by numerous Chinese travel writers toward the indigenous culture of Taiwan. That is, while Chinese observers found the indigenes to be technologically and culturally "backward" in many respects, many writers also romanticized what they saw as the primitive simplicity and naturalness of these people—much as Rousseau romanticized the "noble savage."[7] For these writers, the "primitives" symbolized the innocence, honesty, and virtuousness of the simple life that was lost as Chinese civilization became ever more complex. As is typical in travel writing, then, Qing travelers used the encounter with the "other" as an opportunity for looking back at the self and critiquing their own society.

ORIGINAL TEXT[8]

Supervising Censor Huang Yupu [Shujing], Senior Graduate Yu Canglang [Yonghe],[9] and the various prefectural and county gazetteers all lumped the raw and cooked savages[10] together when they recorded savage customs. But these were things that happened before the Yongzheng era [1723–1736]. Today, most of the cooked savages marry virilocally while few marry uxorilocally, and they pass down a single surname. There is little difference from the Chinese settler population in terms of clothing, food, and conduct. Since the various savages became assimilated, they perform betrothals when they marry, and they bury the dead separately.[11] They distinguish between good and bad foods, and the women wear leggings and blouses, following many of the Chinese customs. However, they rarely have collars or sleeves on their clothing and seldom wear shoes. Nor have they established proper clan names, nor learned to read and write. To begin with, the conditions in the various savage villages already differed; now there is also a difference between the past and the present. So I chose to record the general conditions. Moreover, I'm afraid that in a few more decades once again a description of today's customs will no longer be fitting.

Prefect Deng Chuan'an [style name Shuyuan], native of Fuliang in Jiangxi, wrote in his *Measuring the Sea with a Calabash:*[12] "During the Jiaqing reign [1796–1821], the female native chieftain Baozhu bedecked herself like a Chinese noble lady. In governance she used the law. Someone sent the officials an official communication stating that her tribe followed the law obediently and respectfully, not killing people, and not rebelling. Even though this is beyond the pale, how is this any different from the interior [of China]?" Popular legend has it that during the Zhu Yigui rebellion, a native chieftain of the Beinanmi, Wenji, guided troops to capture the bandits.[13] The general rewarded him with the hat, robe, and shoes of the sixth rank and also made his son a native chieftain.[14] He became dominant over the various native villages. He was presented with coral and pearls. Then he called himself the king of the Beinanmi. He hoped to obtain a beauty for his consort. In Taiwan city there was a courtesan who heard of this and happily volunteered to go. The savages value women *[zhongnü]* to begin with, and since he had gotten a courtesan, he doted on her to the extreme, doing whatever she commanded. Then they got rid of their old customs and were civilized with the rites and laws of China. Therefore, the seventy-odd villages of the Beinanmi are the most orderly, and their customs have long been different from those of other savages. "Baozhu" is not like the name of a savage woman; perhaps this so-called female chieftain is after all a courtesan?

In He Qiaoyuan's *History of Fujian* it is written:[15] "During the Yongle period [1403–1424], Zheng He took to the seas and issued a proclamation to the various barbarian rulers. Only the Eastern Savages northeast of the Pescadores refused to submit to the treaty. Zheng He gave these people a bell to hang around the neck, thus making dogs of them."[16] Since I have traveled to the various savage villages both south and north, I have yet to see anyone wearing a bell. What is written cannot always be trusted.

The *Zhuluo County Gazetteer* says:[17] "Among all the various savages, the husband and wife are mutually devoted. Even when they are wealthy, [the savages] do not have maids and concubines, or boy servants. For their entire lives they never go out the village gate. They hold hands when walking, and they ride together in the same carriage. They do not know the bitterness of being separated in life. They do not steal. They know not of gambling or gaming. They are like an unchiseled block of primeval chaos."

The *Illustrations of the Flora and Fauna of Taiwan* says:[18] "When the harvest is in, the savages invite one another for a celebration. Men and women sit together unsegregated—drinking and making toasts, they enjoy themselves. If a Han Chinese barges in, they pull him in to drink with them. They do not stop until they are drunk. When younger people meet their elders, they stand by the side of the road and wait for them to pass before they continue walking. When they come across one of their peers, they greet one another." These customs have still not changed. One can imagine that this is the world of Lord No-Cares *[Wuhuai shi]* and Getian.[19]

Also, according to the Westerner Giulio Aleni's *World Atlas:*[20] "In North America, the farther north one goes, the wilder the people become. There are no city walls, no chiefs, no writing systems. Several families combined make up one village. By custom they are fond of drink. Attacking and killing is their daily business. Whenever they go out to battle, the entire family fasts and prays for victory. When they are victorious, they return. They cut off the enemy's head and use it to build a wall. If they go into battle again, the elders in the family immediately point to the skulls on the top of the wall to urge them on. Such is the extent of their bravura and belligerence. Recently, there have been European missionaries who have gone amongst them and urged them to worship God and cease their killing. Then they all changed entirely. Moreover, they had firm resolve, so that once they reformed they never transgressed. According to their custom, those who are wealthy are charitable. Whenever a family cooks a meal, they leave some food outside the gate. Passersby can partake as they please." These things that he recorded pertain to the native barbarians of the newly opened northern frontier of North America, but their savagery is no different from the savages of Taiwan. Their ferocity was extreme, yet the Westerners have guided them with their senseless, confused religion and have finally changed their customs. So to say that the raw savages [of Taiwan] have absolutely no human morals despite their human appearance and that they cannot be civilized with our kingly governance *[wangzheng]*, is that not an injustice?![21]

NOTES

1. See Teng, "Travel Writing and Colonial Collecting: Chinese Travel Accounts of Taiwan from the Seventeenth through Nineteenth Centuries."

2. Perdue, "Comparing Empires: Manchu Colonialism," 256.

3. Shepherd, *Statecraft and Political Economy on the Taiwan Frontier, 1600–1800*, 371.

4. See Meskill, *A Chinese Pioneer Family: The Lins of Wu-feng, Taiwan, 1729–1895*.

5. See Teng, "An Island of Women: The Discourse of Gender in Qing Travel Writing about Taiwan."

6. See chapter 5.

7. See Teng, "Taiwan as a Living Museum: Tropes of Anachronism in Late-Imperial Chinese Travel Writing."

8. Source: Ding Shaoyi, *Dongying zhilüe*, 2d ed., 78–79.

9. Huang Shujing and Yu Yonghe were the authors of two famous travel accounts of Taiwan, *Taihai shicha lu* (1736) and *Pihai jiyou* (1697) respectively.

10. I have chosen to translate the Chinese word *fan* as "savage" in order to distinguish it from *yi*, commonly translated as "barbarian." Chinese writers frequently regarded the indigenous people of Taiwan as belonging to a lower order than those termed "barbarians," such as the Koreans and the Japanese. The word "savage" also emphasizes parallels with European accounts of the New World.

11. That is, the dead are buried apart from the living, which is a sign of "progress." Earlier Chinese accounts noted that the dead were placed in the house uncoffined or were buried under the house. Chen Di, for example, wrote in his *Record of the Eastern Savages* (*Dongfan ji*, 1603): "They place the corpse on the ground in the midst of a blazing fire in order to dry it; when it is dried they place it exposed in the house, uncoffined. When the house is dilapidated and they rebuild it, they dig a pit underneath and bury [the corpse] in a standing position, but with no mound to cover it, and the house is then again raised above it" (cited in Thompson, "The Earliest Chinese Eyewitness Accounts of the Formosan Aborigines," 174).

12. Deng Chuan'an, *Lice huichao*, 1830. Deng took his title from the phrase *yili cehai* (to use a calabash to measure the sea), meaning that one's knowledge is shallow and limited. As Deng explains in his preface: "It is not that I dare say that the sea can be measured with a calabash; it is simply that I wish for those who come here to know the small goblet of water that is the beginning of the great river" (1).

13. In 1721, a Chinese settler named Zhu Yigui led a rebellion against the Qing forces on Taiwan. The rebellion was initially successful but was eventually put down by Qing troops with the aid of indigenous militia. See Shepherd, *Statecraft and Political Economy*, for more details on the rebellion and its impact on Qing policy in Taiwan.

14. Ding does not specify the name of the general here. This seems fitting, as he is relating an item of local lore, not historical fact.

15. The *Min shu*, compiled by He Qiaoyuan (1558–1632), was published ca. 1628.

16. Zheng He was the famous palace eunuch and admiral who made a series of seven nautical expeditions during the period 1405–1433. His voyages took him from Java to Mecca and the coast of East Africa. One aspect of his diplomatic missions was to issue imperial proclamations declaring the emperor's majesty and virtue, and then to obtain tribute from the rulers of various domains. It is still a matter of debate whether or not Zheng He ever reached the island of Taiwan. As our author points out, this particular story is most likely apocryphal. One of the earliest references to this story is in Chen Di's *Dongfan ji*.

17. The gazetteer *Zhuluo xian zhi,* compiled by Zhou Zhongxuan, was published in 1717.

18. *Illustrations of the Flora and Fauna of Taiwan (Taihai caifeng tu)* was compiled by Censor Liushiqi about 1746. The work contains text and twelve illustrations of the flora and fauna of Taiwan. Although "flora and fauna" is a specifically Western concept, I have chosen to translate the title in this manner to reflect the contents of the work and to distinguish it clearly from another work by Liushiqi, *Illustrations of the Customs of the Savage Villages (Fanshe caifeng tu).* The two works contain some overlap in terms of content. They are published together as *An Illustrated Book of the Savage Villages (Fanshe caifeng tukao)* in the Taiwan Collectanea series, *Taiwan wenxian.*

19. Lord No-Cares and Getian were legendary rulers during a primeval age of peace, simplicity, and natural virtue. The trope of the Taiwan savages as the subjects of Lord No-Cares or Getian seems to have originated with Chen Di's *Dongfan ji.*

20. Giulio Aleni (1582–1649) was an Italian Jesuit who lived in China during the Ming. He is the author of a number of works in Chinese, including the world atlas *Zhifang waiji,* 1623.

21. This is a reference to a statement made by Lan Dingyuan in his *Record of an Eastern Campaign (Dongzheng ji),* 1722, to the effect that the savages had the outer appearance of human beings, but lacked the morals of humans.

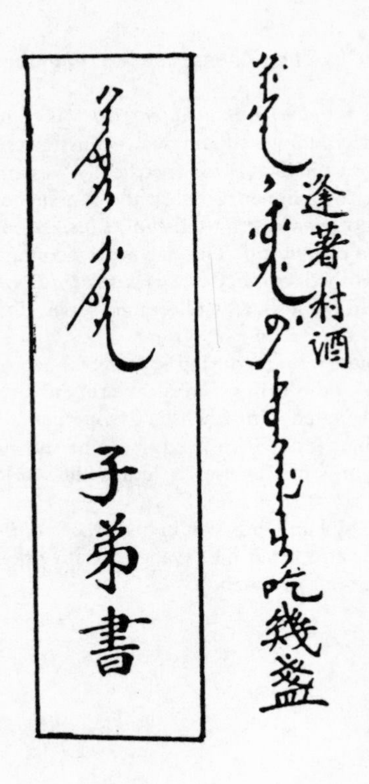

Fig. 18. Lüwucaotang manuscript of the "Eating Crabs" youth book. Left: Title from the first page. The first two words, *katuri jetere* (eating crabs), are written in Manchu, followed by three Chinese characters spelling *zidishu* (youth book). Right: Excerpt from the second line of the story: "When you come upon some good village wine, drink a few bowls." The first five words, *gašan i nure be tunggalaci* (lit., village wine, when [you] encounter [it]), are in Manchu; the last three, *chi ji zhan* (drink a few bowls), are in Chinese. The Manchu phrase is glossed in Chinese. The visual and phonetic contrast between the two languages could not be more strikingly presented. Reproduced in Hatano Tarō, *Pangxie duan'er yanjiu.*

EIGHTEEN

The "Eating Crabs" Youth Book

Translated by Mark C. Elliott

TRANSLATOR'S PREFACE

I chose to translate this text because I think it vividly and humorously illustrates the complexity of both gender and ethnic discourses in eighteenth-century Beijing. As a historian who questions the simplistic assumptions of "sinicization" and the notion that the Manchus and other non-Han peoples were inexorably absorbed by the Chinese, I am always searching for evidence that demonstrates the specific ways in which Manchus and Chinese interacted. In its choice of literary form, its visual presentation on the page (where two different writing systems appear interspersed in the same line), and in the story it tells of a mixed Manchu-Chinese marriage, this unusual text offers convincing proof that while acculturation occurred in the Qing, at the same time, ethnic differentiation remained.

What makes the text even more interesting to me, however, is the introduction of gender conflict into a particularly Qing context, giving familiar tropes of connubial discord a novel ethnic twist. One is forcefully reminded of the sedimentation of social relations: sometimes it is gender categories that are operative, while other times it is ethnic or class categories, and sometimes (as with the case of the Auntie who comes to the rescue) all three.

The "Eating Crabs" youth book differs markedly from most of the other translations in this volume. Instead of a normative text participating consciously in the dominant moral discourse of the day, we have a performance text that is neither serious nor especially "Confucian." The tale it tells—of a henpecked Manchu husband, his impatient Han wife, and their crustacean adversaries—is humorous, an eighteenth-century *Annie Hall* meant mainly to entertain. Rather than putting its message in a dry and didactic format, the story makes its point by exploiting absurd situations and stereotypes for their comic value. And whereas most texts in this volume were written in classical Chinese, the language of "Eating Crabs" is the vernacular of mid-Qing Beijing, combining the city's main languages, Chinese and Manchu, with a little Mongolian thrown in for good measure. As a whole, the text provides a valuable and rare glimpse of gender and ethnic relations in contemporary metropolitan society.

INTRODUCTION

"Eating Crabs" belongs to a literary genre known as *zidishu,* usually translated into English as "youth books."[1] *Zidishu* are storytelling texts that were sung, and they constitute a distinctive sub-type of *guci* (drum rhymes) peculiar to the Qing capital, Beijing. They differ from other types of sung texts such as *tanci* (plucking rhymes) mainly in their shorter length, their varied line lengths, and the absence of prosodic sections. In the case of mixed-language youth books, of which "Eating Crabs" is one of just a few examples that have been preserved,[2] the combination of two languages makes it difficult to achieve a consistent meter. This is because whereas Chinese words are predominantly mono- and bi-syllabic, Manchu words are generally polysyllabic.[3] However, while the text presented here lacks regular meter (length generally varies between eight and fifteen syllables), it does display a consistent rhyme scheme, seen in the consistent preference for the sound "-a" (or "-ia"; rarely, "-an," "-iang") at the end of every couplet.[4] At any rate, the main attraction held by youth books may not have been their musicality so much as their clever use of language, along with the colorful stories they told.[5]

The origins of the youth book genre lie most likely in the Yongzheng reign (1723–1735).[6] The first *zidishu* were printed in 1756, and the genre probably reached its heyday during the Jiaqing reign (1796–1820).[7] By the Guangxu period (1875–1908) there were many published collections. But unlike Peking opera—another performance art that thrived in the culturally rich and diverse Manchu capital—*zidishu* did not survive long into the twentieth century. Exactly when the form died out is unclear. One turn-of-the-century Manchu writer, Zhen-jun, remarked that *zidishu* were no longer being sung. This may have been a premature judgment, for another Manchu memoirist, Dun Lichen ([Fuca] Duncung), writing about Beijing's local culture at the same time, included youth books in his list of "popular forms of entertainment."[8] This would suggest that the genre was yet alive—which the continued publication of youth book texts into the early Republican era also suggests.[9] Youth books are also mentioned in the 1917 miscellany *Qingbai leichao*.[10] The genre probably vanished soon thereafter, and was certainly gone by the late 1930s, when the form first came to scholarly attention. As a result, the exact style of performance is unknown today.[11] We do know, however, that texts were sung by one or two performers. If two, one sang and the other accompanied him on a three-stringed lute *(sanxian);* if one, then the performer played as he sang.[12]

In general, *zidishu* have been divided into two distinct types, an "East City style" and a "West City style."[13] The former was somewhat older, more emotionally moving, and more heroic. The latter, developing slightly later, was more melodious and better suited to love stories, its prolonged and low vowels lending themselves to extended melismas.[14] "Eating Crabs" " would appear to straddle this division. The couple's valiant battle with the crabs is told in appropriately (mock-)heroic fashion, while the description of Auntie's toilette dwells on the finer details of the preparations a proper lady made before leaving the house.

Zidishu appear by their number—close to four hundred are known today, but undoubtedly many more have been lost—to have been a very popular form of entertainment in eighteenth-century and nineteenth-century Beijing, particularly among the city's large banner population.[15] Members of the imperial clan were noted enthusiasts, but *zidishu* audiences were above all the ordinary residents of the Qing capital. These were men and women of the Manchu, Mongol, and Chinese banners who gathered at teahouses, temple festivals, and friends' parties to hear both professionals and amateurs perform.[16] The role of the banners in popularizing this literary form is recalled in the very name *zidishu,* which is taken from the phrase *baqi zidi,* "Eight-Banner youth," a contemporary expression referring to young people in the banners, especially young men.[17] One imagines it was these people, many of whom lacked employment and thus on whose hands time hung the heaviest, who provided the primary audience for youth-book performances.

That *zidishu* were meant for a banner audience is one reason for the common assertion that they are a specifically "Manchu" contribution to the Chinese literary tradition.[18] Authorship is the other reason, even though of the four hundred or so extant *zidishu* texts' exact authorship is unclear in all but a very few instances.[19] It was believed in the late Qing that bannermen originated the genre,[20] and literary historians have tended to accept that youth books were texts originally written or adapted by Manchu or others in the banners. Performers, too, were drawn from the banner population, since Beijing's Inner City was off-limits to Han Chinese after dark. One of the earliest detailed descriptions of the youth-book form suggests the following history:

> It is said that these songs *[zidishu]* were produced by the Eight Banners. They never charged for them. Most of the performers were from the nobility and the imperial lineage; hence the name *"zidi."* When they wanted to perform, they had to find someone to invite them using the requisite *quantie* [a large sheet of red paper specially folded for ceremonial use]. At the appointed time, everyone assembled to perform at a designated place and waited for the host family to greet

> them. They were not to be bothered by the serving of tea. When the singing was done, everyone went home. Late in the day, when it was inconvenient to carry the lights back and forth, the hosts might prepare a dinner [for the performers].[21]

This version of the origin of the youth book genre, with its emphasis on the role of the well-to-do, is challenged by more recent scholars, who insist that *zidishu* was from the beginning an art form of the common people in the Manchu banners.[22]

Whatever their class origins, it seems beyond dispute that youth books trace their beginnings to innovations on Chinese literary/musical forms first introduced by Manchu bannermen. Later, when restrictions on the Han presence in the city were relaxed, Chinese professionals took over—though the author of the preceding passage disparages such performances as "not authentic." In the process, the main venues for youth-book performance migrated to the Outer City, south of walled Beijing, where Han Chinese legally resided during the Qing. Once this happened, the original dual-language texts were gradually replaced by texts solely in Chinese that were written in a more elegant style—a development that meshed with the decline of Manchu as a spoken language. For this reason, the vast majority of the *zidishu* texts that remain today are written only in Chinese.[23] The polished pieces that have come down to us, which rely heavily on Tang and Song poetry for their vocabulary,[24] are likely very different from the original texts listened to by Beijing audiences two hundred years ago.

The mixed-language text of "Eating Crabs" dates from around 1800 and is one of the few remaining examples of what *zidishu* were probably like in the 1700s.[25] It is for this reason one of the best-known *zidishu* texts. Seven editions of the text are extant, including five manuscripts and two wood-block-printed texts.[26] Reflecting its hybrid origins, "Eating Crabs" goes by three different titles: a Manchu title, "Katuri jetere juben i bithe" (lit., the book of the tale of eating crabs), a Chinese title, "Pangxie duan" (The eating-crabs story), and a Manchu-Chinese title, "Katuri jetere zidishu" (The eating crabs youth book), which is the title chosen here. An annotated Japanese translation also exists. As far as I know, the translation that follows is the first English translation of the complete text.[27]

One of the most unusual features of these texts is the appearance of the printed page, where Manchu and Chinese are combined in every single line. Romanized, with Manchu words in italics, the first lines of the main text thus read as follows:

you yige *age* buzhi shi *hala ai*
ye buzhi *colo* jiaozuo *ai niyalma*
you buzhi *Manju Monggo* shi *ujen cooha*
geng buzhi neige *nirui ya gūsa.*

(Once there was a young gentleman—don't know his clan name,
Don't even know what name he was called or what man was he,

> Don't know if he was Manchu, Mongol, or "heavy troops,"
> Much less what banner or what company.)

Reproducing this in a mixed English-French text perhaps provides something of the feel of the original:

> Once there was a *jeune homme*—I don't know *comment était son nom de famille,*
> Don't even know *comment il s'appelait,*
> Or if he was *Mandchou, Mongol,* or *un Chinois des bannières,*
> Much less *de quelle bannière ou compagnie.*

The text is written vertically, but is read from left to right across the page, following Manchu (and European) practice. (Chinese texts, of course, were traditionally printed vertically but read from right to left.) This is one of the best indications that the authors of *zidishu,* although strongly influenced by Chinese culture, were themselves Manchu. As is true for most *zidishu,* the author of "Eating Crabs" is unknown. But whoever the author was, it is obvious from the very nature of the text that he (or she?) was bilingual, and that the audience was, too. For listeners whose command of either language was weak, the frequent repetition of phrases with similar meanings in both Chinese and Manchu was no doubt a boon to fuller comprehension. This sort of redundancy is common enough in Chinese performance genres.

Bilinguality was not unusual in eighteenth-century Beijing, especially among the educated minority, who were very often able to read and write (as well as speak and understand) both Chinese and Manchu. After all, Beijing was an official town, and these were the two most important official languages of the Qing dynasty (when the "national language," that is, *guoyu,* was Manchu, not Chinese).[28] A linguistic paradigm was set by the emperors themselves, who were fluent in both languages until the mid-1800s and sometimes even switched back and forth between them in the same sentence when responding to palace memorials. This mixed style is reminiscent of that found in "Eating Crabs" and is to be distinguished from the formal use of parallel texts in joint Manchu-Chinese *hebi* memorials. Even among the less educated, however, Manchu and Chinese were combined in regular daily use, a fact reflected in numerous linguistic studies of the Altaic nature of the northern dialect (i.e., Mandarin) and especially in local Beijing speech.[29]

The story told in "Eating Crabs" is a simple one and falls into four main episodes. As the story opens, we meet an *age* (pronounced "ah-geh"), or Manchu "gentleman," and his wife, who live in a village in the Beijing suburbs. The wife is often referred to in the text, somewhat tongue-in-cheek, as a *jiaren* (Chinese for "beauty"). Attractive and clever, she is a "southerner" (Chinese, *manzi* in the text), or Han Chinese, but learns to speak fluent Manchu, becoming a "half-Manchu, half-Han wildwoman." During one particularly lean year they move to the city to be near relatives. One day the husband, with nothing to do, goes shopping and buys some crabs, which he brings home for his wife to prepare for supper. She has no idea what they are or what to do with them and ends up getting badly pinched. The second episode begins as they manage, after much effort, to get the crabs into a pot of water and boil them, but then they have no idea how to eat them. The wife loses patience, first with the crabs ("Devil take them! These are so hard! / They're all nothing but bone. Where's the meat?"), and then with her husband ("You lout! / Buying such useless things, / Wasting all our precious money").

At this point, the servant girl becomes alarmed and runs next door to alert the husband's aunt to the trouble between her master and mistress. The third episode, the longest, narrates in excruciating detail the preparations the aunt makes before going out. This description parodies female vanity and at the same time celebrates female beauty. When she finally leaves the house to go next door, her splendid appearance and coquettish demeanor create considerable commotion in the street as everyone stops to stare, including a couple of passing Mongols who liken her to a living bodhisattva. The story concludes with a short episode in which the urbane and sophisticated aunt laughs at her relatives' ignorance and sharply upbraids the wife for having scolded her husband. ("You've been scolding your husband for no good reason. / It's a good thing he's such a nice fellow and lets you rant. / If it were my husband you were married to, he'd have beaten you to death!") Then she proceeds to instruct them in the art of eating crabs. The enlightened couple devour the crabs with gusto, the wife sends her husband out to buy more ("It doesn't matter how much they cost!"), and all are happy and satisfied.

Though space does not permit a lengthy discussion here, the reader will no doubt find "Eating Crabs" to be a rich source for information on urban domestic settings in late-imperial Beijing. In this connection, it is noteworthy that three of the story's four characters are women, two of whom—the wife and the aunt—receive by far the greatest attention from the author. The wife has much in common with the classic "shrew" type found elsewhere in Chinese fiction—quick-tempered, sharp-tongued, domineering.[30] It is she who is expected to figure out what to do with the crabs, and her antics drive the story. Her husband, in contrast, is meek, hardly speaks, and is slow to react when the trouble with the crabs begins. His only response once his wife has finished cursing him is to sit, "quiet as a mute, without making a sound." The husband's general dullness and lack of initiative may have been intended as a humorous send-up of the stereotypical *age,* whose status as a bannerman guaranteed him a livelihood even if he did little or no real work, resulting in an image of the *age* as a craven loafer lacking ambition and enterprise. Hence, for most of the story the wife seems to enjoy the advantage. Yet "proper" relations between husband and wife are finally restored in the conclusion, as she is enjoined to show him more respect, or at least deference. Here the intrusion of neo-Confucian norms into an otherwise purely comical narrative may be observed. Once administered, however, the lesson is quickly passed over as all present turn to the repast at hand. The language focuses again on the crabs, eaten with much relish. One wonders how effectively "Eating Crabs" really operated as a cautionary tale and whether the audience left satisfied that the imbalance in the marriage had been suitably addressed—or hungry for a plate of crabs they could consume themselves while retelling the jokes they had just heard.

In some ways the real "star" of the show is "Number Two Auntie," a stylish flirt who clearly knows the woman's proper place in the household and acts as peacemaker between the couple. Yet her intervention stops short of being sanctimonious—in part because of the absurdity of the marital spat, which is, after all, over a pot of crabs ("Such strange little monsters, spitting out foam, / I don't even know what the hell name to call them"), and in part because she herself has already been well caricatured before she arrives. Much more sophisticated than her country relatives, she puts on a grand display of the city woman's vanity, as the minute description of her toilet makes plain:

> She evenly powdered her face, as pretty as the hibiscus,
> Dabbed crimson on her tiny mouth, as red as the fragrant cherry.
> In the part of her hair, ever so narrow, she traced perfumed powder,
> The hair on her temples, cut ever so neatly, she daubed with light ink.

Despite the urgency of the servant-girl's appeal, we see that nothing can interfere with Auntie's careful preparations for appearing in public, although, as it turns out, she is only walking a few houses down the block. Yet even a short stroll provides an opportunity to turn a few heads and win a few compliments.

Apart from its portrayal of male and female types, "Eating Crabs" also reminds readers of the complex ethnic picture in late-imperial China, particularly in and around Beijing. As already mentioned, the bilingual text itself reflects the city's bicultural milieu. In addition, of course, there is the fact of "mixed marriage" that begins the story: he is a bannerman and she is a Han Chinese. Though the narrator of the story professes ignorance as to the husband's name and place in the Eight-Banner system, this is likely a literary device to enable all in the audience—which would have included members of the banners and perhaps Han commoners as well—to identify with the hero. That the wife learns Manchu once she marries strongly suggests that she has married into a Manchu, not a Mongol or Chinese banner, household. The matter-of-fact mention of their marriage suggests, moreover, that primary marriages between bannermen—including Manchus—and Han women were not uncommon in the mid-Qing period.[31]

The parody of the feckless bannerman in the depiction of the husband—even his marriage seems to come about in a haphazard fashion—has been alluded to. This was probably an ethnic stereotype familiar to all in the audience and good for a few laughs. To what extent the aunt represents an ethnic stereotype is harder to say. She, too, is Manchu. This is apparent from a number of clues: her coiffure, including the carefully groomed side-locks; the three earrings in each ear, typical of Manchu women; the tobacco pouch; the milk tea she orders for her husband; and her free movement out of the house onto the street. Manchu women—along with other bannerwomen, one imagines—enjoyed considerably more physical freedom than did Han women, and it is hard to picture a respectable Chinese society woman attempting the same sort of one-woman parade that the aunt makes as she sashays down the street to her nephew's house.[32]

One obvious question that arises from a reading of the text is whether the aunt's feet were bound. Since she is Manchu, one would certainly not expect this; bannerwomen were forbidden from binding their feet, and it does not appear that the custom ever spread widely, although there are reports of the occasional Chinese bannerwoman who has bound her feet. Nothing in the description of the aunt's ablutions mentions her feet, but the description of her movement down the street is highly suggestive:

> That body so fragile, those feet so small,
> The twin dragons on her shoes like water at the seashore.
> Her gait so light and sauntering,
> The traces of each step the imprint of a lotus.

And again, a few lines later:

> Trembling softly like a willow in the wind as she moved,
> Each step so easy and so fetching.

These passages emphasize the attractiveness of small feet and convey the impression of a woman not quite steady on her too-tiny feet, swaying sensuously and provocatively. But were her feet bound? It is hard to say. Once her admirers have dispersed, the author notes that she reached her destination "in the wink of an eye." This might mean that she could move quickly if she so wished, or merely that she did not have far to go. The evidence is inconclusive, but I think it is more likely that the author wished to describe her movements as being extremely feminine. The language here is fairly conventional as a description of feminine beauty, and one could easily argue that at the time a "feminine" walk was by literary definition a bound-footed walk. Even if one lacked bound feet, one might wish to affect the walk in order to look attractive. Certainly it was for this reason that the odd-shaped platform "horse-heel shoes" sported by elite Manchu women came into fashion: such shoes guaranteed a tottering gait that males were supposed to have found so fetching.[33]

A final point of interest in regard to the text's ethnic texturing is the appearance on the street of Mongol admirers, whose praise of the aunt is given in Mongolian (using Manchu writing). This is a wonderful touch that strikingly emphasizes the plurality of Beijing society under the Qing.

Translating a popular text such as "Eating Crabs" poses a number of special challenges, not the least of which is getting the meaning right. Apart from the difficulties posed by the constant switching between Chinese and Manchu, many of the expressions used are Beijing colloquialisms. Other problems arise when the nuance of the Chinese gloss suggests something not found in the main Manchu text (here I have generally preferred the meaning in Manchu). A different sort of challenge is posed by the desirability of preserving the lively, informal tone of the text without sacrificing comprehensibility. Should *eniyegei monio,* referring to the crab that is pinching the wife's fingers, be translated literally as "my mother's monkey" or more loosely as "the little rascal"? My decision has been to translate colloquial expressions in Chinese and Manchu into colloquial expressions in English that approximate the sense and emotion of the original. This is not, then, a literal translation, and doubtless I have made some poor choices. Whatever the limitations that may burden the following translation, I hope it may nevertheless provoke a few smiles and allow the reader a glimpse into the little-known universe of hybrid Beijing.

ORIGINAL TEXT[34]

To live to one hundred merits some praise,
But it doesn't compare to taking advantage of the pleasures of springtime.
If you come upon some good village wine, drink a few bowls;
When you see flowers in the field, stick a few in your hair.
For where in the underworld are there fresh flowers to wear?
And after all, winehouses around the gates of Hades are few.
If you don't believe me, brother, take a look in the mirror—
Your face is even more lined this year than last.
But let's cut the fancy talk and dispense with the poetry,
And go on to the crab-eating for some good laughs.
Although it's an ordinary story in plain language,
Take care you don't laugh so much that your mouth hurts!

Once there was a young gentleman—don't know his clan name,
Don't even know what he was called or what man was he,
Don't know if he was Manchu, Mongol, or "heavy troops,"
Much less what banner or what company.
He'd lived on the manor for two years and a half
When he took a wife from a Southerner family on the estate.
He didn't ask the surname of the bride's side or her pedigree;
He just up and married her.
Now this beauty was clever and sharp, and she had a way with
 words as well,
And before six months were up she learned to speak Manchu.
She was a lively woman, too, and fond of jokes;
Soon she became a half-Manchu, half-Han wildwoman.

Without any warning, one year a drought hit,
Making it tough just to eat and keep the clothes on your back.
The two had no choice, so they moved into the city,
A place not far from here, right off the main street.
One day, with nothing to do, the young gentleman went out and,
 on a lark,
Bought a few pounds of crabs and brought them home.
Entering the house, he put them in a basin;
"Yikes!" said the wildwoman when she saw them. "What in the
 world are those?"
The gentleman laughed, saying, "Don't ask me!
I'm astonished, too! I don't know what they are."
While the man and wife were busy guessing and making mischief,
The crabs clambered and crawled out of the basin.
The beauty shouted at them, "Where do you think you're going?"
She tucked up her sleeves and quickly went after one with her hands,
But before she could grab it, the crab seized her hand between its
 two pincers.
"The little rascal's got my hand!" cried the wildwoman,
In such pain that she could only shake her delicate wrist frantically
While the crab hung on for dear life, its legs writhing in the air.
The young gentleman watched in alarm. "Oh, no!" he cried. Rushing
 forward, he
Began pulling desperately at the claw.
But the more he pulled, the tighter the crab pinched, and the more it hurt;

Again and again she shook her hand, but the crab just wouldn't let go, until finally
With a mighty flick she hurled the crab onto the floor with a loud crack!
It hurt so much all she could do was grit her teeth and yell, "Ouch! Ouch!" at the top of her lungs.
The tears and snivel were still streaming down her face
When the remaining crabs surrounded her with much clattering,
Scaring her so that she trembled and changed her expression,
As from her mouth poured an uncontrollable stream of curses.
She spun wildly all about the room,
Her hands fluttering in the air, just as if she were dancing.
As long as she didn't catch them, she had to watch out for their biting;
Yet if she tried to pick one up, she was afraid of being pinched.
So the beauty was at wit's end with no idea what to do;
Whenever she saw an opening, she flung here and grabbed there.
Watching all this from the side, the gentleman's ire rose, and
Rolling up his sleeves, he went after them.
The two of them worked together, so that
All you could hear were the shouts that filled the air.
The beauty was throwing her hair pins at the crabs,
While the gentleman took his knife and stabbed at them as hard as he could.
The lady finally took off her blouse and laid it over the floor
As the gentleman removed his summer hat and tried clumsily to catch them.
The husband capped them, his wife flapped them;
The wife wrapped them, her husband trapped them.
So busy were they that the gentleman's head steamed,
And sweat dripped down the girl's face.
Half the day they spent till all the crabs were finally caught
They were panting in exhaustion from all their jumping about.

Then she called to him: "Sir! Why don't you come here and ladle up some water?
Together we can cook these stupid things and kill them."
They covered the basin with the pickle-jar lid and put a ceramic bowl on top,
Then weighed all that down with a big rock they brought over.
They broke some stalks of millet to build a fire,

And did all they could to get the water to a fast boil.
Once it had boiled for a good long while,
The young beauty lifted up the lid to have a look:
"This is really an amazing fish!
No wonder people prize it so much.
Alive, it's blue like indigo, but
Once it's cooked it's as red as cinnabar.
Let's give them a try to see how they taste!"
Quickly they picked up their chopsticks,
One on the left and the other on the right, but they just couldn't get a grip.
Aloud she cursed them: "Freaks of nature! How come you're so slippery?"
Putting down her chopsticks and holding her breath,
She hiked up her sleeves and grabbed one.
With the crab in her hands she gave it a bite.
"Devil take them! These are so hard!
They're all nothing but bone. Where's the meat?
How am I supposed to chew something as hard as this?"
The beauty's temper flared again as she
Cursed the gentleman, "You lout!
Buying such useless things,
Wasting all our precious money.
Steam it and steam it, but it doesn't get cooked. Boil it and boil it, and it
doesn't get soft.
I can't believe what an idiot you are!"
Her scolding made the young gentleman pout his lips
And stay as quiet as a mute, without making a sound.

When the servant girl saw the couple so angry,
She rushed off to get Number Two Auntie,
Who, when she saw the girl, broke into a big smile and asked,
"What have you come to see me about?"
The girl explained, "They're quarreling in the master's house!
Oh, Auntie, please go and make them stop. Hurry!"
Now, this fine lady made a little bleating sound and ordered the girl,
"Be quick! Go get my toilet case."
With a "Yes, ma'am," the girl ran into the house
And in a great flurry got her cosmetics.
All kinds of things she brought out to
Set in front of her master's aunt, including

A carved-dragon basin brimming with perfume, and
An embroidered mandarin duck pillow with mallows.
With skilled hands the aunt undid her jet-black hair,
A tortoise-shell comb in her grasp.
She combed and straightened, straightened and combed;
When her hair was all combed, she put cassia oil in the tresses.
Ribbons of shiny black artfully supported the now-dressed hair,
Golden ear-picks of pure yellow pinned it sideways.
With crystal-clear warm water she washed her face,
Then wiped it dry with a downy white silken kerchief.
She cleaned and rinsed her delicate tongue, then
Brushed her teeth as white and sparkling as sticky rice.
She evenly powdered her face, as pretty as the hibiscus,
Dabbed crimson on her tiny mouth, as red as the fragrant cherry.
In the part of her hair, ever so narrow, she traced perfumed powder,
The hair on her temples, cut ever so neatly, she daubed with light ink.
Her fine and delicate eyebrows she lined with a silver hairpin,
While glittering pearl earrings dangled down, three on a side;
A modish, large flower she fastened in her hair,
Along with many different hairpins all over her head.
Taking the mirror and breathing on it,
With her black tresses she wiped it meticulously; then,
Holding the shiny clean mirror high, looked both in front and in back,
Checking everything carefully, point by point, with fluttering eyes.

When the servant girl saw her mistress had completed her toilet,
She sprang over to the wardrobe to get her clothes.
Slowly, gently, the lady arose and extended her delicate wrists to
Put on a colorful satin-lined gown.
The girl put some tobacco in a pipe and handed it to her, and
Without thinking about what she was doing, also brought tea.
Shyly, the lady called the girl over:
"What do you think? How do I look?"
The servant raised her head when she heard the question;
Looking up and down for a long time, she clicked her mouth in approval.
Her face wreathed in smiles, she respectfully pronounced, "Mistress!
Your appearance is truly marvelous.
I'll just say that while it is hard for people to compete with the beauty
 of flowers,

Who would have known how much like a flower is your visage!
No wonder the elder master cherishes and dotes on you so,
His warm affection added to his favor and love.
Who has ever seen a goddess?
Yet you are like a fairy descended from the moon!"
The lady's cheeks beamed with pleasure at such praise,
But she scolded the girl: "That's enough jawing, you misbegotten
little monkey!
I have to go now to your mistress's house.
Since there's no one here, you stay behind and watch the house.
When the elder master returns, you be sure to look after him well and
Make his milk tea with a lot of cream."
These preparations complete, she set on her way,
Entering the main street right after leaving the house.

Before moving, she first affected a pose,
So that people on both sides of the street were all watching her.
What they saw was a vision of an immortal
Made up to look just like a blossom in her appearance.
Her body was sheathed in a sky-blue satin dress decorated with a
"prosperity-cloud" pattern,
Out of which came the long sleeves of her moon-white satin camisole.
Wrapped loosely around her neck, a scarf draped down over her bosom,
Making the little embroidery purse she carried look all the more precious.
One had only to look to see her curved brows, seductive almond eyes,
Crimson lips behind which showed silvery teeth,
Snow-white complexion, fresh like a mirror of jade, and
The fine line of her beautiful hair, black like a nest of crows.
How magnificent the kerchief that lazily adorned her hair,
How brilliant the gold and jewels that glittered on her head.
That body so fragile, those feet so small,
The twin dragons on her shoes like water at the seashore.
Her gait so light and sauntering,
The traces of each step the imprint of a lotus.
The sweet smell of incense struck people's faces,
Her slender, precious hands clutching a colorful fan.
Every manner of gentility and good taste so pleasing,
So much to commend in her charm and elegance.
Everyone who saw her was full of praise,

Clicking their tongues in amazement.
When the beauty saw so many people gathered and cheering,
She deliberately slowed her pace,
Fluttering the moon-white scarf about her neck,
With skilled hands she pulled the sidelong hem of her gown.
Both eyes flitting anxiously, watchfully, recklessly, she
Purposefully adjusted her hair ornaments and tamped down the locks on her cheeks.
Trembling softly like a willow in the wind as she moved,
Each step so easy and so fetching,
You could even hear the bell-like sound of her delicate cough and
Watch as she dabbed her mouth with her kerchief.
Every glance of those smiling eyes left its mark,
Enticing everyone to stare.
Passersby stopped in their tracks, such that
In a moment all of Taiping Street was full.
Several stopped their sedan chairs and pulled aside the curtains to look;
Several reined in their horses and whipped but lazily;
Several secretly stole a peek and forgot what they were doing;
Several just stood and stared stupidly for a long, long time.
Several Mongols on the street blinked their eyes and said, "Mercy!
Bless my soul! It's the Mother of Buddha in the flesh, a living bodhisattva."
A few businessmen were also busy looking,
Exchanging looks with each other with gaping yellow-toothed mouths.

After everyone had had their look and gone their way,
The lady arrived at her sister's house in the wink of an eye.
The couple sat in morose, angry silence
When they heard the sound of someone's steps.
The young gentleman raised his head and opened his eyes;
His wife looked up to see who was there.
But the woman they saw walk in from outside was a
Colorfully made-up fairy princess.
"Who are you?" they asked, when upon closer inspection they saw
It was in fact their Number Two Auntie from next door.
"How are you?" she asked as she entered,
"And what are the two of you quarreling about?"
The wildwoman cried out, "Dear sister! You've come at the right time.
Can you take a look and see what these things are here?

Their bodies are roundish and flat,
They have neither head nor tail.
Such strange little monsters, spitting out foam,
I don't even know what the hell name to call them."
Number Two Auntie glanced in the pot and saw the crabs;
Looking down, she broke out instantly into uproarious laughter.
She called her niece over, still laughing and laughing:
"You country girl, don't you know what these are?
Clearly, sister, you're in the wrong here.
You've been scolding your husband for no good reason.
It's a good thing he's such a nice fellow and lets you rant.
If it were my husband you were married to, he'd have beaten you
to death!
From now on, I'd suggest you do your best to yield to him
And don't you go fighting again!"
When she was through talking, she called the servant girl to bring the
crabs over,
While the husband and wife watched in dumb amazement.
Number Two Auntie spoke: "This thing is called a crab.
There is an excellent way to eat it."
As she spoke, she took one, removed the carapace,
Opened the shell, and removed the gills.
She broke the crab in two halves and handed it to them,
Saying, "Brother-in-law! Sister! Try it, try it!"
Wife and husband took some in their hands and
Put some of the yellow meat in their mouths, smacking as they chewed.
The beauty ate, smiling and happy,
The gentleman ate joyfully, laughing.
His wife said, "Dear husband! Go buy some more,
It doesn't matter how much they cost!"
With great relish they finished off every one,
Laughing themselves into exhaustion before they separated.

NOTES

I would like to express my thanks to my teachers James Bosson and Okada Hidehiro, who first introduced this text to me; to Ding Yizhuang of the Chinese Academy of Social Sciences for translation help; and to my colleague Kathryn Lowry for her careful reading of the preface. Thank you also to Yu-Yin Cheng for many helpful suggestions on the translation itself.

1. Literally "sons and younger brothers," *zidi* is best rendered, I think, simply as "youth." See the entry in Morohashi Tetsuji, *Dai Kan-Wa jiten,* 6930/647, 3:3067. Translated directly as *juse deote,* the phrase was in regular use in Manchu, with this same meaning.

2. Two other well-known mixed-language *zidishu* are "Chaguan" (The frontier sentinel) and "Xunfu qu" (Looking for a husband). The former is translated by Wadley in "The Mixed-Language Verses from the Manchu Dynasty in China." See also the discussion of this work in Okada Hidehiro, "Mandarin, a Language of the Manchus: How Altaic?" Both stories are translated by Tulli in "Due esempi di zidishu sino-mancesi." Neither, however, duplicates the interspersed use of both languages found in "Eating Crabs." "Chaguan" is mainly in Chinese with Manchu words occurring primarily in the speeches of one character; "Xunfu qu" is completely parallel, with all text in both Chinese and Manchu. The only other youth book whose language might mirror that of "Eating Crabs" is one titled "Shengguan tu" (A plan for promotion to office), described in a footnote in Guan Dedong, *Quyi lunji,* 88, n. 2.

3. On the other hand, as the existence of Manchu-Chinese "mixed verse" attests, it was not impossible to combine Chinese and Manchu together in regular metrical poetry. See Stary, "Fundamental Principles of Manchu Poetry"; and Tulli, "Analisi metrico-formale di una raccolta di poesie ibride sino-mancesi."

4. Thus the final words of each couplet in the first twenty lines after the introductory section are *niyalma**, *gûsa**, *jia, jia, bahanaha**, *mama**, *mangga**, *giyai**, *jia, jaka**, *ta, pa, zhua, jia, la, la, sa, ya, ta, la.* This rhyming pattern holds true for the entire text. (Asterisked words are Manchu.)

5. Hatano Tarō, "Shiteisho Man-Kan ken 'Pangxie duan'er' kaidai," 6. Cf. the remarks of someone who no doubt had heard youth books performed: "The songs of the *zidishu* are sad and lovely, and their words are refined" (Tun Li-ch'en, *Annual Customs and Festivals in Peking,* 97).

6. Hatano Tarō, "Shiteisho Man-Kan ken 'Pangxie duan'er' kaidai," 2.

7. Guan Dedong, *Quyi lunji,* 92–93. I rely on the authoritative accounts by Hatano and Guan for many of the following characterizations of the youth book genre.

8. Zhen-jun, *Tianzhi ouwen,* 7:175; Tun Li-ch'en, *Annual Customs and Festivals in Peking,* 96, 115. It is not entirely clear from the passage in *Tianzhi ouwen* if Zhen-jun meant that the genre had disappeared entirely or if the best tradition of blind *zidishu* performers had been cut off.

9. Hatano Tarō, "Shiteisho Man-Kan ken 'Pangxie duan'er' kaidai," 4.

10. Xu Ke, *Qingbai leichao,* 10:4954. The language here is suspiciously close to that in Zhen-jun, *Tianzhi ouwen,* however.

11. Fu Xihua was the first scholar to examine the youth book genre. Hatano says Fu began his work in 1938 and for years searched in vain for anyone who could sing *zidishu.* He also cites a Beijing guidebook of 1919 to the effect that *zidishu* were no longer being performed in the Inner City. See Hatano Tarō, "Shiteisho Man-Kan ken 'Pangxie duan'er' kaidai," 7.

12. Hatano Tarō, "Shiteisho Man-Kan ken 'Pangxie duan'er' kaidai," 3, 7; Zhang Juling, *Qingdai Manzu zuojia wenxue gailun,* 213.

13. This division is understandable when one recalls that what is now central Beijing's primary east-west thoroughfare, Chang'an dajie, did not exist in the Qing. The placement of the imperial city *(huangcheng)* in the middle of the walled "inner" (or "Tartar") city *(neicheng)* made crossing from east to west and vice-versa impossible except in the north of the city.

14. Zhen-jun, *Tianzhi ouwen,* 175, on the special sound of the West City style.

15. The "banner" (Chinese *qi,* Manchu *gūsa*) was the basic unit of social, political, and military organization in Manchu society. Banners were distinguished by eight color patterns as well as by three ethnic subdivisions: Manchu, Mongol, and Chinese (called *ujen cooha* or "heavy troops" in Manchu). Banner people were required to live separately from Han Chinese. A wide range of legal and economic privileges accentuated their distinct ethno-social status. For more on the banner system and Manchu identity generally, readers are referred to Elliott, *The Manchu Way: The Eight Banners and Ethnic Identity in Late Imperial China.*

16. Tun Li-ch'en says that *zidishu* were performed by "amateur singers who go in groups to the houses of friends, temple festivals, etc." (*Annual Customs and Festivals in Peking,* 115).

17. This is my sense after reviewing thirty-odd occurrences of the relevant Manchu expression, *juse deote,* in Manchu documents from the early eighteenth century. In only one instance did it seem that the phrase referred to bannermen generally; everywhere else it referred either to young people or to children.

18. Guan Dedong and Zhou Zhongming, *Zidishu congchao,* 1; Liu Liemao and Guo Jingrui, *Qing Che wangfu chaocang quben, zidishu ji,* 2; Nienhauser, *The Indiana Companion to Traditional Chinese Literature,* 844. It should be noted, however, that phrasing it this way sidesteps the problem of how the hybrid banner culture that developed in Beijing is taken to stand for "Manchu" culture.

19. The names of just twenty-six youth-book authors are identifiable today, and only by pseudonyms, at that. Hatano Tarō, "Shiteisho Man-Kan ken 'Pangxie duan'er' kaidai," 5.

20. Zhen-jun, *Tianzhi ouwen,* 175.

21. Hatano Tarō, "Shiteisho Man-Kan ken 'Pangxie duan'er' kaidai," 3, citing an anonymous Chinese work of 1940, *Dushi congtan.*

22. Guan Dedong and Zhou Zhongming, *Zidishu congchao,* 3.

23. See the two important collections: Guan Dedong and Zhou Zhongming, *Zidishu congchao;* and Liu Liemao and Guo Jingrui, *Qing Che wangfu.*

24. Liu Liemao and Guo Jingrui, *Qing Che wangfu,* 4.

25. Hatano Tarō, "Shiteisho Man-Kan ken 'Pangxie duan'er' kaidai," 1–2; Okada Hidehiro, "Mandarin, a Language of the Manchus," 168.

26. Hatano Tarō, "Shiteisho Man-Kan ken 'Pangxie duan'er' kaidai," 11, 588; Guan Dedong, *Quyi lunji,* 90.

27. A full Japanese translation is found in Jin Jiujing (Jin Majin), "Chi pangxie," (*Man-Mō zasshi* [September] 1935), reproduced in Hatano Tarō, *Pangxie duan'er yanjiu.* A partial English translation (based on the same manuscript text used here) is given in Okada Hidehiro, "Mandarin, a Language of the Manchus." The present translation is based on the version in Hatano Tarō, *Pangxie duan'er yanjiu,* that is, the so-called Lüwucaotang manuscript, ca. 1800. See note 34.

28. For more on the role of Manchu at this time, see Crossley and Rawski, "A Profile of the Manchu Language in Ch'ing History."

29. Okada Hidehiro, "Mandarin, a Language of the Manchus"; Hashimoto Mantarō, "The Altaicization of Northern Chinese"; Guan Jixin and Meng Xianren, "Manzu yu Shenyang yu, Beijing yu"; and Chang Yingsheng, *Beijing tuhua zhong de Manyu.* A good overview is Wadley, "Altaic Influences on Beijing Dialect."

30. On the classic "shrew," see the work by McMahon: *Misers, Shrews, and Polygamists: Sexuality and Male-Female Relations in Eighteenth-Century Chinese Fiction;* also Wu, *The Chinese Virago: A Literary Theme.*

31. It was matches between bannerwomen, especially Manchu women, and Han

men that were prohibited by the court. This double standard makes sense if one bears in mind that marriage was an important site of acculturation and that acculturation was something the court was quite concerned about. Han commoner women marrying into banner households would presumably ease into a Manchu lifestyle, whereas Manchu women marrying into commoner households would theoretically lose their "Manchu-ness" and become sinified. More on banner marriage patterns may be found in Ding Yizhuang, *Manzu de funü shenghuo yu hunyin zhidu yanjiu.*

32. On the status of Manchu women in Qing society, see the work cited in the previous note; also Elliott, "Manchu Widows and Ethnicity in China; and Zhang Juling, *Qingdai Manzu zuojia,* 110–16.

33. See the illustration in Garrett, *Chinese Clothing: An Illustrated Guide,* 61.

34. Source: Hatano Tarō, *Pangxie duan'er yanjiu.* See note 27. Fortunately, modern editions of the youth book provide helpful annotations, but I have dispensed with annotating the translated text that follows. Readers who wish further information are encouraged to refer to the notes, particularly to the studies by Hatano and Guan. Some editions, such as that used here (ca. 1800), provide a Chinese gloss for the Manchu text. I have been guided by this gloss, but in some cases have opted for English phrasing that seemed to me to better reflect the original sense of the Manchu. I have also introduced breaks in the text between the four main scenes.

Glossaries and References

References marked with an asterisk are recommended for further reading.

1. BIOGRAPHY OF THE DAOIST SAINT WANG FENGXIAN BY DU GUANGTING

Glossary

Dangtu	當塗
Dao (Tao)	道
dong	洞
Dongting	洞庭
Du Shenquan	杜審權
Guanyin	觀音
Huai	淮
Huang Chao	黃巢
Jiangdu	江都
Jinling	金陵
li	里
lienü	列女
Lingbao	靈寶
Linghu Tao	令狐綯
Pang Xun	龐勛
Penglai	蓬萊
Qianqing	千頃
qilin	麒麟
Qin Yan	秦彥
Sanhuai	三淮
Shangqing	上清
Shi Tao	師鋾
Sun Ru	孫儒
Tian Zun	天尊
Wang Fengxian	王奉仙
Wanling	宛陵
Xinghan	星漢
Xuan	宣
Yangzhou	揚州
Yuhang	餘杭
Zhao Hongbi	趙宏畢
zhen ren	眞人
Zhongni	仲尼
Zhuang zi	莊子

References

Benn, Charles D. *The Cavern-Mystery Transmission*. Honolulu: University of Hawaii Press, 1991.

Bokenkamp, Stephen R. *Early Daoist Scriptures*. Berkeley: University of California Press, 1997.

Bynum, Caroline Walker. *Holy Feast and Holy Fast: The Religious Significance of Food to Medieval Women.* Berkeley: University of California Press, 1987.

Cahill, Suzanne E. "Pien Tung-hsuan: A Taoist Holy Woman of the T'ang Dynasty (618–907 AD)." In *Women Saints in World Religions*, ed. Arvind Sharma. Albany: State University of New York Press, 2001.

———. "Practice Makes Perfect: Paths to Transcendence for Women in Medieval China." *Taoist Resources* 2, no. 2 (1990): 23–42.

*———. "Smell Good and Get a Job: Verification and Legitimization of Saints in Medieval Chinese Daoism." In *Presence and Presentation: Women in Chinese History and Legend*, ed. Shirley Mou. New York: St. Martin's Press, 1999.

———. *Transcendence and Divine Passion: The Queen Mother of the West in Medieval China.* Stanford: Stanford University Press, 1993.

Chen Baoguang 陳葆光. *Sandong qunxian lu* 三洞群仙錄. HY 1238, vol. 53, 43316.

Daozang 道藏. Zhengtong 正統 edition. Reprint, Taipei: Yiwen shuju, 1976.

Despeux, Catherine. "L'ordination des femmes Taoistes sous les T'ang." *Etudes chinoises* 5, no.1–2 (1986): 53–100.

Du Guangting 杜光庭. *Yongcheng jixian lu* 墉城集仙錄. Included in *Yunji qiqian* 雲笈七籤 (HY 1026, *juan* 114), in *Daozang*, volume 38, 30344–46 (DG).

Hurvitz, Leon. *Scripture of the Lotus Blossom of the Fine Dharma*. New York: Columbia University Press, 1976.

Kohn, Livia. "The Mother of the Tao." *Taoist Resources* 1, no. 2 (1989): 37–119.

Levy, Jean. "L'abstinance des cereales chez les taoistes." *Etudes chinoises* 1 (1983): 3–47.

Liu Xiang 劉向. *Lienü zhuan* 列女傳. Reprint, Taipei: Sibu beiyao edition, 1966.

Liu Xu 劉煦. *Jiu Tang shu* 舊唐書. Beijing: Zhonghua shuju, 1975 (JT).

Maspero, Henri. *Taoism and Chinese Religion*. Translated by Frank Kierman. Amherst: University of Massachusetts Press, 1981.

Ouyang Xiu 歐陽修. *Xin Tang shu* 新唐書. Shanghai: Zhonghua shuju, 1975 (XT).

*Raphals, Lisa. *Sharing the Light: Representations of Women and Virtue in Early China*. Albany: State University of New York Press, 1998.

Robinet, Isabelle. *Taoism: Growth of a Religion*. Translated by Phyllis Brooks. Stanford: Stanford University Press, 1997.

Schafer, Edward. "Three Divine Women of South China." *Chinese Literature: Essays, Articles, and Reviews* 1 (1979): 31–42.

Shi Baochang 釋寶昌. *Biqiuni zhuan* 比丘尼傳. In *Taishō shinshū daizōkyō* 大正新修大藏經, ed. Takakusu Junichirō 高楠順次郎 and Watanabe Kaigyoku 渡邊海旭. Tokyo: (Taishō shinshū daizōkyō kankōkai, 1924–1929), 50: 2063.

Sung, Marina. "The Chinese *Lieh nü* Tradition." In *Women in China: Current Directions in Historical Scholarship*, ed. Richard W. Guisso and Stanley Johannesen. Youngstown, N.Y.: Philo Press, 1981.

*Tsai, Kathryn Ann. *Lives of the Nuns: Biographies of Chinese Buddhist Nuns from the Fourth to the Sixth Centuries*. Honolulu: University of Hawaii, 1994.

Twitchett, Denis, ed. *Sui and T'ang China*. Vol. 3, part 1 of *The Cambridge History of China*. Cambridge, England: Cambridge University Press, 1979.

Verellen, Franciscus. *Du Guangting (850–933): Taoiste de cour à la fin de la Chine medievale*. Paris: College de France, 1989.

*Waltner, Ann. *The World of a Late Ming Visionary: T'an-yang-tzu and Her Followers*. Berkeley: University of California Press, forthcoming.

Weng Tu-chien [Weng Dujian] 翁獨健. *Tao tsang tzu mu yin te* 道藏子目引得: *Combined Indices to the Authors and Titles of Books in Two Collections of Taoist Literature*. Vol. 25. Beijing: Harvard-Yenching Institute, 1935 (HY).

Yü, Chün-fang. *Kuan-yin: The Chinese Transformation of Avalokiteśvara*. New York: Columbia University Press, 2001.

Yunji qiqian 雲笈七籤. HY 1026, *juan* 114. In *Daozang, Zhengtong* edition. Reprint, Taipei: Yiwen shuju, 1976.

Zhuang zi 莊子. Text in *Chuang-tzu yin-te* 莊子引得: *A Concordance to the Chuang-tzu*. Beijing: Harvard-Yenching Institute, 1947.

2. BIOGRAPHY OF THE GREAT COMPASSIONATE ONE OF XIANGSHAN BY JIANG ZHIQI

Glossary

Cai Jing	蔡京	"Guanshiyin pusa zhuan lüe"	觀世音菩薩傳略
Dabei	大悲	Guanyin	觀音
Daoxuan	道宣	Huaizhou	懷晝
Guan Daosheng	管道昇		

Huizhen	惠眞	Miaoshan	妙善
Jiang Zhiqi	蔣之奇	Miaoyan	妙顏
Jin'gang keyi	金剛科儀	Miaoyin	妙音
Juelian	覺璉	pusa	菩薩
Longxing fojiao biannian	隆興佛教編年通論	Zhao Mengfu	趙孟頫
		Zuxiu	祖琇

References

Dudbridge, Glen. *The Legend of Miao-shan.* Oxford Oriental Monographs, no. 1. London: Ithaca Press, 1978.

———. "Miao-shan on Stone: Two Early Inscriptions." *Harvard Journal of Asiatic Studies* 42, no. 2 (1982): 589–614.

Lai Swee-fo [Lai Ruihe] 賴瑞和. "Miaoshan chuanshuo de liangzhong xin ziliao" 妙善傳說的兩種新資料. *Zhongwai wenxue* 9, no. 2 (1980): 116–26.

———. "Wanli xunbei ji" 萬里尋碑記. *Zhongguo shibao* 中國時報, April 6, 7, 8 (1993).

Lu Zengxiang 陸增祥 (1833–1889). "Dabei chengdao zhuanzan" 大悲成道傳贊. In *Baqiongshi jinshi buzheng* 八瓊室金石補正, 109:19a–25b. Edition of 1925.

Wang Guanghao 王光鎬, ed. *Mingdai Guanyin dian caisu* 明代觀音殿彩塑. Taipei: Yishu tushu gongsi, 1994.

*Yü, Chün-fang. "The Cult of Kuan-yin in Ming-Ch'ing China: A Case of Confucianization of Buddhism?" In *Meeting of Minds: Intellectual and Religious Interaction in East Asian Traditions of Thought*, ed. Irene Bloom and Joshua A. Fogel. New York: Columbia University Press, 1997.

*———. *Kuan-yin: The Chinese Transformation of Avalokiteśvara*. New York: Columbia University Press, 2001.

3. THE *BOOK OF FILIAL PIETY FOR WOMEN* ATTRIBUTED TO A WOMAN NÉE ZHENG

Glossary

Ban Zhao	班昭	*Nü jie*	女誡
Chen Miao	陳邈	*Nü xiaojing*	女孝經
kun	坤	qian	乾
Lienü zhuan	列女傳	*Shuofu*	說郛
Liu Xiang	劉向	Zheng (Miss)	鄭

References

Chen Menglei 陳夢雷, comp. *Qinding gujin tushu jicheng* 欽定古今圖書集成. Reprint, Beijing: Zhonghua shuju and Bashu shushe, 1985.

Ch'en, Yu-shih. "The Historical Template of Pan Chao's *Nü Chieh*." *T'oung Pao* 72, no. 4–5 (1996): 229–57.

*Ebrey, Patricia Buckley. *The Inner Quarters: Marriage and the Lives of Chinese Women in the Sung Period*. Berkeley: University of California Press, 1993.

Fang Xuanling 房玄齡. *Jin shu* 晉書. Beijing: Zhonghua shuju, 1974.

Ji Yun 紀昀 et al., comp. *Siku quanshu zongmu tiyao* 四庫全書總目提要. Shanghai: Commercial Press, 1933.

Legge, James, trans. *The Chinese Classics*. 5 vols. Oxford: 1865–1895. Reprint, Hong Kong: Hong Kong University Press, 1961.

Liu Xiang 劉向. *Lienü zhuan* 列女傳. Reprint, Taipei: Sibu beiyao edition, 1966.

Liu Xu 劉昫 et al. *Jiu Tang shu* 舊唐書. Beijing: Zhonghua shuju, 1975.

Lynn, Richard John. *The Classic of Changes: A New Translation of the I Ching as Interpreted by Wang Bi*. New York: Columbia University Press, 1994.

Martin-Liao, Tienchi. "Traditional Handbooks of Women's Education." In *Women and Literature in China*, ed. Anna Gerstlacher et al. Bochum: Studienverlag Brockmeyer, 1985.

*Murray, Julia K. "Didactic Art for Women: The *Ladies' Classic of Filial Piety*." In *Flowering in the Shadows: Women in the History of Chinese and Japanese Painting*, ed. Marsha Weidner. Honolulu: University of Hawaii Press, 1990.

———. "The *Ladies' Classic of Filial Piety* and Sung Textual Illustration: Problems of Reconstruction and Artistic Context." *Ars Orientalis* 18 (1988): 95–129.

O'Hara, Albert Richard. *The Position of Woman in Early China according to the* Lieh nü chuan, *"The Biographies of Eminent Chinese Women."* Washington, D.C.: Catholic University, 1945.

Raphals, Lisa. *Sharing the Light: Representations of Women and Virtue in Early China*. Albany: State University of New York Press, 1998.

Shi jing 詩經. In *Shisanjing zhushu*. Edition of 1821. Reprint, Taipei: Yiwen yinshuguan, 1981.

Shu jing 書經. In *Shisanjing zhushu*. Edition of 1821. Reprint, Taipei: Yiwen yinshuguan, 1981.

*Swann, Nancy Lee. *Pan Chao: Foremost Woman Scholar of China*. New York: The Century Company, 1932.

Tao Zongyi 陶宗儀. *Shuofu sanzhong* 說郛三種. Shanghai: Shanghai guji chubanshe, 1988.

4. FUNERARY WRITINGS BY CHEN LIANG

Glossary

Chen Liang	陳亮	jiwen	祭文
guwen	古文	"Liu furen He shi muzhiming"	劉夫人何氏墓誌銘
He Ke (Maogong)	何恪 (茂恭)	Liu Shuxiang	劉叔向
Huang	黃	muzhiming	墓誌銘
"Ji meifu Zhou Yingbo wen"	祭妹夫周英伯文	Runeng	汝能
"Ji mei wen"	祭妹文	sui	歲
"Ji yimu Zhou furen Huang shi wen"	祭姨母周夫人黃氏文	wenji	文集
jinshi	進士	xing ying gao chang	行營高敞
		yin	陰
		Zhou Yingbo	周英伯

References

Bossler, Beverly J. *Powerful Relations: Kinship, Status, and the State in Sung China*

(960–1279). Cambridge and London: Council on East Asian Studies, Harvard University, 1998.
Chaffee, John W. *The Thorny Gates of Learning in Sung China: A Social History of the Examinations*. Cambridge: Cambridge University Press, 1985.
Chen Liang 陳亮. *Chen Liang ji* 陳亮集. Beijing: Zhonghua shuju, 1974.
Ebrey, Patricia Buckley. *Family and Property in Sung China: Yüan Ts'ai's Precepts for Social Life*. Princeton: Princeton University Press, 1984.
———. *The Inner Quarters: Marriage and the Lives of Chinese Women in the Sung Period*. Berkeley: University of California Press, 1993.
Tillman, Hoyt Cleveland. *Utilitarian Confucianism: Ch'en Liang's Challenge to Chu Hsi*. Cambridge and London: Council on East Asian Studies, Harvard University, 1982.
Tuo Tuo 脫脫 et. al., ed. *Song shi* 宋史. Beijing: Zhonghua shuju, 1977.
Watson, James L., and Evelyn S. Rawski, ed. *Death Ritual in Late Imperial and Modern China*. Berkeley: University of California Press, 1988.

5. "THE CUSTOMS OF VARIOUS BARBARIANS" BY LI JING

Glossary

a ye wei	阿也韋	Moxie	末些
ba	巴	naide	耐德
Bai	白	Naxi	納西
Bo	僰	piaoxin	縹信
buxie	布燮	Pu Man	蒲蠻
cigong	次工	Puzi Man	朴子蠻
cuan nong	爨弄	ren	人
Dai	傣	Saidianchi	賽典赤
daxipo	大奚婆	sheng	生
Fu Youde	傅友德	shiseng	師僧
Hani	哈尼	shou	手
husun	胡孫	shu	熟
Jinchi Baiyi	金齒百夷	suo	索
Jingpo	景頗	tanchuo	坦綽
jue	鵙	Tulao	土獠
jueshe	鵙舍	Wa	佤
juke	苴可	Woni	斡泥
kowtow [ketou]	磕頭	Wu Man	烏蠻
luohou	落後	xinju	信苴
Luoluo	羅羅	Ye Man	野蠻
miao	苗	zhuang	庄
miaozi	妙子	Zhuang	壯
Mosuo	摩娑		

References

Armijo-Hussein, Jacqueline. "Sayyid 'Ajall Shams al-Din: A Muslim from Central Asia, Serving the Mongols in China and Bringing 'Civilization' to Yunnan." Ph.D. diss., Harvard University, 1997.

———. "Young People and Social Change in China: A Survey on Risk Factors for HIV/AIDS in Yunnan Province." Report on the Yunnan HIV/AIDS Youth Survey conducted by the Australian Red Cross in collaboration with the Yunnan Red Cross. Kunming, China. December, 1996.

Blum, Susan. "Han and the Chinese Other: The Language of Identity and Difference in Southwest China." Ph.D. diss., University of Michigan, 1994.

Caldwell, Harry R., and John C. Caldwell. *South China Birds*. Shanghai: Hester May Vanderburgh, 1931.

Chow, Rey. "Ethnic Minorities in Chinese Films: Cinema and the Exotic." *The East-West Film Journal* 1, no. 2 (1987): 15–32.

Cohn, Bernard S. *Colonialism and Its Forms of Knowledge: The British in India.* Princeton: Princeton University Press, 1996.

Cooper, Frederick, and Ann L. Stoler. "Tensions of Empire: Colonial Control and Visions of Rule." *American Ethnologist* 16, no. 4 (1989): 609–21.

Deng Qiyao, and Zhang Liu, eds. *The Festivals in the Mysterious Land of Yunnan.* Kunming: Yunnan People's Publishing House, 1991.

Dikötter, Frank. *The Discourse of Race in Modern China.* Stanford: Stanford University Press, 1992.

Eberhard, Wolfram. *The Local Cultures of South and East China*. Leiden: E.J. Brill, 1968.

Gladney, Dru. "Representing Nationality in China: Refiguring Majority/Minority Identities." *Journal of Asian Studies* 53, no. 1 (1994): 92–123.

Goodrich, L. Carrington, and Chaoying Fang, eds. *Dictionary of Ming Biography, 1368–1644*. 2 vols. New York: Columbia University Press, 1976.

Harrell, Stevan. "Introduction: Civilizing Projects and the Reaction to Them." In *Cultural Encounters on China's Ethnic Frontiers*, ed. Stevan Harrell. Seattle: University of Washington Press, 1994.

He Hongzuo 何弘佐. "Zhongqinglu xue liyue ji" 中慶路學禮樂記. In *Xinzuan Yunnan tongzhi* 新纂雲南通志, ed. Zhou Zhongyue 周鐘嶽, *juan* 94:5–6. Reprint, Kunming:Yunnansheng difangzhi weiyuanhui, 1988.

Hostetler, Laura. "Chinese Ethnography in the Eighteenth Century: Miao Albums of Guizhou." Ph.D. diss., University of Pennsylvania, 1995.

Hyde, Sandra. "Sex Tourism Practices on the Periphery: Eroticizing Ethnicity on the Lancang." In *China Urban: Ethnographies of Contemporary Culture*, ed. Nancy N. Chen et al. Durham, N.C.: Duke University Press, 2001.

Li Jing 李京. *Yunnan zhilüe* 雲南志略. See Wang Shuwu.

Said, Edward. *Orientalism.* New York: Vintage Books, 1979.

Schein, Louisa. *Minority Rules: The Miao and the Feminine in China's Cultural Politics*. Durham: Duke University Press, 2000.

The Travels of Marco Polo: The Complete Yule-Cordier Edition. 2 vols. New York: Dover Publications, 1993.

Van Gulik, R.H. *The Gibbon in China: An Essay in Chinese Animal Lore*. Leiden: E.J. Brill, 1967.

Von Glahn, Richard. *The Country of Streams and Grottoes: Expansion, Settlement, and the Civilizing of the Sichuan Frontier in Song Times*. Cambridge: Cambridge University Press, 1987.

Wang Shuwu 王叔武, ed. *Dali xingji [jiaozhu]; Yunnan zhilüe [jijiao]* 大理行記 [校注]; 雲南志略 [輯校]. Kunming: Yunnan minzu chubanshe, 1986.

Watson, James L. "The Structure of Chinese Funerary Rites: Elementary Forms, Ritual Sequence, and the Primacy of Performance." In *Death Ritual in Late Impe-*

rial and Modern China, ed. James L. Watson and Evelyn S. Rawski. Berkeley: University of California Press, 1988.

West, Stephen. "Mongol Influence on the Development of Northern Drama." In *China under Mongol Rule*, ed. John D. Langlois, Jr. Princeton: Princeton University Press, 1981.

Yule, Colonel Henry. *Cathay and the Way Thither: Being a Collection of Medieval Notices of China*. Vol. 2. London: The Hakluyt Society, 1866.

6. SELECTED WRITINGS BY LUO RUFANG

Glossary

ai 愛
bian 變
chang 常
changfen 常分
Chen Mingshui 陳明水
Chen Shiwei 陳世爲
Chongren 崇仁
ci 慈
Cijie tang 慈節堂
Dong 董
Ershisi xiao shi 二十四孝詩
Fan Zhongyan 范仲淹
fu dao 婦道
Fu Shijing 傅石井
Fuzhou 撫州
Guan 官
heyou zhi xiang 何有之鄉
Huagai 華蓋
jiangxue 講學
Jiangyou 江右
jie 節
kongdong zhi yu 崆峒之域
kongkong dongdong 空空洞洞
kun 坤
liangxin 良心
liangzhi 良知
Lienü zhuan 列女傳
Linchuan 臨川
muzhiming 墓誌銘
Nancheng 南城
nianjing xiangdao 念經向道
Ning 甯
Ningguo 寧國
qian 乾
qing 情
Taihu 太湖
taixu 太虛
Taizhou 泰州
ti 悌
tianyi 天彝
Wang Danxuan 王澹軒
Wang Wanshan 王萬善
Wen Tianxiang 文天祥
Wu 吳
Xi 璽
xian nainai 賢奶奶
xiao 孝
Xiaoxue 小學
xin 心
yang 陽
yin 陰
yiqie fangxia 一切放下
Zhongbao 重寶
Zhu Xi 朱熹
ziji qiancheng 自己前程

References

Araki Kengo 荒木見悟. *Mindai shisō kenkyū* 明代思想研究. Tokyo: Sobunsha, 1972.

Chan, Wing-tsit, trans. *A Source Book in Chinese Philosophy*. Princeton: Princeton University Press, 1963.

Cheng, Yu-Yin. "Pursuing Sagehood without Boundary: The T'ai-chou School's Message and Lo Ju-fang's Intellectual Development, 1515–53." In *Tradition and*

Metamorphosis in Modern Chinese History: Essays in Honor of Professor Kwang-Ching Liu's Seventy-Fifth Birthday, ed. Hao Yen-p'ing and Wei Hsiu-mei, vol. 2. Taipei: Institute of Modern History, Academia Sinica, 1998.

———. "Sagehood and the Common Man: T'ai-chou Confucianism in Late Ming Society." Ph.D. diss., University of California, Davis, 1996.

———. *Wan Ming bei yiwang de sixiangjia: Luo Rufang shiwen shiji biannian* 晚明被遺忘的思想家: 羅汝芳詩文事蹟編年. Taipei: Guangwen shuju, 1995.

Ching, Julia. "Lo Ju-fang." In *Dictionary of Ming Biography*, ed. L. Carrington Goodrich and Chaoying Fang. New York: Columbia University Press, 1976.

Handlin, Joanna F. *Action in Late Ming Thought: The Reorientation of Lü K'un and Other Scholar-Officials*. Berkeley: University of California Press, 1983.

*Hsiung Ping-chen. "Constructed Emotions: The Bond between Mothers and Sons in Late Imperial China." *Late Imperial China* 15, no. 1 (1994): 87–117.

Luo Rufang 羅汝芳. *Luo Mingde gong wenji* 羅明德公文集. Edition of 1632.

———. *Mingdao lu* 明道錄. Reprint, Taipei: Guangwen shuju, 1987.

———. *Xutan zhiquan* 盱壇直詮. Reprint, Taipei: Guangwen shuju, 1967.

Mou Zongsan 牟宗三. *Xinti yu xingti* 心體與性體. 2 vols. Taipei: Zhengzhong shuju, 1973.

Tang Junyi 唐君毅. *Zhongguo zhexue yuanlun: Yuanjiao pian* 中國哲學原論: 原教篇. 2 vols. Reprint, Taipei: Xuesheng shuju, 1979.

Wang Liqi 王利器. *Lidai xiaohua ji* 歷代笑話集. Hong Kong: Xinyue shudian, 1962.

Watson, Burton, trans. *The Complete Works of Chuang Tzu*. New York: Columbia University Press, 1968.

7. *FINAL INSTRUCTIONS* BY YANG JISHENG

Glossary

"Bao Ren Shaoqing shu"	報任少卿書	xin	心
		Yan Song	嚴嵩
Erzhen	二貞	Yang Jisheng	楊繼盛
Futang	福堂	Yanhao	燕豪
gong dao	公道	Yanjie	燕傑
Huai	槐	Yanxian	燕賢
Jiaoshanzi	椒山子	Yanxiong	燕雄
jinshi	進士	Yingji	應箕
junzi	君子	Yingwei	應尾
li	理	zhang xie zhiqi	長些志氣
li zhi	立志	Zhang Zhen	張貞
nianpu	年譜	zhen jie	貞節
tian li	天理	zhiqi	志氣
Wang Lin (Jijin)	王遴 (繼津)	zhong	中
wu dao li	無道理		

References

Birch, Cyril, ed. *Anthology of Chinese Literature*. New York: Grove Press, 1967.

Birge, Bettine. "Levirate Marriage and the Revival of Widow Chastity in Yuan China." *Asia Major*, 3d ser., 8, no. 2 (1995): 107–46.

*Carlitz, Katherine. “Shrines, Governing-Class Identity, and the Cult of Widow Fidelity in Mid-Ming Jiangnan.” *Journal of Asian Studies* 56, no. 3 (1997): 612–40.
Ebrey, Patricia Buckley. *Chu Hsi's Family Rituals*. Princeton: Princeton University Press, 1991.
———. *Confucianism and Family Rituals in Imperial China: A Social History of Writing about Rites*. Princeton: Princeton University Press, 1991.
Goodrich, L. Carrington, and Chaoying Fang, eds. *Dictionary of Ming Biography, 1368–1644*. 2 vols. New York: Columbia University Press, 1976.
Holmgren, Jennifer. “The Economic Foundations of Virtue: Widow-Remarriage in Early and Modern China.” *The Australian Journal of Chinese Affairs* 13 (1985): 1–27.
Leung, Angela Ki Che. “To Chasten Society: The Development of Widow Homes in the Ch'ing, 1773–1911.” *Late Imperial China* 14, no. 2 (1993): 1–32.
*Mann, Susan. “Widows in the Kinship, Class, and Community Structures of Qing Dynasty China.” *Journal of Asian Studies* 46, no. 1 (1987): 37–56.
Mingren zhuanji ziliao suoyin 明人傳記資料索引. 2 vols. National Central Library, comp. Taipei: Guoli zhongyang tushuguan, 1965.
Mote, Frederick W., and Denis Twitchett, eds. *The Cambridge History of China*. Vol. 7. Cambridge: Cambridge University Press, 1988.
Yang Jisheng 楊繼盛. *Yang Jiaoshan xiansheng yan xing lu* 楊椒山先生言行錄. Shanghai: Privately sponsored printing, 1932.
———. *Yang Zhongmin gong yibi* 楊忠愍公遺筆. Congshu jicheng edition. Shanghai: Shangwu yinshuguan, 1939.

8. “RECORD OF PAST KARMA” BY JI XIAN

Glossary

Ban Zhao 班昭
Cai Yan 蔡琰
caiyuan 才媛
Chen Weisong 陳維崧
Fangsheng wen 放生文
gegu 割股
Guan Yu (Lord Guan) 關羽
Ji Kaisheng 季開生
Ji Xian 季嫻
Ji Yuyong 季寓庸
Ji Zhenyi 季振宜
Jiesha wen 戒殺文
jinshi 進士
Jingyang 靜姎
Li Chang'ang 李長昂
Li Qingzhao 李清照
Li Sicheng 李思誠
Li Weilin 李爲霖
Li Yan 李妍
lienü 列女
Mulian 目連
Qianshou jing 千手經
Sanguo yanyi 三國演義
shi 詩
Shiji shuo 施濟說
shilu 實錄
Taixing 泰興
Tan jing 壇經
Wang Duanshu 王端淑
Wang Shizhen 王士禎
Wang Zhaoyuan 王照圓
Weizhang 維章
Xinghua 興化
Xingyi 興邑
Xuanyi nüzi 玄衣女子
yu 予
zixu 自序
Zou Siyi 鄒斯漪

References

Brook, Timothy. *Praying for Power: Buddhism and the Formation of Gentry Society in Late-Ming China*. Cambridge: The Council on East Asian Studies, Harvard University, 1993.

Chang, Kang-i Sun. "Ming and Qing Anthologies of Women's Poetry and Their Selection Strategies." In *Writing Women in Late Imperial China*, ed. Ellen Widmer and Kang-i Sun Chang. Stanford: Stanford University Press, 1997.

Chen Weisong 陳維崧. *Furen ji* 婦人集. Xiangyan congshu edition. Preface dated 1908.

Fong, Grace S. "Writing Self and Writing Lives: Shen Shanbao's (1808–1862) Gendered Auto/Biographical Practices." *Nan Nü: Men, Women and Gender in Early and Imperial China* 2, no. 2 (2000): 259–303.

Frankel, Hans. "Cai Yan and the Poems Attributed to Her." *Chinese Literature: Essays, Articles, Reviews* 5, no. 2 (1983): 133–56.

Guangxu Taixing xian zhi 光緒泰興縣志. Edition of 1886.

Heyin Siku quanshu zongmu tiyao ji Siku weishou shumu jinhui shumu 合印四庫全書總目提要及四庫未收書目禁毀書目. 5 volumes. Reprint, Taipei: Taiwan shangwu yinshuguan, 1986.

Hu Wenkai 胡文楷. *Lidai funü zhuzuo kao* 歷代婦女著作考. Shanghai: Shanghai guji chubanshe, 1985.

Ji Xian 季嫻. "Qianyin ji" 前因紀. In *Yuquankan heke* 雨泉龕合刻. Vol. 2, *wenji* 文集, 1a–5b. Preface dated 1657. Copy in Beijing Library.

———. *Yuquankan shixuan* 雨泉龕詩選. Preface dated 1653. Copy in Beijing Library.

Johnson, David, ed. *Ritual Opera, Operatic Ritual: "Mu-lien Rescues His Mother" in Chinese Popular Culture*. Berkeley: Publications of the Chinese Popular Culture Project, no. 1, 1989.

Owen, Stephen. *Remembrances: The Experience of the Past in Classical Chinese Literature*. Cambridge: Harvard University Press, 1986.

Roberts, Moss, trans. *Three Kingdoms: A Historical Novel*. Berkeley: University of California Press, 1991.

Soothill, William, comp. *A Dictionary of Chinese Buddhist Terms*. Reprint, Taipei: Cheng Wen Publishing Company, 1972.

Swann, Nancy Lee. *Pan Chao: Foremost Woman Scholar of China*. New York: The Century Company, 1932.

Wang Duanshu 王端淑, comp. *Mingyuan shiwei* 名媛詩緯. Edition of 1667. Copy in Beijing University Library.

Wu, Pei-yi. *The Confucian's Progress: Autobiographical Writings in Traditional China*. Princeton: Princeton University Press, 1990.

Yampolsky, Philip. *The Platform Sutra of the Sixth Patriarch*. New York: Columbia University Press, 1967.

Yangzhou fu zhi 揚州府志. Edition of 1664. In *Xijian Zhongguo difangzhi huikan* 稀見中國地方志彙刊, vol. 13. Beijing: Zhongguo shudian, 1992.

Zou Siyi 鄒斯漪, comp. *Shiyuan ba mingjia ji* 詩媛八名家集. Preface dated 1655. Copy in Beijing Library.

Zurndorfer, Harriet. "The 'Constant World' of Wang Chao-yuan: Women, Education, and Orthodoxy in Eighteenth-Century China." In *Family Process and Political Process in Modern Chinese History*, vol. 1. Taipei: Institute of Modern History, Academia Sinica, 1992.

9. "LETTER TO MY SONS" BY GU RUOPU

Glossary

Gu Ruopu	顧若璞	Huang Maowu	黃茂梧
Gui fan	閨範	Lü Kun	呂坤

References

Cole, Alan. *Mothers and Sons in Chinese Buddhism.* Stanford: Stanford University Press, 1998.

Eastman, Lloyd E. *Family, Fields, and Ancestors: Constancy and Change in China's Social and Economic History, 1550–1949.* New York: Oxford University Press, 1988.

Ebrey, Patricia. "Women, Marriage, and the Family in Chinese History." In *Heritage of China: Contemporary Perspectives on Chinese Civilization*, ed. Paul Ropp. Berkeley: University of California Press, 1990.

Fu Xihua 傅惜華, comp. *Zhongguo gudian wenxue banhua xuanji* 中國古典文學版畫選集. Shanghai: Renmin meishu chubanshe, 1981.

Ko, Dorothy. *Teachers of the Inner Chambers: Women and Culture in Seventeenth-Century China.* Stanford: Stanford University Press, 1994.

*Mann, Susan. *Precious Records: Women in China's Long Eighteenth Century*. Stanford: Stanford University Press, 1997.

Robertson, Maureen. "Changing the Subject: Gender and Self-inscription in Authors' Prefaces and *Shi* Poetry." In *Writing Women in Late Imperial China*, ed. Ellen Widmer and Kang-i Sun Chang. Stanford: Stanford University Press, 1997.

*———. "Voicing the Feminine: Constructions of the Gendered Subject." *Late Imperial China* 13, no. 1 (1992): 63–110.

Waltner, Ann, and Pi-ching Hsu. "Lingering Fragrance: The Poetry of Tu Yaose and Shen Tiansun." *Journal of Women's History* 8, no. 4 (1997): 28–53.

Wang Qi 汪淇. *Chidu xinyu chubian* 尺牘新語初編, 23:1a–2b. N.p., 1663. Copy in the Naikaku bunko.

Weidner, Marsha, et al., ed. *Views from Jade Terrace: Chinese Women Artists, 1300–1912.* Indianapolis: Indianapolis Museum of Art; New York: Rizzoli, 1988.

*Widmer, Ellen. "The Epistolary World of Female Talent in Seventeenth-Century China." *Late Imperial China* 10, no. 2 (1989): 1–43.

———. "The Huanduzhai of Hangzhou and Suzhou: A Study in Seventeenth-Century Publishing." *Harvard Journal of Asiatic Studies* 56, no. 1 (1996): 77–122.

10. PERSONAL LETTERS IN SEVENTEENTH-CENTURY EPISTOLARY GUIDES

Glossary

bi shi	鄙詩	Fan Caiyun	范彩雲
chidu	尺牘	fengyue men	風月門
ci bujin yi	詞不盡意	"Fengyun qingshu"	丰韻情書
dai	代	fuqi fengyun	夫妻丰韻
dongfang chunyi	洞房春意	jiashu	家書
miaofang	妙方	jizhou fu	箕帚婦

Liu Chen	劉晨	Ruan Zhao	阮肇
milou	迷樓	shu	書
mou	某	shujian huotao tishi	書柬活套體式
nieguo	孽果	"Wu ye ti"	烏夜啼
pengyou fengyun	朋友丰韻	xianqi	賢妻
qing	情	xunchang jiaxin shi	尋常家信式
qinghao	情好	yougui fengyun	幽閨丰韻
qingji fengyun	情姬丰韻	yue fu	樂府
qingshu	情書	zhi duan yi chang bujin	紙短意長不盡
qingzhao youshang	請召遊賞	zhuju zhaiyu	逐句摘語
riyong leishu	日用類書		

References

Bai, Qianshen. "Chinese Letters: Private Words Made Public." In *The Embodied Image: Chinese Calligraphy from the John B. Elliott Collection*, ed. Robert E. Harris and Wen C. Fong. Princeton: The Art Museum, Princeton University, 1999.

Boreau, Alain. "The Letter-Writing Norm: A Medieval Invention." In *Correspondence: Models of Letter-Writing from the Middle Ages to the Nineteenth Century*, ed. Roger Chartier, Alain Boreau, and Cecile Dauphin, trans. Christopher Woodall. Princeton: Princeton University Press, 1997.

Brook, Timothy. *The Confusions of Pleasure: Commerce and Culture in Ming China*. Berkeley: University of California Press, 1998.

Chartier, Roger. "Secretaires for the People?" In *Correspondence: Models of Letter-Writing from the Middle Ages to the Nineteenth Century*, ed. Roger Chartier, Alain Boreau, and Cecile Dauphin, trans. Christopher Woodall. Princeton: Princeton University Press, 1997.

Chen Shao 陳詔 (pseud. Qingpu shuijing shanfang 青浦水鏡山房), comp. *Mingyuan chidu* 名媛尺牘. Wuyunlou edition, 1863.

Danshan feng. See under Mei Fengting.

Ebrey, Patricia. "Tang Guides to Verbal Etiquette." *Harvard Journal of Asiatic Studies* 45 (1985): 581–613.

Feng Menglong 馮夢龍. *Feng Menglong quanji* 馮夢龍全集. Edited by Wei Tongxian 魏同賢. Shanghai: Shanghai guji chubanshe, 1993.

Hanmo quanshu. See under Liu Yingli.

Hansen, Valerie. *Negotiating Daily Life in Traditional China: How Ordinary People Used Contracts, 600–1400*. New Haven: Yale University Press, 1995.

Knechtges, David R., trans., annot., ed. *Wen xuan, or, Selections of Refined Literature*. Vol. 3. Princeton: Princeton University Press, 1996.

Li Yunxiang 李雲翔, comp. *Jinling baimei* 金陵百媚. Preface dated 1618. Naikaku bunko.

Liu Xin 劉歆, comp. *Xijing zaji* 西京雜記. In *Guanzhong congshu* 關中叢書, vol. 3. Taipei: Yiwen yinshuguan, 1970.

Liu Yingli 劉應李, ed. *Xinbian shiwen leiju Hanmo quanshu* 新編事文類聚翰墨全書. Edition of 1307. Gest Oriental Library, Princeton University.

Liu Yiqing 劉義慶. *Youming lu* 幽明錄. Annotated by Zheng Wanqing 鄭晚晴. Beijing: Wenhua yishu, 1988.

Lowry, Kathryn. "The Transmission of Popular Song in Late-Ming China." Ph.D. diss., Harvard University, 1996.

———. "Writing and Reading Letters in Late-Ming China" (unpublished manuscript).

Mei Fengting 梅鳳亭, ed. *Xinke zhushi yasu bianyong Yizha sanqi Danshan feng* 新刻註釋雅俗便用一札三奇丹山鳳. Ming edition, n.d. Printed by Yu Changgeng 余長庚. Original edition in Naikaku bunko.

Oki Yasushi 大木康. "Minmatsu Kōnan ni okeru shuppan bunka no kenkyū" 明末江南における出版文化の研究. *Hiroshima daigaku bungakubu kiyo* 50, spec. issue no. 1 (1991): 1–176.

Owen, Stephen, ed. and trans. *An Anthology of Chinese Literature, Beginnings to 1911*. New York: W.W. Norton, 1996.

Pattinson, David. "The Chidu in Late Ming and Early Qing China." Ph.D. diss., Australian National University, 1998.

Qian Zhongshu 錢鍾書, comp. *Songshi xuan zhu* 宋詩選注. Beijing: Renmin wenxue, 1958.

Qizha qingqian. See under *Xinbian shiwen leiyao Qizha qingqian*.

Quanbu wenlin miaojin Wanbao quanshu 全補文林妙錦萬寶全書. Preface dated 1612. Anzheng tang 安正堂 reprint by Liu Ziming 劉子明 (style name Double Pines 雙松). Harvard-Yenching Library.

Shen Jin 沈津. "Mingdai fangke tushu zhi liutong yu jiage" 明代坊刻圖書之流通與價格. *Guojia tushuguan guankan* 1 (1996): 101–18.

Wanbao quanshu. See under *Quanbu wenlin miaojin Wanbao quanshu*.

Wang Shifu 王實甫. *Xixiang ji* 西廂記. Beijing: Renmin wenxue chubanshe, 1995.

Wanhua gu. See under *Zengbu Huijun yuan [ ] shishi tongkao Wanhua gu*.

Wenlin zhaijin. See under *Xinke titou wanshi quanshu leiju wenlin zhaijin*.

West, Stephen H., and Wilt L. Idema, intro. and trans. *The Moon and the Zither: The Story of the Western Wing*, by Wang Shifu. Berkeley: University of California Press, 1990.

Widmer, Ellen. "The Epistolary World of Female Talent in Seventeenth-Century China." *Late Imperial China* 10, no. 2 (1989): 1–43.

Xiao Tong 蕭統, comp. *Wen xuan zhu* 文選注. Annotated by Li Shan 李善. Taipei: Shijie shuju, 1962.

Xinbian shiwen leiyao Qizha qingqian 新編事文類要啓劄青錢. 1324 edition by the Liu printing establishment Rixin tang 日新堂. Modern reprint, with notes by Niida Noboru 仁井田陞, Tokyo: Koten kenkyū kai, 1963.

Xinke titou wanshi quanshu leiju wenlin zhaijin 新刻提頭萬事全書類聚文林摘錦. Wanli edition. Niida Collection, Tokyo University.

Zengbu Huijun yuan [ ] shishi tongkao Wanhua gu 增補徽郡原［ ］世事通考萬花谷. Published by Yu Kaiming 余開明, ca. 1621–1627. Harvard-Yenching Library.

Zhemei jian 折梅箋. Attributed to Feng Menglong 馮夢龍. Late-Ming edition. Printed by Yu Changgeng 余長庚 (style name Dweller in the Purple Clouds 紫霞居). Facsimile reprint in *Feng Menglong quanji* 馮夢龍全集, ed. Wei Tongxian 魏同賢, vol. 43. Shanghai: Shanghai guji chubanshe, 1993.

11. LETTERS BY WOMEN OF THE MING-QING PERIOD

GLOSSARY

baifeng 白鳳
Cao Cao 曹操
Chen Chengkuang 陳承纊
chidu 尺牘
chishu 尺書
dajia guifan 大家規範
Dao 道
dao yun yafeng 道蘊雅風
Fang 方
Gu Ruopu 顧若璞
Guo Pu 郭璞
huma 胡麻
jian (fine paper for writing poetry) 箋
jian (simple) 簡
Jiang Yan 江淹
"Li sao" 離騷
Li Shuzhao (Duanming) 李淑昭(端明)
Lin Yining (Yaqing) 林以寧(亞清)
Liu Bei 劉備
luan 亂
Luo Rufang 羅汝芳
Meng Haoran 孟浩然
Qi Biaojia 祁彪佳
Qian Feng Xian (Youling) 錢馮嫻(又令)
Qian Tingmei 錢廷枚
qingniao 青鳥
Qinlou hegao 琴樓合稿
Qu Yuan 屈原
Sanguo zhi 三國志
Shang Jinglan 商景蘭
shudu 書牘
shuqi 書啓
Sun Quan 孫權
Tang Xianzu 湯顯祖
Tao Qian 陶潛
tongguan 彤管
Wuling 武陵
xingqing 性情
Yang Jisheng 楊繼盛
yuxie 玉屑
zha 扎
Zhang Chayun 張槎雲
Zhang Dehui 張德蕙
zhiji 知己
Zhou Geng 周庚
Zhou Lianggong 周亮功
Zhu Derong 朱德蓉

REFERENCES

Chang, Francois. *Chinese Poetic Writing*. Translated by Donald A. Riggs and Jerome P. Seaton. Bloomington: Indiana University Press, 1982.

*Chang, Kang-i Sun. "Ming-Qing Women Poets and the Notions of 'Talent' and 'Morality.'" In *Culture and State in Chinese History: Conventions, Accommodations, and Critiques*, ed. Theodore Huters, R. Bin Wong, and Pauline Yu. Stanford: Stanford University Press, 1997.

Chen Shao 陳韶 (pseud. Qingpu shuijing shanfang 青浦水鏡山房), comp. *Mingyuan chidu* 名媛尺牘. Wuyunlou edition, 1863.

Chen Weisong 陳維崧. *Furen ji* 婦人集. Reprint, *Xiangyan congshu* 香艷叢書. Guoxue fulunshe edition. Shanghai: Zhongguo tushu gongsi, 1914, vol. 1, 2: 15a–35a.

Fu Xihua 傅惜華, comp. *Zhongguo gudian wenxue banhua xuanji* 中國古典文學版畫選集. 2 vols. Shanghai: Shanghai renmin meishu chubanshe, 1981.

Fujian tong zhi 福建通志. Edition of 1938.

*Ko, Dorothy. "Pursuing Talent and Virtue: Education and Women's Culture in

Seventeenth- and Eighteenth-Century China." *Late Imperial China* 13, no. 1 (1992): 9–39.
*———. *Teachers of the Inner Chambers: Women and Culture in Seventeenth-Century China*. Stanford: Stanford University Press, 1994.
Legge, James, trans. *The Chinese Classics*. Vol. 1, *Analects*, and vol. 4, *The Book of Odes*. Oxford: Clarendon Press, 1892.
Li Fang 李昉. *Taiping guangji* 太平廣記. Beijing: Renmin wenxue chubanshe, 1959.
McDermott, Joseph P. "Friendship and Its Friends in the Late Ming." In *Family Process and Political Process in Modern Chinese History*, ed. Institute of Modern History, Academia Sinica, vol. 1. Taipei: Institute of Modern History, Academia Sinica, 1992.
Shi Hongbao 施鴻保, comp. *Min zaji* 閩雜記. Fuzhou: Fujian renmin chubanshe, 1985.
Shi Shuyi 施淑儀, comp. *Qingdai guige shiren zhenglüe* 清代閨閣詩人徵略. Shanghai: Shanghai shudian, 1987.
Tang Xianzu 湯顯祖. *Yuming tang chidu* 玉茗堂尺牘. Taipei: Guangwen shuju, 1990.
Wang Xiuqin 王秀琴, and Hu Wenkai 胡文楷, comp. *Lidai mingyuan shujian* 歷代名媛書簡. Changsha: Shangwu yinshuguan, 1941.
Watson, Burton. *The Columbia Book of Chinese Poetry: From Early Times to the Thirteenth Century*. New York: Columbia University Press, 1984.
Widmer, Ellen. "The Epistolary World of Female Talent in Seventeenth-Century China." *Late Imperial China* 10, no. 2 (1989): 1–43.
Xin Yi 辛夷. *Zhongguo diangu da cidian* 中國典故大辭典. Beijing: Beijing Yanshan chubanshe, 1991.
Xu Yitang 徐益棠, comp. *Lidai mingxian chushi jiashu* 歷代名賢處世家書. Taipei: Laogu wenhua chubanshe, 1982.
Yuan Ke 袁珂. *Shanhai jing jiaoyi* 山海經校譯. Shanghai: Guji chubanshe, 1985.
Zhang Qiyun 張其昀, comp. *Zhongwen da cidian* 中文大辭典. Taipei: Zhongguo wenhua xueyuan, 1968.
Zhou Lianggong 周亮功. *Min xiaoji* 閩小記. Fuzhou: Fujian renmin chubanshe, 1985.
———, comp. *Mingxian chidu xinchao* 名賢尺牘新鈔. In Congshu jicheng chubian 叢書集成初編. Shanghai: Shangwu yinshuguan, 1936.

12. SELECTED SHORT WORKS BY WANG DUANSHU

Glossary

Bimu yu	比目魚
Chen Hongshou	陳洪綬
Chen Suxia	陳素霞
Ding Junwang	丁君望
Ding Shengzhao	丁聖肇
Guochao guixiu zhengshi ji	國朝閨秀正始集
Hengxin ji	恆心集
Huang Yuanjie	黃媛介
Li Yu	李漁
Lidai diwang houfei kao	歷代帝王后妃考
Liu Rushi	柳如是
Liuqie ji	留篋集
Meng Chengshun	孟偁舜
Mingyuan wenwei	名媛文緯
Qi Biaojia	祁彪佳
Qian Qianyi	錢謙益

Shang Jinglan 商景蘭
Shen Yunying 沈雲英
Shigui shu 石匱書
Shiyu 史愚
Wang Duanshu 王端淑
Wang Jingshu 王淨淑
Wang Ruqian 汪如謙
Wang Siren 王思任
Wang Youding 王猷定
Wang Zhenshu 王貞淑
Wu Guofu 吳國輔
Wu Shan 吳山
Wucai ji 無才集
"Xingzhuang" 行狀
Xu Wei 徐渭
Yilou ji 宜樓集
Yun Shouping 惲壽平
Yun Zhu 惲珠
Yuying tang ji 玉映堂集
Zeng Yi 曾益
Zhang Dai 張岱
Zhu Kuangding 諸匡鼎
Zhoushan 舟山
Zou Siyi 鄒斯漪

References

*Chang, Kang-i Sun. "Ming and Qing Anthologies of Women's Poetry and Their Selection Strategies." In *Writing Women in Late Imperial China*, ed. Ellen Widmer and Kang-i Sun Chang. Stanford: Stanford University Press, 1997.

Chang, Kang-i Sun, and Haun Saussy, eds. *Women Writers of Traditional China: An Anthology of Poetry and Criticism*. Stanford: Stanford University Press, 1999.

Deng Hanyi 鄧漢儀. *Shiguan chuji* 詩觀初集. Edition of 1672. In Naikaku bunko.

Hanan, Patrick. *The Invention of Li Yu*. Cambridge: Harvard University Press, 1988.

Hu Wenkai 胡文楷. *Lidai funü zhuzuo kao* 歷代婦女著作考. Shanghai: Shanghai guji chubanshe, 1985.

Lin Meiyi 林玫儀. "Wang Duanshu shilun zhi pingxi—jian lun qi xuan shi biaozhun" 王端淑詩論之評析兼論其選詩標準. *Jiuzhou xuekan* 6, no. 2 (1994):45–62.

Ren Xiong 任熊. *Yu Yue xianxian zhuan* 於越先賢傳. Edition of 1856.

Wang Duanshu 王端淑, comp. *Mingyuan shiwei* 名媛詩緯. Edition of 1667. Originals in Beijing University Library and National Central Library, Taipei.

———. *Yinhong ji* 吟紅集. Original in Naikaku bunko.

Wang Qi 汪淇 and Xu Shijun 徐士俊, ed. *Chidu xinyu* 尺牘新語. 3d collection. Edition of 1668. In Nanjing Library.

Weidner, Marsha, et al., ed. *Views from Jade Terrace: Chinese Women Artists, 1300–1912*. Indianapolis: Indianapolis Museum of Art; New York: Rizzoli, 1988.

Xu Fuming 徐扶明. *Yuan Ming Qing xiqu tansuo* 元明清戲曲探索. Hangzhou: Zhejiang guji chubanshe, 1986.

Yu Jianhua 俞劍華. *Zhongguo meishujia renming cidian* 中國美術家人名詞典. Shanghai: Renmin meishu chubanshe, 1981.

Zhang Dai 張岱. *Shigui houji* 石匱後集. Beijing: Zhonghua shuju, 1959.

*Zhong Huiling 鐘慧玲. "Qingdai nü shiren yanjiu" 清代女詩人研究. Ph.D. diss., Zhengzhi University, 1981.

Zhu He 朱睢 (Suchen 素臣). "Qinlou yue" 秦樓月. In *Gudian xiqu cunmu huikao* 古典戲曲存目彙考, ed. Zhuang Yifu 莊一拂. Shanghai: Shanghai guji chubanshe, 1982, p. 11.

Zou Siyi 鄒斯漪, comp. *Shiyuan ba mingjia ji* 詩媛八名家集. Preface dated 1655. In Academy of Sciences Library (Beijing) and Beijing Library.

13. TWO GHOST STORIES FROM *LIAOZHAI'S RECORDS OF THE STRANGE* BY PU SONGLING

Glossary

Chen Yuanlong	陳元龍	Qiaoniang	巧娘
Gao Heng	高珩	Qinnü cun	秦女村
leiran	纍然	qing	情
Liansuo	連瑣	wei	幃
Nongyu	弄玉	yingqin	迎親
qi	氣	Zichuan	淄川

References

Barr, Allan. "A Comparative Study of Early and Late Tales in *Liaozhai zhiyi*." *Harvard Journal of Asiatic Studies* 45, no. 1 (1985): 157–202.

———. "Disarming Intruders: Alien Women in *Liaozhai zhiyi*." *Harvard Journal of Asiatic Studies* 49, no. 2 (1989): 501–17.

———. "Pu Songling and *Liaozhai zhiyi*: A Study of Textual Transmission, Biographical Background and Literary Antecedents." Ph.D. diss., Oxford University, 1983.

———. "The Textual Transmission of *Liaozhai zhiyi*." *Harvard Journal of Asiatic Studies* 44, no. 2 (1984): 515–62.

Birch, Cyril, trans. *The Peony Pavilion*. Bloomington: Indiana University Press, 1980.

Chang, Chun-shu, and Shelley Hsueh-lun Chang. *Redefining History: Ghosts, Spirits, and Human Society in P'u Sung-ling's World, 1640–1715*. Ann Arbor: University of Michigan Press, 1998.

Giles, Herbert A., trans. *Strange Stories from a Chinese Studio*. 1916; New York: Dover, 1969.

Li, Wai-yee. *Enchantment and Disenchantment: Love and Illusion in Chinese Literature*. Princeton: Princeton University Press, 1993.

Mair, Denis C., and Victor H. Mair, trans. *Strange Tales from Make-Do Studio*. Beijing: Foreign Languages Press, 1989.

Pu Songling 蒲松齡. *Liaozhai zhiyi [huijiao huizhu huiping ben]* 聊齋誌異 [會校會注會評本]. Edited by Zhang Youhe 張有鶴. 1962; Shanghai: Shanghai guji chubanshe, 1983.

———. *Liaozhai zhiyi*. Facsimile reprint of the author's manuscript. Beijing, 1955.

———. *Xiangzhu Liaozhai zhiyi tuyong* 詳注聊齋誌異圖詠. Originally published, Tongwen shuju (preface dated 1887). Facsimile reprint, Beijing: Beijing shi Zhongguo shudian, 1981.

Spence, Jonathan. *The Death of Woman Wang*. Harmondsworth: Penguin, 1978.

Tang Xianzu 湯顯祖. *Mudanting* 牡丹亭. Edited by Xu Shuofang 徐朔方 and Yang Xiaomei 楊笑梅. Beijing: Renmin wenxue chubanshe, 1978.

Yu, Anthony C. "'Rest, Rest, Perturbed Spirit!' Ghosts in Traditional Chinese Prose Fiction." *Harvard Journal of Asiatic Studies* 47, no. 2 (1987): 397–434.

Yuan Zhen 元稹. "Lianchanggong ci" 連昌宮詞. In *Yuan Bo shixuan* 元白詩選, ed. Su Zhongxiang 蘇仲翔. Shanghai: Gudian wenxue chubanshe, 1957.

Zeitlin, Judith T. "Embodying the Disembodied: Representations of Ghosts and the Feminine." In *Writing Women in Late Imperial China*, ed. Ellen Widmer and Kang-i Sun Chang. Stanford: Stanford University Press, 1997.

———. *Historian of the Strange: Pu Songling and the Chinese Classical Tale*. Stanford: Stanford University Press, 1993.

Zhang Peiheng 章培恆. "Xinxu" 新序. In *Liaozhai zhiyi [huijiao huizhu huiping ben]* 聊齋誌異 [會校會注會評本], by Pu Songling 蒲松齡, edited by Zhang Youhe 張有鶴, 1962; Shanghai: Shanghai guji chubanshe, 1983.

14. TWO BIOGRAPHIES BY ZHANG XUECHENG

Glossary

Dai	戴	Wu	吳
Dao	道	xiao hu, wei	孝乎惟孝友
"Fu xue"	婦學	xiao you yu	于兄弟施
Hanyang	漢陽	xiong di, shi	於有政是
Hubei tong zhi	湖北通志	yu you zheng,	亦爲政奚
Huizhou	徽州	shi yi wei	其爲爲政
Ji	紀	zheng, xi qi	
Jiang Lan	江蘭	wei wei zheng	
Li ji	禮記	xingshi	行事
lienü zhuan	烈女傳	Xun	荀
Lienü zhuan	列女傳	Yingcheng	應城
Liu	劉	Zhang Biao	章鑣
Nüzong	女宗	Zhang Shuting	張叔珽
Wang	王	Zhang Yuanye	章垣業

References

Lau, D. C., trans. *Confucius: The Analects*. New York: Penguin Books, 1982.

Liu Xiang 劉向. *Gu lienü zhuan* 古列女傳. Edited by Ruan Fu 阮福. Facsimile edition of 1825.

Mann, Susan. "'Fu xue: Women's Learning,' by Zhang Xuecheng." In *Women Writers of Traditional China: An Anthology of Poetry and Criticism*, ed. Kang-i Sun Chang and Haun Saussy. Stanford: Stanford University Press, 1999.

———. "Women in the Life and Thought of Zhang Xuecheng." In *Chinese Language, Thought, and Culture: Nivison and His Critics*, ed. Philip J. Ivanhoe. Chicago: Open Court Press, 1996.

Nivison, David S. *The Life and Thought of Chang Hsüeh-ch'eng (1738–1801)*. Stanford: Stanford University Press, 1966.

Zhang Xuecheng 章學誠. *Zhang shi yishu* 章氏遺書. Jiayetang edition, 1922.

15. POEMS ON TEA-PICKING

Glossary

Cao Weijie	曹偉皆	Gao Qi	高啓
Chen Zhang	陳章	guyu	谷雨
Dongting	洞庭	Huangfu Zeng	皇甫曾
Fan Chengda	范成大	Huangyangjian	黃楊尖
Fang Youjiang	方右將	Kuizhou	夔州
Fenghuang	風篁	Lu Hongjian	陸鴻漸

Nanyue	南岳	Wang Fuzhi	王夫之
qing	磬	Wu Lan	吳蘭
qingming	清明	Xin'an	新安
Shu Yuexiang	舒岳祥		

References

Bray, Francesca. *Technology and Gender: Fabrics of Power in Late Imperial China*. Berkeley: University of California Press, 1997.

Cao Weijie 曹偉皆. "Huangyangjian shan" 黃楊尖山, *Dinghai ting zhi* 定海廳志. In *Zhongguo difangzhi chaye lishi ziliao xuanji* 中國地方志茶葉 歷史資料選輯, ed. Wu Juenong 吳覺農 (Beijing: Nongye chubanshe, 1990), 123.

Chen Zhang 陳章. "Caicha ge" 采茶歌. In *Qing shi duo* 清詩鐸, comp. Zhang Yingchang 張應昌 (1869 edition; reprint, Beijing: Zhonghua shuju, 1983), 174.

Dianshizhai huabao 點石齋畫報. 1884–1898. Reprint, Guangzhou: Guangdong renmin chubanshe, 1983.

Ebrey, Patricia Buckley. *The Inner Quarters: Marriage and the Lives of Chinese Women in the Sung Period*. Berkeley: University of California Press, 1993.

Fan Chengda 范成大. "Kuizhou zhuzhi ge" 夔州竹枝歌. In *Fan Shihu ji* 范石湖集 (Hongkong: Zhonghua shujü Xiang'gang fenju, 1974), 220.

Fang Youjiang 方右將. "Xin'an zhuzhi ci" 新安竹枝詞. In *Ming-Qing Huishang ziliao xuanbian* 明清徽商資料選編, ed. Zhang Haipeng 張海鵬 and Wang Tingyuan 王廷元 (Hefei: Huangshan shushe, 1985), 20–21.

Gao Qi 高啓. "Caicha ci" 采茶詞. In *Daquan ji* 大全集 (Siku quanshu wenyuange edition; reprint, Taipei: Shangwu yinshuguan, 1986), 1230: 24b.

Huangfu Zeng 皇甫曾. "Song Lu Hongjian shanren caicha hui" 送陸鴻漸山人採茶回. In *Quan Tang shi* 全唐詩, comp. Peng Dingqiu 彭定求 (Beijing: Zhonghua shuju, 1996), 492.

Judd, Ellen R. "*Niangjia*: Chinese Women and Their Natal Families." *Journal of Asian Studies* 48, no. 3 (1989): 525–44.

Mann, Susan. *Precious Records: Women in China's Long Eighteenth Century*. Stanford: Stanford University Press, 1997.

Robertson, Maureen. "Changing the Subject: Gender and Self-inscription in Authors' Prefaces and *Shi* Poetry." In *Writing Women in Late Imperial China*, ed. Ellen Widmer and Kang-i Sun Chang. Stanford: Stanford University Press, 1997.

———. "Voicing the Feminine: Constructions of the Gendered Subject." *Late Imperial China* 13, no. 1 (June 1992): 63–110.

Shu Yuexiang 舒岳祥. "Zi gui geng zhuan qi, jian cunfu you zhaicha . . ." 自歸耕篆畦,見村婦有摘茶 . . . In *Langfeng ji* 閬風集 (Siku quanshu wenyuange edition; reprint, Taipei: Shangwu yinshuguan, 1986), 1187: 358b.

Wang Fuzhi 王夫之. "Nanyue zhaicha ci" 南嶽摘茶詞. In *Chuanshan yishu quanji* 船山遺書全集 (Taipei: Zhongguo Chuanshan xuehui, Ziyou chubanshe lianhe yinxing, 1972), 11042.

Wu Lan 吳蘭. "Caicha xing" 采茶行. In *Qing shi duo* 清詩鐸, comp. Zhang Yingchang 張應昌 (1869 edition; reprinted Beijing: Zhonghua shuju, 1983), 179.

"Xia ci" 夏詞. In *Gujin tushu jicheng* 古今圖書集成, comp. Chen Menglei 陳夢雷 (Beijing: Zhonghua shuju, 1985), 47706.

16. *DRINKING WINE AND READING "ENCOUNTERING SORROW": A REFLECTION IN DISGUISE* BY WU ZAO

Glossary

Chen Wenshu	陳文述	shi bu yu	世不與
Chu ci	楚辭	Su Shi	蘇軾
ci	詞	"Wang Dongting Hu zeng Zhang Chengxiang"	望洞庭湖贈張承相
Du Fu	杜甫	Wu Zao	吳藻
duoduo guaishi	咄咄怪事	Xiang	湘
Gu Lanzhou	顧蘭洲	xiao	嘯
Hua lian ci	花簾詞	Xie Daoyun (Xie Xucai)	謝道韞 (謝絮才)
Huang Shan	黃衫	xu	絮
Huo Xiaoyu zhuan	霍小玉傳	"Yexia du zhuo si shou"	夜下獨酌四首
Jialing	迦陵	Yin Hao	殷浩
Li Bo	李白	"Yinjiu baxian ge"	飲酒八仙歌
"Li sao"	離騷	"Zhao hun"	招魂
Liu Mengde	劉夢得	Zhu Shuzhen	朱淑眞
Lu Eting	陸萼庭	Zijin (Wang Ziqiao)	子晉 (王子喬)
Mengjiao	夢焦	"Zui ge"	醉歌
Penglai	蓬萊		
Pingxiang	蘋香		
Qiao ying	喬影		
Qingping	青萍		
Qu Yuan	屈原		
Renhe	仁和		

References

Bo Juyi 白居易. *Bo Juyi ji* 白居易集. Shanghai: Shangwu yinshuguan, 1934.

Chou Zhao'ao 仇兆鼇, ed. *Du shi xiangzhu* 杜詩詳注. Beijing: Zhonghua shuju, 1979.

Fang Xuanling 房玄齡. *Jin shu* 晉書. Beijing: Zhonghua shuju, 1974.

Hawkes, David. *The Songs of the South: An Ancient Chinese Anthology of Poems by Qu Yuan and Other Poets*. London: Penguin Books, 1985.

Hua Wei 華瑋. "Ming Qing funü juzuo zhong zhi 'ninan' biaoxian yu xingbie wenti" 明清 婦女劇作中之 [擬男] 表現與性別問題. In *Ming Qing xiqu guoji yantao hui lun wen ji* 明清戲曲國際研討會論文集, ed. Hua Wei 華瑋 and Wang Ailing 王璦玲. Taipei: Dawen yinshua youxian gongsi, 1998.

Ji Yun 紀昀, ed. *Shaoshi jianwen houlu* 邵氏見聞后錄. Beijing: Zhonghua shuju, 1983.

Kaltenmark, Max. *Le Lie-sien tschouan*. Beijing: Publications du Centre d'études sinologiques de Pékin, 1953.

Ko, Dorothy. *Teachers of the Inner Chambers: Women and Culture in Seventeenth-Century China*. Stanford: Stanford University Press, 1994.

Li Bo 李白. *Li Bo ji jiao zhu* 李白集校注. Edited by Qu Tuiyuan 瞿蛻園 and Zhu Jincheng 朱金城. Shanghai: Shanghai guji chubanshe, 1990.

Liu Xiang 劉向. *Liexian zhuan* 列仙傳. Wenyuange siku quanshu edition. Vol. 1058. Taipei: Shangwu yinshuguan, 1983.

Liu Yiqing 劉義慶, comp. *Shishuo xinyu* 世說新語. Shanghai: Shanghai guji chubanshe, 1996.

Lu Eting 陸萼庭. *Qingdai xiqu jia cong kao* 清代戲曲家叢考. Shanghai: Xuelin chubanshe, 1995.

Mann, Susan. *Precious Records: Women in China's Long Eighteenth Century*. Stanford: Stanford University Press, 1997.

Mather, Richard, trans. and ed. *"Shih-shuo Hsin-yü": A New Account of Tales of the World*. Minneapolis: University of Minnesota Press, 1976.

Rexroth, Kenneth, and Ling Chung. *Women Poets of China*. New York: New Directions, 1972.

Sima Qian 司馬遷. *Shi ji* 史記. Beijing: Zhonghua shuju, 1959.

Wu Zao 吳藻. *Yinjiu du "Li sao" tu: Qiao ying* 飲酒讀離騷圖: 喬影. In *Qingren zaju erji* 清人雜劇二集, ed. Zheng Zhenduo 鄭振鐸. Hong Kong: Longmen shudian, 1969.

———. *Yinjiu du "Li sao" tu: Qiao ying* 飲酒讀離騷圖: 喬影. In *Qingdai zaju xuan* 清代雜劇選, ed. WangYongkuan 王永寬, Yang Haizhong 楊海中, and Yao Shuyi 么書儀. Henan: Zhongzhou chubanshe, 1991.

Xiao Tong 蕭統, comp. *Wen xuan* 文選. Reprint, Shanghai: Shanghai guji chubanshe, 1986.

Zeng Yongyi 曾永義. *Shuo xiqu* 說戲曲. Taipei: Lianjing chubanshe, 1976.

Zhang Shuqiong 張淑瓊, ed. *Meng Haoran* 孟浩然. Taipei: Diqiu chubanshe, 1990.

17. A BRIEF RECORD OF THE EASTERN OCEAN BY DING SHAOYI

Glossary

Baozhu	寶珠
Beinanmi	卑南覓
Deng Chuan'an (Shuyuan)	鄧傳安 (菽原)
fan	番
Fanshe caifeng tu	番社采風圖
fansu	番俗
Getian	葛天
He Qiaoyuan	何喬遠
Huang Yupu	黃玉圃
Min shu	閩書
she	社
shefan	社番
sheng	生
shengfan	生番
shu	熟
shufan	熟番
Taihai caifeng tu	台海采風圖
Taiwan wenxian	台灣文獻
tuman	土蠻
wangzheng	王政
Wenji	紋吉
Wuhuai shi	無怀氏
Wuxi	無錫
yi	夷
yili cehai	以蠡測海
Yu Canglang	郁滄浪
Zheng He	鄭和
zhongnan qingnü	重男輕女
zhongnü	重女
zhongnü qingnan	重女輕男
Zhou Zhongxuan	周鍾瑄
Zhu Yigui	朱一貴

References

Aleni, Giulio. *Zhifang waiji* 職方外紀. Reprint, Shanghai: Wenruilou, 1903.

Chen Di 陳第. *Dongfan ji* 東番記. Edition of 1603. In Shen Yourong 深有容, comp. *Minhai zengyan* 閩海贈言. Reprint, Taiwan wenxian congkan (TWWX) 56. Taipei: Taiwan yinhang, 1959.

Deng Chuan'an 鄧傳安. *Lice huichao* 蠡測彙鈔. Edition of 1830. Reprint, TWWX 9. Taipei: Taiwan yinhang, 1958.

Ding Shaoyi 丁紹儀. *Dongying zhilüe* 東瀛識略. Fuzhou: Wu Yutian kanben, 1873; 2d ed., TWWX 2. Taipei: Taiwan yinhang, 1957.

Huang Shujing 黃叔璥. *Taihai shicha lu* 台海使槎錄. Edition of 1736. Reprint, TWWX 4. Taipei: Taiwan yinhang, 1957.

Lan Dingyuan 藍鼎元. *Dongzheng ji* 東征集. Edition of 1722. Reprint, TWWX 12. Taipei: Taiwan yinhang, 1958.

Liushiqi 六十七. *Fanshe caifeng tukao* 番社采風圖考. Edition of c. 1746. Reprint, TWWX 90. Taipei: Taiwan yinhang, 1961.

*Meskill, Johanna Menzel. *A Chinese Pioneer Family: The Lins of Wu-feng, Taiwan, 1729–1895*. Princeton: Princeton University Press, 1979.

Perdue, Peter C. "Comparing Empires: Manchu Colonialism." *The International History Review* 20, no. 2 (1998): 255–61.

*Rubinstein, Murray A., ed. *Taiwan: A New History.* Armonk, N.Y.: M.E. Sharpe, 1999.

*Shepherd, John. *Statecraft and Political Economy on the Taiwan Frontier, 1600–1800.* Stanford: Stanford University Press, 1993.

Teng, Emma Jinhua. "An Island of Women: The Discourse of Gender in Qing Travel Writing about Taiwan." *The International History Review* 20, no. 2 (1998): 353–70.

———. "Taiwan as a Living Museum: Tropes of Anachronism in Late-Imperial Chinese Travel Writing." *Harvard Journal of Asiatic Studies* 59, no. 2 (Dec. 1999): 445–84.

———. "Travel Writing and Colonial Collecting: Chinese Travel Accounts of Taiwan from the Seventeenth through Nineteenth Centuries." Ph.D. diss., Harvard University, 1997.

Thompson, Laurence, trans. "The Earliest Chinese Eyewitness Accounts of the Formosan Aborigines." *Monumenta Serica* 23 (1964): 163–204.

Yu Yonghe 郁永河. *Pihai jiyou* 裨海記遊. Edition of 1697. Reprint, TWWX 44. Taipei: Taiwan yinhang, 1959.

Zhuluo xian zhi 諸羅縣志. Edition of 1717. Reprint, TWWX 141. Taipei: Taiwan yinhang, 1962.

18. THE "EATING CRABS" YOUTH BOOK

Glossary

baqi zidi	八旗子弟	*Pangxie duan*	螃蟹段
Chaguan	查關	quantie	全帖
guci	鼓詞	sanxian	三弦
guoyu	國語	*Shengguan tu*	升官圖
hebi	合璧	tanci	彈詞
jiaren	佳人	*Xunfu qu*	尋夫曲
manzi	蠻子	zidishu	子弟書

References

Chang Yingsheng 常瀛生. *Beijing tuhua zhong de Manyu* 北京土話中的滿語. Beijing: Beijing yanshan chubanshe, 1993.

Crossley, Pamela Kyle, and Evelyn S. Rawski. "A Profile of the Manchu Language in Ch'ing History." *Harvard Journal of Asiatic Studies* 53, no. 1 (1993): 63–102.

*Ding Yizhuang 丁宜莊. *Manzu de funü shenghuo yu hunyin zhidu yanjiu* 滿族的婦女生活與婚姻制度研究. Beijing: Beijing Daxue chubanshe, 1999.

Elliott, Mark C. *The Manchu Way: The Eight Banners and Ethnic Identity in Late Imperial China*. Stanford: Stanford University Press, 2001.

*———. "Manchu Widows and Ethnicity in Qing China." *Comparative Studies in Society and History* 41, no. 1 (1999): 33–71.

Garrett, Valery M. *Chinese Clothing: An Illustrated Guide*. Hong Kong: Oxford University Press, 1994.

Guan Dedong 關德東. *Quyi lunji* 曲藝論集. Shanghai: Shanghai guji chubanshe, 1958.

*Guan Dedong 關德東, and Zhou Zhongming 周中明, ed. *Zidishu congchao* 子弟書叢鈔. Shanghai: Shanghai guji chubanshe, 1984.

Guan Jixin 關紀新, and Meng Xianren 孟憲仁. "Manzu yu Shenyang yu, Beijing yu" 滿族與沈陽語北京語. *Manzu yanjiu* 1 (1987): 73–81.

Hashimoto Mantarō. "The Altaicization of Northern Chinese." In *Contributions to Sino-Tibetan Studies*, ed. J. McCoy and T. Light. Leiden: E. J. Brill, 1986.

*Hatano Tarō 波多野太郎. *Pangxie duan'er yanjiu* 螃蟹段兒研究. Asian Folklore and Social Life Monographs 9. Taipei, 1970.

———. "Shiteisho Man-Kan ken 'Pangxie duaner' kaidai" 子弟書滿漢兼〈螃蟹段兒〉解題. In *Pangxie duan'er yanjiu*. Asian Folklore and Social Life Monographs 9. Taipei, 1970.

*Liu Liemao 劉烈茂, and Guo Jingrui 郭精銳, eds. *Qing Che wangfu chaocang quben, zidishu ji* 清車王府鈔藏曲本子弟書集. 2 vols. Suzhou: Jiangsu guji chubanshe, 1993.

McMahon, Keith. *Misers, Shrews, and Polygamists: Sexuality and Male-Female Relations in Eighteenth-Century Chinese Fiction*. Durham, N.C.: Duke University Press, 1995.

Morohashi Tetsuji 諸橋轍次, comp. *Dai Kan-Wa jiten* 大漢和辭典. Tokyo: Taishukan shoten, 1955–60.

Nienhauser, William H., Jr., et al. *The Indiana Companion to Traditional Chinese Literature*. 2nd rev. ed. Bloomington: Indiana University Press, 1986.

*Okada Hidehiro. "Mandarin, A Language of the Manchus: How Altaic?" *Aetas Manjurica* 3 (1993): 165–87.

Stary, Giovanni. "Fundamental Principles of Manchu Poetry." *Proceedings of the International Conference on China Border Area Studies*. Taipei, 1970: 187–221.

Tulli, Antonella. "Due esempi di zidishu sino-mancesi." *Aetas Manjurica* 3 (1993): 290–391.

———. "Analisi metrico-formale di una raccolta di poesie ibride sino-mancesi." *Aetas Manjurica* 3 (1993): 222–89.

Tun Li-ch'en [Dun Lichen] 敦禮臣. *Annual Customs and Festivals in Peking* (original title: *Yanjing suishi ji* 燕京歲時記). Trans. Derk Bodde. Beijing: Henri Vetch, 1936; reprint, Hong Kong: Hong Kong University Press, 1987.

Wadley, Stephen A. "Altaic Influences on Beijing Dialect: The Manchu Case." *Journal of the American Oriental Society* 116 (1996): 99–104.

*———. "The Mixed-Language Verses from the Manchu Dynasty in China." *Indiana Papers on Inner Asia* 16: 60–112. Bloomington: Research Institute for Inner Asian Studies, University of Indiana, 1991.

Wu, Yenna. *The Chinese Virago: A Literary Theme*. Cambridge: Harvard University Press, 1995.

Xu Ke 徐珂. *Qingbai leichao* 清稗類鈔. 13 vols. 1917. Reprint, Beijing: Zhonghua shuju, 1984.

Zhang Juling 張菊玲. *Qingdai Manzu zuojia wenxue gailun* 清代滿族作家文學概論. Beijing: Zhongyang minzu xueyuan chubanshe, 1990.

Zhen-jun 震鈞. *Tianzhi ouwen* 天咫偶聞. Beijing: Beijing guji chubanshe, 1982.

Contributors

JACQUELINE M. ARMIJO-HUSSEIN is Andrew W. Mellon Postdoctoral Fellow in the Humanities, Department of Religious Studies, Stanford University.

BEVERLY BOSSLER is Associate Professor, Department of History, University of California, Davis.

SUZANNE CAHILL is Adjunct Associate Professor, Department of History, University of California, San Diego.

YU-YIN CHENG is Assistant Professor, Department of History, Marymount Manhattan College.

PATRICIA BUCKLEY EBREY is Professor, Department of History, University of Washington.

MARK C. ELLIOTT is Associate Professor, Department of History, University of California, Santa Barbara.

GRACE S. FONG is Chair, Women's Studies Program, and Associate Professor, Department of East Asian Studies, McGill University.

DOROTHY KO is Professor, Department of History, Barnard College, Columbia University.

KATHRYN LOWRY is Assistant Professor, Department of East Asian Languages and Cultural Studies, University of California, Santa Barbara.

WEIJING LU is Assistant Professor, Department of History and American Studies, Mary Washington College.

SUSAN MANN is Professor, Department of History, University of California, Davis.

EMMA JINHUA TENG is Assistant Professor, Department of Foreign Languages and Literatures, Massachusetts Institute of Technology.

SOPHIE VOLPP is Assistant Professor, Department of East Asian Languages and Cultures, University of California, Davis.

ELLEN WIDMER is Professor, Department of Asian Languages and Literatures, Wesleyan University.

CHÜN-FANG YÜ is Professor and Chair, Department of Religion, Rutgers, The State University of New Jersey.

JUDITH T. ZEITLIN is Associate Professor, Department of East Asian Languages and Civilizations, University of Chicago.

Text:	9.5/12 and 9.5/13.5 Sabon
Display:	Sabon
Composition:	Binghamton Valley Composition
Printing and binding:	Friesens Corporation